Annual Editions: Human Resources, 23/e

Maria Nathan

http://create.mheducation.com

ISBN-10: 1259873447   ISBN-13: 9781259873447

Contents

Detailed Table of Contents

Unit 5: Implementing Compensation, Benefits, and Workplace Safety

Making Benefits Matter, Torry Dell, *Management Accounting Quarterly*, 2010

It is not just salary that will attract and keep employees. The total compensation package becomes important, and a big part of that package is the benefits offered by the employer. Health care, retirement, and life insurance all play a role in the total compensation package, and more and more, workers look at the total picture.

Cash-Back Program Puts Money into Workers' 401(k)s, Andrea Davis, *Employee Benefit News*, 2013

This online program doesn't require employees to change behavior or make other sacrifices to save for retirement.

Individual and Social Factors Associated with Workplace Injuries, Ashwin Kumar, *International Journal of Human Sciences*, 2011

While individual worker factors, such as gender, age, personality, ethnicity, and substance use, do contribute to workplace injuries and fatalities, broader social and organizational workplace factors, such as workload, work hours, work environment, safety culture, provision of quality supervision, and provision of occupational health and safety training, socially structure and influence individual worker attitudes and behaviors in workplace injury and fatalities.

Unit 6: HR and Sustainable Organizations

The Importance of Human Resource Management in Strategic Sustainability: An Art and Science Perspective, Harold Schroeder, *Journal of Environmental Sustainability*, 2012

Strategic sustainability is associated with significant business benefits and positive environmental impacts, yet many organizations fail to recognize the potential of this approach, and neglect the factors necessary for its successful implementation. This article recommends an art and science based approach to strategic sustainability and discusses the important role of human resource professionals in contributing to the success of this approach. A number of key areas of responsibility for the HR department in relation to strategic sustainability are discussed and the importance of a more proactive approach on the part of HR professionals is noted.

Building Sustainable Organizations: The Human Factor, Jeffrey Pfeffer, *Academy of Management Journal*, 2010

There has been much talk and research on the sustainability of the physical environment. Corporations are going to great lengths to "GO GREEN." But there has been relatively little discussion about how to sustain the organization's single greatest asset—its human resources. This is explored here.

Discrimination and the Aging American Workforce: Recommendations and Strategies for Management, Frank J.Cavico and Bahaudin G. Mujtaba, *SAM Advanced Management Journal*, 2011

This article seeks to provide managers with practical strategies, tactics, and recommendations to comply with age discrimination laws, to maintain fair employment practices, and to handle an actual age-based discrimination lawsuit.

Generational Differences in the Workplace: Personal Values, Behaviors, and Popular Beliefs, Jane Whitney Gibson, Regina A. Greenwood, and Edward F. Murphy, Jr., *Journal of Diversity Management*, 2009

This paper uses popular and academic literature to describe the distinguishing characteristics that differentiate baby boomers, Gen X and Gen Y. The authors then further examine these differences by comparing the results of a survey of 5,057 members of these cohorts, using the Rokeach Value Survey, to the previously generated profiles. Both terminal and instrumental values of the respondents were analyzed. Results generally confirm the popular profiles and suggest that managers should take these profiles into consideration when leading, motivating, and communicating with employees belonging to these generations.

Preface

Human resource management (HRM) has advanced as a field in practically every facet. It has become more strategic as it seeks to connect its operations meaningfully and measurably to the C-suite within organizations. In fact, an entire course within HRM programs has been spawned—strategic HRM—that seeks to connect the activities of HRM to the strategy of the organization. Furthermore, HRM professionals are now more frequently seen as agents of strategic change who are able to also talk the language of line management.

Other ways in which HRM has advanced include advances in measuring HR impact and connecting HRM to meaningful bottom-line measures such as return on investment. HRM information systems have helped greatly to this end, including sophisticated dashboards that permit the HR leader to monitor all key activities of HRM over time, including external HRM forces and numerous indicators of employee productivity.

Just as the ability to capture difficult to measure employee indicators such as employee attitude have advanced, so too has the HRM function advanced in its ability to serve as a key agent in organizational change. The HRM professional guided by rich and interesting theories and capable of measuring effectively, advances the organization through internal change consultation. It is as if the HRM function sits at the very heart of the organization and as a key facilitator of heartfelt concern for employee productivity.

HRM as an academic discipline is integrally linked to applied psychology. So much has been done to enhance HRM offerings from a psychological viewpoint. For example, concepts like emotional intelligence, emotional labor, job insecurity, and employee motivation—all topics treated in this volume—permit the HR professional to help employees to grow and develop alongside their managerial leaders.

Managerial leaders can turn to the HRM function as a source of support in the many difficult decisions pertaining to employees, including hiring, firing, promotion, demotion, reductions in force, layoffs, and more. HRM serves to link managers with needed training and development as these managers themselves seek to advance in their careers.

Finally, HRM is the key function that serves as employee advocate addressing delicate issues such as employee assistance, sexual harassment, bullying, incivility in the workplace, and much more. The skills of the HRM officer in such matters cannot be underestimated.

Yet even as HRM has grown up in the past few decades, it also is confronted by distinct challenges from those within the organization who suggest that HR should do still more, faster, and better. This volume is dedicated to educating those who will be managers in particular. These agents must understand what HRM is up against as well as the many HRM-related managerial challenges they will take on in just doing their jobs.

This volume contains a number of features designed to make it useful for both students and instructors. The articles are organized into units, each dealing with specific interrelated topics in HRM. Each unit provides an overview with necessary background information for informed reading of the articles.

Within each article, *Learning Outcomes* outline key concepts. *Critical Thinking* questions encourage the reader to think beyond the article they've just read. *Internet References* are provided for students who want to explore more deeply into a topic.

We believe this collection of articles provides the reader with the most complete and current readings available on the subject of Human Resource Management.
Maria Nathan

Editor of This Volume

Dr. Maria Nathan is a professor of Management in the School of Business and Economics at Lynchburg College, Lynchburg, Virginia. She earned her doctorate in Management and Organization from the University of Southern California in Los Angeles, California. She has also been a visiting scholar in diverse schools around the globe, including the University of California at Los Angeles (UCLA), Chinese University of Hong Kong, Hong Kong, SAR, China; Fachhochschule Voralberg, Voralberg, Austria, and Ramkhamhaeng University, Bangkok, Thailand, among others. Dr. Nathan has authored or co-authored over 50 books, chapters, and scholarly journal articles and is highly active as an editorial review board member for over nine scholarly journals. She has won many awards for her work.

Academic Advisory Board Members

Members of the Academic Advisory Board are instrumental in the final selection of articles for the *Annual Editions* series. Their review of the articles for content, level, and appropriateness provides critical direction to the editor(s) and staff. We think that you will find their careful consideration reflected in this book.

Lashun R. Aron
Lincoln College of New England

Januarius Asongu
Santa Monica University

Arthur Bowes
University of Massachusetts, Boston

Bruce Caine
Belmont University

Donna K. Cooke
Florida Atlantic University

Jeffrey Fahrenwald
Rockford College

Otha Hawkins
Alamance Community College

Gwendolyn Jones
University of Akron

Mark Kendrick
Methodist University

Gyongyi Konyu-Fogel
Walsh College

Elizabeth Langevin
University of Phoenix

Daniel O. Lybrook
Purdue University

Roosevelt Martin, Jr.
Chicago State University

Ken Moore
State University of New York, Albany

Carlton R. Raines
Lehigh Carbon Community College

David Schlocker
University of California Berkeley

Rieann Spence-Gale
Northern Virginia Community College

Robert Tanner
DeVry University

Valerie Wallingford
Bemidji State University

Ignatius Yacoub
Loma Linda University

Unit 1

UNIT

Prepared by: Maria Nathan, *Lynchburg College*

Human Resource Management in Perspective

Virtually every organizational function has been strained in recent years as demands both from outside and within the organization is made. Marketing, information systems, finance, and other core staff functions are experiencing the demand that they change with the times, react to key changes from outside the organization (e.g., the gig economy), and even be proactive sources of sustainability mindedness, competitive advantage, and more.

The HRM function is experiencing the stresses of growth as they translate ubiquitous and important changes within the external environment into actionable employee-centered responsibilities. HRM as an advocate for employees must focus upon refined and fine grain understanding of laws and regulations that constrain organizational behavior. The aging workforce, diversity, disability, health reform, retirement, and more require that the HRM professional is highly knowledgeable and competent.

The HRM function experiences pressure to justify itself as an agent that directly affects the bottom line. Thus, HRM must become much more measurement-astute as they seek to demonstrate both cost savings and revenue generation. HRM must speak the language of line management and its bottom line even while they are ever conscious of employee needs and employee welfare. Several readings in this volume explore, for example, information systems that permit the HRM function to keep tabs on spending and productivity.

The HRM function further experiences stress to be relevant and useful to employees. Career planning, retirement planning, concerns for employee well-being and quality of life must be state of the art and help the employees to live their lives more effectively. For some time now, the HRM function is challenged to initiate programs that permit employees to lead more balanced work-home lives.

The HRM function is also at the heart of competitive advantage through people. It is suggested by scholars such as Jeffrey Pfeffer that competitive advantage through employees is a chief means by which an organization can expect to achieve competitive advantage that can sustain over time. This is because such advantage would be very difficult for another organization to copy. This focuses the organization upon a new and heightened regard for its human capital and what they are capable of achieving. This focus is quite distinct from previous perspectives in which employees were but operatives of the strategic managerial mind of the organization. So many employees with active and intelligent minds are guided by the various HRM programs that seek to assist employees to grow and develop over time.

Sustainability is also not just about competitive advantage relative to organizational rivals, but the ability of organizations to use existing resources without depleting them for future generations. Sustainability consciousness has been sweeping through the global corporate world, with many of the sustainability-minded activities centered in the HRM function. For example, employees who plateau in their careers, employees who are overqualified within their current jobs, employees who seek to reinvent themselves—are all about sustaining the interest, value, and contributions of employees over time.

As the HRM function seeks to address the many pressures placed upon it, a distinct growth opportunity presents itself to the HRM professional. Tough minded yet compassionate; bottom line focused yet employee centered . . . Such challenges can be expected to produce HRM professionals who are much refined in the process.

Article   Prepared by: Maria Nathan, *Lynchburg College*

Is HR at Its Breaking Point?

Some companies are choosing to do away with traditional HR departments and divvy up the duties to other departments, but not everyone agrees that's such a good idea.

TODD HENNEMAN

Learning Outcomes

After reading this article, you will be able to:

- Recognize that HR functions may not be addressing important organizational requirements.

- Understand how Ulrich's business partner model of HR might be a preferred alternative to traditional HRM structure.

- Consider the possibility that HR as a function may need to evolve over time.

Three years ago, Toronto-based G Adventures held a funeral for its human resources department.
"We had a company function where I put up crossbones and skull with the title 'Death of HR,' " says Bruce Poon Tip, founder of the adventure-travel company, which employs 1,500 people.

Poon Tip took the drastic action after spending a year looking for a veteran of the field to become vice president of human resources, which would have been a new position overseeing the five-person department. He received 600 resumes and spent months interviewing candidates.

"Every meeting I had, I couldn't wait for it to end," he says. "It seemed like HR was the art of oppression. I knew I didn't want that in my company."

The debate over HR's shifting function and format continues, but it is apparent that as executives shift their corporate priorities, HR is following suit. Some companies have chosen to outsource their HR functions; others have shifted responsibilities to front-line managers in efforts to transform HR leaders

into business leaders; and some, like G Adventures, have no HR department whatsoever.

Poon Tip moved administrative tasks into the finance department and created two new departments. The so-called "talent agency" focuses on recruiting and talent management. The "culture club," where everyone has the title "karma chameleon"—named after the hit 1980s song sung by Boy George—organizes everything from fundraisers for the company's nonprofit foundation to holding celebrations whenever G Adventures wins an award.

Poon Tip's approach wouldn't work for many organizations, but a growing number of companies are reimagining their HR structures along with who executes their people strategies. Almost 45 percent of organizations indicated that they will change their HR structure by the end of 2013, according to Towers Watson & Co.'s 2012 HR Service Delivery Survey, up from 28 percent in the previous year's survey.

Jac Fitz-enz, founder of the consulting firm Human Capital Source, says it's time for the C-suite to forget tradition. Organizations should pull apart HR departments and place pieces where they fit naturally. "We have patched together a function that isn't working very well," Fitz-enz says.

If it's the sunset of HR as we know it, the new era's dawn can't come soon enough for Robert Bolton, a partner in KPMG's HR Transformation Center of Excellence. The field has "relentlessly pursued best practices and generic models" with a blind eye to business strategies or even industries. "If people are significant for your organization in relation to achieving a competitive advantage, and if you are trying to steal a march on your competition, then that calls for a differentiated HR function, not one that looks like everybody else's," Bolton says. This never-ending chase of best practices and copycat models has put HR in a "doom cycle," he says. "To my mind," he says, "HR has got to break out of that or die."

Deerfield, Illinois-based Beam Inc. might be a bellwether of how larger organizations can branch out. The maker of Pinnacle vodka and Maker's Mark bourbon is midway through reinventing its approach to HR and talent management, a process that began 18 months ago.

In October 2011, Beam became a stand-alone spirits company after Fortune Brands Inc. split up its three enterprises. Fortune Brands sold its golf business, best known for its Titleist golf balls. It then spun off Fortune Brands Home & Security, whose brands include Moen faucets. The remaining business, which includes the Jim Beam whiskey brand, became Beam Inc. It has 3,400 employees.

At the new Beam, executives wanted a culture that encouraged managers to think and act more like entrepreneurs. Based on that concept, they thought about what entrepreneurs do.

"If I'm an entrepreneur running a small business, the first thing I don't do is go out and hire an HR person," says Steve Molony, Beam's director of people strategy and solutions. "If I'm starting a small business, I should be making all these decisions. Big companies get bloated with bureaucracies and these big, huge back offices that remove the business leaders from making some of these decisions. We wanted to reverse that trend when we were still lean and nimble enough to do this."

Beam hopes to nurture what Molony calls "holistic managers," who take on deeper HR responsibilities. "That means they don't just have their job of operational and financial management of whatever part of the business they're in," Molony says. "But their responsibilities are to attract, develop, retain and compensate the people on their team, which are traditional HR roles that would have been done by centralized HR teams."

Take plant managers. In the past, they would tell HR what role needed to be filled, wait for a list of candidates and then be told the new hire's start date after making the selection.

In the future, plant managers first will decide whether the job is necessary. If it is, they next would decide whether they have an internal successor or need to look outside. They also would look at market data about salaries, negotiate the pay and onboard the new hire.

The change isn't happening overnight. It requires training, such as helping managers and other leaders understand what would happen if they paid everyone at the 75th percentile of the market, for example. And they won't be without help from seasoned HR professionals—just fewer of them.

As part of its transformation, Beam is centralizing its disparate HR departments.

It has adapted the business-partner model first championed in 1997 by Dave Ulrich, a business professor at the University of Michigan. His model rests on three pillars: a shared service center, whose centralized staff handles administrative and transactional tasks; centers of excellence, which offer specialized consultants on topics such as training or labor relations; and business partners who advise business-unit leaders on talent strategy such as succession plans.

Beam didn't adopt Ulrich's framework wholesale. Its tailored tactic lets the company have a leaner business-services staff and fewer HR business partners, Molony says. In the traditional framework, those HR practitioners would have handled many of the activities Beam envisions managers taking on.

The goal: Develop a better caliber of business leaders that will help Beam outperform its competition. It's not an HR cost-cutting exercise, Molony says. "We feel like if we give our business leaders these skills, it will differentiate us in the market," he says.

The goal of HR leaders becoming business leaders and front-line supervisors taking on more HR-like work remains an aspiration, not a reality, particularly for small to midsize employers. "The HR people are absolutely drowning in many cases in the transactional-type stuff," says management consultant Susan Heathfield, who covers HR for About.com.

At some companies, talent leaders see the potential for other departments to take over aspects of HR. At digital advertising agency Razorfish, Anthony Onesto, director of technology talent development, has asked his recruiting and marketing teams to get together so they work more closely and think about recruiting as a marketing effort. He acknowledges that recruiting likely will not become part of the marketing department, but he also thinks that much of what an HR department does could be done elsewhere.

"This HR group could be dissolved, and folks could be handed some of the responsibilities, and I think we would be OK," says Onesto, emphasizing it's a theory, not a plan. But if it happened? "There would be no need for someone like me," he says. "I would have to reinvent myself. I've done it before."

Other companies already rely on managers to lead aspects of what an HR department does elsewhere. The Container Store Inc., a Coppell, Texas-based retailer with 58 locations nationwide, holds store managers responsible for career development and employee morale, says Eva Gordon, vice president of stores. The Container Store also is famous for its training—263 hours for full-time employees in their first year.

"We hire fantastic people, we train them really well to understand leadership and communication, so who better to manage careers and guide people and answer their questions than their manager?" Gordon says.

Susan Meisinger isn't so sure. "You can't tell me there isn't somebody who is making sure that no matter how they're doing their talent recruitment, that it is being done in accordance with law and that they're reaching a pool of candidates who have a higher likelihood of success," says Meisinger, a consultant who retired as president and CEO of Society of Human Resource Management in 2008. "You can't tell me there isn't going to be some consultation going on when there are performance issues, sort of an adviser somewhere in the corporation to help managers improve performance when there are performance issues."

At Netflix Inc., recruiting largely is considered the responsibility of the hiring manager. The recruiting team handles transactional aspects, and managers determine the market price for salaries through multiple channels, according to spokesman Jonathan Friedland. He declined to elaborate or comment further.

The video-streaming company raised eyebrows in 2011 when it sought a new HR director. Netflix specified that it wanted someone who "thinks business first, customer second, team and talent third" and did not want "a change agent, an OD practitioner, a SHRM certificate, a people person."

Some observers saw the job posting as a reflection of the C-suite's frustration with the HR field, which struggles to shed its image as little more than open-enrollment gurus and rule enforcers.

"HR has been for many years scoring on its own score card," says Dick Beatty, professor of human resource management at Rutgers University.

A recent study suggests Beatty's right. "Help people grow" was the No. 1 reason HR leaders cited for entering the profession, according the New Talent Management Network, a group of HR professionals started by Avon Products Inc.'s former vice president of global talent management.

"It's lovely to talk about 'business partner' and 'seat at the table,' but the challenge for HR leaders is: Do they understand what's being served at that table?" says Marc Effron, president of the consulting firm The Talent Strategy Group and founder of the network. "It's a business meal. It's not an HR meal."

This gap may explain why CEOs rank talent as a top priority but don't mention the HR function.

For example, Irv Rothman, president and CEO of HP Financial Services, a wholly owned subsidiary of the Hewlett-Packard Co., keeps talent management as a standing item on his executive team's agenda. But he doesn't see it as something the HR department should lead.

"It's not an HR process," Rothman says. "It's a business process because it's the business that sees people in action. HR has a role. They have a role in creating the environment and creating the infrastructure. For HR to conduct talent management to me seems a little . . . I don't know."

In his book, *Out-Executing the Competition,* Rothman recommends that no CEO delegate the cultural implications of a merger to the HR department, which he describes as good at

such things as benefits. "If the HR department is delivering that message and achieving that visibility, it's not the inspirational leadership that people are looking for in the aftermath of a merger when just about everybody is as nervous as cat in a roomful of rocking chairs," Rothman tells Workforce.

Survey after survey continues to find that HR leaders are viewed as low status and better at transactional tasks than strategic planning. "If we're doing our job well, people don't say those things," Effron says. "It's very easy for HR to whine that people don't respect us, but people respect those who deliver results." The solution? Attract a fresh pool of talent into the field that understands business and wants to maximize profits, Effron says. "In many ways, it's not: 'Can we teach those in the field to do it better?'—it's: 'Can we get different people in the field who truly understand what it takes to succeed in this area?' " he says.

During the recession, many global organizations learned that they could do more with less if they had flatter HR departments, fewer job grades and health plans, and used more self-service tools, says Harry Osle, The Hackett Group's global HR transformation and advisory practice leader.

The result: Leaner HR departments that add more value for every dollar spent than their peer groups and run by professionals skilled in analytics and consulting. "HR organizations in the future are going to be a lot thinner," Osle says, "but they're not going to disappear."

Meisinger, the former SHRM president, says HR departments historically have become leaner during economic downturns. It's more efficient to have managers do a better job of managing than wait for people problems to emerge and be pushed over to HR.

But even companies that boast that they have no HR department retain someone with HR expertise to help guide recruitment and talent management, she argues.

Still, technological advances will continue to transform the field. Companies have "dramatically" more self-service tools available now than they did 10 years ago, Meisinger says.

"That's freeing up HR to focus on what it should be: getting in the right talent and making sure they're developed appropriately and looking at the strategy of the business—where is the business going and what are the talent needs?" Meisinger says. "There are a lot of folks in HR who grew up in the transactional world who aren't equipped to operate in the strategic world."

Critical Thinking

1. Does the centrality of the HR function vary depending upon the industry within which an organization operates?
2. How might the HR function need to reinvent itself to address criticisms lodged against it?

Internet References

Evolution of Human Resource Management - HR Dictionary

http://hrdictionaryblog.com/2012/10/28/evolution-of-human-resource-management

HRM Guide - Alternative HRM Models

www.hrmguide.co.uk/introduction_to_hrm/alternative-hrm-models.htm

Is Your Current HR Service Delivery Model Working for You?

www.oracle.com/us/solutions/hcm/wsd-whitepaper-03-2011-333243.pdf

The Evolution of Human Resource Management

www.shrm.org/Education/hreducation/Pages/TheEvolutionof HumanResourceManagement.aspx

Article   Prepared by: Maria Nathan, *Lynchburg College*

The Leadership Challenges Facing HR

Top CHROs Share Learnings and Advice on What's Next

The Chief Human Resources Officer's job has never been more crucial, and, at the same time, more challenging. The severe economic downturn and slow recovery has impacted leader and employee engagement across industries and across the country. Frequent CEO succession, new financial regulations and ethics scandals, along with more active and engaged boards of directors, have added to the complexity that confronts HR leaders. And many of us still are locked into what seems the HR function's never-ending search for relevance and impact.

STEVE STECKLER

Learning Outcomes

After reading this article, you will be able to:

- Become acquiainted with diverse perspectives on the most important thing the CHRO can do.

- Understand what are the biggest personal challenges CHROs face.

- Understand what are considered the top leadership challenges faced by HRM in the future.

With this as context and leadership as the focus of this special issue, this is the right moment to engage in a rare and candid conversation with a small group of CHROs. We asked what they learned about having impact, being successful and about the serious challenges facing both HR leaders and the function.

You will recognize many of these leaders; they are well-known within our field, some reaching business media fame. They are from iconic brands and companies and have been acknowledged for their impact and for developing great business and human resources talent.

We specifically selected a group largely made-up of those who already have completed their careers as CHROs, although one or two said that they might be tempted to re-enter the arena. Most are currently consulting, teaching, writing or serving on

boards. This created a singularly high level of candor and openness, including some raw self-reflection. We also included a relative newcomer to the role for her comparative perspective. Our interviews occurred during the final weeks of summer 2010.

The level of exchange exceeded our expectations. A small number of common themes emerged, including what was particularly difficult about being successful in the role, in what areas many of these leaders felt ill-prepared and what they learned about their leaders and the HR function. In addition, they shared a loud warning to current HR leaders about what may be next.

Steve Steckler: Mark Hurd's story at Hewlett Packard was just reported, so let's talk about ethics and the responsibility that human resources and HR leaders should have in company ethics. With so many scandals over the years in U.S. companies, what role does HR play?

Ursie Fairbairn: Well, I think HR definitely has a role. I think that, to play that role successfully you have to have facts, you have to be connected and you need to be courageous. And sometimes that means you are placed in a very vulnerable position whether that scandal is a business scandal or whether that scandal is a personal scandal.

Bill Conaty: I think that the best thing that HR can do and that the CEO can do is make integrity the all-encompassing value of the company. Sure, we all have got a list of values that are important that describe how you work and how you behave and what is expected of you, but integrity has got to be the center-piece of the whole deal. I know in GE when it came to integrity violations, we said one strike and you're out. You weren't going to get a second chance.

Libby Sartain: I think that it is our job to monitor the behavior of our people and ensure that ethical behavior is a way of life in our organizations. My experience is that most of us take it seriously and we partner with our CEOs. As part of that partnership, we point out where there are issues that are concerning. HR can have a separate relationship with the board. If a situation cannot be resolved inside, is serious, or involves the CEO or a top executive, we must talk with the board when these things happen and recommend a course of action. I have known several CHROs that have had to go to the board and recommend that their bosses be fired over these situations.

Dick Antoine: HR is the guardian of the values of any company or organization. It's what we are uniquely charged with doing. We must protect those values and we must defend employees who have small voices and smaller jobs in organizations. And we do this through a combination of training and education and reinforcement of the values. We also do it by consistently enforcing discipline in cases where values are

---

Our CHRO Panel and Their Former Companies:

- **Dick Antoine;** Global Human Resources Officer at Procter & Gamble
- **Bill Conaty;** Senior Vice President of Human Resources, General Electric
- **Ursie Fairbairn;** Executive Vice President of Human Resources and Quality at American Express. Prior to that, she was senior vice president of human resources at Union Pacific
- **Libby Sartain;** Executive Vice President of Human Resources at Yahoo! Inc. Prior to that, she was vice president of people at Southwest Airlines
- **Dick Sibbernsen;** Executive Vice President of Human Resources for AT&T. Prior to that, he was chief human resources officer for BellSouth Corporation
- **Ian Ziskin;** Corporate Vice President of Human Resources and Chief Administrative Officer at Northrop Grumman Corporation. Prior to that he was executive vice president and chief human resources officer at Qwest Communications

Our current CHRO is **Kalen Holmes.** She is executive vice president of partner resources at Starbucks.

---

violated that normally will mean termination regardless of level in the organization.

Ian Ziskin: The short answer is yes, HR does play a role and should play a role going forward. HR contributes, perhaps most uniquely, by ensuring that there are mechanisms in place in the organization to make it safe for people to tell the truth, to surface things that are wrong and to surface things that are right for that matter. There should be tools that you use to solicit input and feedback and make it safe for people to tell you what is on their minds. I don't believe that HR has sole responsibility over that, but somebody has to be the advocate. I think the law department would say that it has a role to play and the finance organization would say that it has a role to play.

Steckler: Let's talk about what was most surprising to you when you first took the CHRO role?

Sartain: Well, I had two very different situations at the two companies where I was the head of HR. I had been at Southwest for seven years before I was promoted to become head of HR. In working for the same company, my biggest surprise was that as you reach a new level in the organization, there is sort of a new culture, a new set of unspoken norms and rules at that level. If you are not aware of that, you can make some mistakes. After a few years as head of HR, I was put on the executive committee, and at that point, I was the first HR person ever at the table. Even though I believed that I had been placed onto the executive committee because of what I had accomplished as the head of HR, I still had to earn my seat on the executive committee once I was there. At Yahoo, when I joined the company as head of HR, the company was so young that I had a lot of surprises. There was not any organized executive committee and no cadence about how decisions were made and no one really felt that was necessary. So we had to create an informal operating committee, and I worked with the COO to do that. Later, we had to establish formal decision rules so that we could get "stuff" done.

Dick Sibbernsen: For me, at both companies, the surprise was how each company you are at, has a different business model with different ways of making money. There were different ways that power was structured and decision rights created. It really brought home that there is not a prescription for success, but a range of solutions and that how you get the performance needed to achieve strategy is going to be different from company to company.

Fairbairn: Although I had held senior HR roles before at other companies, each time I became head of HR, first at Union Pacific and then at American Express, I was always surprised about the ability to influence and that the amount of opportunity to have an impact was so huge. There were so many ways that you could make a big difference, including helping leaders

Recent Research on the CHRO Role

In 2009, the Cornell Center for Advanced Human Resources Studies (CAHRS) published the results of their first Chief Human Resources Officers Survey, "Strategies and Challenges of the Chief Human Resource Officer: Results of the First Annual Cornell/ CAHRS Survey of CHRO's." Our colleague Pat Wright led the study. Many of its conclusions mirror perfectly the comments of our interviewees.

The survey was sent to CHROs at U.S. Fortune 150 companies and to 10 additional CHROs at CAHRS partner companies. The study focused on a number of areas, including the different roles and responsibilities that CHROs considered to be the key parts of their jobs and how they allocated their time to different stakeholders and to these roles. The study found that there were seven distinct roles of the CHRO:

- Leader of the HR function (22% of time spent)
- Strategic adviser to the executive team (21% of time spent)
- Counselor/confidante/coach to the executive team (17% of time spent)
- Talent architect (17% of time spent)
- Liaison to the board of directors (10% of time spent)
- Workforce sensor (8% of time spent)
- Representative of the firm (5% of time spent)

Consider how closely these findings reflect what our CHRO panel said.

Moreoever, when the seven areas are combined based on total time spent with stakeholders, CHROs spend the majority of their time with their peers and the CEO.[1]

Here is a portion of the 2009 report:

"The results reveal that CHROs focus their attention in two general directions. They serve as business leaders who spend significant amounts of time with the CEO, the executive leadership team and the individuals making up the team, and the board of directors. They also devote considerable time with the HR leadership team and individuals who make up that team. In other words, they must be both business leaders and HR leaders."

"In addition, CHROs view their roles as strategic advisor, counselor/confidante/coach to the executive team, and talent architect as being the most important aspects of their job in terms of impact on the business, and the ones in which they spend significant amounts of time. In addition, while they spend the greatest amount of time as leaders of the HR function, they do not view that role as particularly high impact."

In 2010, the survey was expanded to the U.S. Fortune 200 and asked many of the same questions. Additionally, Wright and Mark Stewart, PhD also focused on the CHRO's relationship with the board of directors, along with identifying innovative practices that had been developed and implemented within their HR organizations. They found that the financial crisis that influenced 2009 survey responses had been replaced with a more optimistic view. They describe the move from "bunker" to "building."[2]

Wright and Stewart found that CHROs were now increasing their focus on retaining talent, building HR capability, spending more time with their HR leaders and addressing high potential talent.[3] CHROs were also giving more time to their role as HR leaders and as the talent strategist/architect.[4] For their CEOs, talent tops the agenda, and the lack of HR talent is one of the key obstacles to achieving the CEO's agenda for HR.[5]

Both the 2010 CHRO Survey Report and the Executive Summary of the 2009 CHRO Survey can be downloaded from: www.ilr.cornell.edu/cahrs/research.

[1]Wright, Patrick M. (2009). "Strategies and challenges of the chief human resource officer: Results of the first annual Cornell/CAHRS survey of CHRO's." 6.

[2]Wright, Patrick M. and Stewart, Mark. (2010). "From bunker to building: Results from the 2010 chief human resource officer survey Cornell center for advanced human resource studies (CAHRS)." 4.

[3]Wright, Patrick M. and Stewart, Mark. (2010). "From bunker to building: Results from the 2010 Chief human resource officer survey. Cornell center for advanced human resource studies (CAHRS)." 4.

[4]Wright, Patrick M. and Stewart, Mark. (2010). "From bunker to building: Results from the 2010 Chief human resource officer survey. Cornell center for advanced human resource studies (CAHRS)." 4.

[5]Wright, Patrick M. and Stewart, Mark. (2010). "From bunker to building: Results from the 2010 chief human resource officer survey. Cornell center for advanced human resource studies (CAHRS)." 4.

be more effective, helping the board select the right successor, helping to implement new technology, helping the leadership team be more effective.

Antoine: When I was named CHRO at Procter & Gamble, except for being a plant HR manager 20 years prior, my

background was exclusively in operations rather than HR, so a lot of it was surprising and a learning experience. One specific area of surprise was that I was able to shape the role. It evolved from a narrower definition when I started, to a pretty broad role that included a significant role with the board of directors.

Conaty: Although, I spent my entire career with GE and moved up within the company, when I took the top HR role for all of corporate human resources for the entire company, the stakes became much higher. You are now dealing with the CEO of the corporation and you know at GE, a dozen or 15 different business units, versus working for just one singular business unit and one CEO. The job was much broader with stronger constituencies. You really learn whether you have the ability to see the bigger picture and really make a significant impact on a much larger stage.

Ziskin: For me, the most surprising thing was that sometimes what leaders said they wanted from HR, didn't really match their own behavior. I have had this experience twice, as head of HR for Qwest and then at Northrop Grumman. People seemed very clear at first about the things that they were looking for out of the HR function and out of the CHRO: Generally, the things that you typically hear, be a good business partner, lead change and invest in talent and help improve the performance of the business. But as I stepped into both jobs, I found that there was much greater resistance to actually making some of those things happen then you would imagine. It also meant that peers on the leadership team might also have to change, do things differently and be more receptive to the concepts that you were trying to sell as the new head of HR. This also included other people in HR, who were clamoring for more of a voice and for more of a seat at the table. They wanted to influence more things that they saw could be done differently and better, but even they were reluctant to change to achieve some of the things that they said they wanted.

Kalen Holmes: Compared to this group, I am a new CHRO. I have been in this role at Starbucks for just about a year. I spent a lot of time with Howard Schultz, our president, chairman and CEO and with others on the senior leadership team during the interview process. Through those discussions, it became apparent that Starbucks was entering a very exciting time as a company. The most surprising aspect for me entering this role is the pace at which we are entering our new evolution of growth; and, therefore, the immediate focus we are putting toward organizational capability and process to ensure we are readying the organization for this evolution.

Steckler: How did being in the role change your perspective about the company, leadership and HR?

Fairbairn: Several things come to mind: When you have more information, you are better able to prioritize and diagnose the issues. Sometimes you do all of your homework when you are not yet the head of human resources, but when you are inside, you understand it so much better and you, therefore, are more able to do your job superbly well. The second would be the importance

of leadership. Leadership is so crucial in differentiating between the just average, the good, the very good and the excellent.

Ziskin: I agree. Great leadership does matter. Sometimes you might be able to convince yourself that any large, complicated organization can succeed despite itself and keep things chugging along irrespective of who is in charge. But at the same time, you know that who's in charge does make a difference in terms of the tone they set, the priorities on which they focus, the questions they ask and the people with whom they surround themselves. Great leadership has a multiplier effect that goes deeper down into the organization. I think that I learned a lot about the importance of quickly figuring out whether the leaders that you have are the ones who are going to take you to the next level. The role that HR has is in bringing that question up and then taking responsibility for doing something about it.

Sibbernsen: I believe that the main job of the CHRO is to set up the context in which the senior leaders can really do a deep dive and deep thinking about their people issues. Set the context, start the conversation and set up the going forward priorities. Identify five or six priorities, and then come up with the solutions. I would say that there are four categories that the CHRO is going to spend 75 percent of his or her time around: defining what the key organization implications of the business strategy are; facilitating a real deep discussion and deep thinking; the third bucket is then working up the solutions. Fourth is developing a project plan to go forward and to get these solutions into the operating system of the company. Delivery of all of this has to be linked to business outcomes. Did we lift revenue? Did we lift the productivity? Most companies are pretty good at strategy. The performance gap is execution. This is the sweet spot for the CHRO. What are the capabilities to perform this work? That is where I think the very value of an effective CHRO comes into play.

Conaty: When I took the top HR job at GE, I felt that I had become a true insider of the company. Literally and figuratively, you become a corporate insider from the standpoint of the technical, compensation and reporting rules. The other thing from an HR perspective, which I think is critical here, is that you become the HR face of GE, and people want to know who the face of GE is from an HR standpoint. You become part of the outside world with the HR Policy Association, later the National Academy of Human Resources. Your network expands.

Steckler: Do you think that the leader of HR should come from the HR function? What about coming from outside the function?

Sartain: A lot of people are threatened by someone from outside the function, I am not. If there is a solid leader in the business that the company wants to move into the position for a while, that can be a good situation. We can then feel good when that leader then acquires a much better understanding about what it takes to deliver HR and can go to their peers with that insight. At the same time, I have seen people come in and not know what they are doing and make big mistakes. The only way it can work is if they have very strong lieutenants in the HR function below them and they listen to those folks while helping them better serve the organization. I also think that it is great for an HR person to move into a business role and add value there.

Fairbairn: I think that it can be done, and there are certainly companies who have a history of that. I think that they generally go through a period where the HR function is at a disadvantage. On the other hand, I have learned that for every organizational situation, there are no absolutes. There can be a line person who can become a great head of HR, if they have the right mindset, the right learning, if they have the right team, if they listen and not only talk and if they have a leader who supports them. And here is a perfect parallel. Many companies believe in picking a CEO from inside, but if that hasn't worked then you have to go outside.

Antoine: Understanding my background, which was almost totally from operations, I will now give you the blanket statement. I think it's a really bad idea to put someone in charge of HR who doesn't know and understand HR. So putting me in charge of it was a really bad idea. It turned out some people would say it was a great idea, but I don't agree with that assessment. Unfortunately, there is a belief among many, I won't say the majority, but certainly a lot of CEOs and a lot of senior leaders of companies that anyone can do HR. And I think that's wrong, completely, absolutely wrong. HR has a technology and a methodology and skills around it just like finance does, or research and development or marketing or any other function. Would you have a CFO with no finance or accounting experience? Why would it be OK to have a CHRO without previous HR experience?

Steckler: What was most personally challenging for you about the role?

Conaty: I would say for me it was learning the HR role from the standpoint of dealing with the board of directors. That is the only HR job in the company where you have direct involvement with the GE Board of Directors, and as you might imagine the GE Board of Directors is a pretty star-studded group of rock stars.

Fairbairn: I agree. Working with the board was the most challenging part of the role. When you take on this role the first time, there are so many things that you need to understand and no HR person has done it all; if you had, you would be too

old to then take on the CHRO role. You need to learn how to deal with the board in an effective way, recognizing that you have to balance between the board as the representative of the shareholder and your boss, the CEO, who is the leader of the organization. Once you have done it once, it gets easier.

Ziskin: Yes, it's in working with the board. Prior to taking on the CHRO role, you have much more limited exposure to and experience with the board then you really need to have to be effective in the role, and so there is really no great proxy for that. It is a shortcoming in how we develop and prepare our future HR leaders.

Antoine: Managing the boundary between senior leaders and the CEO. On the one hand, you are trying to help the senior leaders with advice and career perspective and on the other hand, you are trying to keep the CEO informed of critical concerns and development issues while protecting the confidences of the senior leaders that talk to you.

Steckler: So how do you better prepare HR leaders for working with the board?

Conaty: Look at what we have done with the National Academy of Human Resources. We have established the CHRO Academy where we spend a day and a half with newly minted VPs of HR. We spend a lot of time of talking about these kinds of issues, dealing with a board on succession, dealing with the board on strategy. I wish that I had had this before 1 took the SVP job at GE.

Steckler: What about other areas that were personally challenging about being in the CHRO role?

Sartain: The most challenging work is long-term strategic workforce planning. It was a little easier at Southwest because we had one business and we could plan our growth. We had to plan ahead to order the number of airplanes we needed in the future up to five years in advance. We didn't always know the cities we wanted to open that far in advance, but we had a long list of possibilities. With every plane ordered, we knew the number of workers we needed to add and HR could plan for staffing. The unknowns were what the economy and the competition would be doing in the future. At Yahoo, even though we knew that there were not enough software programmers in the United States to meet all of the needs that we had in software programming, it was difficult to plan ahead for the next tech center. We needed to open tech centers in other parts of the world, but we knew that we did not want to put a tech center where everyone else was putting one, and the competition didn't tell us where they were going. Yet, sometimes we would tend to focus more on the here and now or the next week, rather than three years from now. We were growing fast, so we didn't always have all of the planning tools we needed. I think that some of the bigger, more mature, companies were better at it than we were.

Ziskin: The other thing that was most personally challenging to me was being able to figure out who the people were within HR that I needed to invest in, to try to give them the tools that they needed to help me be part of the changes that I was attempting to bring about versus the people who were probably just good people, had good experience, but they are weren't really going to help me. You believe that if you give everyone enough information, enough feedback, enough rationale, enough support, they will eventually come around to join what you want them to be part of. But that doesn't always happen.

Steckler: What is so difficult about being successful in the CHRO role?

Holmes: In my view, HR leaders are not any less—or more—successful than other senior leaders. The CHRO plays multiple roles and you have to manage and prioritize your focus. First and foremost, you are the leader of a global function and you have to lead that global function, no one else will do it for you. So I think it is important to spend a lot of time developing your own function, putting the right attention and direction to it, along the way ensuring that you have the right talent, and the right kind of team around you to drive the business forward. At the same time, you have to be the senior generalist for the CEO and for the senior leaders.

Sartain: Everybody has a point of view about talent and about people. If you are the finance person or the head technologist or the chief counsel or whatever else, you don't have as many people who think they know as much as you do about what it is that you do. You really have to have an expertise that adds value beyond what everybody else thinks they know about it. And often, we are the people who have to say "no," or have to make the toughest decisions and that doesn't always make us the most popular leader in the room.

Fairbairn: Three things: One, there is so much to do. Two, the issues are really complex—they are not simple but interrelated, global, and they are complicated. Three, the issues are people issues and people issues that you deal with are never simple. So I think it is the complexity and then balancing the complexity of the issues with the appetite for solutions. It is a hard job, and it never ends, and that is another element. It just goes on and on.

Ziskin: I think that the things that make it most difficult are that the fact that you are in a role that is viewed by most people as a support, advisory and influence role. But you also have accountability for driving change, making unpopular decisions in some cases like we talked about earlier. You are making hard calls about how the business should be organized and

who should be in key leadership roles. Not that you are making those decisions by yourself, but you are influencing certainly the CEO and others who have to make those decisions. You are trading on your own personal relationships with people and credibility, and they can choose to support you or not. And then you have to make decisions about how much you are willing to battle to fight for something that you believe is right and important but perhaps less important than other things.

Antoine: I think the difficulty is twofold. For people who are coming from operations or from the line, you have to get used to getting things done through influence with little formal authority. I think most people who come into the role struggle with it for that reason. All of a sudden you've got this incredibly broad portfolio, lots of responsibility, but little authority. The second thing that I found difficult and I think most people do, is the breadth of the role. It's from the mundane cost control to needing to be knowledgeable in all of the expert areas within HR like compensation or benefits or organization behavior, organization design and more. At the same time, you have your relationships with the C-suite team, other members of the senior management team, the senior HR team, the CEO and the board.

Conaty: I think that it is balancing that delicate tightrope walk of being a business partner at one end and an employee advocate on the other. I actually see some HR leaders become so ingrained and obsessed with becoming a business partner that they forget why they are at the table. They become so business- and analytically focused that they miss their role. Unless you can be both, you really are not going to be successful. So when I was in the CHRO role, I had to balance that and not be hesitant to be that employee advocate for all 350,000 people.

Sibbernsen: It goes back to getting the priorities right. That's number one. You have to avoid coming into an organization with a set of prescriptions and prescriptive solutions in your briefcase and start to find problems to solve. That is just the opposite of what is needed and what you should do. Build the priorities and then build up the relationships. Use power effectively and understand who has got the power and who doesn't. You have to use power constructively and establish key relationships.

> **It goes back to getting the priorities right . . . Build the priorities and then build up the relationships. Use power effectively and understand who has got the power and who doesn't. You have to use power constructively and establish key relationships.**

Steckler: I have seen top HR leaders try to elevate themselves almost a half-step or full step above their peers on the management team to get closer to the CEO because they believed that is part of their role. What do you think about that?

Fairbairn: I am in the school that you do not do that. It is not helpful to accomplishing your goals to put yourself ahead of your business colleagues as peers. You have a very special relationship with the CEO by the very nature of what you do. But you need to make your relationship really bring value to your colleagues and to your peers as well. And if you are seen as in the pocket of the CEO, or seeing yourself as one step closer to the CEO, I think that that has a possible detriment to your effectiveness overall.

Conaty: If the organization deems you to be in the CEO's pocket and that is how you carry yourself, you are dead. I can list a dozen CHROs who have been fired after enjoying an initial strong relationship with the CEO. I tell people who think that their role is to establish great rapport only with the CEO that will keep you alive for about a year. Then, something will hit you that you don't know where the hell it came from and it's your peer group and it's your subordinates that take you out.

Steckler: What are the most serious challenges facing the HR function in the future?

Holmes: The continued globalization of the world, specifically the growth of Asia Pacific and what that means to heads of HR in helping to ensure that the right talent, the right capability and the right processes are in place to become truly global. I think that there are very few companies today that are truly global, and it is going to become even more important as you look at the growth estimates for the next five to 10 years in Asia. The other challenge is the workforce demographic that is going to be entering the workforce over the next five to 10 years and their expectations of aligned real-time communication channels that flow both ways, as well as their ability to craft and shape their jobs. I think that the traditional hierarchical management structure is going to become even more challenged if we don't better understand how to organize, align, galvanize and energize the workforce that is about to join us.

Fairbairn: I think one of the challenges is having enough talented, motivated, experienced people ready to take on the top HR job. It's a combination of things. The job has grown, expectations are higher, and there are more companies that really want a strong contributing HR function, and we are not filling that pipeline effectively enough. To clarify, it's supply and demand. Most of us have done a good job at developing talent; it's when you assess the supply and you look at jobs that are open and for how long they remain open, there is just not enough of a pipeline. To have choice because the selection process is skills, experiences and chemistry and that means you need a larger supply of truly good successors, and I think we as a function are not doing enough of that.

Ziskin: I would pick a few. One is making sure that you have the right quality and quantity of leadership talent. Leadership depth is important because even the best companies increasingly are going to have a hard time holding onto people, and so you can't just have one solution for each job. You need to have more because it is equally likely that that good person is going to be courted by somebody else. The second challenge is around the reconciliation of performance with ethics. CEOs and other people who are moving into leadership positions are really under the microscope to show whatever performance they are going to show in much shorter periods of time. In that type of environment and the pressure that comes from budget cuts and the economic downturn and all of the other things that are going on out there in the world, even the most ethical people are going to be challenged. It is about creating an environment where you have a culture that is based on driving performance while at the same time you have a culture that highly values ethical behavior.

Sartain: We are all going to have to do more with less. I do not think that we are going to have all the resources we need at our disposal the way we might have in the past. So how do we continue to deliver the most important things without all the resources that we feel we need?

Sibbernsen: When I look back on it, I think that HR has got to do a better job of aggregating and analyzing the business intelligence around the workforce. When their line managers come and say, I have to remodel the structure, I have to consolidate these operations, I have to merge product lines—that is going to become more and more of a frequent item. And companies have to do it faster. Number two is that HR has got to be much better at quickly identifying the high-performing talent, the mission-critical talent. The third challenge would be that HR has got to do a better job of getting a common set of definitions around people investments and people processes. Get them better aligned, better understood and more user-friendly for line leaders.

Antoine: Making sure that HR is a good business partner. In a lot of organizations, we are in really good shape. In a lot of others, we are not. Until you fix that, these questions about a seat at the table, which drive me crazy, will continue. I think the ability to be flexible and adaptable is really critical because we are in a chaotic world, and look what's happened in the past year or two. That's what I worry about the most, because nothing stays the same for very long anymore.

Conaty: I believe that the biggest challenge for HR is the credibility of the organization itself. This is the time that HR leaders really need to step up and be counted. Because right now, I'm convinced that in most companies, employees are on the short end of the stick and that in these tough economic times where "take-aways" are the name of the game, you know you better have somebody that is in there plugging for employees and making sure that you don't overreach on the "take-aways." Employees do understand when you're in dire straits and you've got to take tough actions, but when the sun starts to come back out again, they expect you to react to that too. So I would say that these companies who have reinstated 401(k) matches, as an example, those companies are probably getting "high fives" from their employees saying, "Hey this company does care, they took it away from us but as things got better they gave it back." And then there are other companies where employees are saying, "Hey what gives, our earnings are up, everything is moving in the right direction but they don't seem to want to give us our perks back, and the reason they don't is because they know no one is going to leave anyway." Until things really get better in the economy, companies won't really feel the pinch of departures, but people who have been true blue and loyal over the years and have not answered the head hunters calls are now going to do so.

Steckler: Any other challenges facing HR?

Conaty: As mentioned before, one of the greatest challenges for HR going forward is the developing and growing our own future HR leaders. And my point there is that seldom, with few exceptions, do we develop our own HR leaders for major corporations. I did it at GE. I had four people who could do my job when I left. Dick Antoine had a few people. Name me some other major corporations where that has happened. We all too often, are the biggest violators of succession. We talk and preach about CEO succession and developing internal candidates and the like and we are the shoemaker's children when it comes to HR. Still the majority of top HR slots go to somebody from outside the company.

Steckler: What was the toughest decision you made or action you had to take as head of HR?

Fairbairn: For me, I think those are always the individual people decisions when you have to deliver a tough message. A message that communicates that someone is not doing a good job, when you need to tell someone that we are all finished waiting for the good job to make itself apparent. I think that if those decisions at some point become no longer difficult, it may not be the right job for you anymore.

Sartain: Any decision that affects another's livelihood is a difficult one. For me, the toughest ones have been when there has been a reduction in force and you know not only do you have to help the whole company reduce, but you have to reduce your own team.

Ziskin: I agree. I have been involved several times in making decisions that somewhat dramatically reduced headcount to take cost out of the business in the name of survival or in the name of improved performance. No matter how many times I've done that, I always find that is the single most difficult decision; and I promised myself that if I ever stopped feeling badly about doing these things, I should probably get out of HR and do something else.

Sibbernsen: The hardest decisions, I agree, are those that involve letting people go, even if you do it for the right reason and you do it right. And you have to take care of the people that remain, too.

Antoine: I think one of the really tough aspects of our job is when you have to separate senior managers of the company for the violation of ethics or principles of the company. In the 10 years, I had fortunately only a few of those situations to deal with. Now I'm distinguishing between decision and action here. The decision was easy. At least in P&G, if you violate the ethics or the values of the company, you go. But then doing it, having to talk to those people, who were individuals that I knew as colleagues usually for many years, the action was really hard.

Holmes: I agree that, by far, the toughest decisions are when you have to let an employee go. Any time you are impacting someone's life it is a difficult situation. Therefore, it's important that all actions surrounding these situations are handled respectfully—for all involved.

Conaty: I had so many tough ones that it is hard to pick one out. But probably the toughest was when I was in the aircraft engines business and we had a major integrity issue in marketing. I don't want to talk about the specifics, but in the end we had to get rid of 23 high-level executives within the aircraft business. And I really put my job on the line arguing back and forth with the corporate office as to why we should discipline our people based on the role they played. You can imagine dealing with Jack Welch on that issue. He literally wanted everybody involved in any way to be let go. I disagreed and persevered, at that time when I didn't have a long relationship with Jack. I told him that that would be absolutely the wrong thing to do. I asked him to trust me to make sure that anybody that was really a violator receives the appropriate action. While if there were other people who were part of the organization but were not directly involved, I could mete out the discipline in an equitable way. And, quite honestly, that is how I ended up with the SVP job. Welch really loved the way I handled it, loved the way that I would fight back.

Steckler: Let's talk about the economy. With the economic "reset" and continued turbulence, what are the implications for HR leaders and their organizations?

Ziskin: Everybody who has gotten comfortable with the fact that retention is up and that their attrition is down, shouldn't get too comfortable. I believe that as the economy continues to improve, I think even happy people—those that are perfectly happy where they are—are going to be chased after by other companies. Also, we are going to have to pay attention to the people who want to stick around versus those who don't and segment the way that we treat talent, because companies aren't going to have the resources or the time to focus equally on everyone.

Antoine: I agree. I think a big challenge is how do you re-engage employees. Especially if you are one of the companies that had let a lot of people go and you cut back benefits, trimmed wages and so on. You have a lot of work to do to earn back the appropriate level of loyalty and commitment. If you had to have layoffs, but you did it in the right way, I would argue then I think it's easier. If employees saw you doing everything you could to avoid what had to be done, and that that pain was shared equally all the way up to the top of the company, then I think it's a lot easier to get them back.

Fairbairn: I think that the implications for HR are probably similar to the implications to lots of organizations. But the adjectives that come to my mind are: flexibility, comfort with high velocity and resilience. You just need you need to be ready for every change and for creating change, for selling change and then realizing that you, too, have to change.

Steckler: I want to express my appreciation to each of you for participating in these interviews. Your level of openness and candor about the CHRO role, leadership overall and the future challenges facing HR, are all important contributions. Thank you!

Critical Thinking

1. What are the top leadership challenges facing human resource professionals?

2. What are some strategies that could be used to address those challenges?

3. How could these challenges be implemented? Panel and Their Former Companies:

Internet References

Challenges and Opportunities Facing Today's HR Professional
   http://blog.randstad.ca/news/bid/231814/Challenges-and-Opportunities-Facing-Today-s-HR-Professional

Challenges Facing HR Over the Next 10 Years
   www.shrm.org/research/surveyfindings/articles/pages/challengesfacinghroverthenext10years.aspx

5 Great Challenges Ahead for HR and Leaders, Forbes
   www.forbes.com/sites/meghanbiro/2012/11/11/5-greatest-challenges-ahead-for-hr-and-leaders

The Biggest Challenges Facing HR Today
   www.tlnt.com/2013/04/17/the-biggest-challenges-facing-hr-today

---

STEVE STECKLER has held senior HR line and staff positions at WPP, Marriott International, TRW, Citibank and Ciba-Geigy. Most recently, he was director of HR Integration for Microsoft's Venture Integration team, responsible for integrating acquired companies and leaders. Steckler joined Microsoft as director of Strategic Talent Planning, managing a team focused on senior talent development and succession management. Steckler is an associate article editor of *People & Strategy* journal and is a member of HRPS's Board of Directors.

Article   Prepared by: Maria Nathan, *Lynchburg College*

Grooming the Next Generation

Sustain competitive advantage through succession planning and an early career development program.

KASTHURI V. HENRY

Learning Outcomes

After reading this article, you will be able to:

- Understand how the Early Career Development Program at Aon Corp. works.

- Understand Aon's implementation plan that supports the Career Development Program.

- Consider why this article focuses upon knowledge workers in particular.

A viable succession plan for ensuring business continuity is crucial for a company to be able to sustain value for its stakeholders. To create a successful plan, the corporation must have a steady stream of resources that are valuable, rare, and not imitable. When the company belongs to the service industry, its most valuable resource is its intellectual capital, represented by its team of knowledge workers, so attracting, retaining, and developing the best minds to collaborate and deliver cutting-edge solutions to customers becomes the underpinning of the business. Aon Corporation built such a culture.

A major part of Aon's succession plan is the development of young talent to effectively contribute in the social exchange process and establish trust-based, business-to-business relationships that will nurture and grow the business. This pipeline of future knowledge workers comes from universities in the communities in which the company operates. Acquiring, retaining, and serving the client base necessitates a relationship-based approach to business development, so the social network and the ability to leverage relationships are required skills for doing business.

Motivation for the Plan

Aon provides risk management services, insurance and reinsurance brokerage, and human capital consulting through its 59,000 employees in more than 500 offices in more than 120 countries. The company grew through acquisitions. In the early 2000s, it integrated its various business segments and streamlined its operations to better deliver the customer value proposition. During this process, management made key observations about the organizational resources, customer base, and success factors necessary for an effective partnership between them. Here's a summary of the observations.

The existence of a generational gap in the workforce: Baby Boomers dominated the senior team, and there was no tangible game plan for when they retired. Also, 45% of the workforce was composed of Baby Boomers.

Growth and related needs: Business growth required additional knowledge workers. Since the business was specialized, recruiting needed to be strategized to guarantee long-term success.

Shift from male to female client contacts: The landscape of risk managers was changing in the United States. More women were entering the field of risk management at the customers' businesses, which resulted, for example, in a shift from clients wanting to do business over a game of golf to clients wanting to do business over a spa outing. Yet Aon's workforce continued to remain predominantly male.

Technological progress in the industry: Technology became all-pervasive, which started influencing how business was done as people were constantly connecting at all hours via mobile devices and social media as well as traditional means. Thus, a technology-savvy generation of knowledge workers became necessary to backfill the human resource pipeline.

Diversity: Aon had become increasingly conscious of the varied ideas and thought processes encompassed in a diverse workforce and made a targeted effort to build such a dynamic team.

These findings became the motivation for exploring equitable business solutions and culminated in Aon creating an Early Career Development Program (ECDP). The goal was to develop a scalable program that addressed the needs of the immediate future while remaining flexible to evolve as the dynamics of the business warranted. As the regional CFO based out of the corporate office, I was in a position to partner with the human resources team at Aon to develop the program and the model.

The Plan Model

The Early Career Development Program consisted of Rotational and Direct Development Programs that became a pipeline for future talent and business-unit long-term added value. The internship program was the feeder program, and the employee retention rate was 96% when entry into Aon was via this route.

Campus champions were identified from within the existing workforce to cultivate and nurture strategic partnerships with 15 national universities. The universities were selected based on the areas of specialization corresponding to the company's needs, which were risk management, consulting, human resources, accounting, and finance. Through these ongoing partnerships, the campus champions interacted with student organizations, faculty, and the administration to build brand awareness across the university community as well as identify potential talent. Based on campus interviews, the company selected third-year undergraduates to participate in its annual three-month summer internship program. The internship program was department-specific with performance goals and targeted deliverables identified. This way, Aon could evaluate the

young talent in the context of day-to-day business performance and help the interns develop soft as well as technical skills that were necessary for a full-time career transition when they graduated. Both the intern and the manager had the opportunity to determine if a long-term engagement could be possible. At the end of their internship, the participants identified for a continued partnership were offered a permanent position as an associate through either the Rotational Development Program or Direct Development Program.

The associates embraced the idea of already having accepted a job offer when they returned to the university to complete their senior year. Aon embraced the internship program as its sustained recruiting pipeline and leveraged it to serve as the early career development initiative feeder program. This turned out to be a win-win partnership. But the ECDP associates weren't limited to the internship route. Recruiting from the national university partners and local university strategic partners filled the remaining talent pool opportunities. For example, if a strong candidate from a nonpartner university applied for the ECDP Direct Development Program, they were given fair consideration as a means for evaluating alternate partnership opportunities. When the candidates wanted to limit their engagement to the city of their university, the university was considered a local strategic partner. When the candidates were willing to relocate across the U.S., the university they came from was considered a national strategic partner. The local universities play a critical role in recruiting for offices outside big cities like Chicago (home of Aon Corporation world headquarters), New York, and Los Angeles.

It was clear as the program began rolling out that the associates preferred the Rotational Development Program because it gave them an opportunity to sample practical aspects of their field of education and training, but the managers preferred the Direct Development Program since it ensured that designated talent remained within the team. Associates in the Rotational Development Program needed to find a "permanent home" or job in the company when they completed their rotation, but those in the Direct Development Program already had a specific full-time role.

Table 1   Rotational Development Program and Direct Development Program

Rotational Development Program	Direct Development Program
Students are hired within one particular track in large offices (Chicago, New York, Los Angeles).	Students are hired within one particular track in offices across the country.
They rotate three times within 18 months, and the length of each rotation is defined by the track.	Students are hired into a single role and don't formally rotate.
Predetermined business rotations are selected prior to start date.	
Upon successful completion of the program, participants secure full-time placement.	

Here are the program criteria for selecting the associates:

- **Description of potential associate**
  - Undergraduate student of any major
  - Graduating in December of the previous year or May-June of the current year
  - A minimum 3.0 GPA
- **18-month program** (12-month development plan corresponding to the plan year and a new six-month development plan for the second year congruent with the new annual plan)
- **Seven tracks:** Aon Risk Services, Aon Consulting, Actuarial, Human Resources, Accounting & Finance, Strategy, and Aon Re (Aon Reinsurance Brokerage Service)
- **Established development plans for each track**
- **Ongoing performance management**

Table 1 shows the differences between the Rotational Development Program and Direct Development Program.

Implementation Plan

The ability to sustain the ECDP is contingent on a robust university-company partnership to keep the flow of talent into Aon and on Aon's ability to nurture the recruited talent and retain the brain trust. Naturally, the implementation cycle starts with an annual campus recruiting process. The recruiting interviews are two parts: oncampus screening interviews conducted by campus champion teams and a final interview at Aon with the Early Career Development Program participating managers. Interview sessions at Aon also give the potential associates the opportunity to experience the real work environment and the respective work groups. Associates selected for the program are brought in for an orientation before they begin their assignments. The Chicago-based three-day orientation typically includes in-depth transition training by HR coupled with:

- Executive and business unit speakers,
- Program overview/expectations/development plans,
- Networking activities,
- Business etiquette, and
- Discussion about Aon's leadership model.

HR has an Early Career Development Program team dedicated to the talent management initiative. The team is headed by the vice president of HR for Americas, which assures executive sponsorship of the strategic efforts. The ECDP director, two HR managers, and an HR specialist work in unison with the campus champions and ECDP participating managers to make the plan come to life and stay focused. The onboarding process takes place at the local offices before the Chicago-based orientation, giving a two-week lead time for the various logistical steps to be coordinated.

After the first ECDP was complete, Aon conducted a survey to see how the participants felt about the program. The company found that training managers, work groups, and HR representatives are equally important for a successful program. The survey results also showed that associates have better experiences and more fulfilling programs if their managers are supportive and are engaged in the program. In addition, if the work groups and HR contacts were supportive of the associates, then the associates had an incrementally beneficial experience.

Transplanting students from universities into work groups won't automatically harness their potential talent. To bring about an effective transition, the talent has to be nurtured and developed as part of the ECDP curriculum, which encompasses core, track, and department curricula.

Core Curriculum

This is made up of required common learning and development components for all associates. The curriculum aims at developing associates' soft skills in the areas of value-centric leadership; communication, including listening; decision making; team building; collaboration; critical thinking; basic finance; technology; and mentoring. This curriculum spans the first 12 months and culminates in a graduation presentation to the management team.

Track Curriculum

This is track-specific to provide technical skills and expertise in effective utilization of track-specific processes and tools. Track-specific licenses are incorporated into this curriculum, and associates are required to earn the necessary professional credentials corresponding to their tracks. For example, an associate going through the risk management track is prepared for risk manager licensing, and an associate in the accounting and finance track is prepared for the Certified Public Accountant (CPA) credential. Since insurance is a regulated industry, risk managers are required to be licensed insurance brokers in the state in which they practice.

Department Curriculum

This includes departmental knowledge necessary for associates to function effectively in their roles. For example, the accounting and finance track will train the associate on the processes around journal entries, monthly close, rolling 12-month forecasting, and monthly variance analysis along with teaching how the systems are used to perform the tasks.

The mentoring program, performance management, and peer discussions during networking sessions add to the program's success because they highlight the collaborative nature of the program and emphasize the common stake.

Progress Evaluation and Continuous Strategic Realignment

Program success is tracked and analyzed for university partnership performance, candidate work performance, track-based performance, associate satisfaction rate, manager satisfaction rate, financial impact, retention rate, and overall added value. The company also performs an ongoing SWOT (Strengths, Weaknesses, Opportunities, and Threats) analysis to directionally align the continuous progress with the dynamic business needs. This program evaluation survey is based on a 360-degree approach to identify what aspects of the program work and what aspects need improvement. Here are more results from the first program survey.

Areas of success:

- Manager/team training was highly appreciated.
- Work assignment experience was fulfilling to the associates.
- Sixty-nine percent of the associates indicated that their developmental goals were met.
- Eighty-eight percent of the associates said they had good working relationships with managers and work teams.
- There was a 91% rate of satisfaction with the availability of managers and the assignment team to aid in candidate development.

Areas of opportunity:

- Quantity of work could be higher.
- Associates can take on more challenging work.
- There should be more discussions between the manager and the associates about performance management and the process for establishing objectives or setting goals.

After the initial rollout and feedback, Aon made some changes to enhance the program. One such enhancement was that the roles and responsibility definitions establish functional clarity and streamlined coordination.

The program management role includes responsibilities such as setting program vision and strategy with business leaders, establishing consistent program definitions and timelines, collecting and reporting key deliverables and metrics, developing and clarifying program roles and responsibilities, recognizing key contributors to the program, and communicating about the program efforts.

The manager role includes ownership of the ultimate accountability for positive and meaningful early career professional experience. The manager works in partnership with the track champion, specifies and drives the development of

assignment-related competencies, and carries out the performance development process. Providing continual feedback to associates, maintaining flexibility to support associates in completing all early career development plans, attending all manager training sessions, completing the required performance management training component, managing associates' day-to-day activities, and providing challenging assignments that create opportunities for continual growth are some additional aspects of the manager's role.

Champion roles are scattered across the country and represent all business lines. Champions act as business liaisons to the ECDP team and can take one of four forms, namely track champions, location champions, HR champions, and campus champions. Campus champions build the university partnership as well as establish working relationships with faculty, administrators, and student organizations. They have a campus presence and help establish brand awareness through various campus-based initiatives of the student organizations.

Another program modification was the alignment of the performance management plan with the Aon leadership model. Since the goal was to develop the talent pool, it made sense to instill the leadership values at the point of entry—or when the associates started with the company. The leadership model provides every employee with the fundamental tools to achieve the company's strategic imperatives and is grounded in its core value of acting with integrity across everything Aon does:

- Deliver distinctive customer value by leveraging relationships, client and industry knowledge, and the "Best of Aon," which means to bring the best cross-functional team to meet the complex client needs and to present the best possible solution, regardless of geography. In other words, a natural resource client in the Midwest will get the benefit of the Texas-based Aon Natural Resources Practice in order to provide distinctive solutions, such as risk management solutions, benefits solutions, etc.
- Develop unmatched talent and high-performing teams through continuous learning, honest feedback, rigorous development, and disciplined talent management.
- Build differentiated capability through innovation, proven solutions, and deep content expertise.
- Deliver business results with excellence and the best balance of investment and efficiency.
- Live Aon's values by always acting with integrity and by working every day in a way that positively impacts clients, colleagues, and communities.

Future Outlook

Recent events have led to a greater number of Direct Development Program associates than Rotational Development Program associates. Clients' need for an uninterrupted service relationship, managers' need for an uninterrupted resource pool, and economics have been the drivers for this shift. Rotational associates will continue working in the accounting and finance track, given the diverse skill set requirement of that professional track coupled with the fact that it doesn't require customer interfacing. Also, consulting, HR, and finance need more resources. Compared to 2007, associate roles at local offices outside major metropolitan areas have increased by 88%, and the 2009 program year saw a 48% increase over 2008 in actuarial roles.

The Early Career Development Program has opened the door for experienced employees to engage in a personally and professionally fulfilling endeavor—to leave their legacy through the development of the emerging generation of knowledge workers. The overall experience has allowed Aon to partner with national and local universities to develop future leaders. And the program has given students the chance to obtain corporate work experience in a career development program. The result of this collaborative long-term effort is a better, more powerful workforce and good community relationships.

Critical Thinking

1. What does it mean for the baby-boomers to be retiring?

2. How are companies dealing with the fact that many of their key personnel are leaving?

3. What are some of the steps that firms can take to get the best new employees?

Internet References

Examples of Employee Development Activities
http://smallbusiness.chron.com/examples-employee-development-activities-11195.html

Implementing an Employee Training and Development Program
http://hrcouncil.ca/hr-toolkit/learning-implementing.cfm

The Manager's Role in Employee Learning - ASTD
www.astd.org/Digital-Resources/Webcasts/TD/2013/09/The-Managers-Role-in-Employee-Learning

Six Tips for Effective Career Development Programs
www.cio.com/article/29169/Six_Tips_for_Effective_Career_Development_Programs

The National Career Development Association
www.associationdatabase.com

KASTHURI V. HENRY, CTP, is the president of Kas Henry Inc, a consulting and training firm serving the corporate finance space. She is a visiting assistant professor at Southern Illinois University and an adjunct faculty member at North Park University (NPU) in Chicago. She is also a member of IMA's Northwest Suburban Chicago Chapter.

From *Strategic Finance*, January 2011, pp. 37–42. Copyright © 2011 by Institute of Management Accountants-IMA.Reprinted by permission via Copyright Clearance Center.

Article   Prepared by: Maria Nathan, *Lynchburg College*

What Does the Gig Economy Mean for HR?

CATH EVERETT

Learning Outcomes

After reading this article, you will be able to:

- Understand what is meant by "gig economy."
- Appreciate how the gig economy relates to HR practice.

The "gig economy" has firmly entered employment vocabulary, becoming a catch-all term for anything from Uber taxi drivers to freelance professionals. But what does this hyper-flexible way of working mean for HR? Cath Everett reports.

The buzz around the so-called gig economy—the "Uberfication" of work—has been growing louder in recent months, even making it into a speech by US presidential hopeful Hillary Clinton—where she aired concerns over what this growing hiring trend could mean for workers.

But interestingly, the definition of what the "gig economy" actually is varies tremendously depending on who you speak to.

One characterisation is an environment in which people buy and sell services via online service brokering platforms, such as TaskRabbit and PeoplePerHour, a tech-enabled marketplace for freelancers.

In the consumer world, perhaps, the best illustrations of this phenomenon are apps, such as Uber for taxi rides, or the home rental service Airbnb. Customers bid for specific services or types of property at their best price, while the drivers or owners fight for business at the back end.

But the term also stretches to include the idea of "portfolio working." This phrase describes people who work on a number of different projects for different organisations, sometimes combining such activity with other more formal employment.

Whichever the preferred definition, Alex Swarbrick, senior consultant at leadership institute Roffey Park, points out that this kind of workforce, although still only relatively small at the moment, tends to consist of two tiers with "radically different working conditions."

"You can characterise the workforce in this model like an hourglass. So the people at the top comprise highly-skilled, sought-after talent that is relatively well paid and expects to work flexibly," he says.

"Workers at the bottom end of the hourglass, however, are likely to be on temporary, fixed-term, zero-hour contracts and have a number of jobs that could be characterised as insecure, low-paid work."

Employment on-demand

Gig economy—a system where work is contracted on a freelance short-term basis, often using technology to connect workers and hirers.

Uberfication—the disruptive application of Uber-convenient technologies to more traditional marketplaces, for example, Uber taxis, Airbnb hotels, Deliveroo takeaways, Rover dog-sitting.

In other words, at the top of the hourglass, it is and will remain an employee's market, and at the bottom, an employer's market.

This scenario plays into equally widespread optimistic and pessimistic world views of future employment trends, depending on which end of the spectrum you choose to focus on.

Early Days

It is still only early days for the gig economy, which, according to research by PwC, makes up a mere 2 percent of the total recruitment market.

But by 2020, it is forecast to be worth nearly $63 billion globally, and £2 billion in the United Kingdom alone.

Its My life connected report suggests that, while technology is definitely contributing to the trend, it is also being driven by growing numbers of millennial workers keen to take more control over their careers.

And they are not the only ones. There is also mounting interest among older employees, who are moving towards the end of their career and, in many instances, are looking less for more flexible ways of working too.

David Knight, associate partner at KPMG's people and change practice agrees with this trajectory: "The gig economy and portfolio working is still in its infancy and is quite immature as many organisations have yet to see the value of employing people in this way."

"But rolling the clock forward over the next two or three years, I anticipate a groundswell of interest from employers, driven by demand from old and young alike."

Lost in the Numbers

Mark Beatson, chief economist at the CIPD, on the other hand, cautions against getting too carried away.

"Most forecasts tend to be overoptimistic in the short term as change is often much slower to catch on than people expect," he says. "But gig working may also be difficult to pick up in the statistics, especially if people are just doing a few hours here and there, so we may not see it coming for a while."

The types of jobs likely to be affected most are those that are either quite specialised or subject to volatility in demand.

So at the top of the hourglass, this might include IT work, such as software testing or web design, or auditing activities in an accountancy context.

At the bottom, it could include cleaning services or hotel roles, such as chambermaids or bar staff.

But the big question, of course, is whether or not HR is ready for all of this and/or in a suitable position to handle the multifarious challenges thrown up as labor models start to shift?

Is HR Ready?

A separate PwC report, the future of work, implies that most HR departments are failing to get to grips with the issues.

It found that less than 1/3 of employers are basing their future talent strategies on the rise of the portfolio career, even though a huge 46 percent of HR professionals expect at least 20 percent of their workforce to be made up of contractors and temporary workers by 2020.

A 2014 CIPD survey into agile working echoed this, with the majority of HR leaders who responded saying their primary concern with employing non-permanent staff related to quality of work issues.

Furthermore, only about half provided training to casual workers and a mere third offered them performance appraisals. The figures were even worse for agency staff and self-employed people.

And despite worries over such workers' lack of engagement, less than half of employers bothered to include them in internal communications or consider them for recognition awards.

Adding Value

As a result, Roffey Park's Swarbrick says: "We're seeing a polarisation of the HR profession—some are persisting in maintaining a commodity management model where workers are seen as resources and HR is there to manage the risk they pose."

"But others see their role as making it easy to fulfill the enterprise's purpose by starting to open up relations with people working at the top, bottom and middle of the hour glass."

Although this move to the gig economy undoubtedly poses numerous organisational challenges, it also provides HR with a "great opportunity to add value to the organisation"—if they can get it right ("see box 'Gig Economy: Key Challenges for HR'").

"I'm not sure there are any slick models for dealing with any of this just yet, but as a starting point, it's important for HR to grasp what this kind of agility requires of them and to start turning some of the traditional preconceptions of their role and ideas

---

Gig Economy: Key Challenges for HR

- Managing a talent pool and developing an employee value proposition that works across a blend of permanent and portfolio workers.
- How to integrate contract terms and conditions into a cohesive, seamless whole and offer pertinent benefits and rewards—and become an employer of choice for "gig workers".
- Ensuring that the right technology is in place to automate joining and leaving processes and ensure they are smooth and easy to manage so as not to increase the HR admin burden
- Working out what risk management and governance ground rules should be put in place for portfolio staff working for multiple employers, including rivals.
- Managing quality control and ensuring that contracts do not simply end up going to the cheapest rather than most reliable and/or best bidder.
- Line managers operating beneath the radar without being aware of working time, health and safety and minimum wage legislation.

Source: Alex Swarbrick, Roffey Park

such as careers, reward recognition and talent and succession management on their heads," Swarbrick says.

Gary Browning, chief executive of HR consultancy Penna, agrees. "I don't think HR has focused much on this yet, but people need to," he says.

"As they start to focus, they'll ask 'what are the implications for policies, procedures, systems and processes?'

"This is important, but even more important is how to change mindsets about the workforce and how you embrace gig workers."

A key issue here relates to the need to shift the organisation's leadership culture from one of command-and-control to one of collaboration, partnership and mentoring.

Another involves moving from a performance-management approach based on formal appraisals to a performance culture based on individuals taking responsibility for their own output.

A further consideration is about reevaluating matters around career development. This means that, should employees decide to leave the organisation to embrace gig working, taking the attitude of "never darken my door again" simply will not cut it in an increasingly transient employment world. Giving people your blessing and creating an alumni network in order to keep in touch and encourage them to share their new-found skills in future will prove much more fruitful.

As Browning concludes: "There's a huge opportunity for HR to take on a more strategic role here."

"Changing systems and the like is relatively easy, but where people can really add value is in taking their organisations through a transformation to change everything from culture and leadership to recruitment and marketing. It's where HR can really add value and most already have the skills in place to do it."

Cath Everett has been a journalist and editor for more than 20 years, specialising in HR and technology issues.

Critical Thinking

1. What is meant by "gig economy" and why is it important to Human Resource Management?
2. In what ways must HR management adapt its practices to the demands of the gig economy?
3. Do you think that the "gig economy" is here to stay?

Internet References

A Tricky Task: Government Tries to Define the Gig Economy
http://blogs.wsj.com/economics/2016/06/27/a-tricky-task-government-tries-to-define-the-gig-economy/

Defining "Employee" in the New Gig Economy
http://www.nytimes.com/2015/07/19/opinion/sunday/defining-employee-in-the-gig-economy.html?_r=0

Working in the Gig Economy
http://www.bls.gov/careeroutlook/2016/article/what-is-the-gig-economy.htm

Article   Prepared by: Maria Nathan, *Lynchburg College*

Are You a Leader or a Laggard?

HR's Role in Creating a Sustainability Culture

Human Resources Management (HRM)—function, practices and systems—may be missing the next source of real competitive advantage. Leading and facilitating sustainability initiatives and creating a sustainability culture are the critical tasks confronting human resources professionals now. HRM, particularly in the specific practices impacting recruiting, hiring, training, compensation, knowledge management and development, holds tremendous opportunity to shape the firm's sustainability agenda.

ROBERT SROUFE, JAY LIEBOWITZ, AND NAGARAJ SIVASUBRAMANIAM

Learning Outcomes

After reading this article, you will be able to:

- Understand how human resource management can serve to shape an organization's sustainability agenda.

- Understand how/why sustainability in a culture is built in a stair-step process.

- Recognize three primary obstacles to implementing sustainability initiatives and develop strategies for overcoming these obstacles.

W e find an immediate need for understanding the possibilities of transformation to a sustainable organization, and the range and type of actionable practices suitable for HRM and HR professionals. A small number of firms, including industry leaders like Nike and Starbucks, have recognized the emerging paradigm of sustainability and have taken steps to make sustainability a central component of their strategy (Epstein, 2008). Despite the increasing clamor for more sustainable business practices from multiple stakeholders, many firms are reluctant to move quickly, due possibly to a lack of understanding of policies and actions leading to sustainability.

We are concerned that HR professionals may be missing an opportunity to develop and capture unique resources and competencies that customers will value and the competition will find difficult to imitate. Instead, they find themselves waiting to see what emerges, as firms transition out of an emphasis on compliance and pollution prevention activities to those in which social and environmental impacts will be the basis of strategic opportunities and competitive advantage.

Our Investigation

We focus on two primary questions: (1) How do firms organize and manage themselves to promote and integrate new sustainability initiatives, and (2) How do HR practices influence a firm's ability to integrate and collaborate on a myriad of emerging sustainability-focused business practices? Our analysis of both quantitative and qualitative data helped us to:

- uncover three distinct types of firms integrating sustainability activities into the work place;
- identify three primary obstacles to implementing sustainability initiatives;
- develop strategies for overcoming these obstacles to implementation; and
- propose a stairway to sustainable opportunities for HR to take a leadership role.

Sustainable practices are those that go beyond process improvement and waste reduction (typically found in the operational approaches of the past), and focus on developing innovative social and environmental practices that promote collaborative efforts across functions, create unique social capital and build long-term economic value for the firm. A dominant theory in the literature, the resource-based view of the firm, stipulates that companies can gain sustainable competitive advantages if they are built on and supported by organization-level competencies (Barney, 1991). These competencies reflect unique combinations of resources that are rare, non-substitutable, difficult to imitate and valuable to customers (Barney and Wright, 1998). Organizations integrating organizational-level competencies within sustainability activities are predicted to have highly motivated and engaged employees who can focus their efforts on the reduction of materials and energy by several orders of magnitude, the development of new, innovative "green" products or services and new business models that they can design to have a strategic impact on sustainability (Epstein, 2008).

So what can HRM professionals do to increase the opportunities that await them in the new, "green collar" economy? An organization's culture and entrenched business practices, and the strategic importance given to human resources may be critical determinants of building a sustainable organization. Every day, managers are charged with developing new, "sustainability" focused programs and strategies in a way that will most benefit the firm. Yet, researchers and practitioners have few examples of what has been tried that focus on HR elements such as organizational design, recruiting, training and management practices; and several questions still remain unanswered.

After conducting an HR-focused forum on sustainability sponsored by the local chapter of the Human Resource Planning Society[1], and through the collection of survey data, we are able to highlight the importance of the HR function and offer an explanation for why some firms adopt certain sustainability practices and others do not. There is a significant opportunity to build upon an emerging paradigm of sustainable development and explore how the HR function can play a strategic role to help lead the efforts to build a sustainability culture.

Study Design

We designed and conducted a Web-based survey of executives of firms located in western Pennsylvania, eastern Ohio and northern West Virginia. The survey, sponsored by the local chapter of the Human Resource Planning Society, was designed to identify the extent to which firms had implemented various sustainability initiatives, and the role of the human resource function in creating and implementing these sustainability initiatives. Based on an extensive review of literature, we pooled many initiatives that had been identified as examples of environmental and social dimensions of sustainability. We rewrote the items to avoid redundancy and ensure clarity, and pre-tested them with

a group of academics and practitioners. The Web-based survey, administered during October and November 2008 resulted in 76 complete responses. The sample consisted primarily of HR professionals (49 percent) along with operations (14 percent), sales and marketing (13 percent) and senior management (8 percent). Three-fourths of our respondents had nine or more years of experience in their field. Both small and large firms were represented in our sample. The firms represented a variety of industry sectors including manufacturing, healthcare, retail and services.

We identified six sustainability dimensions based on a factor analysis of responses to 21 items that measured whether the respondent firm implemented particular sustainability initiatives. These ranged from employee-related efforts, such as promoting ethics and integrity and encouraging community volunteer programs, to environmental protection initiatives such as conserving electricity and pollution reduction/prevention. We computed the dimension score by adding the responses to the initiatives that comprise each dimension. We then classified the 76 firms based on their score on the six dimensions spanning social (employee orientation and volunteerism) and environmental (conserving materials, environmental protection, employee conservation and sustainability measurement) sustainability initiatives. We identified three distinct groups of firms using cluster analysis; we labeled them *Leaders, People-focused* and *Laggards*. We conducted further analyses to validate the cluster membership, as well as examine the presence of any systematic differences across these three clusters of firms (additional details on the statistical procedures are provided in the sidebar).

Key Findings

Our analysis revealed four conclusions:

1. Firms differed significantly in the extent to which they had implemented sustainability initiatives. Those firms simultaneously integrating social and environmental sustainability initiatives were considered *Leaders.* Next, *People-focused* firms focused on social initiatives to a greater extent than environmental initiatives. Finally, *Laggard* firms had not implemented, to any significant extent, either the social or the environmental sustainability initiatives.
2. *Leader* firms saw a significant role for HR in facilitating and leading the sustainability efforts within their organizations.
3. *Leader* firms utilized a range of human resource systems to reinforce their firm's people practices and environmental practices to build a sustainability culture.
4. *People-focused* firms utilized a range of human resource systems to implement their firm's people practices to a greater extent than their environmental practices.

Sustainability Dimensions and Diffusion of Sustainability Practices

The six sustainability dimensions and the 15 specific sustainability practices that comprise them are summarized in Table 1. We also examined the extent to which the responding firms adopted or diffused these practices. The firms more widely adopted employee wellness, safety and ethics-related initiatives than environmental initiatives. For instance, 75 percent of the responding firms implemented employee health and wellness programs and promoted ethics and integrity as an integral part of their organizational culture. In contrast, fewer than 12 percent of the firms indicated that they conduct life cycle analysis of new products or calculated the carbon footprint of their companies. We captured the patterns of these differences in the adoption of sustainability initiatives using cluster analysis, and have summarized the results.

Leaders, People-focused and Laggards

A cluster analysis of the sustainability initiatives across the six dimensions revealed three distinct groups of firms that were most similar to each other within a group, and least similar across groups. We examined the profile of each group and labeled them as *Leaders, People-focused* and *Laggards* based on the extent to which they implemented social and environmental sustainability practices. Characteristics of these three clusters are summarized graphically in Figure 1.

We validated our classification by looking at two indicators. Firms that we classified as *leaders* and *people-focused* were significantly more likely to have a sustainability policy than firms classified as laggards (50 percent, 35 percent and 7 percent respectively, x^2 significant). We also examined whether the three clusters differed in their responses (using a three-point scale) to the question: *To what extent is your organization developing a sustainability culture/work environment?* Again *leaders and people-focused* firms were engaged in developing such a culture to a greater degree than laggards (2.20, 1.82 and 1.25 respectively, $p < .001$). While *leaders* and *people-focused* firms were not significantly different in either having a sustainability policy or developing a sustainability culture, their extent of adoption of many of the environmental initiatives was significantly different. These results confirm the existence of three groups of firms.

Leaders (N = 20)

These firms, comprising 26 percent of our sample, were far ahead of others on all six dimensions of sustainability practice, and were the most comprehensive in their approach to implementing both social and environmental sustainability

Table 1   Sustainability Dimensions[1]

	Sustainability Dimension	Sustainability Business Practices[2]
SOCIAL	1. Employee Orientation	• Value diversity & inclusion • Promote ethics & integrity • Encourage innovation & risk-taking
	2. Employee Volunteerism	• Support community volunteer programs on company time • Encourage biking to work & taking mass-transit
ENVIRONMENTAL	3. Employee Conservation	• Promote conservation at home • Encourage telecommuting
	4. Environmental Protection	• Address climate change • Conserve electricity • Reduce pollution
	5. Conserving Materials	• Develop "green" products & services • Purchase recycled products
	6. Sustainability Measurement	• Establish an internal sustainability team • Conduct life-cycle analysis of new products • Calculate the carbon footprint of the company

[1] We did not include an economic dimension, as corporate financial performance is an outcome of social and environmental practices and not a strategic initiative in and of itself.

[2] The dimensions were identified using factor analysis; an index was constructed for each dimension by summing up the Yes/No (1/0) responses to the set of practices that comprised each dimension.

initiatives. A typical firm in this group implemented at least two employee orientation and two environmental protection initiatives, and at least one employee conservation, materials conservation and sustainability measurement initiative. These firms were more likely than other firms to establish an internal sustainability team, address climate change or promote conservation at employees' homes.

People-focused (N = 28)

This group, comprising 37 percent of the sample, had a strong showing on two of the six sustainability dimensions: employee orientation and volunteerism. These firms clearly excel at becoming an employer of choice and creating a great place to work. Our results suggest that these firms have just begun implementing environmental initiatives, and are significantly behind the leaders on the environmental dimensions.

Laggards (N = 28)

This group showed no discernible strength in any of the six sustainability dimensions and lagged behind the other firms on five of the six dimensions. Virtually none in this group had implemented initiatives such as valuing diversity, encouraging innovation and risk taking, reducing pollution, encouraging telecommuting, promoting conservation at employees' homes, establishing an internal sustainability team or conducting life cycle analysis of new products.

The Role of HR in Sustainability

To gauge the level of involvement of the HR function in implementing sustainability initiatives, we asked the respondents to rate the extent to which the HR function either facilitated or led their sustainability efforts. Results of our analysis are

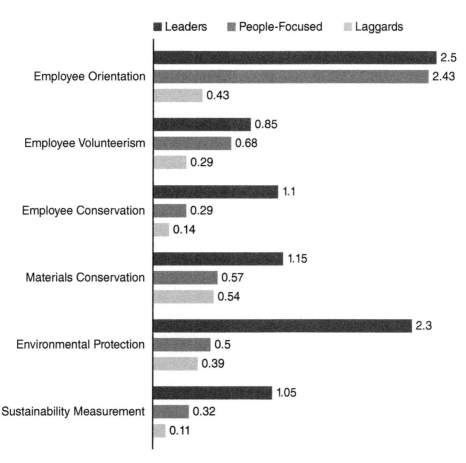

Score for each dimension was computed by summing up the Yes/No (1/0) responses to the set of initiatives that comprise each dimension (see Table 1 for information on specific practices).

Figure 1   Characteristics of leaders, people-focused and laggards

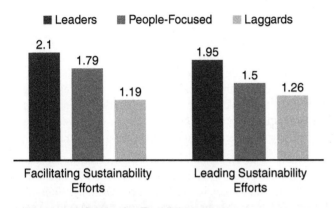

Response Scale: 1 – To a little extent;
2 – To a moderate extent; 3 – To a great extent

Figure 2   Role of HR in sustainability efforts

summarized in Figure 2. As expected, *leaders* and *people-focused* firms were significantly different from *laggards* in the facilitating role played by the HR function. However, when it came to the HR function leading the sustainability effort, *leaders* were significantly different from both *people-focused* and *laggard* firms. Our results suggest that a leading role for the HR function can be crucial for firms implementing the full-range of sustainability initiatives. HR possesses an array of tools that can help to change an organization's culture (e.g., employee selection, training and reward systems).

We examined the extent to which specific HR practices were changed to support developing a sustainability culture within an organization. The results are summarized in Figure 3. In general, *leaders* and *people-focused* firms had modified their HR practices to a significantly greater extent than *laggard* firms, and ANOVA tests confirmed this. This was most apparent for

Response Scale: 1 - To a very little extent; 2 - To a little extent; 3 - To some extent
4 - To a significant extent; 5 - To a very great extent

Figure 3   Role of HR practices in sustainability efforts

recruiting, employee selection and new employee orientation—practices that enable organizations to change their culture, one hire at a time. This strategy of changing these practices first also might be prudent given the dual benefits of attracting an applicant pool with different characteristics and the possibility of encountering minimal resistance within the organization to implement new strategy. Training, development and mentoring practices also were modified to support sustainability initiatives, though not to the same extent as the recruiting and selection practices.

Modifying HR practices to help build a sustainability culture is an evolutionary process, with the firms we observed at different stages of implementing their sustainability strategies. Our results suggest that HR practices targeted at the external community, i.e., potential applicants, were modified to a greater extent than HR practices governing internal stakeholders, i.e., current employees. Logically, we expect HR managers to modify performance management and compensation practices at a later date. Our results imply a natural progression beginning with modifying recruiting and selection practices to impact the characteristics of new hires, then to alter training and development practices to help current employees develop new competencies, and finally changing the way employee performance is measured and rewarded.

We analyzed the correlations between the eight HR practices and the six sustainability dimensions. As expected, firms that are doing more sustainability practices also changed their HR practices to a greater extent than other firms. Firms that are leading in the social dimensions of sustainability practices (employee orientation and employee volunteerism) modified all eight HR practices to a greater extent than others (correlations ranged from .28 to .48, all significant at p < .01). When it comes to the environmental dimensions, the pattern also is clear. HR practices were modified to support employee conservation and materials conservation, but not the other two environmental dimensions (environmental protection or sustainability measurement). For employee conservation, modifying HR practices related to recruitment, selection, orientation, training, development and performance management have the greatest impact, with correlations ranging from .21 to .31. Firms that implemented materials conservation initiatives to a greater extent also significantly altered HR practices, especially with regard to training and development.

In summary, our results suggest that *leaders* differed significantly from *people-focused* and *laggard* firms in the extent to which they implemented different sustainability initiatives. The human resource function played a critical role in these firms in leading and facilitating their sustainability efforts. *Leaders* and *people-focused* firms modified their HR practices to a greater extent than *laggards* to support their sustainability agenda. These changes in HR practices also are aligned with certain sustainability initiatives: supporting our argument that

HR practices play a strategic role in implementing specific sustainability initiatives and creating a sustainability organizational culture.

Obstacles on the Pathway to Sustainability

Despite a growing consensus that firms can "do well by doing good" and considerable empirical evidence confirming a positive relationship between a firm's social and environmental performance and financial performance (Orlitzky, Schmidt & Rynes, 2003), our results suggest a lack of widespread adoption of sustainability initiatives. Either there is no acceptance of the basic premise, despite evidence to the contrary, or the task of building a sustainability culture may be considerably more challenging and complex.

We asked the respondents what challenges and obstacles they encounter in creating a sustainability culture. We reviewed these open-ended responses for common themes and how frequently they occurred across the three distinct types of firms. Our research suggests three possible reasons for why firms either have not undertaken any sustainability initiatives or continued building on their early efforts to become a sustainable organization. These were (1) lack of commitment and buy-in from both management and employees, (2) lack of resources, and (3) cultural and institutional resistance to change. We also found systematic differences in the obstacles identified by *laggards* versus *leaders*.

Lack of Commitment and Buy-in
As we expected, this was a primary obstacle among *laggards* and an important issue for *people-focused* firms who felt there was widespread "apathy," and "lack of interest from top management" regarding environmental issues. This was not the case for *leader* firms. Without top management support and employee buy-in, it is very difficult to generate the momentum needed to implement any new sustainability initiatives (Wirtenberg, Harmon, Russell & Fairfield, 2007). One respondent stated the difficulty of building a sustainability culture without senior management commitment as follows:

> I work for XYZ Co. and they just don't care about sustainability . . .

We also heard other comments such as "lack of understanding and endorsement at the top of the organization" and the need for "changing the mindset of middle managers," reinforcing our conclusion that the lack of commitment and buy-in is a major obstacle. These comments suggest that it might be due to lack of awareness of sustainability issues or the fear of dealing with change.

Lack of Resources

This was a critical issue for *people-focused* firms and an important issue among *leaders* as well. Only two *laggard* firms identified lack of resources as an obstacle to creating a sustainability culture. Resources were broadly defined to include financial, human and knowledge resources. A respondent

Description of Statistical Procedures Used in This Study

Identification of Sustainability Dimensions

We asked respondents to indicate whether or not they had implemented 21 different sustainability initiatives. We subjected their Yes/No responses (coded 1/0) to these 21 questions to an exploratory factor analysis to identify the underlying dimensions. We next used the principal components extraction method with varimax rotation procedure to obtain six coherent factors. Questions that were not loading highly on one factor (factor loading less than .5) or were loading highly on more than one factor were eliminated from further analysis. Descriptions of the six factors, represented by 15 sustainability initiatives, are summarized in Table 1.

Because we used a Yes/No response for each of the initiatives, we computed the score for each dimension by adding the number of initiatives that the responding firm had implemented. For example, the first factor, *employee orientation,* comprises three specific initiatives: "Value diversity & inclusion"; "Promote ethics & integrity"; and "Encourage innovation & risk-taking." Hence the score for this factor ranged from 0 (had implemented none of the initiatives) to 3 (had implemented all three initiative). This dimension score was used in all further analyses.

Identification of Distinct Groups

Finally, we used the scores on the six sustainability dimensions to group firms into clusters. We used the K-means clustering procedure to identify groups of firms, and compared the group profiles for multiple solutions (2, 3, 4 & 5 cluster solutions). We also compared these results to cluster solutions derived from an alternative method of clustering procedure (2-step clustering). We sought to identify the smallest number of clusters that best explain the variance in the scores for the six dimensions. A three-cluster solution was identified as the best representation of the data based on analysis of variance results and the convergence with alternative methods. Based on the mean scores on the six sustainability dimensions, we labeled these three clusters of firms as *leaders, people-focused* and *laggards*.

from a *people-focused* firm captured the need for specialized knowledge to create support and buy-in among employees:

> . . . having a hard time coming up with a clear definition of sustainability that can make sense and be motivating to employees

Another respondent expressed the difficulty of "getting employees to understand why we are pursuing this and understand the benefits rather than just comply," due to lack of knowledge or the resources to provide additional education/training to their employees. Respondents recognized that they are asked to do more with less resources and indicated that they "do the best they can" with limited resources.

Cultural and Institutional Resistance

This was a primary obstacle among *leader* firms. Even when there was commitment from the top—buy-in from employees and available resources, albeit limited, for sustainability initiatives—there remained cultural and institutional resistance to creating a sustainability culture. "Changing behavior and habits" is possibly the biggest and the most deep-seated hurdle. Comments such as the ones reproduced below confirm how hard it is to manage this cultural transformation effectively:

> . . . silos, business as usual, and established business metrics that do not yet reflect sustainability"

> . . . large company, so layers of politics and hierarchy"

This effort to change the culture and "educate employees of the alternatives" may "take more time upfront, but produce better, longer-lasting, successful outcomes."

Strategies for Dealing with the Obstacles

We also asked respondents to identify possible solutions to the obstacles and challenges they identified. A content analysis of the responses indicated significant differences among the three groups of firms. *Laggard* firms identified "education and communication" to improve awareness as the single best strategy to deal with the obstacles and challenges. *People-focused* firms wanted information and tools for building the "business case" for sustainability, and *leaders* unanimously pointed out the strategic benefit of sharing "best practices" in sustainability.

Education and Communication

Only respondents from *laggard* firms identified education and communication as the primary strategy for overcoming the obstacles, possibly due to their position. Suggestions for educating both management and employees ranged from "information posters" and ". . . radio, newspaper, billboards, etc. telling of the importance" to "... trained executive leadership on the models (of sustainability), otherwise you'll experience flavor of the month." For *laggard* organizations starting on the path to sustainability, education and communication of all employees is a first step to build a shared understanding of sustainability, generate interest and support for the initiatives, and lay the foundation for the sustainability culture.

Building the Business Case

Having identified lack of knowledge resources as primary obstacles for implementing sustainability initiatives, respondents from *people-focused* firms sought information and tools to make the business case. They wanted to convince other internal stakeholders of the benefits of such initiatives. Comments such as "(need) documentation of how it impacts profitability" and "... the benefits of functioning with greater efficiency, saving $ and resources" highlight the need for making the winning argument to other stakeholders, using language and metrics critical to their decision making.

Sharing Best Practices

Respondents from *leader* firms recognize the importance of collaboration both within and across firms, and seek the sharing of best practices to further their sustainability agenda. They commented on the need for sharing "... best practices for metrics that make sustainability everyone's responsibility" and "tips on how to create excitement within the organization." This is consistent with the observation by Wirtenberg, Harmon, Russell and Fairfield (2007) that some firms view sustainability not necessarily as a source of competitive advantage, but as an opportunity for holistic integration to build and be part of a sustainable ecosystem. After all, as one of their respondents indicated, it is not possible to be a sustainable company when the ecosystem, as a whole, is unsustainable. Seeking and sharing best practices is possibly one way of creating a sustainable ecosystem.

Stairway to Sustainability

Past research in both TQM (Blackburn & Rosen, 1993) and Environmental Management Systems (Daily & Huang, 2001) argued for the human resource function to play an active role in implementing these new systems. Blackburn and Rosen (1993), in their research of Baldrige Quality Award winners, found the HR function played a leading role in designing HRM policies and practices to create quality-oriented work cultures. Specifically, HR policies and practices helped communicate the importance of quality initiatives, empower employees to contribute to the initiatives and design appropriate rewards and reinforcements to ingrain the total quality orientation into the firm's DNA.

Implementing a comprehensive sustainability strategy is no different a challenge than the TQM challenge of the 1980s and 1990s. Like TQM, sustainability is about managing change. We believe the HR function can and should play an active role in ensuring that change toward sustainability happens.

One of the biggest blunders in leading change toward sustainability is the failure to institutionalize sustainability within the firm (Doppelt, 2003). If the internal policies and practices are inconsistent with the needed sustainability culture, "the risks are high that old thinking and behavioral patterns will eventually rise up and overwhelm efforts to adopt more environmentally and socially responsible paths" (Doppelt, 2003, p. 36). We recommend an active and early role for HR to help create the systems and processes (for example, selection, training and reward systems) to reinforce the wide range of sustainability initiatives and institutionalize the change.

Our earlier observation that the adoption rates of different sustainability initiatives are not uniform across firms suggests that firms might not adopt a practice, either because of its relative difficulty or the need to follow a sequence for maximal effectiveness. Extending this logic, we suggest a definitive pathway to sustainability that incorporates three decision-making dimensions:

1. the need to maintain a strategic sequence to build on prior efforts,
2. the relative difficulty of adopting the initiative, and
3. the strategic pay-off over the long-term.

In a useful strategic sequence, the first step toward sustainability is to be employee-oriented-valuing employee diversity, ethics, risk taking and innovation. The strategic HRM literature provides convincing evidence of the benefits of starting here: engaged employees resulting in increased organizational identity and commitment leading to superior performance. A quick review of different rankings of "green companies," such as the recent list by *Newsweek,* reveals that the top companies are also among the most-admired companies and the 100-best companies to work for. Absent this "employee-first" philosophy, efforts to promote other sustainability initiatives are unlikely to gain traction, creating a lack of coherence in an organization's sustainability strategy. Makower and Pike (2008) coined the term "random acts of greenness" to identify firms that had no internal coherence or strategy when implementing "green" initiatives. This is primarily due to their weak foundation.

The strategic implementation sequence identified in our Stairway to Sustainability model is based on the assumption that successive stages of building a sustainability culture depend on the successful implementation of the previous steps. This provides coherence to the strategy and organizational readiness to implement the next initiative. If a well-thought-out strategic implementation sequence is not followed, the likely result is the "flavor of the month"—leading to the random acts of greenness mentioned previously. Our Stairway to Sustainability framework complements Wirtenberg, Harmon, Russell and Fairfield's (2007) work on the role of human resources in building a sustainable enterprise, by focusing on the "Foundation" and "Traction" stages of their Sustainability Pyramid.

As firms climb up the steps, the relative difficulty of implementing initiatives increases. The assessment of the degree of difficulty includes convincing the relevant stakeholders of the benefits of the focal initiative, as well as the resources required to implement it. Due to their higher adoption rates, there is abundant evidence of the positive effects of early stage initiatives, such as materials conservation (Esty & Winston, 2006). Yet evidence is scarce or the returns unclear as firms take on late-stage initiatives, like conducting life cycle analyses or measuring a firm's eco-footprint. The payback periods on these initiatives may be longer, and the time horizons for returns on investment might be more than the firm generally uses as hurdle rates for new projects. As a result, firms have to base decisions on the cultural and ethical rather than economic rationale.

The impact of a firm's sustainability strategy is indicated by the third dimension—strategic payoffs. As a firm moves up the stairway, there is a greater pay-off in making the firm sustainable. We have evidence of the performance implications of employee orientation and materials conservation; however, the linkages become weaker for other dimensions because of the excessive emphasis on measuring performance concurrently or at best, one or two years ahead. The benefits of the later initiatives are more strategic than financial, long-term than short-term, and as indicated above, the usual decision criteria may not be applicable.

Building a sustainability culture requires the sequential approach suggested here for two reasons. First, there is considerable evidence that the principle of "success breeds success" applies to individuals as well as organizations.

Building a sustainability culture requires the sequential approach suggested here for two reasons. First, there is considerable evidence that the principle of "success breeds success" applies to individuals as well as organizations. Early tangible wins from employee orientation and materials conservation efforts should increase the likelihood of creating a self-reinforcing, virtuous cycle that creates excitement and potency among stakeholders that changes can become sustainable. Second, successful early initiatives help build organizational capacity for taking on the more challenging late-stage initiatives, increasing the likelihood of both adoption and success.

Second, successful early initiatives help build organizational capacity for taking on the more challenging late-stage initiatives, increasing the likelihood of both adoption and success.

Implications for Managers

The first implication for executives creating a sustainability culture is that they need to start by creating HR policies and practices that embody becoming an employer-of-choice. Then, they should encourage their technical, scientific and environmental managers to work more closely with human resources to change the ways they handle recruiting, selection, orientation, training, development, performance management and compensation to reinforce sustainability as a core organizational value. They should begin their sustainability journey with initiatives on the lower steps of the stairway, and progress toward the highest level.

The three types of firms we identified will face very different sets of challenges to creating a sustainability culture. *Leader* firms already have climbed quite a few steps on the stairway to sustainability, and now have to deal with resource constraints to implement initiatives with less clear pay-offs, amid resistance from forces entrenched in the current system. HR managers in these firms are faced with leading deep change, and will benefit by collaborating with other leader firms to identify best practices. They also may benefit by aligning their performance management and reward systems with a comprehensive sustainability strategy. *People-focused* firms already have taken the first step of becoming an employer of choice and now should focus on building a business case for adopting a broader set of sustainability initiatives and implementing innovative practices to create buy-in and employee commitment. *Laggard* firms would do well to first focus on the social initiatives (i.e. becoming a great place to work) and then invest in education and training in sustainability so as to create awareness of sustainability issues and motivation.

Limitations

Our sample provides a glimpse into current HR practices drawn from a single geographic region. As such, it should be looked at as the tip of an iceberg. What was highlighted here as both obstacles and solutions may reflect the region's industrial history. Still, we strongly believe that the results provide valuable lessons for all managers. The amount and different kinds of sustainability initiatives and the challenges of implementing provide ample opportunity for further discovery and continued research.

Conclusions

Sustainability starts with a guiding philosophy or strategic vision of achieving profits through people, while minimizing one's impact on the planet. Human resource professionals have a very important role to play in developing and implementing sustainability strategies. The success of every sustainability initiative depends on the extent to which the firm's human capital is knowledgeable, engaged and committed to implementing new initiatives. Recognizing the need for a strategic rather than piecemeal approach to sustainability, the HR function can facilitate, if not lead, the sustainability effort by laying the groundwork, designing systems that help build a sustainability culture, and become the champion of the organization's transformation to sustainability.

Note

1. We are grateful to Peggy Fayfich and Michael Couch for their support of our research.

References

Barney, J.B. (1991). Firm resources and sustained competitive advantage. *Journal of Management, 17,* 99–120.

Barney, J.B., & Wright, P.M. (1998). On becoming a strategic partner: The role of human resources in gaining competitive advantage. *Human Resources Management, 37* (1), 31–46.

Blackburn, R., & Rosen, B. (1993). Total quality and human resources management: Lessons learned from Baldrige Award-winning companies. *Academy of Management Executive, 7* (3), 49–66.

Daily, B.F., & Huang, S. (2001). Achieving sustainability through attention to human resource factors in environmental management. *International Journal of Operations & Production Management, 21* (12), 1539–1552.

Doppelt, B. (2003). *Leading change toward sustainability: A change-management guide for business, government and civil society.* Sheffield, UK: Greenleaf Publishing Limited.

Epstein, M.J. (2008). *Making sustainability work: Best practices in managing and measuring corporate social, environmental and economic impacts.* San Francisco, CA: Berrett-Koehler Publishers.

Esty, D.C., & Winston, A.S. (2006). *Green to gold: How smart companies use environmental strategy to innovate, create value, and build competitive advantage.* New Haven, CT: Yale University Press.

Makower, J., & Pike, C. (2008). *Strategies for the green economy: Opportunities and challenges in the new world of business.* New York, NY: McGraw-Hill.

Orlitzky, M., Schmidt, F.L., & Rynes, S.L. (2003). Corporate social and financial performance: A meta-analysis. *Organization Studies,* 24, 403–441.

The Greenest Big Companies in America, (2009). *Newsweek,* Sept. 28, 34–52.

Wirtenberg, J., Harmon, J, Russell, W.G., & Fairfield, K.D. (2007). HR's role in building a sustainable enterprise: Insights from some of the world's best companies. *Human Resource Planning,* 30 (1), 10–20.

Critical Thinking

1. What is the importance of sustainability for corporations?

2. How can human capital participate in the effort to increase and maintain an organization's efforts in sustainability?

3. What role can human resource management play in this effort?

Internet References

Sustainability Now!
sustainability-now.org

HRM's Role in Corporate Social Responsibility and Sustainability, SHRM Foundation Executive Briefing
www.shrm.org

HR and Sustainability: An Odd Couple?
www.GreenBiz.com

ROBERT SROUFE, (PhD, Michigan State University) is the Murrin Chair of Global Competitiveness in the Palumbo-Donahue Schools of Business at Duquesne University, Pittsburgh, PA. His research interests include environmental management systems, sustainable business practices, green supply chain management, performance measurement and human resource management. **JAY LIEBOWITZ,** SPHR (PhD, from the University of Tennessee, Knoxville) is an associate professor of Organizational Behavior & Human Resource Management in the Palumbo-Donahue Schools of Business at Duquesne University, Pittsburgh, PA. His research interests include the role of HR in sustainability, and new product development teams. **NAGARAJ SIVASUBRAMANIAM,** (PhD, Florida International University) is an associate professor of Leadership in the Palumbo-Donahue Schools of Business at Duquesne University, Pittsburgh, PA. His research focuses on measurement of sustainability orientation, climate protection strategies & models, and organizational impacts of individual and team leadership.

Unit 2

UNIT

Prepared by: Maria Nathan, *Lynchburg College*

Human Resource Recruitment, Selection, and Retention

Years ago the HR function was usually a small office in which pay and benefits were managed and usually by an individual who was not necessarily among the organization's most gifted or promotable. HRM has come a long way since then. Now, highly talented individuals with high aspiration levels can expect to find rewarding careers in this highly people-focused function.

There is no end to the number of significant and valuable activities that have come to be integral to HRM. Recruitment and selection are now conducted with much more data to support HR initiative to hire the best talent. Organizations have full staffing plans, career plans, succession plans, and other supports to forecasting. Recruitment uses social media extensively (if cautiously) to reach those talented individuals out in the labor market. Selection has become much refined in past decades as supports such as biographical information blanks, realistic job previews, and more permit the organization to make the very difficult decision of choosing the best for a job from among a slate of talented applicants. Talent management HRM professionals now work in teams of cross-HRM specialists who strive to ensure optimal support for each employee.

How do you retain these talented employees? Although an organization may not be able to guarantee lifetime employment, they can be expected to provide compensation that focuses employee efforts upon rewards that are intrinsically motivating, benefits that can be tailored to the needs of individual employees, and training and development that doesn't just make the employee more competent at his/her job, but competent in life in general . . . What makes an employee want to stay, produce, give their best, and be loyal to their organization? HRM in many ways holds the key that unlocks the answers to this critically important question.

Some employers in certain industries in particular have found it difficult to assure a steady flow of desirable applicants as jobs become available. Therefore, employers have turned to contingent workers, off-shore workers, part time and temporary workers. Recent research evidence shows that these contingent workers contribute much more value, including hard work and loyalty, when they are treated the same as standard employees. This is just one more way in which HRM can advance the organization—by knowing how to retain contingent workers by treating them as valued resources.

What motivates employees to provide superior results? What should managers do and what supports should their HRM function provide to this end of employee motivation? Fundamentally, managers must take a personal approach to employees. Rewards that are attuned to individual needs and wants are generally found to be the most rewarding. Furthermore, nonmonetary rewards are sometimes found to be more motivating to employees than those monetary. Most employees don't tend to believe that until they really think about what makes them tick. Nonmonetary rewards are very effective at accessing employees' intrinsic motivation and motivation to do great things. One author wrote a book—*1001 Ways to Reward Employees Even When You Don't Have Any Money to Give*. Then why don't more managers use nonmonetary rewards? One author suggests that it is because such rewards take more time to administer. Time well spent!

For some time now, employees and employers have been cautioned about the erosion of the old employment contract. Employees may not be guaranteed lifetime employment. However, they can be given employability security skills that serve to ensure that employees are managing their careers over time. This lack of employment security has been seen as a negative. Yet seen in a positive light—the employee becomes more self-sufficient and can be encouraged to appreciate the benefits and joys of lifelong learning and change. If in the past some employees relied upon the organization to give them career opportunities, employees now themselves seek out these opportunities.

Article   Prepared by: Maria Nathan, *Lynchburg College*

The Contingent Quandary

Today's HR leaders must recognize and understand the opportunities the so-called gig economy presents to their organizations, but must steer clear of potential legal problems it poses, too.

ANDREW R. MCILVAINE

Learning Outcomes

After reading this article, you will be able to:

- Understand what is meant by "gig economy."

- Understand why the "gig economy" has developed over recent years.

- Understand implications of the "gig economy" for the HR function.

Eric Castro has never even seen, let alone met, the overwhelming majority of the people who work for his company.

An army of approximately 2,300 technicians who work as independent contractors make up the bulk of Atlanta-based Ammacore's workforce. Their work includes installing cabling and rack servers, and performing other electronic maintenance and troubleshooting work at the firm's clients around the country.

The company uses a crowdsourcing platform to find these workers and assign them to clients. Once a job is finished, Ammacore rates the technicians on the quality of their work and their reliability—and, likewise, the techs rate the company on its reliability, support and the timeliness of its payments.

"We've always used this model," says Castro, Ammacore's chief operating officer, who oversees its HR function.

The arrangement is beneficial to both Ammacore and the technicians, he says. In fact, Castro thinks it's a model for the employment relationship of the future.

"People enjoy being their own boss and having the ability to turn down work they don't want, and crowdsourcing gives them visibility into the companies that want to hire them," he says.

Castro is far from alone. Proponents of the "gig economy"—also referred to as the sharing economy, the 1099 economy,

etc—say it gives workers more freedom to choose who they work for, and when and how they work. Smartphone apps have enabled companies, such as Uber, Lyft, and Taskrabbit to assemble virtual workforces that can be summoned by customers with a few taps—while giving the workers themselves the freedom to accept or decline assignments.

"I'm seeing a gradual movement to people being able to realize a bit more entrepreneurial freedom," says Steve Cadigan, the former chief human resource officer of LinkedIn who's now started his own consulting firm, Cadigan Talent Ventures. Cadigan, whose recruiting staff at LinkedIn consisted of 40 percent contingents, cites the Affordable Care Act as one of the enablers of the "1099 workforce," as it makes it easier for people to obtain health insurance that isn't tied to a full-time job.

Statistics on the size of the gig workforce are hard to come by. The Bureau of Labor Statistics' last attempt to measure the number of freelance workers was in 2005, when it found that 31 percent of the U.S. population worked as freelancers.

Much more recent studies—one from MBO Partners, the other from the Freelancers Union and Upwork—suggest the current number of freelancers accounts for 19 percent and 34 percent of the U.S. workforce, respectively. Both sources have skin in the game, it should be noted—MBO Partners sells products and services to freelancers and the Freelancers Union/ Upwork offers job listings for these workers—and their surveys were not scientifically conducted.

However, the number for the category of jobs performed mostly by part-time freelancers or part-time independent contractors grew from 20 million to 32 million between 2001 and 2014, rising to almost 18 percent of all jobs, according to Economic Modeling Specialists International, a labor market and analytics firm based in Moscow, Idaho.

The gig economy is also controversial—a lawsuit filed against ride-sharing service Uber in California asserting the company's drivers are misclassified as independent contractors is just one of a number of cases being filed against these sharing-economy companies. Although the Uber case is specific to California law, "what happens in California doesn't necessarily stay in California," warns employment attorney Robert Whitman, a partner at Seyfarth Shaw in New York (see sidebar).

The use of contingent labor draws scrutiny from states as well as the federal government due to the potential for missed tax revenue (companies don't pay federal or state payroll taxes when they use contingents), experts warn.

Even so, proponents say the gig economy—in its various forms—brings with it too many benefits for it to be considered just a trend. And HR leaders, they say, need to understand it and determine whether and how it fits in with their organization's talent-management strategy.

"HR [leaders have] not done a great job of acknowledging the gig-economy concept and committing themselves to go[ing] through all the different channels to find the right person," says Jason Averbook, CEO of Los Angeles-based The Marcus Buckingham Cos. "Most of the time, they just open a requisition and try to recruit a full-timer."

Connecting with Talent

Castro oversaw a major shift to contract workers at his previous employer, computer retailer CompUSA. Under his direction, the firm changed its computer repair and services arm from a traditional employment model to one comprised almost entirely of independent contractors.

Under the old model, uneven customer demand meant full-time technicians and their vans were often idle while waiting for calls.

"We let go of 80 percent of the technicians we had and switched to a 100-percent outsourced model," says Castro. "We ended up having no backlogs, we were no longer constricted by the skill sets we had on hand and we were thus able to take on a greater variety of jobs."

Castro says companies and independent contractors benefit from the crowdsourcing model, in which both parties rate each other on their reliability, dependability and results. To find its technicians, Ammacore uses Work Market, a New York-based "freelance-management system" designed to connect clients with independent contractors. Work Market offers screening and credentialing services designed to help companies find qualified workers in a given geographic area. Other vendors that offer similar services include Upwork (formed by the merger of Elance and oDesk); MBO Connect, from MBO Partners; and Freelancer.com.

Ammacore employs a community manager who communicates with the techs before, during and after a project to ensure they have all the information they need. The company rates the techs via Work Market on their promptness, performance and reliability. Meanwhile, the techs rate Ammacore on factors such as the timeliness of their payments, reliability and communication during projects.

It's a symbiotic relationship, says Castro.

Techs who perform poorly are warned they risk being grouped into "the bottom 10 percent," he says. Those who perform well—including individuals who receive compliments from customers—receive small bonuses. At the same time, Ammacore depends on the good ratings it receives to attract talented workers.

"1099s live paycheck to paycheck, so pay timeliness is very important to them," says Castro. "If they weren't paid on time, it would affect our ratings and make it harder for us to attract the best people." He's proud of the company's 98.4 percent rating from techs on Work Market.

"You can't push people in this model—they can choose whether to do business with you or not and, if you don't treat people well, you could find yourself out of business," he says.

The "Human Cloud"

Organizations that would rather not deal with the hassle of finding contingent workers themselves also have options other than relying on full-time employees.

Tammy Browning, senior vice president for field operations at Philadelphia-based Yoh Staffing, says a growing number of companies are contracting out major chunks of work—such as building new software or creating new video games—to outside staffing firms.

"We're seeing changes in terms of managed-services business, in which companies outsource a particular line of business for another company to manage—that way, there are no blurred lines in terms of who's managing whom," she says. "It's a growing sector of our business."

Another option is to "crowdsource" a job by breaking it down into components and having outsiders do it. Amazon's Mechanical Turks, People Per Hour, Archability and Topcoder, which was acquired by San Francisco-based Appirio in 2013, are examples of these so-called "human cloud" services.

"I describe it as our clients using us to find results, not talent," says Harry West, Appirio's vice president of services product management.

On Topcoder, companies create a challenge—solve this problem, build an app that does this, etc.—and offer prize money for whoever comes up with the best solution. One of the firm's clients, Honeywell, used Topcoder to create a mobile app that can tap into Internet-connected sensors embedded in a building's HVAC systems to make it easier for customers to monitor their facilities via a tablet.

"They'd tried building it themselves for several months but lacked the skills to take all those requirements and turn them into a compelling mobile customer experience," says West.

So who are these people on Topcoder who can do this sort of work?

Many are scientists, while others are software engineers who work at places such as Google, and some are talented coders from overseas, in countries where a cash prize of $6,000 can be equivalent to several months' salary, says West.

"A lot of them have full-time jobs elsewhere, but view working on Topcoder as a development opportunity," he says. "These tend to be people who like to learn."

Similar to other crowdsourcing platforms, Topcoder has a ranking system for its members: Red is the top rating, while gold is second best.

Although crowdsourcing eliminates the need to screen and hire people, HR still has an important role to play, says West.

"It makes sense for HR to learn about which areas of work lend themselves to the crowd so they can intervene when a department can't find a qualified person [and ask], 'Is there a crowd equivalent that would get us a better result, rather than trying to add headcount to our organization?'" he says.

"How much sense does it make to fight a talent war you're never going to win?" says West. "You don't need to own the talent to have the capability."

Like other aspects of the gig economy, crowdsourcing platforms haven't been immune to legal problems. CrowdFlower, a "microtasking" crowd service, recently paid a $600,000 settlement to plaintiffs who filed a lawsuit claiming their compensation for assignments via CrowdFlower amounted to far less than minimum wage.

Nevertheless, crowdsourcing's proponents say it's an intriguing option that HR needs to pay attention to, especially in an era when the pressure some companies are under from upstarts in their industry can make hiring for the long-term costlier and riskier.

"Crowdsourcing is a very creative approach, and I would like to see the HR community get more aggressive in this regard," says Averbook.

Training Still Matters

Regardless of whether gig workers do their work in your office or in a far-off country, manager training is crucial.

For on-site workers, "If HR doesn't do a good job of blending these workers together, there's a high probability

that some of these workers could get bullied and those companies will have a harder time leveraging the gig economy than those that are prepared for it," says Averbook, whose company counts at least 50 gig workers among its total workforce of about 100.

Companies that successfully manage freelancers do several things, says Donna Wells, CEO of Palo Alto, California-based online training firm Mindflash: They take the time to orient the freelancers on the "big picture" of what they're working on to help give them context, and they work to make themselves "clients of choice" among freelancers, the same way companies strive to be employers of choice for full-time talent.

"You also need to think seriously about your headquarters managers—very few people are great managers, but it's an order of magnitude easier to manage people who are co-located compared to remote freelancers and independent contractors," says Wells.

HR needs to train managers in how to interview effectively over the phone, how to onboard freelancers remotely and how to know when the work is getting done—and done based on a quality standard—when you're not seeing them every day, she says.

Interestingly, freelancers have the opportunity to serve as "reverse mentors," considering the opportunities they've had to observe firsthand what works and what doesn't work at other companies in the field, she says.

"I think there's a reverse-training opportunity, where the freelancer—who's seen the best and worst practices in a given industry—can put together a presentation on it," says Wells. "I've always found freelancers to be delighted to be asked to be the teacher and not the student."

When it comes to freelance talent, one of the biggest challenges is maintaining an "alumni base" of such talent and, of course, knowing which ones to choose, says Averbook. "It's really understanding who's worked with us before and who we call on again before we start searching for new gig talent," he says.

Many core HR systems, including those from Workday, SuccessFactors and Oracle, have the ability to store data on contingent workers.

"Most HR people don't use their systems for that, which is a tragedy and a travesty—instead, they end up storing this information with accounts payable," says Averbook.

By doing this, HR is missing an opportunity to track freelance talent—how successful they were, work histories, security clearances and their performance.

"Teams these days are almost always made up of full-timers and freelancers, so in order to truly understand a team's performance, you can't just look at the employees—you also have to look at the freelancers and contractors," he says.

Instead, many business leaders go out and hire freelancers on their own without involving HR, he says.

Human resource professionals should also—to the extent that is legally possible—try and help contingent workers stay engaged, says Averbook.

"We often communicate to employees, but because we don't want to share confidential information with contractors, we don't include them in communications and don't include them in employee meetings," he says. "That ends up driving down engagement among these workers."

At TMBC, Averbook now includes gig workers in all employee meetings, and addresses confidentiality concerns by having them sign strict nondisclosure agreements as part of their contract.

"When you have all these rules around how you deal with gig workers, at a certain point they start asking, 'Why do I want to get treated like this?' Treat them as close to employees as humanly possible."

Critical Thinking

1. What is the "human cloud"?
2. What differences does the gig economy precipitate in the HR function?
3. Do you think the "gig economy" is here to stay?
4. Do you know someone who is a contingent worker? What's their employment experience with this type of work?

Internet References

10 More Great Sites to Find Gigs and Part Time Work
http://www.forbes.com/sites/nextavenue/2016/06/13/10-more-great-sites-to-find-gigs-and-part-time-work/#759997916789

The 4 Best Resources for Gig Economy Workers
https://www.fastcompany.com

The Gig Economy
http://gig-economy.biz/

The Gig Economy: 100 Plus Ways to Make Extra Money
https://www.diygenius.com/the-gig-economy/

Article

Prepared by: Maria Nathan, *Lynchburg College*

Love It and Leave It

HR has a big role to play in parsing and contending with the job-engagement paradox.

PAT TOMLINSON AND MARCELO MODICA

Learning Outcomes

After reading this article, you will be able to:

• Appreciate how and employee may be well treated within an organization and still want to leave.

• Appreciate the need for a changed perspective about employee retention practices.

For too long, HR leaders have embraced an employee-value proposition based on the simple logic that engaged, happy employees are more productive and committed to their jobs, and that such loyal employees form a stable, sustainable workforce.

But this comforting paradigm has become something of a paradox. More specifically, it's an engagement paradox, in which even happy employees—including senior managers—are looking to leave their organizations in greater numbers, despite their contentment with most aspects of their pay, healthcare, career, and retirement prospects.

For today's multigenerational workforce, engagement is becoming disconnected from retention. Employees are committed for now, but many of them would happily move on tomorrow. Employers face a loss of key talent, and the threat of being left with too many disaffected workers who can drain productivity and morale.

Organizations need to counter these trends with a new value proposition that recognizes this love-it-and-leave-it work ethic—and even makes it easier for employees to return to the organization as they continue to advance their health, wealth and careers.

Those are among the conclusions of a new Mercer survey, *Inside Employees' Minds*, which polled more than 3,000 U.S. and 1,000 Canadian employees on their attitudes regarding everything from pay and benefits to engagement, leadership, performance and culture. The data shows that nearly two in five U.S. workers (37 percent) are seriously considering leaving their jobs—up from 33 percent in the 2011 *Inside Employees' Minds* survey.

More to the point, that 37 percent includes many workers who are very satisfied with their jobs and organizations. For example, 46 percent of those considering leaving strongly agree that they have sufficient opportunity for growth and development, while 48 percent of those considering leaving strongly agree that they are paid fairly given their performance and contributions.

As for senior managers in the United States, the statistics are even more dramatic. Three out of five (63 percent) of them are considering looking for a new job, despite high levels of satisfaction with their jobs (93 percent) and organizations (94 percent). For many companies, the potential strategic-leadership void of even the threat of such transience can be severe. It calls for an emphasis on programs to ensure that robust knowledge transfer is in place for new employees and an increased emphasis on succession planning lies further down in the organization.

Generational Divide

Not surprisingly—but significantly—there's a divide in the views of older and younger workers. Across all age groups in the United States, base pay was the most important element of the value proposition, but younger workers—millennials, ages 18 to 34—cared more about flexible work schedules and career opportunities than did older workers.

Clearly, employers can't offer one-size-fits-all rewards and expect them to satisfy all employee segments. It's also important to acknowledge that not all millennials share precisely the same attitudes. Some may be inspired to stay if they are engaged by their firms' commitment to concepts such as innovation hubs and performance/project challenges.

But with millennials and Gen Xers (the latter group comprised of ages 34 to 50) now representing the dominant share of the workforce—68 percent, according to the Pew Research Center—their preferences and behaviors are driving workforce phenomena, especially the happy-but-leaving trend, more than ever. This calls for action on the part of HR leadership, a close examination not only of value propositions but also a commitment to change in order to ensure future success and a sustainable workforce.

This begins, as do most strategic shifts, with the right questions. For example, how much do your organization's employee surveys reflect the happy-but-leaving trend? Do reward programs and HR policies reflect a more fluid mobile workforce, and allow the flexibility and career development younger workers value? Is the workforce transition being actively addressed, as baby boomers retire and the younger cohorts define the workforce?

If the answers are troubling, or unclear, it's time to reanalyze or update employee-survey findings, and go further: Survey employees about the trade-offs they are willing to make in terms of rewards and benefits, and then pinpoint the differences between demographic groups. Is there an opportunity for more flexible reward programs allowing employees to place increased emphasis on components they value more? From there, it becomes easier to evolve an employee value proposition that better reflects the changing workforce.

Beyond the Traditional

Organizations need to go beyond traditional approaches, though. The most dramatic finding of the Mercer survey—that 63 percent of senior managers are seriously considering leaving for new pastures, despite being very happy with their companies—demands new thinking to solve the engagement paradox. After all, this segment of the workforce, right below C-level, is comprised of the people who are driving strategy, client relationships, product development, operations and other core functions. If they are highly engaged yet still thinking of leaving, what's the strategy?

In part, it requires some redefinition and different expectations. Organizations must think in terms of getting their core talent engaged quickly in order to maximize their contributions in a shorter amount of time if they are going to rotate within or outside of the organization at a faster rate.

This calls for better strategic workforce planning, with more predictive modeling based on the evolving fluidity of talent—a redefinition of the traditional "Build, Buy, Borrow" approach to the workforce. Rather than relying on the long-term building of talent from within—training and developing over more than a decade—organizations must be ready to replace key talent more frequently and efficiently, either from within or through external channels.

An extra focus on succession planning and leadership development must go hand in hand with this redefinition, with a focus on the population right below the senior-management level. HR must be able to determine whether the right talent is in the pipeline, both internally and externally, and start to rapidly address the development of those that would have been traditionally ready in one to three years so that they are "Ready Now."

Indeed, this emphasis on employee fluidity reflects a larger transformation now under way: career portability. What began with the introduction of 401(k)s and the decline of defined-benefits pensions has extended to healthcare with the introduction of the Affordable Care Act, resulting in a greater degree of job mobility for workers and less obligation for employers.

But success in managing the human-capital challenge of this change requires a new, almost radical approach, in which employers commit to providing key talent with the skills and experience they will need for their career growth—even at a different company, or even with a competitor.

The messaging of this new employer-value proposition is one of help with career building, no matter where it leads. It also includes maintaining strong connections to employees who move on to other organizations, given the reasonable prospect that they will be your best sources of external talent after developing their careers elsewhere. Few organizations invest enough in the robust alumni programs it takes to maintain successful connections.

Ultimately, HR leadership must embrace the fact that flexibility and fluidity—in pay, benefits, retirement, work/life and career progression—are critical factors, as the multigenerational workforce of today becomes increasingly dominated by workers whose career and life goals differ from many of their current coworkers, on whom traditional human capital practices and policies have been based. Employment-value propositions are always evolving, but that fact has never been more apparent than it is today.

Critical Thinking

1. What is the engagement paradox?
2. Do you think that engaged and happy employees are more productive and committed to their jobs?
3. What is the "love it and leave it" work ethic?

Internet References

Employee Engagement and Commitment: A Guide to Understanding, Measuring and Increasing Engagement in your Organization
https://www.shrm.org/about/foundation/products/Pages/Employee Engagement.aspx

'Harvie' Information for Employees
http://hr.harvard.edu/news/new-hhr-website-launched

The Employee Engagement Group
http://employeeengagement.com/

PAT TOMLINSON is a Mercer senior partner and the North American region business leader for Mercer's talent business.

MARCELO MODICA is the chief people officer for Mercer, responsible for developing its talent strategy. Both are based in New York.

Article   Prepared by: Maria Nathan, *Lynchburg College*

Hiring Right

Recruiting the Wrong Person Is Costly. Follow This Expert Advice to Make Smart Hiring Decisions.

CAROLYN HEINZE

Learning Outcomes

After reading this article, you will be able to:

- Offer some guidelines for assuring the employer is hiring the right candidate.

- Explore the three Cs of hiring.

- Understand why it is so important for the employer to check candidate references.

Running a successful equine practice presents its fair share of challenges but none quite so crucial as bringing in a new veterinarian. After all, the process of hiring is time-consuming and expensive, and can have either a positive or negative effect on the practice's business. Not only should potential recruits possess the skills required, they need to fit in with the culture of the practice. For owners and practice managers, this demands an investment of time in an effort that, for many, can be a daunting—and, at times, discouraging—task.

According to the Society for Human Resources Management, an association that supports HR professionals, you can determine the cost-per-hire for each associate or practitioner by adding together all the expenses required to recruit and then hire the individual, including travel, advertising and other costs. If you add up all the costs per hire of each associate, it can be quite a substantial sum of money, so making sure you hire the right person to begin with is key. When you hire the wrong person, it's even more costly: 100 to 150 percent of their annual salary, according to SHRM.

So how do you know if you're making the right hiring decision? According to Kurt A. Oster, practice management consultant at Oster Business Solutions in Sterling, Connecticut,

practice owners can begin by envisioning an ideal candidate: what characteristics, exactly, are you seeking in a veterinarian? And, once you've established these criteria, Oster emphasizes that you should stick with those attributes, no matter what.

"What happens is, people say: 'I think I want somebody who can do this and this.' Then someone else who doesn't fit that mold will show up, but they're there, they're interviewing, they're interested, and they end up hired," he says. In many cases, veterinarians and practice managers aren't fond of the recruiting and interviewing process, leading them to make quick—and not always wise—decisions to get it all over with.

Articulating a list of attributes—both personal and professional—that you want in a candidate before you start looking is as important as job description. When you meet someone at a meeting, a conference or in another practice that you think would be a good fit in your operation, take note of his or her information and keep it on file. Then, when you're ready to hire, you'll have a starting list of potential candidates. Even if that individual isn't interested, he or she may know of someone else who would be a good fit.

David Grant, DVM, founder of Animal Care Technologies in Denton, Texas, advises that when seeking associates and practitioners, practices should cast their nets wide. "Recruiting doesn't necessarily mean geography; it also implies time," he says. "You want to be looking for people all the time—not in that reactionary, two-week window when most people do all of their resume-gathering, and then they make a quick decision."

Refer to Their References

We've all heard it, but it merits stating once again: One of the biggest errors recruiters commit is being remiss when it comes to checking references. "Believe me, if you have a problem employee, you will spend a lot more time fixing mistakes than you will checking references," warns Kurt A. Oster, practice management consultant at Oster Business Solutions in Sterling, Connecticut.

Oster suggests that recruiters go above and beyond the references listed on the candidate's resume. "If you know a practice that they worked at before, or if you know the university they attended, contact somebody there and ask some questions," he says. He cites a case in his own business, where not long ago he hired a doctor who happened to have served on a committee on veterinary medicine. "I talked to some of the other people who were on the committee. They weren't people listed as references, but they were people who had contact and experience with them." It's often these individuals who will give you the most candid assessments on the candidate in question.

Depending on the practice's focus, market and location, the definition of the ideal practitioner or associate varies. In many cases, owners and practice managers are seeking to diversify in order to grow the business. Some practices, for example, may need someone specializing in lameness, while others may want to branch out into reproduction, necessitating a practitioner with these particular skills.

The Three Cs

Regardless of a practice's specific needs, when assessing a candidate, Grant believes in applying the "Three Cs": character, competence and confidence. The "character" element combines maturity, emotional I.Q. and good communication skills. "Competence" comprises hard skills, such as those associated with either general medicine or specialties, such as lameness or reproduction. "Confidence" is the trickiest—again, especially in relation to younger doctors. "What we find in young practitioners who lack experience is a lack of confidence," he says. "They haven't seen the diseases and conditions as much, so their diagnoses are oftentimes shadowed by a lack of confidence. That is almost impossible to hide from a client, so confidence is key."

Which, in a way, points back to "character," since good communication skills—and the confidence therein—are important in reassuring clients. "Good communication skills make a good veterinarian," Grant says. "Oftentimes, we are too quick to associate skills, training and advanced degrees [with competency], but having hired hundreds of veterinarians, I would take communications skills and bedside manner any day of the week." He adds that in equine veterinary medicine, clients tend to demand even more communication than in other areas of veterinary medicine. "Whatever it is, I find that they're going to be a more particular decision-maker when it comes to who is vetting the needs of their horses." Thus, an increased need for equine practitioners to be communicative.

Oster notes that while skills sets and personality are the primary factors in determining whether or not a candidate will be a good fit, "soft" items can often act as deal-breakers . . . and should be examined before both the practice and the candidate sign on the dotted line. "Scheduling is huge," he says. Do you require your practitioner to be on call? How is scheduling handled on weekends? Do your vets work five consecutive days, or are they scheduled for four long days, followed by four days off? "A lot of times, you start these relationships by looking at the hard criteria like skill sets and experience, and the relationship goes south because of things like disagreements over the schedule," he adds.

Beyond Veterinary Medicine

When assessing resumes, Oster advises owners and practice managers to look for any listed job experience that may have little to do with veterinary medicine—especially if you're hiring younger practitioners. "There is a tendency on the part of how they train younger veterinarians on putting together a resume. They tell them to only list their veterinary experience," he says. General job experience, however, often provides certain skills that are useful for veterinarians. "If I had two veterinarians that were equally trained, equally experienced, equally skilled, with equal personalities—everything was perfectly the same, only one flipped hamburgers at McDonald's and one didn't—that shows me that the person who flipped hamburgers for two years can get along with coworkers, they can follow a routine, they can show up on time, they have basic job and interpersonal skills and have demonstrated some responsibilities." A candidate in his or her late 20s who has either been in school or only practiced veterinary medicine may not possess the work ethic or discipline your veterinary practice demands.

It seems like there are as many books out there on the art of interviewing as there are opinions on recruiting itself, but one thing for interviewers to remember is that their job is to listen more and talk less. "It goes back to the old saying: Two ears, one mouth," Oster says. "One should use that ratio when interviewing." He points out that problems arise when practice owners and managers who dislike the interviewing process use the job interview as a way to sell their practice to the candidate: This is the equipment we have on hand. These are the types of clients we service. These are the benefits we offer. "They spend the whole time selling the practice, and they never really find out what that candidate is about. During an interview, you want to learn about that candidate to see if they fit into your mix."

This is especially important in today's economy, where the market for jobs—even among veterinarians—has dwindled. "With student loan debt and everything else, a candidate will grab a job that is a less than an ideal fit thinking: Well, in six months or a year, if something better comes along, I will jump," Oster notes. "That doesn't help the owner of the practice."

Stephanie Keeble, operations manager at Campbellville, Ontario's McKee-Pownall Veterinary, explains that at McKee-Pownall Veterinary, interviewers apply behavior-based questioning, asking candidates to give examples of how they handled themselves in specific situations. "We find this more effective than questions like, 'In this situation, what would you do?'" she says. She adds that candidates must demonstrate open-mindedness and an emphasis on customer service. "Customer service is extremely important to us, so what's their experience with that? What's their viewpoint on treating customers?" A sense of humor and an acceptance of change are also important. "We've grown a lot over the last little while and the people who work for us have to be willing to go with the flow. If you can't stand change, then this is not the place for you." After the initial interview process, candidates undergo a "working interview," during which they spend several days working with associates and staff to determine if they will integrate well into the practice's culture.

Temp to Perm

Many companies hire temporary help as a way to fill gaps and as a way to "vet," as it were, potential employees. In fact, the temporary-to-permanent phenomenon is well ensconced in American business. According to the American Staffing Association, 59 percent of companies that use temporaries do so to find good, permanent employees.

So, one way to determine whether a practitioner or potential associate is a good fit with your practice is to enlist him or her in relief work. Grant notes that some of his company's most successful placements resulted out of such an arrangement. "I don't think you can replace the benefit of actually working with that person, even for an extended period of time if that's an option," he says. "It's kind of like a low-pressure date—they're not even thinking in terms of putting on their best face." In this scenario, both the temporary practitioner and permanent staff

are more relaxed, giving both the opportunity to see each other for who they really are. "Whenever possible, hiring relief veterinarians as a way of looking for future associates or partners can be valuable," he explains.

Few successful relationships are born out of rapid-fire decisions, and this applies to hiring as well. Oster advises that owners and practice managers spend the necessary time to find the right candidate rather than settling for the wrong candidate and then trying to fix him or her. "I see so much heartache and people trying to fix things down the road," he says. "Not only is it your time and energy, but it also has an impact on your client base as well. You're better off short-staffed than with the wrong staff."

Critical Thinking

1. Why is it so important to hire the right people for the right job?
2. Does this also apply to professionals as well as blue-collar jobs?
3. What do you think happens when you don't hire the right person for the right job?

Internet References

Answering the Question, "Why Should We Hire You"?
www.linkedin.com/today/post/article/20130617055559-52594-answeringthe-question-why-should-we-hire-you

Methods for Hiring the Right Person for the Job
www.aerotek.com/employment-agency/methods-to-help-hire-theright-person-for-the-job/445

Top 10 Interview Questions and Sample Answers
www.hireheroesusa.org/top-10-interview-questions-sample-answers

CAROLYN HEINZE is a freelance writer/editor.

Article   Prepared by: Maria Nathan, *Lynchburg College*

Beat the Overqualified Rap

Finding a new job is extra challenging when you've been labeled overqualified. Here are 4 common concerns hiring managers have when a candidate's qualifications exceed the job requirements, and tips for overcoming them.

JULIE ANN SIMS

Learning Outcomes

After reading this article, you will be able to:

- Understand the employer's perspective on candidate overqualification.

- Know what the overqualified employee can do to counter employer objections to overqualification.

You've steadily worked your way up the career ladder, earning a greater salary and increased responsibilities over the years. Then, the unthinkable happens: You lose your job and find that the experience you've worked so hard to acquire isn't helping you in your search for work. In fact, it's causing many employers to turn you away, claiming that you're overqualified for the role.

That's the position Michael Sinanan found himself in last year when he was laid off from his position as an art director at a financial services firm in Vancouver, British Columbia. Career-driven Sinanan had worked as a high-level art director for a magazine before accepting the position with the financial services firm. Both jobs focused on print, and the long hours he put in left him very little time to acquire in-depth web skills. Given the sluggish economy and the emphasis on digital design within many organizations, Sinanan received a weak response to the high-level jobs he might typically be considered for, so he set his sights a little lower—to no avail. Instead of employers jumping at the chance to add someone of his caliber to their teams, they told him he was too experienced for the jobs he sought.

"I could see in their faces that they knew I would be pretty bored there," Sinanan says. "People also were saying, 'You're overqualified. We can't afford you.'"

Given the state of the job market, an increasing number of creatives are in the same position. Although they're willing to accept jobs at a lower level than they've held before, they find employers are reluctant to hire them, for fear that they'll be a flight risk once the economy picks up.

If you're one of the many people trying to beat the overqualified rap, the first step is to take a stroll in the employer's shoes. Following are some of the common concerns hiring managers have when presented with applicants whose qualifications exceed those needed for the position at hand, as well as tips for overcoming these objections:

You're Too Expensive

Budgets are lean within most organizations, and companies have less leeway than they used to when it comes to negotiating higher salaries. That's why a fancy résumé with previous positions that paid a pretty penny may give hiring managers pause. This was the objection Sinanan found himself up against with a potential employer who owned a small design studio. "He was concerned I wouldn't be interested in the position because it paid less than my previous job," Sinanan says. "However, the compensation was still quite good, and the role was a great fit for me,"

For Sinanan, the lower pay was mitigated by the fact that the role offered a flexible schedule and more creative freedom than he had before. He also felt there was significant growth potential. Once Sinanan explained to the employer that compensation wasn't a concern, he was able to land an extended interview. The takeaway from this situation? Address an employer's concerns about pay head-on. Here are a few suggestions for doing so:

- Bring up the fact that you're more interested in the position itself than the pay and that you're flexible about salary.
- Discuss aspects of the job that are appealing to you and could compensate for a lower salary, such as creative freedom or flexible scheduling.
- If the position is in a different city, research average salaries and the cost of living in that area. If prices are lower in the new location, point out to the employer that you can maintain the same standard of living on a smaller salary.

Demonstrate enthusiasm about the company. Describe the things about the firm that you find most appealing, such as a good corporate culture, a start-up feel or the ability to develop fresh concepts.

You'll Get Bored and Leave

If you're accustomed to working on strategy and managing a design team, and the role you're applying for involves hands-on production work and no direct reports, employers may be concerned that you'll find the position humdrum and set your sights on something more challenging as soon as the job market picks up. Before an employer expresses this concern, it's wise to do a little soul-searching to see just how much of an issue this will be, says Julie Jansen, career coach and author of the career book "I Don't Know What I Want, But I Know It's Not This: A Step-by-Step Guide to Finding Gratifying Work."

"People's values and motivators change over time, and if the person will be satisfied doing a job he did 10 years ago, then it's absolutely a good idea to go for it," she says. "If, on the other hand, the person is taking any job because he needs one but has his eye on a more senior role as soon as he can find one, then it's not a good idea."

Those pursuing a certain job because they lack other options might want to consider project work until something more suitable comes along. If, however, a lower-level job truly appeals to you, you might be able to turn the tables in your favor by

explaining what interests you about the role. Following are some tips that can help:

- Explain how much the job duties appeal to you. Perhaps they include tasks you've enjoyed the most throughout your career.
- Demonstrate enthusiasm about the company. Describe the things about the firm that you find most appealing, such as a good corporate culture, a start-up feel or the ability to develop fresh concepts.
- Emphasize that you can take the job and run with it. There will be no learning curve.
- When discussing your previous experience, focus on your former duties—rather than previous job titles—and how they're a match for the position.
- If you have a stable work history, discuss your longevity with previous employers to demonstrate loyalty.

You Seem Desperate

Underlying the concern that candidates will be underpaid and bored if they accept job offers for which they have excess qualifications is the idea that these professionals are desperate for a job, any job—an image that, unfortunately, detracts from any applicant's appeal. Although it's only natural to feel anxious and frustrated during an extended job search, it's important not to make those feelings apparent to hiring managers. Rich Stoddart, president of Leo Burnett, North America, says candidates who have a good story to tell and present themselves well have an edge, no matter their level of experience. "Show hunger, curiosity, passion and confidence." he advises. "Who are you? What makes you tick? What are you passionate about? What kind of things in your work bring you joy?"

Stoddart says the answers to these types of questions can help creative professionals craft a compelling story that grabs a potential employer's attention in a positive way. If the last year or so has left you battered and bruised, take a fresh look at yourself and come up with a new narrative—one that's uniquely you and helps define the skills, ideas and passion you bring to the table. Following are some ideas that can help:

- Re-examine how you present yourself in your application materials and in person from a personal branding perspective: What message does your brand convey? Does it highlight your key strengths and abilities?
- Are you putting out subtle signals that you're desperate or frustrated? If so, consider taking a break from your job search so you can recharge. Even a few days can put you in a better mindset.

- Develop anecdotes that demonstrate your passion for your work and the industry. These are useful stories to tell in cover letters and during job interviews.
- Be sure to take good care of yourself during your unemployment period, socializing with friends and getting plenty of exercise.

Re-examine how you present yourself in your application materials and in person from a personal branding perspective: What message does your brand convey? Does it highlight your key strengths and abilities?

You're Obsolete or Power-Hungry

Although the concerns above are the most common when it comes to overqualified candidates, occasionally an employer will have other, more negative ideas. If you've spent a good portion of your career with a single employer or working with more traditional media, for example, the hiring manager may fear that you're set in your ways or that your skills haven't kept pace with changes in the industry, A prospective employer may even worry that you'll soon set your sights on her job, especially if you've held a similar role in the past. Following are some tips that can help you overcome these obstacles:

- Avoid intimidating a less experienced hiring manager by emphasizing the teamwork involved with past successes, rather than your individual performance. Also, don't use phrases that can make you seem condescending, such as, "At my last job, we . . ." or "I would recommend that you . . ."
- To show that your skills are current, discuss any training or coursework that you've recently participated in, and

how you've put these skills into action, even if it's been through volunteer work.
- Demonstrate that you're up to speed on current trends, not only within the industry as a whole, but as they pertain to the potential employer. Talk as specifically as possible about how your skills could help the firm address its challenges.

Unfortunately, the overqualified label can be tough to shake. The best strategy is to proactively address an employer's concerns and try to convince the hiring manager that your creative experience and expertise are a benefit, not a disadvantage, "Don't forget that we're in the idea business, not the technology or widget business," Stoddart says. "People who can design and nurture big ideas are in short supply and are incredibly valuable."

Critical Thinking

1. How can being experienced be a bad thing?
2. What can experienced employees do to beat the "overqualified rap"?
3. Is overqualified sometimes a hidden way to discriminate based on age?

Internet References

Job Recruiting
www.jobrecruiting.com
Reasons for Being Overqualified for a Job
www.recruiter.com/i/reasons-for-being-overqualified-for-a-job
Should You Hire Overqualified Workers?
http://management.about.com/od/careerdevelopment/a/HireOverqualified.htm
What to Do When You Are Labeled Overqualified
www.careerpath.com/advice/what-to-do-when-youre-labeled-overqualified

JULIE ANN SIMS is director of communications strategy for The Creative Group, a specialized staffing service placing creative professionals, and HOW's official career partner. www.creativegroup.com

From *HOW Magazine*, November 2010, pp. 42–45. Copyright © 2010 by F+W Media, Inc. Reprinted by permission www.howdesign.com

Unit 3

UNIT

Prepared by: Maria Nathan, *Lynchburg College*

Performance Management for Employee Productivity

Among the latest trends in HR can be found a focus on human capital, an investment perspective to HR, and productivity (and competitive advantage) through people. This focus unlocks amazing potential of so many employees to make contributions, innovate, brainstorm, and more.

How do you get employees to be productive over time? This complex question is tackled by HR personnel. They are the team that generates state of the art ideas about motivation training, incentive programs, nonmonetary benefits. . . . At its very core, human motivation is centered in the individual. We have over a dozen theories of motivation. They explore varied facets of the human motivation to produce. McClelland theorized about need for power, need for achievement, need for social relationships. . . . Adams theorized about employee perceptions of equity and inequity. He provided a simple equation that helps the manager to consider how an employee will feel about what they get given what they produce vs. what a significant another will receive given what they've produced. Expectancy theory, goal setting theory, decision theory. . . . So many theories, so little time. . . . What is a person to do?

At the base of all of these theories is the insight that employees are each distinct in what motivates them. This means that the manager must find out what motivates each employee and then seek to provide a reward system that uniquely meets the needs and wants of the employee. This is not as difficult as it seems even when an employer has well developed compensation/reward systems. This is so because managers have not just monetary awards available to them to administer. They have a whole set—a vast set—of nonmonetary rewards they can administer to complement the monetary reward. Wonderful idea that permits the personalization that we know works so well with employee rewards (even as there may be much standardization within the organization). Nonmonetary rewards are readily personalized and inexpensive.

So why don't organizations use nonmonetary rewards more often? Funny thing. Managers don't use them because they are more time consuming to administer. Of course they are; many nonmonetary rewards are personalized and require the time and care of the manager who must know what serves to motivate each individual employee.

Are motivation and corresponding rewards the same no matter the industry? Not entirely. For example, in the cruise ship service industry, employees may accept low wages and paltry tips . . . but they may be motivated by other facets of the job that other jobs couldn't provide. For example, foreign travel and the opportunity to work and live very closely with your associates—which may promote deeper friendships and even mating—may be unique to only certain industries.

We like to say that people are the same wherever they may live and whatever their origins. Yes, the same, but different too. Hofstede is an international researcher who studied the personalities of many managers the world over. He found that there were reliable differences between nations of the world in important ways. One culture may be highly money and career focused and promotions and money are what are found most rewarding. Another culture may be clan focused and find money is not as important as collegiality.

Motivation is so fundamental. What motivates you? Has what motivates you changed over time? What works; what doesn't? We are still learning. What about group pay plans like Scanlon or Gain-sharing? Employee stock ownership plans in which employees buy their company among them? Even given national culture differences and team versus individual reward differences, one basic we can count on—know your employee. Ask him or her what s/he finds rewarding.

Article

Prepared by: Maria Nathan, *Lynchburg College*

Rewarding Outstanding Performance: Don't Break the Bank

Some of the most effective methods of rewarding outstanding performers involve little or no money.

ELIZABETH (BETSY) MURRAY AND ROBYN RUSIGNUOLO

Learning Outcomes

After reading this article, you will be able to:

- Differentiate between monetary and nonmonetary rewards.

- Consider how nonmonetary reward use may promote superior performance.

- Know why nonmonetary rewards are not used as frequently as might be expected.

In these challenging economic times, it may be tempting to focus solely on the bottom line, and to forget the importance of motivating your employees. After all, don't employee incentives cost money, and who has extra money to spend on-raises or bonuses? While money certainly is a contributing factor to employee happiness, it is not the only cause of employee satisfaction.

Employees who are happy are more productive than those who are dissatisfied. Therefore, it makes economic sense to encourage excellence. Moreover, if you can find ways to reward your outstanding performers and keep them motivated, you are more likely retain these top players—which in and of itself is a savings. Importantly, some of the most effective methods of rewarding outstanding performance involve little or no money. Create your own employee stimulus without breaking the bank.

Employees who are happy are more productive.

Praise, Recognition: Simple, Cost-Free and Effective

Praise and recognition are simple, cost-free and effective ways to reward individual employees, or even a group of deserving employees. Indeed, many studies show that thanking employees for outstanding work is one of the most effective ways to reward your staff. Employees who perform a job well should be told their work is recognized and appreciated.

Praise is most effective when the employee is told how his or her performance merited acknowledgement. Rather than a general "good job," provide some specific information (for example, "You did a good job handling that customer complaint. You politely listened to what he had to say, you apologized for and fixed the error and then thanked the customer for bringing the matter to your attention so you could resolve it. That goes far in creating customer loyalty.") Where possible, provide this feedback immediately, when it is fresh on everyone's mind.

Praise should be delivered in public (remember the adage, "praise in public; punish in private"). A public congratulations and a "thank you" makes the employee who performed well feel good about his or her work and motivates that individual to continue to work hard. It is also a lesson for the employee's co-workers. When they hear a peer being celebrated, they learn exactly what behavior the employer considers commendable.

In addition to informal praise, consider implementing a formal recognition program. An "Employee of the Month" or "Customer Service Star of the Month" award does not have to include a monetary component, or it can include a low cost financial gift. To make such a program successful, the criteria should be announced to employees. If an "Employee of the Month" is being selected, the winner may be the employee with the best overall performance, or one month the winner may be the employee with the best customer service and the next month the winner is the employee who most successfully upsold your product or service. The award for being Employee or Customer Service Star of the Month could be as simple as a certificate, presented publically to the winner. Employees could also be given a small prize, such as movie passes or a DVD rental and popcorn.

Allow Top Performers to Set Their Schedule

Your best performers are probably also your most reliable employees. You can schedule them when and how often they are needed, and they will consistently arrive at work on time. In fact, these employees will change their personal schedules to meet your organization's needs. Nevertheless, all employees would appreciate the flexibility of being able to set their own schedule, or to have first choice of a preferred schedule. If your operations permit, consider rewarding a top performer with the ability to choose his or her schedule for a set period of time (for example, one or two weeks). This well-regarded employee may want to use his or her week to choose the prime shifts or to request time off from work. Either way, the employee will consider this to be a perk, and other employees will strive for the same reward. And from the employer's perspective, this flexibility should cost little or nothing to implement.

Reward Excellent Performance

Paying an employee when he or she is not at work is definitely a cost to the employer, but everyone enjoys having some time off, especially when they are paid for being away from work. If your employees currently do not have paid vacation or sick leave, a bonus day off is an excellent motivator. Even if employees do have paid time off, most would appreciate an extra paid day.

A bonus day off is an excellent motivator.

Discount Your Own Product or Service

Giving away or discounting your own product or service is not cost free, but it could be cost effective. Even if your staff can currently obtain a discount on the product or service you sell, consider enhancing this benefit for your top performers. For example, if your franchise is a restaurant, employees may be allowed to eat a free or discounted meal immediately before or after their shift, as long as the meal is consumed on the premises. For a set number of shifts or for a set number of meals (not necessarily coinciding with a shift), allow deserving employees to take the meal home; or give such employees a free meal certificate and allow the employee to use the certificate him or herself, or give the certificate away to a friend or relative. If your franchise provides a service, reward outstanding performance by discounting your service; if you already provide a discount, provide a deeper discount, or allow the employee to choose a friend or relative who will receive the employee discount on a one-time basis.

Provide Training and Advancement Opportunities

Your most valuable employees should be rewarded with advancement opportunities. If formal promotions are not available, keep these employees engaged and interested in their work by cross-training them on different aspects of your operation. This investment of time will pay off in the long run. In this regard, as employees learn new skills, they become more valuable to your organization; they also feel more connected to the company, which results in enhanced loyalty. On a related note, choose your top performers to train new employees. The trainer will understand his or her efforts are being recognized, and the new employees will learn good habits and skills from a star player.

Time with Company Leaders Is Valued

Employees who have invested their hard work in the organization will view one-on-one time with a company leader as a bonus. This time can be a lunch or a cup of coffee, or just a brief private meeting in which the leader solicits feedback about the work environment, and answers the employee's work-related questions. Employees like to be "in the know" about company issues, and meetings such as this can tie valued employees to the organization.

Best Workers, Best Parking Space

If most of your employees drive to work and you exercise some control over your parking lot, celebrate your best employees by rotating access to the best parking space in your lot. Yes, customers should have parking spaces that provide the easiest access to your establishment, but most will enjoy meeting the employee who merited the great parking space. And the chosen employee will relish the recognition.

There are numerous cost-effective (and in some instances, cost-free) ways an employer can acknowledge its best employees. While difficult economic conditions may present challenges to increasing profits, you can easily—and inexpensively—increase workplace satisfaction and motivate your employees. Whether implementing a suggestion discussed above or designing your own employee incentive, you can celebrate your top performers without breaking the bank.

Critical Thinking

1. What are some of the ways that people can be rewarded for outstanding performance besides money?

2. Why would you want to keep cost under control?

3. How do you think people feel about getting nonmonetary rewards?

Internet References

How to Reward Employees on a Budget
www.inc.com/guides/2010/04/rewarding-employees-on-a-budget.html

101 Ways to Recognize People
www.hr.unt.edu/main/pdf/training/101_WAYS_TO_RECOGNIZE_PEOPLE.pdf

Performance Management: Overview and History
www.opm.gov/policy-data-oversight/performance-management/reference-materials/historical/handbook.pdf

25 Ways to Reward Employees Without Spending a Dime
www.hrworld.com/features/25-employee-rewards

ELIZABETH (BETSY) MURRAY is chief legal officer and vice president of human resources and **ROBYN RUSIGNUOLO** is assistant senior counsel and human resources manager of Modern Business Associates.

Article   Prepared by: Maria Nathan, *Lynchburg College*

Ahead of the Curve: The Future of Performance Management

BORIS EWENSTEIN, BRYAN HANCOCK, AND ASMUS KOMM

Learning Outcomes

After reading this article, you will be able to:

- Differentiate between performance management and performance appraisal.

- Consider new ways to make performance management more useful to managers.

- Reconsider the traditional relationship between performance appraisal and salary increases.

The worst-kept secret in companies has long been the fact that the yearly ritual of evaluating (and sometimes rating and ranking) the performance of employees epitomizes the absurdities of corporate life. Managers and staff alike too often view performance management as time-consuming, excessively subjective, demotivating, and ultimately unhelpful. In these cases, it does little to improve the performance of employees. It may even undermine their performance as they struggle with ratings, worry about compensation, and try to make sense of performance feedback.

These aren't new issues, but they have become increasingly blatant as jobs in many businesses have evolved over the past 15 years. More and more positions require employees with deeper expertise, more independent judgment, and better problem-solving skills. They are shouldering ever-greater responsibilities in their interactions with customers and business partners and creating value in ways that industrial-era performance-management systems struggle to identify. Soon enough, a ritual most executives say they dislike will be so outdated that it will resemble trying to conduct modern financial transactions with carrier pigeons.

Yet, nearly 9 out of 10 companies around the world continue not only to generate performance scores for employees but also to use them as the basis for compensation decisions.[1] The problem that prevents managers' dissatisfaction with the process from actually changing it is uncertainty over what a revamped performance-management system ought to look like. If we jettison year-end evaluations—well, then what? Will employees just lean back? Will performance drop? And how will people be paid?

Answers are emerging. Companies, such as GE[2] and Microsoft,[3] that long epitomized the "stack and rank" approach have been blowing up their annual systems for rating and evaluating employees and are instead testing new ideas that give them continual feedback and coaching. Netflix[4] no longer measures its people against annual objectives, because its objectives have become more fluid and can change quite rapidly. Google transformed the way it compensates high performers at every level.[5] Some tech companies, such as Atlassian,[6] have automated many evaluation activities that managers elsewhere perform manually.

The changes these and other companies are making are new, varied, and, in some instances, experimental. But patterns are beginning to emerge.

- Some companies are rethinking what constitutes employee performance by focusing specifically on individuals who are a step function away from average—at either the high- or low-end of performance—rather than trying to differentiate among the bulk of employees in the middle.

- Many companies are also collecting more objective performance data through systems that automate real-time analyses.

- Performance data are used less and less as a crude instrument for setting compensation. Indeed, some companies are severing the link between evaluation and compensation, at least for the majority of the workforce, while linking them ever more comprehensively at the high and low ends of performance.

- Better data back up a shift in emphasis from backward-looking evaluations to fact-based performance and development discussions, which are becoming frequent and as-needed rather than annual events.

How these emerging patterns play out will vary, of course, from company to company. The pace of change will differ, too. Some companies may use multiple approaches to performance management, holding on to hardwired targets for sales teams, say, while shifting other functions or business units to new approaches.

But change they must.

Rethinking Performance

Most corporate performance-management systems don't work today, because they are rooted in models for specializing and continually optimizing discrete work tasks. These models date back more than a century, to Frederick W. Taylor.

Over the next 100 years, performance-management systems evolved but did not change fundamentally. A measure like the number of pins produced in a single day could become a more sophisticated one, such as a balanced scorecard of key performance indicators (KPIs) that link back to overarching company goals. What began as a simple mechanistic principle acquired layers of complexity over the decades as companies tried to adapt industrial-era performance systems to ever-larger organizations and more complicated work.

What was measured and weighted became ever more micro. Many companies struggle to monitor and measure a proliferation of individual employee KPIs—a development that has created two kinds of challenges. First, collecting accurate data for 15–20 individual indicators can be cumbersome and often generates inaccurate information. (In fact, many organizations ask employees to report these data themselves.) Second, a proliferation of indicators, often weighted by impact, produces immaterial KPIs and dilutes the focus of employees. We regularly encounter KPIs that account for less than 5 percent of an overall performance rating.

Nonetheless, managers attempt to rate their employees as best they can. The ratings are then calibrated against one another and, if necessary, adjusted by distribution guidelines that are typically bell curves (Gaussian distribution curves). These guidelines assume that the vast majority of employees cluster around the mean and meet expectations, while smaller numbers overperform and underperform. This model typically manifests itself in three-, five-, or seven-point rating scales,

which are sometimes numbered and sometimes labeled: for instance, "meets expectations," "exceeds expectations," "far exceeds expectations," and so on. This logic appeals intuitively ("aren't the majority of people average by definition?") and helps companies distribute their compensation ("most people get average pay; overperformers get a bit more, underperformers a bit less").

But bell curves may not accurately reflect the reality. Research suggests that talent-performance profiles in many areas—such as business, sports, the arts, and academia—look more like power-law distributions. Sometimes referred to as Pareto curves, these patterns resemble a hockey stick on a graph. (They got their name from the work of Vilfredo Pareto, who more than a century ago observed, among other things, that 20 percent of the pods in his garden contained 80 percent of the peas.) One 2012 study concluded that the top 5 percent of workers in most companies outperform average ones by 400 percent. (Industries characterized by high manual labor and low technology use are exceptions to the rule.)[7] The sample curve emerging from this research would suggest that 10–20 percent of employees, at most, make an outsized contribution.

Google has said that this research, in part, lies behind a lot of its talent practices and its decision to pay outsized reward to retain top performers: compensation for two people doing the same work can vary by as much as 500 percent.[8] Google wants to keep its top employees from defecting and believes that compensation can be a "lock-in"; star performers at junior levels of the company can make more than average ones at senior levels. Identifying and nurturing truly distinctive people is a key priority given their disproportionate impact.

Companies weighing the risks and rewards of paying unevenly in this way should bear in mind the bigger news about power-law distributions: what they mean for the great majority of employees. For those who meet expectations but are not exceptional, attempts to determine who is a shade better or worse yield meaningless information for managers and do little to improve performance. Getting rid of ratings—which demotivate and irritate employees, as researchers Bob Sutton and Jeff Pfeiffer have shown—makes sense.

Many companies, such as GE, the Gap,[9] and Adobe Systems,[10] have done just that in a bid to improve performance. They've dropped ratings, rankings, and annual reviews, practices that GE, for one, had developed into a fine art in previous decades. What these companies want to build—objectives that are more fluid and changeable than annual goals, frequent feedback discussions rather than annual or semiannual ones, forward-looking coaching for development rather than backward-focused rating and ranking, a greater emphasis on teams than on individuals—looks like the exact opposite of what they are abandoning.

The point is that such companies now think it's a fool's errand to identify and quantify shades of differential performance among the majority of employees, who do a good job but are not among the few stars. Identifying clear overperformers and underperformers is important, but conducting annual ratings rituals based on the bell curve will not develop the workforce overall. Instead, by getting rid of bureaucratic annual-review processes—and the behavior related to them—companies can focus on getting much higher levels of performance out of *many more* of their employees.

Getting Data that Matter

Good data are crucial to the new processes, not least because so many employees think that the current evaluation processes are full of subjectivity. Rather than relying on a once-a-year, inexact analysis of individuals, companies can get better information by using systems that crowdsource and collect data on the performance of people and teams. Continually, crowdsourcing performance data throughout the year yields even better insights.

For instance, Zalando, a leading European e-retailer, is currently implementing a real-time tool that crowdsources both structured and unstructured performance feedback from meetings, problem-solving sessions, completed projects, launches, and campaigns. Employees can request feedback from supervisors, colleagues, and internal "customers" through a real-time online app that lets people provide both positive and more critical comments about each other in a playful and engaging way. The system then weights responses by how much exposure the provider has to the requestor. For every kind of behavior that employees seek or provide feedback about, the system—a structured, easy-to-use tool—prompts a list of questions that can be answered intuitively by moving a slider on the touchscreen of a mobile device. Because the data are collected in real time, they can be more accurate than annual reviews, when colleagues and supervisors must strain to remember details about the people they evaluate.

Employees at GE now use a similar tool, called PD@GE, which helps them and their managers to keep track of the company's performance objectives even as they shift throughout the year. The tool facilitates requests for feedback and keeps a record of when it is received. (GE is also changing the language of feedback to emphasize coaching and development rather than criticism.) GE employees get both quantitative and qualitative information about their performance, so they can readjust rapidly throughout the year. Crucially, the technology does not replace performance conversations between managers and employees. Instead, these conversations center around the observations of peers, managers, and the employees themselves

about what did and didn't help to deliver results. GE hopes to move most of its employees to this new system by the end of 2016.

In other words, tools can automate activities not just to free up time that managers and employees now spend inefficiently gathering information on performance but also transform what feedback is meant to achieve. The quality of the data improve, too. Because they are collected in real time from fresh performance events, employees find the information more credible, while managers can draw on real-world evidence for more meaningful coaching dialogues. As companies automate activities and add machine learning and artificial intelligence to the mix, the quality of the data will improve exponentially, and they will be collected much more efficiently.[11]

Finally, performance-development tools can also identify the top performers more accurately, though everyone already knows subjectively who they are. At the end of the year, Zalando's tool will automatically propose the top 10 percent by analyzing the aggregated feedback data. Managers could adjust the size of the pool of top performers to capture, say, the best 8 or 12 percent of employees. The tool will calculate the "cliff" where performance is a step function away from that of the rest of the population. Managers will therefore have a fact-based, objective way to identify truly distinctive employees. Companies can also use such systems to identify those who have genuinely fallen behind.

Relatively easy and inexpensive to build (or to buy and customize), such performance-development applications are promising—but challenging. Employees could attempt to game systems to land a spot among the top 10 percent or to ensure that a rival does not. (Artificial intelligence and semantic analysis might conceivably distinguish genuine from manicured performance feedback, and raters could be compared with others to detect cheating.) Some employees may also feel that Big Brother is watching (and evaluating) their every move. These and other real-life challenges must be addressed as more and more companies adopt such tools.

Take the Anxiety Out of Compensation

The next step companies can take to move performance management from the industrial to the digital era is to take the anxiety out of compensation. But this move requires managers to make some counterintuitive decisions.

Conventional wisdom links performance evaluations, ratings, and compensation. This seems completely appropriate: most people think that stronger performance deserves more pay, weaker performance less. To meet these expectations, mean performance levels would be pegged around the market average. Overperformance would beat the market rate, to attract and retain top talent. And poor scores would bring employees below the market average, to provide a disincentive for under-performance. This logic is appealing and consistent with the Gaussian view. In fact, the distribution guide, with its target percentages across different ratings, gives companies a simple template for calculating differentiated pay while helping them to stay within an overall compensation budget. No doubt, this is one of the reasons for the prevalence of the Gaussian view.

This approach, however, has a number of problems. First, the cart sometimes goes before the horse: managers use desired compensation distributions to reverse engineer ratings. To pay Tom x and Maggie y, the evaluator must find that Tom exceeds expectations that Maggie merely meets. That kind of reverse engineering of ratings from *a priori* pay decisions often plays out over several performance cycles and can lead to cynical outcomes—"last year, I looked out for you; this year, Maggie, you will have to take a hit for the team." These practices, more than flaws in the Gaussian concept itself, discredit the perfor-mance system and often drown out valuable feedback. They breed cynicism, demotivate employees, and can make them combative, not collaborative.

Second, linking performance ratings and compensation in this way ignores recent findings in the cognitive sciences and behavioral economics. The research of Nobel laureate Dan-iel Kahneman and others suggests that employees may worry excessively about the pay implications of even small differ-ences in ratings, so that the fear of potential losses, however small, should influence behavior twice as much as potential gains do. Although this idea is counterintuitive, linking perfor-mance with pay can demotivate employees even if the link pro-duces only small net variances in compensation.

Since only a few employees are standouts, it makes little sense to risk demotivating the broad majority by linking pay and performance. More and more technology companies, for instance, have done away with performance-related bonuses. Instead, they offer a competitive base salary and peg bonuses (sometimes paid in shares or share options) to the company's overall performance. Employees are free to focus on doing great work, to develop, and even to make mistakes—without having to worry about the implications of marginal rating dif-ferences on their compensation. However, most of these com-panies pay out special rewards, including discretionary pay, to truly outstanding performers: "10x coders get 10x pay" is the common way this principle is framed. Still, companies can remove a major driver of anxiety for the broad majority of employees.

Finally, researchers such as Dan Pink say that the things which *really* motivate people to perform well are feelings like autonomy, mastery, and purpose. In our experience, these increase as workers gain access to assets, priority projects, and customers and receive displays of loyalty and recognition. Snapping the link between performance and compensation allows companies to worry less about tracking, rating, and their consequences and more about building capabilities and inspir-ing employees to stretch their skills and aptitudes.

A large Middle Eastern technology company recently con-ducted a thorough study of what motivates its employees, look-ing at combinations of more than 100 variables to understand what fired up the best people. Variables studied included mul-tiple kinds of compensation, where employees worked, the size of teams, tenure, and performance ratings from colleagues and managers. The company found that *meaning*—seeing pur-pose and value in work—was the single most important factor, accounting for 50 percent of all movement in the motivation score. It wasn't compensation. In some cases, higher-paid staff were markedly less motivated than others. The company halted a plan to boost compensation by $100 million to match its competitors.

Leaders shouldn't, however, delude themselves into think-ing that cutting costs is another reason for decoupling compen-sation from performance evaluations. Many of the companies that have moved in this direction use generous stock awards that make employees up and down the line feel not only well compensated but also like owners. Companies lacking shares as currency may find it harder to make the numbers work unless they can materially boost corporate performance.

Coaching at Scale to Get the Best from the Most

The growing need for companies to inspire and motivate per-formance makes it critical to innovate in coaching—and to do so at scale. Without great and frequent coaching, it's difficult to set goals flexibly and often, to help employees stretch their jobs, or to give people greater responsibility and autonomy while demanding more expertise and judgment from them.

Many companies and experts are exploring how to improve coaching—a topic of the moment. Experts say three practices that appear to deliver results are to change the language of feedback (as GE is doing), to provide constant, crowdsourced vignettes of what worked and what didn't (as GE and Zalando are), and to focus performance discussions more on what's needed for the future than what happened in the past. Concrete vignettes, made available just in time by handy tools—and a shared vocabulary for feedback—provide a helpful scaffolding. But managers unquestionably face a long learning curve for effective coaching as work continues to change and automation and reengineering configure job positions and work flows in new ways.

Companies in high-performing sectors, such as technology, finance, and media, are ahead of the curve in adapting to the future of digital work. So it's no surprise that organizations in these sectors are pioneering the transformation of performance management. More companies will need to follow—quickly. They ought to shed old models of calibrated employee ratings based on normal distributions and liberate large parts of the workforce to focus on drivers of motivation stronger than incremental changes in pay. Meanwhile, companies still have to keep a keen eye on employees who are truly outstanding and on those who struggle.

It's time to explore tools to crowdsource a rich fact base of performance observations. Ironically, companies like GE are using technology to democratize and rehumanize processes that have become mechanistic and bureaucratic. Others must follow.

Notes

1. See "The measure of a man," *Economist*, February 20, 2016.
2. "Why GE had to kill its annual performance reviews after more than three decades," *Quartz*, August 13, 2015, qz.com.
3. Nick Wingfield, "Microsoft abolishes employee evaluation system," *New York Times*, November 13, 2013, nytimes.com.
4. Patty McCord, "How Netflix reinvented HR," *Harvard Business Review*, February 2014, hbr.org.
5. Richard Feloni, "Inside Google's policy to 'pay unfairly'—why 2 people in the same role can earn dramatically different amounts," *Business Insider*, April 11, 2015, businessinsider.com.
6. "8 automations that improved our HR team's productivity," *Atlassian blogs*, blog entry by jluijke, November 29, 2011, atlassian.com.
7. Ernest O'Boyle Jr. and Herman Aguinis, "The best and the rest: Revisiting the norm of normality of individual performance," *Personal Psychology*, 2012, 65, pp. 79–119. Researchers canvassed studies involving more than 600,000 people in academia, politics, entertainment, and sports. They found performance power curves consistent across different jobs, performance measures, and time frames.
8. Google's senior vice president for people operations, Laszlo Bock, wrote about these practices in his book, *Work Rules: Insights from Inside Google That Will Transform How You Live and Lead*, New York, NY: Hachette Book Group, 2015.
9. Vauhini Vara, "The push against performance reviews," *New Yorker*, July 24, 2015, newyorker.com.
10. *Adobe Life Blog*, "The dreaded performance review? Not at Adobe," adobe.com.
11. For additional insights, see Aaron De Smet, Susan Lund, and William Schaninger, "Organizing for the future," *McKinsey Quarterly*, January 2016.

Critical Thinking

1. How do the authors anticipate performance management will change in the future?
2. How can performance management sharply reduce the subjectivity that has been found in performance management?
3. What are some technology-based performance-management tools that can enhance the performance-management process?

Internet References

Performance Management
http://www.phf.org/focusareas/performancemanagement/Pages/Performance_Management.aspx

Performance Management
https://www.shrm.org/about/foundation/products/Pages/PerformanceManagement.aspx

Performance Management: Keeping the Right People
http://hrcouncil.ca/hr-toolkit/keeping-people-performance-management.cfm

Performance Management Solutions
http://www.silkroad.com/hr-resource-center/performance-management-solutions/

BORIS EWENSTEIN, BRYAN HANCOCK, AND ASMUS KOMM are expert principals in McKinsey's Johannesburg, Atlanta, and Hamburg offices, respectively.

Motivating Employees: What Works? What Doesn't Work? by Woodruff Imberman

69

Article

Prepared by: Maria Nathan, *Lynchburg College*

Motivating Employees: What Works? What Doesn't Work?

Injured by the Great Recession, scarred by the recovery, and fearful of the future, metalcasting workers can be motivated to improve their efforts when they find their rewards in their paychecks.

WOODRUFF IMBERMAN

Learning Outcomes

After reading this article, you will be able to:

- Understand how perceived effectiveness of economic and non-economic rewards has changed in the past 10 years.

- Know which motivators work and which don't.

- Define gainsharing and explain why is it so effective.

It is not surprising that our latest survey of how 427 companies are persuading workers to improve productivity in today's uncertain economy finds growing numbers of employees now are motivated primarily by basic provisions of employment—job security and pay. They are only secondarily influenced by employers' efforts using the latest "employee engagement" fad.

In 2002, well before the Great Recession, we visited 427 manufacturers nationwide—32 being foundries and diecasters—asking executives how they were trying to persuade employees to make greater on-the-job efforts, and which ways were most effective. ("Improving Your Profitability Pattern," *Foundry Management and Technology,* September 2002.) We repeated the survey five years later ("Work Harder, Work Smarter, to Motivate Your Employees," *FM&T,* November 2007), as the Great Recession was just starting, and again early this year, during its sullen recovery. Trends in the metalcasting industry's efforts to persuade employees to improve on-the-job performance—and the effectiveness of these efforts—are shown in the following chart.

The chart documents five important facts:

- First, due to the 2008–2009 recession's impact, workers now focus on basic rewards (job security) and economic motivators (the value of their paychecks).

- Second, short-term economic motivators like Gainsharing that match employees' short-term horizons had the greatest impact on productivity.

- Third, employees expect "extra" rewards for any "extra" efforts asked of them. Fulfilling these expectations is critical to the long-term success of any new initiative for boosting productivity and eliminating waste. If the "extra" is absent, employee cooperation is short-lived.

- Fourth, although many employers have reemphasized "engagement" efforts to influence employees' behavior, employees considered these to be of only secondary importance. Economics remained their priority.

- Fifth, jargon has gone steroidal. Efforts to improve worker performance were called "motivators" in 2002 and "involvement efforts" in 2007. By early 2012 these efforts had become "engagement." "Engagement" has morphed now into the "science of engageonomics," at least by those promoting the latest jargon and trying to sell their version of it.

Don't misunderstand: there are advantages to jargon. It gives those using it an aura of omniscience. Because it is not well defined and its goals are vague, jargon can mean anything its practitioners say it means, and the positive results they claim will be just as specious as is their jargon.

As to jargon's disadvantages, one can recall marketing guru John Sculley, recruited by Steve Jobs to run Apple. In 1991, the Wall Street Journal reported Sculley declaring, "… We have a new agenda … empowering individuals." Apple's mid-1990s near-death experience let the world know the effectiveness of Sculley's vague empowerment efforts.

Motivators That Work

Eschewing jargon, our surveys show the obvious: recent events have affected workers' attitudes and changed how to influence their behavior with effectiveness. The Great Recession devastated Americans' pocketbooks, and the continuing impact of high gas prices on consumer spending isn't helping either. Unless Washington faces up to its fiscal crisis, the non-partisan Congressional Budget Office reports the U.S. will fall off a "fiscal cliff" early next year, triggering another recession.

Consumer confidence and workers' attitudes remain shaken. With today's concerns and tomorrow's uncertainties, metalcasting executives have learned that short-term, transparent economic motivators paired with supporting communications efforts are most effective at persuading employees to boost productivity and cut per-unit costs. Using them improves worker performance, reduces employee insecurities, bolsters future job security, and shows workers they can control their

own destinies—the smarter they work, the better their future will be.

Non-economic motivators have a long history, always aiming to bolster workers' pride. These include preferred parking places, service awards and special recognition for those that reach certain milestones, service lunches and Christmas parties. Although they offer little positive motivation, their absence or curtailment is resented, which perhaps explains why, as the chart shows, companies continue these efforts although they question their effectiveness.

These efforts should be continued because they sustain employee morale. However, they have little direct effect on workers' daily effort or on-the-job behavior.

Economic Rewards

Most executives expect economic rewards for their own better "performance." Such performance might be seen in improved company profitability, increased per-share earnings, or higher stock prices. As the 2002–2012 responses show, astute foundry and diecaster executives have learned that what is good for the goose is good for the gander, and are extending economic incentive programs deep within their organizations.

Profit-sharing plans are widespread, as are merit raises and discretionary year-end bonuses. Unfortunately, many merit

	2002	2002	2008	2008	2012	2012
	Percent of companies trying this method	Percent of companies thinking method is effective	Percent of companies trying this method	Percent of companies thinking method is effective	Percent of companies trying this method	Percent of companies thinking method is effective
Rewards for good attendance	81%	27%	74%	25%	56%	19%
Merchandise/gift cards for achievements	77%	11%	72%	8%	54%	8%
Recognition tokens (hats, caps, etc.)	61%	18%	83%	22%	88%	26%
Service awards	58%	11%	76%	6%	75%	4%
Educational assistance	56%	12%	68%	6%	44%	5%
Short term monetary awards for achievement	56%	49%	65%	57%	79%	69%
Public recognition (milestones, achievements)	53%	22%	77%	28%	81%	32%
Company parties (to recognize achievements, share information)	52%	24%	68%	11%	72%	9%
Recognition in company publications	47%	15%	72%	4%	80%	3%

raise programs are disguised general increases (if everybody receives the same "merit raise," what's the incentive?) And, most discretionary year-end bonuses are based on ill-defined, illusory criteria.

Many executives think their discretionary year-end bonus programs are highly effective. Unfortunately, vague programs produce vague results, rather than specifically focusing employees on daily performance. Year-end bonuses are popular—nobody says no to them—but, when asked, few employees can answer: "What specifically did you do to earn your year-end bonus, and why did you earn the amount you received?"

Economic motivators that affect day-to-day behavior are effective if they are easy to understand and match the short-term horizons of the workers whose efforts they are designed to influence. Few blue-collar workers have a "line of sight" long enough to equate what they do today with an ill-defined year-end raise or bonus, to say nothing of a profit-sharing plan paid 20 years from now on retirement.

Casting industry executives said pay-for-performance programs with frequent payouts coupled with vigorous supporting communications efforts are the most effective at "engaging" employees to focus on daily productivity requirements, and reinforcing their desire to cooperate with management to eliminate waste. That short-term rewards are effective is not surprising, not when Wal-Mart reports the number of customers living paycheck-to-paycheck "remains pronounced," due to "continuing economic pressures." (*Wall Street Journal*, Aug. 16, 2012.) Perhaps this need for immediacy explains why, as the chart again shows, companies feel that deferred reward programs are becoming less effective.

Employees expect "extra" rewards when they make "extra" efforts, executives said. Recognizing this is critical for the success of any productivity program a company starts, like "lean manufacturing." In the past, the successes of similar plans like Quality Circles, Total Quality Management, or Statistical Process Quality Control frequently were brief. When workers asked "what's in it for me?" to make extra efforts, they received vague answers. Based on the Toyoda System for eliminating waste, Lean emphasizes the "5 S's," the last being Sustainability. When the extra reward was absent, employee cooperation was unsustainable, and the Lean initiative soon petered out.

The Forgotten Side of Gainsharing

As the chart shows, Gainsharing was the most effective short-term motivator. Gainsharing is a group pay-for-performance program under which employee performance is quantified and assigned a dollar value. The value of their improvement is

split among them. So, for every dollar paid out to workers in Gainshare bonuses earned by specific measures of short-term performance, a metalcaster saves a like amount in higher productivity, better quality, and improved safety. Because Gainsharing plans provide pay-offs earned on a short-term basis (often monthly), employee notions that Gainsharing is an entitlement are negated.

Many executives think workers respond automatically to earn a Gainshare bonus. They are wrong: effective Gainsharing plans do require "engageonomics," i.e., vigorous communications programs to engage workers to cooperate in improving production efficiency and product quality.

Especially now, employees welcome opportunities to earn extra money. Although no metalcasting executive we surveyed singled out communications as a motivational tool, it is the root of employee satisfaction. With Gainsharing, frequent communications to employees regarding quality and productivity "engaged" them to do their best to keep their company competitive and their jobs secure. Workers respond to the opportunity to contribute. When they see management honestly soliciting ideas to work smarter by identifying and removing impediments to their performance and then responding to them, workers realize their efforts are important–and valued. Call it motivation, involvement, or engagement … the process is effective.

The subtleties of persuading employees to make increased efforts are lost on many metalcasting executives, who focus on data to check costs while ignoring the importance of good employee communications.

Most of these executives have little time to debate what is effective—economic or non-economic motivators. They need immediate, practical answers on how to influence worker behavior so their goals of high productivity and better profit margins can be reached. The chart shows most executives use both ways: first, providing group economic rewards to employees working as a team to help achieve company productivity and profitability goals; and second, using effective "engagement efforts" (communications programs) to reinforce the economic motivators and create a sense of unity.

Injured by the Great Recession of 2008–2009, scarred by the anemic recovery, and fearful of the future, today's employees are oblivious to buzz words but can be convinced to try their best when they find their rewards in their paychecks. What are you doing to give them the rewards they value?

Critical Thinking

1. Why do you think employees become skeptical about incentive systems in the workplace?
2. What incentives work for you personally? Why?

Internet References

How to Motivate Employees to Work Harder
www.openforum.com/articles/how-to-motivate-employees-to-work-harder

What Motivates Us at Work? 7 Fascinating Studies That Give Insights
http://blog.ted.com/2013/04/10/what-motivates-us-at-work-7-fascinating-studies-that-give-insights

The Top 9 Things That Ultimately Motivate Employees to Achieve
www.forbes.com/sites/glennllopis/2012/06/04/top-9-things-that-ultimately-motivate-employees-to-achieve

Article   Prepared by: Maria Nathan, *Lynchburg College*

The Endless Conversation

Many employers are adopting real-time dialogues in place of traditional performance-management approaches. But are they really working? And what's the best approach?

JULIE COOK RAMIREZ

Learning Outcomes

After reading this article, you will be able to:

- Appreciate how traditional performance appraisal has some clear limitations.

- Understand how technology can be used to improve the performance appraisal process.

W hen Ellyn Shook assumed her post as chief human resources officer in the Minneapolis office of Accenture in March 2014, she was intent on shaking things up at the global management-consulting, technology services and outsourcing firm. Long opposed to the concept of performance management—which she says is counterintuitive to the "holy grail" of unlocking human potential—Shook dove deep into the firm's talent strategy, challenging conventional wisdom. She determined Accenture had long embraced a performance-management process that focused on looking backwards, the exact opposite of the direction she wanted to take the future-oriented company.

"If you look at how dynamic the context is in which we are working, how quickly our clients' businesses are changing, how the whole digital revolution is changing the way people work and live, it was those drivers that made us realize we needed something that was much more dynamic," says Shook. "Instead of trying to fix something we weren't happy with, we decided to recreate our own future."

Seeking to learn what Accenture employees—and the public at large—would like to see in an employer, Shook and her team set out to "crowdsource the employee experience," as she puts it. Reaching out to Accenture employees and people who follow the company on social media, they learned individuals

want to work for "an organization that helps them achieve their expectations" and they crave real-time feedback. Shook and her team delved into what that meant, researching what practices, if any, were already being used in the marketplace. They then took those insights and went about revolutionizing the way the firm assesses and develops its 336,000 employees.

At the heart of the revolution was a seismic shift from performance management to what Shook calls performance achievement.

"Performance achievement is about putting our people front and center," says Shook. "It's about giving people the opportunity to set priorities on a real-time basis and get feedback on-demand, which not only entails telling them how they are doing as it relates to their priorities, but also how to move forward."

Under the new approach, which just rolled out in September, Accenture is focusing on performance conversations—frequent, informal, real-time coaching discussions—instead of formal performance reviews or rankings. These conversations are intended to occur naturally, whenever a suitable occasion arises. Managers can initiate such a discussion following completion of a project or whenever they want to commend an employee for a job well-done or make suggestions for ways to improve his or her performance. Likewise, employees are encouraged to ask for feedback to ensure they are progressing in the right direction.

According to Ravin Jesuthasan, global leader of talent management and managing director in the Chicago office of Towers Watson, companies would be wise to incorporate more real-time conversations into their performance-management processes.

"If you look at all the HR programs and processes, performance management is the one where there is the most hope and expectation, but the one that consistently fails to deliver," says Jesuthasan. "Companies are saying, 'We want performance management to be about improving the performance of the individual.' Waiting for year-end to have such critical conversations won't do much towards accomplishing that goal."

The specific composition of a performance conversation varies from company to company, but the general premise is that managers and employees engage in a continuous dialogue about the employee's performance—whether positive or negative—rather than waiting for a regularly scheduled review.

Whether a company abandons traditional reviews in favor of performance conversations or adopts a hybrid approach that melds ongoing, informal dialogue with a formal review process, HR has a key role to play in preparing managers and employees for this bold new approach to performance management.

Defining the Dialogue

Proponents of performance conversations argue that a process centered around ongoing, informal, in-the-moment dialogues eliminates the challenge of recalling an entire year's worth of accomplishments, developmental activities and shortcomings for an annual—or even a biannual—review.

"Who can remember what they did on the weekend, let alone six or eight or 10 months ago?" says Liam Ackland, president of North America for Acendre, an Arlington, Virginia-based provider of cloud-based talent-management software. "It becomes really challenging come review time."

Traditional reviews are also often criticized for leaving employees in the dark for months on end with no indication of how their efforts are being perceived. That was the case for employees of New York-based PwC, says Lauren Sandor, the firm's managing director of human capital performance. They typically received evaluations at the end of each client engagement. With each engagement averaging four months, employees forged ahead with the work, not knowing how their efforts were being perceived until the job was complete. If there were areas in which they could have done better, they found themselves blindsided, because they had no idea their work was not up to par. This approach is not only demoralizing for employees, it doesn't allow them to make any changes in their performance because the feedback arrived after the fact.

"[An employee] would sit at the end of that four months and [his or her manager would] say, 'It would have been so good if you had done X instead of Y,' " says Sandor. "It was obvious the periodic, episodic mind-set wasn't adequately developing our people."

That led PwC to embark on an initiative to encourage more real-time dialogue with development at the forefront. Rather than waiting until the end of an engagement—or worse, the end of the year—managers are encouraged to share feedback with employees "every day in the course of work because that's where we learn," says Sandor. How frequently managers engage in these developmental dialogues is left to their discretion.

"The expectation is that it's ongoing and constant, but there's no formal target," she says. "It could be daily, once a week or anything in between."

This new approach not only "eliminates any kind of surprise," according to Sandor, it also presents employees with the incredibly valuable opportunity to "course-correct," a concept that lies at the very heart of the performance-conversation movement. It's also the facet of PwC's new approach that has led to widespread acceptance from the moment it was rolled out organization-wide in September 2014.

"The idea of learning on the job is something people appreciate because it accelerates their development," says Sandor. "They like the reinforcement of the positive, along with the corrective actions they can take and apply to their next engagement. It changes the conversation into a much more developmental one they can feel invested in."

Building the Vocabulary

Clearly, there is much to be gained from managers engaging in regular performance-focused conversations with employees. However, some would argue effective managers already take it upon themselves to provide feedback to their reports on an as-needed basis.

"The good managers are already doing these things and they don't need to be told what to do," says Kris Duggan, CEO of BetterWorks, a Palo Alto, Calif.-based provider of goal-setting software. "They are doing them because they are biased to work that way—clear expectations, frequent check-ins, clear feedback. That's just how they are wired."

For those managers, an organization-wide initiative geared toward performance conversations is unnecessary. But not everyone possesses the skill or the natural inclination to pull an employee aside and chat about what they are doing well or where they could stand some improvement.

"There are many folks who really struggle with giving—and getting—feedback, particularly if it's done in the spirit of improving performance," says Jesuthasan. "It takes a lot of organizational maturity to get to this place, and there's a lot of remedial work that needs to be done to build manager capability and transform the culture of the organization around the subject of performance improvement."

The task of preparing managers to hold on-the-spot, real-time, developmental-focused performance conversations falls to HR. According to Marc Effron, president of The Talent Strategy Group, based in New York, the secret lies in making it "embarrassingly easy for the average manager to have the conversation"—so easy, in fact, that "any manager who can't do it shouldn't be a manager in the first place."

Over the past two years, Glenview, Ill.-based Combined Insurance/ACE Group has relied on a series of performance-management-training "road shows" to prepare its workforce of more than 5,000 to engage in "a continuous conversation throughout the year," says Melanie Lundberg, assistant vice president of talent management and corporate communications. Managers participated in leadership-development sessions in which they were taught how to have an effective performance discussion. Meanwhile, employees participated in a session on "owning your career" in which they were taught that they, too, should initiate coaching conversations. According to Lundberg, including both constituencies in the training was key to the company accomplishing its goal of driving a "high-performance culture."

"You need to have feedback to be able to know where to improve and how to improve," says Lundberg. "If you are not getting it, you need to solicit it by proactively asking things like, 'What did you think of that meeting I facilitated? Any reaction? Any tips?'"

At PwC, the entire human capital community was trained as performance-conversation specialists to prepare employees and managers to engage in more real-time dialogue. They relied on information garnered from a four-month pilot of 3,000 employees to determine how best to teach the rest of the workforce. The result was a "multitiered plan," consisting of formal training and on-demand training, workshops, and lunch-and-learn sessions.

"The skills you need to have can take some time to develop, so we've invested heavily in training," says Sandor. "We've been training our people on techniques such as guided inquiry, open-ended questions and helping people understand how to arrive at their own insights, and not just telling them the answer. The idea is not to just get something off your to-do list, but to give somebody an opportunity to grow as they are learning."

Framing the Feedback

Adopting a process of continuous dialogue is one thing. Eliminating the traditional review—and possibly the formal ratings or rankings that often go with it—is an entirely different thing. Experts argue a formal performance-review process is necessary to determine compensation, fire substandard employees or identify which employees may be C-suite bound.

"It's advisable to spread the feedback conversation across the year, but there still needs to be a time when you determine how this person is doing and how [his or her] performance compares to others," says Effron. "This is particularly critical when it comes to pay decisions. If you're going to link bonuses to performance, there has to be a formal time when overall performance during that period is assessed."

While some companies have abandoned formal reviews and rankings altogether, many organizations have discovered that a hybrid approach, combining performance conversations with traditional performance-management practices, better serves their needs. Informal, real-time dialogues take place throughout the year, but annual, biannual or even quarterly reviews are still held to formally assess each employee's performance.

"We are seeing a lot of organizations keeping the annual year-in-review event, because it's a good chance to review the past year and talk about the year coming up," says Dominique Jones, vice president of human resources for Halogen Software Inc., an Ottawa, Canada-based provider of cloud-based software solutions for performance management and other key HR disciplines. "They use it in conjunction with ongoing feedback mechanisms, so it becomes a summary of the conversations they've had throughout the year."

Employees appreciate the opportunity to gain real-time feedback they can use to help improve their performance and advance their careers, but without a formal check-in or rating, Jones says, they lack a firm understanding of where exactly they stand. That's one of the reasons the hybrid approach is particularly effective.

"When you take the scores away, many employees will tell you there's no frame of reference for them as to how they are performing," says Jones. "Without scores, you are relying on the sophistication of your leaders to be able to identify various degrees of performance and articulate that to the employee in a meaningful way."

That's exactly the strategy employed by PwC, which has kept its traditional performance-review process, even while "in-the-moment feedback" has set the stage for a "real-time development culture," says Sandor. Each year, leadership teams hold "career roundtables" to discuss their people's leadership attributes, progression and future growth. PwC also uses a system of "performance tiers," which Sandor defines as "a one-time categorization of where [an employee's] impact fell for the year." Employees are tracked in the system for the purpose of determining compensation and helping them understand where they stand relative to their peer group, she says, but this categorization "doesn't follow you around the same way a rating used to."

For Combined Insurance, performance-rating definitions have replaced a numerical-ratings scale. Rather than being told they are 1, 2, 3 or 4, employees are now told their performance has been deemed as exceeding, meeting, or falling below expectations. According to Lundberg, it's been necessary for the company to continue using ratings despite its push for continuous conversations.

"As our leaders are in the process of becoming better at having honest performance-feedback conversations, we continue to use . . . ratings to give employees a clear understanding of how they measure up against performance standards and established goals and behaviors," says Lundberg. "Until you are completely secure that your leader population is having great, candid, crucial conversations about performance—unless you can confidently say that is happening across the board—I wouldn't stop having some type of performance rating or performance definition."

Critical Thinking

1. Why does Ellyn Shook believe performance management is counterintuitive to unlocking human potential?

2. How are Shook's performance conversations different from and superior to traditional performance management?

3. Why are real-time dialogues considered "endless conversations?"

Internet References

Guide to Performance Management
http://hr.columbia.edu/helpful-tools/hr-manager-toolkit/managing-staff/goal-setting-managing-performance/guide-performance

Performance Management: Keeping the Right People
http://hrcouncil.ca/hr-toolkit/keeping-people-performance-management.cfm

Unit 4

UNIT

Prepared by: Maria Nathan, *Lynchburg College*

Training and Developing Human Resources

HR is highly focused upon the welfare of employees at least as much as line and staff managers who work directly with employees. Both HR and the managers they support maintain this focus upon the employee. Additionally, both HR and managers must work closely with one another if they are to be effective resources for employees. HR holds this integral relationship to managers in virtually every key activity they are responsible for. For example, recruiters aren't just seeking to attract the best player to the organization, but the best player for a particular job that is set within a particular workplace context—the manager's workplace context.

HR translates key external environmental changes into policies, procedures, programs, and projects. For example, diversity characterizes the labor market within the United States in particular. While more and more organizations have embraced diversity in their recruitment and selection, many managers still do not know why diversity can make a positive difference. They also may not know how to actually utilize the opportunities that diversity can present to them. Here again—HR must work closely with managers not just in training and development, but in fostering diversity consciousness itself. For another example—handicap is also a form of diversity. Personnel literature has quite positive things to say about the contributions of handicapped people in the workplace. However, a manager and/or his/her employees may experience discomfort with handicap. The HR professional has an opportunity to help other employees to become more sensitive to the circumstances, wants, and needs of the handicapped.

Evidence is that workplaces within the United States will only become more diverse over time—in all of the many ways that diversity may be manifest. An organization that hires for diversity does not necessarily utilize diversity to benefit. Diversity management also means that those representing various facets of diversity are given opportunities to make significant contributions and be recognized for these contributions.

Another diversity within U.S. organizations is language diversity. More and more—a significant chunk of the employee population may not use English as their primary language. In general, a proficiency with several languages is seen as valuable as employees may be more useful in customer relations, for example. Yet case law has developed in recent years around the matter of organizations with an English only language policy for their workplace. Can you require that employees speak only English in the workplace?

Diversity presents opportunity for the astute organization. However, diversity also presents challenge that the HR professional and managers in general must recognize. The Age Discrimination in Employment Act has been around for some time now. Employees over 40 must not be discriminated against in any aspect of the employment relationship. Our population demographers tell us that there are now more baby boomers in the workplace. Many of these are working even beyond the traditional retirement age. Can an organization dismiss, demote, or fail to promote the older worker? With so many active and healthy baby boomers among us, is it still possible that some managers have negative stereotypes about the aging worker? Here again is an interesting challenge for the HR professional as more and more it is recognized that the retirement age of 65 was a U.S. economy-based construction set in a particular point in time.

No wonder employees may feel somewhat insecure about their jobs nowadays. Organizations in the United States in particular are finding that they cannot promise lifetime employment. Now, there is a new employment contract that is taking shape between organization and employee. Now, HR can serve as an additional source of support in considering how employees can be helped to deal with this job insecurity that may in turn affect their health and productivity. For example, emotional intelligence can serve to reduce employee feelings of job insecurity. As they gain in general self-awareness and social awareness, employees become more capable of managing intense emotions that arise when feelings of job insecurity surface.

Article   Prepared by: Maria Nathan, *Lynchburg College*

Gamification: Win, Lose, or Draw for HR?

Many companies are experimenting with using games and social media challenges to facilitate learning. Could gamification be a win–win for HR and employees?

BILL ROBERTS

Learning Outcomes

After reading this article, you will be able to:

- Know what gamification is.
- Understand how HR can use gamification in its core functions.

From the first Olympics in ancient Greece to "The Biggest Loser" television show to the latest Xbox offering, games have always entertained and enthralled people. They tap into our natural competitive drive and our need to make sense of the world through storytelling. Advances in technology and social media have only multiplied the options, making it possible for people to cultivate their own virtual farms or play Scrabble with a friend in another country.

But, as it turns out, fun and games isn't all, well, fun and games. Increasingly, gaming technology is being used by businesses to engage customers or employees and, ultimately, to change their behavior. So-called "gamification" has been called one of the hottest trends in human resources this year, although the truth is that it has not been adopted in HR as much as it has been hyped.

While it's still early for HR in the gamification game, game mechanics and game design represent promising tools for the field, especially for learning activities, such as onboarding, safety education, product training, career development, and even team building. Game-based learning also has the advantage of being available when and where employees need it, since most options have been developed for computers, tablets and/or smartphones.

There are few hard metrics or return-on-investment numbers to prove the effectiveness of gamification programs to date. However, learning theory works in their favor, and experts predict that games will play a role in the future of organizational learning.

The Games and Players

There are two basic types of gamification, according to Karl Kapp, professor of instructional technology at Bloomsburg University in Bloomsburg, Pennsylvania, consultant and author of *The Gamification of Learning and Instruction Field Book* (Wiley, 2014). The first is structural gamification, in which gaming elements are added to existing content to help people move through it; the elements might include badges, points, leaderboards, and similar devices.

The second type, content-based gamification, turns the content itself into something that resembles a game, but one with business objectives at its core. Some people refer to these learning tools as "serious" games.

SAP Is in the Game

Player: SAP in Walldorf, Germany, which develops enterprise database technology and business applications, including HR information systems and talent management suites.

Objective: Millennial leadership training.

Date of adoption: Pilot program started in April 2014.

Game: Six-week program in which participants complete the first three weeks individually and the second three in a team setting. Participants are asked to read content, watch video and listen to audio. Points are awarded to individuals for completing content and to groups for engaging in discussions and posting relevant material.

Developer: SAP developed its own tool.

Outcome: Too soon to know, but SAP will be looking at increases in employee productivity, engagement and retention, among other factors.

In a global survey of 551 HR, learning and business executives in late 2013 by the American Society for Training & Development (ASTD), 25 percent had integrated structural game characteristics and mechanics into a real-world training program or task to promote changes in behavior. Most often the games were used to motivate and engage people, and they included features, such as achievement badges, levels to clear, and other rewards.

Another 19 percent of companies had used serious game simulations that included elements, such as story, goals, feedback, and play to help people reinforce their skills, practice a task or increase their contact with content.

Not everyone was on board with gamification, however. Nineteen percent of respondents had no plans to use games with structural elements, and 27 percent had no plans to use serious games.

HR was the most-cited area for future growth: 56 percent of respondents declared that gaming was in their plans for uses related to HR. Among those who were using gamification, common applications were in onboarding, all-employee training and the development of high-potential employees.

Think Engagement

While playing games can be fun, that is not the point of them in this context; rather, the goal is to use game elements to drive engagement in learning, Kapp says. He looks for ways to add game elements to instruction and content without turning the whole thing into a game. He says it is easier to pitch "gamification" to business executives than it is to mention a "game," which many leaders consider a four-letter word.

Indeed, it is the ability of games to engage people that may be HR's best argument when trying to convince business executives of gamification's value. After all, recent Gallup data indicates that only 13 percent of employees worldwide are fully engaged with work, and surveys of CEOs repeatedly show engagement as one of their top concerns.

No-Tech Gamification

Ryan Kleps, an IT process analyst at Boeing Co. in Seattle, used games to teach agile software development long before "gamification" became the buzzword du jour.

He and three colleagues developed a two-day football-themed training program to teach agile development as it applies to Boeing's software and other IT projects. Two thousand people, including employees from outside IT, have taken the course since it launched in 2009. Agile development emphasizes incremental software improvements by ad hoc teams instead of traditional big software projects.

The idea of a game occurred to Kleps when he was watching his children in their church school class that used competition as a learning technique. "I wondered what would happen if we applied that to our class," he says. "I had no idea if it would work for adults."

The game is played between two teams, each made up, preferably, of employees from the same workgroup. Classes include a 25-minute instructional module followed by a 25-minute application period.

Yardage and touchdowns are awarded under three circumstances: for correct quiz answers during the instructional module; for accomplishments during the application period, which requires teams to apply the preceding module's content to a workplace problem or agile development challenge of their choice; and during a two-minute drill of 10 questions at the end of each day.

Survey results suggest the approach is well received. There's no company mandate to use agile development, but the training seems to spur willingness to adopt the methods.

Kleps had never heard of gamification until about 18 months ago, when he realized that he had been ahead of the curve all along.

Engagement has been shown to correlate with retention, productivity, and financial results.

At EVault Inc., a San Francisco-based data storage and recovery company that recently implemented a game-based onboarding program, engagement was a key outcome of using gamification. When the company went on a hiring spree two years ago, nearly doubling its staff to more than 500, HR Director Dorothy Serdar wanted to replace the standard employee orientation program of hit-or-miss lectures, readings and meetings with executives.

For a year now, new employees have completed a game-based interactive program on a tablet at their own pace in their first two weeks on the job. It takes about 30 hours to complete, with points given for progress made. The program consists of five "missions" with learning objectives around some aspect of EVault. Each one includes videos, readings, and activities that require the employee to meet other employees in person or virtually and ends with a quiz that tests retention and provides managers with information about where employees need more training.

The program is exactly what Serdar had hoped it would be: consistent, comprehensive, efficient, interactive and, according to employees, highly engaging, if not downright fun. "The biggest positive statement is how much they learned in a short period of time," she says.

Serdar had never heard of gamification before she met with her vendor, Appical, an Amsterdam-based onboarding software developer. Appical offers a software-as-a-service platform, which the adopter populates with its own video, text, audio and other elements along with the game mechanics of its choosing. "I've become a fan of game mechanics," she says. "I think it is the future."

Objectives First

Game mechanics cannot be sprinkled on learning programs like nuts on ice cream, according to HR and learning professionals. A more thoughtful approach is needed for successful implementation. Key steps include the following:

Determine your objective. As with any type of instructional design, the first step is to figure out what behaviors you are seeking to change and/or which learning objectives you want employees to meet.

"Before you sit down and write software for the game, you have to design the program in detail. That was a big lesson for me," says Omar Zaki, senior instructional designer at SAP in Walldorf, Germany, which develops enterprise database technology and business applications, including HR information systems and talent management suites. "Figure out the learning objectives first. Then develop the rules of the game before you write any code."

Decide if game mechanics are appropriate. Gamification is best used for well-defined learning tasks. "Gamification is fantastic in a very targeted way," says Jenny Dearborn, chief learning officer at SAP, who is responsible for the gamification of employee learning, especially sales training, and for some learning aimed at partners and customers.

Develop game mechanics. As game czar (yes, that is her formal title) at the Defense Acquisition University (DAU) in Fort Belvoir, Virginia, the corporate university and training establishment for the Department of Defense and its contractors, Alicia Sanchez has created more than 50 serious games. She emphasizes that performing a "task analysis," or an assessment of which tasks learners should be able to do as a result of training, is critical in guiding development.

"The task analysis is a process through which you understand what the real end performance objective is," Sanchez says. At DAU, content for games is often based on teaching people about procurement policies. Understanding policy is important, but knowing how to apply it is imperative, she says. Serious games give DAU learners simulated opportunities to face situations that are both routine and rare in their work, make decisions, and experience consequences.

Test, test and test again. Scott Thomas, director of global product enablement at ExactTarget, an Indianapolis-based developer of digital marketing tools, owned by Salesforce.com, urges adopters to test as often as possible.

In 2012, ExactTarget used game mechanics to train all 2,000 employees on a major new product, a suite of tools for mobile marketing. One reason game mechanics worked, he says, is his team had a lead time of several months—longer than most product launches. His team had time to work with a consultant to analyze tasks, write objectives, design instruction, choose game mechanics, and then test before rolling out the learning tool to the entire employee base and later to partners and customers.

Ignore the foregoing advice at your own peril, experts caution. Brian Burke, a research vice president at Gartner Inc. a Stamford, Conn.-based technology research and advisory company, predicts that more than 70 percent of Global 2000 companies will use game mechanics this year in at least one area of their business, mostly for marketing purposes. As many as 80 percent of those will fail to meet business objectives primarily due to poor design, Burke says. "Gamification is a powerful tool, but we see a lot of misguided implementations."

What's the Score?

So far, few companies have cited improved metrics or business benefits from gamification. Burke's failure estimate is based, in part, on his review of a couple hundred write-ups about early efforts across organizational domains. They include details about what was done but little about results, he says. "I would assume that if they were improving business benefits, they would write about them, and I didn't find that except in a few cases—less than 10 percent," he explains.

Despite positive anecdotal feedback, many companies have not used game mechanics long enough to produce measurable results. In the ASTD survey, only about a third of respondents that used gamification measured its effectiveness.

By contrast, more than 80 percent of them had measured the effectiveness of traditional classroom training techniques, and 74 percent assessed the effectiveness for other e-learning efforts. Despite the lack of hard data, 37 percent of respondents from organizations that used gamification, and 51 percent of those using serious games, rated the methods as highly effective.

Moreover, many that have measured have seen good results. NTT Data reports several business benefits from a leadership development program that uses gamification. Based in Plano, Texas, and Tokyo, NTT Data is the IT services and consulting company of the NTT Group, which includes various telecom-related businesses. The purpose of the leadership program is to improve employee engagement as measured by certain metrics, says Naureen Meraj, senior global director for gamification and employee engagement practices.

Employees work through modules on leadership skills such as negotiating, time management and delegating.

Giant Eagle Is in the Game

Player: Giant Eagle grocery chain, which has nearly 400 stores in Pennsylvania, Maryland, Ohio and West Virginia.

Objective: Reducing repetitive stress injuries among cashiers.

Date of adoption: January 2014.

Game: A simulation game played on a desktop computer in a dedicated training room. It gives team members the tools and resources to safely perform everyday tasks and reduce work-related injuries.

Developer: Etc. Edutainment, Pittsburgh.

Outcome: It is too soon to measure the results, according to a spokesperson for Giant Eagle.

Modules include readings, videos, puzzles, and scenario-based quizzes that help learners understand the contextual basis for leadership decisions. Not everyone is expected to become a manager, but each person has opportunities to be a project leader, mentor, and teacher.

"We structured this game to give people the ability to experience the skills of being a good leader without the pressure of becoming a manager," Meraj says. "As people complete modules, they get points and move through different levels and appear on a leaderboard."

About 700 of the 7,000 employees completed the pilot program in 2012. Fifty have assumed team lead roles, which is 50 percent more than assumed team lead roles after participating in traditional leadership training and coaching. Those 50 people generated 30 ideas that created $1 million in new revenue or costs savings for clients, Meraj says. Organization-wide employee referrals increased by 30 percent, reducing recruiting costs by $500,000 a year.

ExactTarget also reports business benefits of gamification. In the six to nine months after it concluded its product training program, the company measured improvements compared to traditional product training on three metrics: a higher, faster sales rate with larger average contract values; more support cases closed on first calls; and faster time-to-implement with less scope creep for customers.

"In all three areas, we had positive results compared to other similar products," Thomas says. "Gamification of the product training definitely contributed."

Ultimately, time will tell how gaming technologies can be best integrated into HR. Effectiveness will likely depend on careful planning around well-defined business objectives. With many employers experimenting in this area—or planning to—hopefully, there will be more data on outcomes to come. Game on!

Critical Thinking

1. What are the potential HR applications for the gamification phenomenon?
2. Why does gamification hold so much promise for HRM?
3. What are the key mechanisms of gamification that make them useful to HRM?

Internet References

Gamification
  https://www.trainingindustry.com/wiki/entries/gamification.aspx

Gamification in Business: How Learning and Development Can Take It Beyond the Hype
  https://elearningindustry.com/gamification-in-business-how-learning-and-development-can-take-it-beyond-the-hype

How Deloitte Made Learning a Game
  https://hbr.org/2013/01/how-deloitte-made-learning-a-g

BILL ROBERTS is technology contributing editor for *HR Magazine*. He is based in Silicon Valley.

Article   Prepared by: Maria Nathan, *Lynchburg College*

Hidden Bias

Some employers are implementing training programs that address employee biases head-on—to everyone's benefit.

CAROL PATTON

Learning Outcomes

After reading this article, you will be able to:

- Consider how hidden biases exist in HR work, some of which are unconscious within people.

- Understand how hidden bias training can assist in diversity training.

A nnette Morris first heard the term unconscious bias in 2012, when it was introduced as a global initiative by the head of diversity and inclusion at Nestle, the Swiss food and beverage giant. As the U.S. director of diversity, inclusion and gender balance at Purina, a St. Louis-based subsidiary of Nestle that produces pet food, Morris soon became familiar with the dark side of employee bias.

"We all have biases," she says, adding that, through a variety of educational opportunities, HR at Purina is helping its 7,000 U.S. workers uncover and minimize personal biases when performing their daily responsibilities. "It's all about a holistic approach rather than just training."

Unconscious bias exists everywhere and in everyone. For years, psychologists have believed that humans are naturally attracted to others who look, sound and act like them. These preferences, however, prevent employees and managers from making logical decisions in business operations, such as hiring, succession planning, and employee assignments or promotions. Some HR professionals are helping workers at all levels in changing, multicultural environments recognize their innate biases and push them aside when making key business decisions.

The concept of unconscious bias training was first introduced to Purina's U.S.-based executive-leadership team in 2014 during the CEO's monthly business meeting. Morris says the training was approached as a business imperative based on how employees were making decisions. Were decisions being driven by unconscious employee perceptions regarding different genders, races, nationalities, ethnicities, religions, or even sexual orientation?

"We wanted to reach all of Purina associates to find out what would resonate without focusing so much on the blame and shame piece that typically goes with diversity initiatives," Morris says, adding that, since this was introduced by the corporate office in Switzerland, U.S. executives didn't need much persuasion to climb aboard. "It's more [a matter of] understanding what your world views are [and] how you bring them into the workplace, and challenging those assumptions . . . "

Later that year, HR hired a consulting firm to deliver bias training to the company's estimated 90 HR practitioners and 40 others in its talent-sourcing department. Then, in 2015, Purina produced and launched a 10-minute online video called *Understanding Bias* to introduce the topic to employees. The company also encouraged them to sign up for a half-day workshop called Bias in the Workplace. Offered throughout the year at its St. Louis headquarters, the optional workshop includes interactive videos, simulations, tips for mitigating risk and action planning.

So far, roughly 20 percent of Purina's U.S. employees have watched the video and/or participated in the workshop, says Elizabeth Marengo, manager of organizational development at Purina. "I gave this [video] to my counterparts at other operating companies. . . . It had a broader reach that went beyond Nestle Purina to Nestle North America."

Since HR believed a blended approach would deliver a more powerful message, it developed a suite of different training components and tools. Marengo says HR is constantly thinking about the program's next layer, its next version, and how it can be embedded into company processes to help shape the company's culture and drive employee conversations and behavior within the workforce, community and marketplace.

"We're definitely making a concerted effort to make sure that every year, we're introducing something new so [unconscious bias] stays very relevant in our organization . . .," Marengo says. "This really needs to be a deep dive in multiple facets into the work [employees] do for it to be long lasting and successful."

Last year, for example, Purina integrated a 30-minute training program called Common Biases in Talent Assessment into succession-planning sessions with senior managers and directors. This year, the half-day workshop will be rolled out to Purina factories and remote office locations across the United States. Likewise, bias training will be incorporated into the front end of talent-and performance-management meetings as well as the overall management process.

Although HR is working with the analytics department to put more meat behind program outcomes, Marengo says employee ratings of the workshops have been high—at least 4.5 on a five-point scale. Over the past two years, the gender, racial, and age balance within its workforce has also improved. So has succession planning, which now involves more diverse employees.

Behind-the-Scenes Influences

Many employers, including Purina, encourage employees to complete the Implicit Association Test that was developed by Harvard University to study subconscious bias. By sorting different images and words into categories, the test measures attitudes and beliefs that employees may either be unwilling to admit or unable to recognize.

"If you want your company to [perform] better, unconscious bias is something you need to embark upon," says Gerard Holder of GH Consulting in Providence, Rhode Island, and author of *Hidden Bias—How Unconscious Attitudes on Diversity Undermine Organizations and What To Do About It.*

However, this is not a one-and-done type of training effort. He compares changing people's lifelong biases to stretching a rubber band and then letting go. People can change, he says, but then revert back to old, comfortable habits. "In order for the change to take effect, you have to continuously train your staff."

He points to one company that went one step further. Hiring managers there can no longer see the names of job candidates. By reviewing blind applications, Holder says, candidates won't be unconsciously chosen or disqualified because of their genders or perhaps their ethnic-sounding names.

When making key business decisions, Mike McGinley, managing partner at Element North, a leadership-development consultancy in Washington, suggests that employees also ask themselves three questions:

1. What else could the reality be? For example, do you want to hire, promote or award a special project to an individual because he or she came from your hometown, shares your religious beliefs or previously worked at the same company you did? "A natural affinity may be at play," he says.

2. What data is present that does not support my hypothesis or conclusion? Take a hard look at the evidence. For instance, why promote someone when their productivity over the past year has barely met minimum standards?

3. What's the probability that you're wrong? What's really driving or influencing your decision that may lead you astray?

"There's more power in these questions than there are in the answers," says McGinley. "The discipline to stop and ask yourself [these questions] will bring a level of vigilance that's going to serve you well."

He says his company has been offering customized, unconscious-bias training to hiring managers and recruiters for the past decade. Over the years, he has heard many myths surrounding this topic—one being that smart people don't have biases. However, intelligent workers, or even employees who are familiar with their biases, are still not immune to their power, he says.

The essence of unconscious-bias training is self-awareness. The more self-aware employees are, the more effective they will be when performing their jobs, says McGinley.

To help such training programs gain traction, he says, HR professionals can conduct pilot programs with senior managers so they fully understand their value; otherwise, the programs may be doomed from the start. By gathering recruitment and retention data, HR can also incorporate the cost and impact of the company's hiring process and failures in its business case.

"There's nothing about this that's faddish," says McGinley, explaining that, with more brain scans now being conducted, scientists have been learning a great deal about how the brain works. "We're going to get deeper [into] the forms and forces that drive human behavior."

Outcomes and Strategies

Unconscious-bias training is mandatory for the 500 employees at the Thompson Hine law firm in Atlanta. In 2014, the firm piloted a two-hour program to roughly 25 employees in its Cleveland office, says Roy Hadley Jr., a partner at the firm who also chairs the firm's diversity and inclusion initiative.

Some of the firm's executive managers participated in that first session and immediately bought into the concept, paving the way for Hadley to roll the program out to the firm's remaining offices in Ohio, Georgia, and the cities of New York and Washington. Since then, he says, every employee has completed the workshop. Invitations were also extended to key clients, so they could share lessons with their own workforces.

"The more diversity in the room, the better off you are because people can share their experiences," says Hadley.

The program may be repeated next year. Meanwhile, he says, the firm hired a chief talent officer whose responsibilities include increasing the workforce's diversity and inclusion. Practice team leaders are now more conscious of work assignments, ensuring that all associates receive equal opportunities and equal work. Recruitment and retention of diverse staff is now being measured. Hadley adds that a diversity summit for the firm's top managers, executive-committee members, practice-group leaders and senior attorneys will also be held later this year to develop and institutionalize concrete steps to minimize bias and increase diversity and inclusion.

Several years ago, Capgemini also made its unconscious-bias training program mandatory for its corporate vice presidents and senior vice presidents throughout the United States and Canada, says Janet Pope, North America corporate responsibility and sustainability leader at the global management-consulting organization based in Houston.

"We were looking at where we were in terms of our diversity and inclusion . . . around demographic numbers or head count as related to women and people of color," Pope says, adding that, when diversity was mentioned, not everyone was on the same page. "One leader might think gender diversity. Another might think broader—diversity of thought—and everything in between."

She explains that every business unit at the Paris-based company has an executive sponsor. When Capgemini's program was in its initial phases, the sponsor of diversity and inclusion for North America held a job similar to chief operating officer. Fortunately, that person supported the concept and presented it to Tim Bridges, chief executive officer of North America Application Services, who agreed to pilot the program.

Pope, who partnered with Southern Methodist University in Dallas to develop the initiative, says the program offered enriching exercises that encouraged participants to discuss inclusion, and challenged their thinking about unconscious bias and how it rears its head in the workplace.

In 2013, she says, Bridges participated in the pilot called *Culture Bias and the Brain*. "Immediately, he saw the value of having these conversations across [employee] levels," she says, adding that he wanted the program to be mandatory for his direct reports but optional for the remaining 15,000 employees across the United States and Canada. The pilot intentionally included 20 people with different experiences, ranging from Bridges and his vice presidents to consultants.

The program consists of two one-day sessions that are 30 days apart. Pope says the first session focuses on organizational culture, introduces the bias of familiarity—the idea that people are attracted to those like them—and examines how bias shows up in different ways in the workplace, such as in the forms of sexism or racism. During the next 30 days, participants complete the Harvard University IAT. During session two, they discuss their test results, address the brain science around bias and develop strategies to mitigate bias.

Among Pope's favorite strategies is for employees to stretch their areas of influence or comfort zones through employee-resource groups, which are similar to affinity groups but broader in scope. For example, heterosexuals might become allies of the Lesbian, Gay, Bisexual and Transgender ERG. By meeting people outside their normal spheres, she says, employees can expose their biases or at least peel away some of the layers.

Last year, the company hosted 12 sessions. All of Bridge's direct reports—fewer than 100—have been trained, along with several hundred interested employees.

So far, employee retention is being used as a measuring stick to determine outcomes. According to Pope, retention of the employees who participated in the program over the past two years is 12 percent higher than those who haven't attended the program.

"The ultimate goal is for our 180,000 [employees] to be aligned [with] how we can be inclusive as an employer," Pope says, adding that business units in other countries are interested in running their own versions of this program. "We really wanted to make sure it wasn't a desktop PowerPoint, but had enriching exercises that would get people talking to each other, discussing inclusion, and really challenge their thinking about what unconscious bias means and how it shows up in the workplace."

Critical Thinking

1. How do people bring world views and hidden biases into the workplace?
2. How does bias training work?
3. What is the desired end result in bias training?

Internet References

Employee Diversity Training Module, Office of Diversity and Inclusion
www.diversity.va.gov

Performance Management, Society for Human Resource Management
https://www.shrm.org/india/hr-topics-and-strategy/performance-management/creating-high-performance-culture/Documents/Performance%20Management.pdf

Article   Prepared by: Maria Nathan, *Lynchburg College*

7 E-Learning Best Practices for Maximum Global Workforce Training ROI

Bad training can end up costing more than good training when you calculate the time, resources, and opportunity cost wasted on training that does not provide the desired ROI.

BILL ENGLISH

Learning Outcomes

After reading this article, you will be able to:

- Know how bad training can cost more than good training.
- Consider possible guidelines for e-training.
- Know the challenges associated with global workforce training.

The rapid development of technology means employee training is more critical than ever to ensure that employees have the right technology skills to keep businesses operating at peak performance. If employees are behind the times when it comes to technology, a business risks losing its competitive edge. And while technology is developing more rapidly, it also is becoming more complex. Organizations are investing in complex, enterprise-wide software platforms, such as SharePoint, but often do not receive the expected return on investment (ROI) due, in part, to a lack of employee training.

In addition to keeping up with the pace of rapidly developing new technologies, businesses are faced with additional training challenges as a result of increased globalization. Worldwide employment by U.S. multinational companies reached 34 million in 2010 (U.S. Department of Commerce Bureau of Economic Analysis. April 18, 2012: http://www.bea.gov/newsreleases/international/mnc/mncnewsrelease.htm). With so many businesses establishing locations across the globe, businesses must learn how to train a global workforce efficiently and cost-effectively without sacrificing quality. This means companies must face the daunting task of evaluating the quality of training and establishing consistent training company-wide despite language and cultural barriers, all while keeping the training budget in check.

The Demand for Training

Despite economic woes, employer spending on training is up. According to *Training* magazine's 2011 Industry Report, total 2011 U.S. training expenditures—including payroll and spending on external products and services—jumped 13 percent to $59.7 billion. With the overall demand for technology training increasing, the demand for e-learning is expected to increase globally, as well (Global Industry Analysts, Inc. "Global E-Learning Market to Reach US $107 Billion by 2015, According to New Report by Global Industry Analysts, Inc": http://www.prweb.com/releases/distance_learning/e_learning/prweb9198652.htm). According to a 2011 report by Ambient Insight, the worldwide market for self-paced e-learning products and services reached $32.1 billion in 2010. The five-year compound annual growth rate is 9.2 percent and revenues are expected to increase to $49.9 billion by 2015 ("Ambient Insight Worldwide eLearning Market Forecast," Ambient Insight. July 15, 2012: http://www.ambientinsight.com/News/Ambient-Insight-2010-2015-Worldwide-eLearning-Market.aspx).

Although computer-based e-learning has been established as the most efficient and cost-effective way to train a large group of employees spread across the globe, not all computer-based e-learning is created equal. In the end, bad training can end up costing more than good training when you calculate the time, resources, and opportunity cost wasted on training that does not provide the desired ROI.

Best Practices

Here are seven best practices, as identified by Mindsharp, to help your organization provide high-quality technology training for your global workforce efficiently and cost-effectively for maximum ROI. Mindsharp is a member of the World Education Alliance, a global SharePoint education alliance comprising Combined Knowledge Ltd. (Europe, the Middle East, and Africa) Combined Knowledge Asia Pacific (Australia and New Zealand), and Mindsharp (United States). The best practices are based on Mindsharp's real-world experience in providing computer-based and instructor-led SharePoint training for more than 58 percent of Fortune 500 companies.

1. Measure Training Results

The No. 1 element that affects training ROI is measurement. Training without measurement is an endless black hole that forces employers to make training decisions based on assumptions instead of on concrete data. For instance, employers have to decide if the training was effective. But without tools in place that measure comprehension, employers have no way of knowing if employees retained the information and learned new skills or how much information and skill development they retained. Without measurement, tracking whether or not employees developed the desired skill sets as a result of the training becomes more difficult. Lack of measurement also means employers cannot easily identify potential gaps in employee knowledge and skills to know if more training is needed.

To avoid the training black hole, look for training that includes certification programs that test comprehension and track progress. Training with certification programs should include quizzes throughout the training to help employees identify gaps in knowledge during training. Certification programs also should include final tests to evaluate overall comprehension at the completion of a training session. With certifications, you can quickly track which employees have obtained the desired competencies and which employees need additional training. Human Resource and Training departments also can track how much they have enriched each employee's development, as well as track how much is invested in employee training. In addition, employees can measure their own growth and development, which increases employee satisfaction and

reduces turnover (Society for Human Resource Management (SHRM) 2011 Job Satisfaction and Engagement Research Report: http://www.shrm.org/research/surveyfindings/articles/documents/11-0618%20job_satisfaction_fnl.pdf).

2. Evaluate the Quality of Training

The time to evaluate the quality of training is before you implement a new training initiative. Unfortunately, with the low cost and accessibility of video and recording technologies, subpar computer-based technology training has flooded the market. To evaluate the quality of computer-based training materials, consider the following:

How closely does the training company work with the technology manufacturer?
Look for technology training companies that have an official partnership with the manufacturers of the technology. For instance, is the training company a member of a testing program of the beta software? Does the manufacturer hire the training company to provide training on its own products? Is the training company called upon to write guides on behalf of the manufacturer? Does the training company have access to new products before they are released? A close, mutually beneficial relationship between a technology manufacturer and a training company often results in high-quality, cutting-edge training.

What credentials do course authors and instructors have?
When evaluating the quality of computer-based training, check to see if the course authors and instructors are identified. Where there is identification, there is accountability. Look for course authors who have partnered with reputable publishers to produce training books on the technology. Look for legitimate industry designations obtained from reputable educational institutions or industry associations.

Is the course material professionally produced?
Beware of poorly recorded audio and unprofessional voiceovers, which may distract learners and diminish learning. Look for professional voiceovers recorded in a studio. Also, look for training that is self-paced so employees can return to content when necessary to make sure they learn a concept completely before moving on to new content. Courseware that is peer-reviewed also is more likely to be accurate and complete than non-peer-reviewed content. Technology develops rapidly, so be sure to research how up to date the courseware is. Even a small difference in version can cause significant frustration for users trying to learn new software.

3. Provide Long-Term Access to Training

Short-term training sessions are valuable, but what happens when an employee forgets how to complete a specific function or a new employee is brought on board after a training initiative ends? These situations highlight the need for long-term access to training materials. Look for training programs that provide computer-based access to materials on a long-term basis to supply employees with resources for continued learning and technical support for maximum ROI.

Providing long-term access to training also may help your company save money in the long run. When it comes to technology training, licensing for on-demand computer-based learning can help reduce the need for robust help desk support. Tracking help desk calls can be one method for measuring the effectiveness of a training program. Consider tracking the number of help desk calls before and after training to evaluate if there is a decrease in frequency and volume of calls.

Computer-based training that requires a flat licensing fee for long-term access also helps you increase your ROI by allowing you to train more employees over a longer period of time. With traditional training, the more employees you train, the higher the cost. With e-learning licenses, the more employees you train, the lower your cost of training is per employee because the cost of training goes down per employee as each additional employee uses the content. To further reduce costs, look for training programs that have transferable licenses that can be passed from exiting employees to new employees.

4. Preserve Consistency of Training

One of the greatest challenges in training employees across the globe is to preserve the consistency of training for all employees being trained. If you hire a different local training company in each location, employees will receive incongruent training. To avoid this problem, employees must be trained from the same course content. Instead of hiring local training companies from each country, look for a global training company that can provide the same training for all employees across the globe. When employees receive the same training and learn to use a technology using the same processes and terms, employees in multiple locations are better equipped to communicate with each other effectively. Consistent training also ensures that employees are using the same processes, which then can be replicated and repeated in any part of the globe.

5. Train Multiple Levels of Stakeholders

Traditional training methods involve taking employees out of the work environment and requiring them to attend formal, in-person seminars. With traditional training methods, the cost of training increases with each employee being trained, which means organizations had to be selective regarding which employees to train. Now, with computer-based training, employers have to shift their way of thinking to realize that the cost of training per employee actually decreases as more employees use the content. This allows you to train employees at multiple levels, boosting the skill set of your entire organization.

By training multiple levels of stakeholders that use a new technology, you also are reducing the amount of lost productivity at each level of the organization. For instance, if employees are not provided sufficient training on a new technology and only learn how to use 30 percent of the technology's functionality that relates to their role, your organization is potentially losing 70 percent of the technology's capabilities for that role, not to mention lost productivity as employees fumble through learning how to use a new technology. Employees also might passively resist using the technology and utilize old methods for completing job tasks—a scenario ample training should overcome.

Fortunately, effective training doesn't mean every employee has to be trained on every function of a new technology. Instead, zero in on the training that specific stakeholders need to do their job more effectively, without wasting time training employees on functions that do not apply to them.

6. Integrate Training into Company Culture

With computer-based training, ongoing training is now more affordable than ever for companies that want to develop a highly skilled workforce. However, employees are not going to invest time in training if ongoing training is not a top-down initiative from the executive team. Training must be integrated into the everyday culture of your organization for maximum ROI.

Set an expectation that employees should dedicate a specific amount of time each day, week, or month for completing computer-based training, and then give employees a compelling reason to engage in the training. For instance, consider taking cues from what drives social media. People love to brag about what they've accomplished, win recognition, and compete. Consider establishing a company currency where employees can earn company points for completing certifications. The points later can be redeemed for a bonus, time off, or other rewards. Create a leader board to encourage employees to set goals and compete with their peers. Integrating training into your company's culture also means choosing a training platform that can be deployed into your existing learning management system (LMS) to make it possible to easily track and manage.

7. Provide Technical and Business Training

Some technical training courses are just that—technical. While employees need to understand the technical side of a new software program or system, they also need to understand how it relates to the larger picture of overall business goals. Training on a new technology should include more than instruction on how to perform a certain task or function. It also should help employees connect the technical skills they are developing with the larger business goal. For instance, the larger business goal may be to increase productivity. The training then should not just show employees how to use a function that will increase productivity, but they should be made aware that the skill they are learning will help them increase productivity. The course material also should be tied to real-world business situations and not just focus on the features of the technology. It also include should best practices and not just functional processes.

Critical Thinking

1. What are special training challenges for the global e-learner?
2. How could the e-learner assure better results?

Internet References

The E-Learning Guild: Community and Resources for E-Learning Professionals
www.elearningguild.com

Microsoft IT Academy Program
http://itacademy.microsoftelearning.com

BILL ENGLISH, CEO of Mindsharp, is an industry leader, author, and educator specializing in SharePoint training. As a former psychologist, English uses his knowledge of human behavior to help companies implement change through software platforms. English is the author of 14 books on Exchange and SharePoint products, including the "Administrator's Companion for SharePoint Server 2010," published by Microsoft Press.

Article   Prepared by: Maria Nathan, *Lynchburg College*

Language Diversity in America: Challenges and Opportunities for Management

BAHAUDIN G. MUJTABA, FRANK J. CAVICO, AND STEPHEN C. MUFFLER

Learning Outcomes

After reading this article, you will be able to:

- Understand challenges and opportunities of language diversity in the workplace.
- Consider the advantages and disadvantages having an "English-only" communication policy.
- Understand legal ramifications of English-only policies in the workplace.

Introduction

Language is part of each person's life from birth. As such, it is an important part of a person's learning, living, earning, general well-being, and identity. A manager of one of the authors of this article said that speaking effectively can determine up to 70% of professional success as well as earnings in life. Conversely, a lack of effective oral and written communication may block the path to high personal or professional success. Those who are not able to express themselves effectively through language are bound to do it physically, including stressing themselves and others or, worse, harming others. Unfortunately, prisons are full of spouses who cannot control their emotions and anger and express them violently. A teenager who gets angry and cannot effectively verbalize his or her thoughts is likely to end up in a fight. Language is an important aspect of an individual's personal and professional identity.

This professional identity can be threatened and harmed when working in a different culture and country where people speak another language. Many individuals, however, can speak

several languages fluently, especially in European and Asian countries. At the other end of the spectrum are those who can speak only their native language and may presume their co-workers will have the same level of comprehension of English as themselves. Friction arises when American workers harbor the unreasonable expectation that only spoken English in the workforce is acceptable and proper. Simple misunderstandings between workforce members due to language deficiencies can brew distrust, challenge team cohesiveness, and undermine managers' ability to direct their employees. Such misunderstandings can at times cause undue stress, hardship, and conflict. It is a tightrope that business leaders must be prepared to walk in today's global economy and the rapid diversification of America's workforce. This article, therefore, explores the challenges and opportunities of language diversity, especially the legal and practical ramifications when employers establish language policies for the workplace.

Overview

The increasing diversity of the United States and the country's workforce is clearly reflected by the 2010 census. The Census Bureau reported that as of July 1, 2009, the population of the United States was 307,007,000, of which 12.5% was foreign born. For some states, the foreign-born percentage was much higher, for example, California at 26.8, New York at 21.7, New Jersey at 19.8, Nevada at 18.9, and Florida at 18.5% (U.S. Census Bureau, 2011 Statistical Abstract, Table 38). *The Sun-Sentinel* (2011) newspaper also reported 2010 census data indicating that for the first time in the history of the U.S., a majority of young people in two states, California and New Mexico, now are identified as Hispanic; and in eight additional states—Nevada, Arizona, Texas, Mississippi, Georgia, Florida, Maryland, and Hawaii—white children are in a minority compared with children from other racial and ethnic groups combined. Furthermore, the *Sun-Sentinel* (2011) also reported that for the first time in the history of the U.S., births have surpassed immigration as the main cause of the growth in the Hispanic population. In particular, the *Sun-Sentinel* (2011) indicated that Mexican-American population increased by 7.2 million as a result of births in the decade ending in 2010, whereas new immigrants added 4.2 million people. The point that the *Sun-Sentinel* (2011) made is that the Hispanic population is going to continue to increase regardless of efforts to control immigration and prevent illegal immigration, especially at the U.S.-Mexico border.

The language data provided by the 2010 census are also revealing. The Census Bureau reported that in 2008, out of a total population (age five and older) of 283,150,000, 34,560,000 spoke Spanish at home. Other languages spoken at home included Chinese, 2,466,000, Vietnamese, 1,225,000, Tagalog, 1,488,000, French or French Creole 1,979,000, Korean, 1,052,000, and German, 1,112,000 (U.S. Census Bureau, 2011 Statistical Abstract, Table 53). For the states, the percentage of people over five years of age who spoke a language other than English at home was 42.3% in California, 33.8% in Texas, 35.4% in New Mexico, 29% in New York, 27.9% in Nevada, 27.5% in Arizona, and 25.9% in Florida (U.S. Census Bureau, 2011 Statistical Abstract, Table 54).

Based on 2000 census data, the Equal Employment Opportunity Commission (EEOC) reported that about one in 10 Americans is foreign born, with the largest number of immigrants at that time coming from Latin America and Asia (EEOC, Compliance Manual, Section 13.1, 2011). The EEOC reported that in 2000, one in eight Americans was of Hispanic origin.

The composition of the U.S. workforce has grown increasingly more diverse. Again using 2000 census data, the EEOC reported that immigrant workers numbered 15.7 million in 1999 and represented 12% of U.S. workers. In addition, of the 12.7 million new jobs created in the U.S. between 1990 and 1998, 38% (5.1 million jobs) were filled by immigrants. In 2000, Hispanics, Asians, and American Indians made up 15.2% of the workforce of private employers having 100 or more employees (EEOC, Compliance Manual, Section 13.1, 2011).

Concomitantly, the number of employees who are not native English speakers has also increased substantially. The EEOC reported that in 2002 approximately 45 million Americans, representing 17.5% of the population, spoke a language other than English in the home, and of these, approximately 10.3 million (4.1% of the total population) spoke little or no English—an increase from 6.7 million in 1999. In 1990, according to the EEOC, approximately 31.8 million Americans (13.8% of

the population) spoke a language other than English in the home; and of these 6.7 million (2.9% of the total population) spoke little or no English (EEOC, Compliance Manual, 2011, Note 42). For the fiscal year 2002, the agency received 228 charges challenging English-only policies.

The cultural and language diversity of recent immigrants was plainly underscored by the *Miami Herald* (Torrens, 2011), which reported that a sizable number of Latin American immigrants in New York City not only did not speak English, which is understandable, but did not speak Spanish! They are at a decided disadvantage in finding employment in New York. What languages do these immigrants speak? Torrens (2011) related that they speak as their primary and perhaps only languages the indigenous, pre-Columbian languages of their native lands. For example, many Mexicans in New York City speak Mixteco, Chinanteco, Otomi, Nahautl, and Trque; Guatemalans speak Quiche; and Peruvians speak Quechua. Today, however, these immigrants are reported to be taking Spanish classes to learn the "primary" language of their native countries, as apparently not knowing Spanish in New York City, let alone English, is a barrier to employment (Torrens, 2011).

The major reason for increased language conflicts in the workplace is the greater presence of employees whose primary language is not English. This language trend is bound to continue, and it is a reasonable supposition that many employees will speak their primary, non-English language to fellow employees who are members of the same ethnic, cultural, or national background.

Accordingly, as the U.S. population and composition of the workforce continues to diversify, Title VII of the Civil Rights Act of 1964 prohibiting discrimination based on national origin emerges as even more important in ensuring equality and fairness in employment relationships. As the number of employees who are bilingual or do not speak English at all continues to expand, the legal challenges to employer language restrictions, especially English-only policies, will also rise and acquire greater legal importance. Moreover, employers more frequently seek out bilingual employees and may require that some employees be fluent in languages other than English.

Nonetheless, other employers and their managers and supervisors who may be monolingual, may want to restrict the use of languages other than English in the workplace. For a variety of reasons, they implement workplace policies that limit the communication among employees to "English-only." Civil rights and immigrant rights groups, however, have condemned these policies as illegal, racist, xenophobic, immoral, and as exhibiting the irrational fear of a traditional, Anglo, English-speaking society that it is being swamped by "hordes" of Hispanic, Asian, African, and Afro-Caribbean immigrants. Stoter (2008) asserts that "In recent decades, anti-immigration sentiments have been increasing … and English-only rules seem to be the natural response to the growing uneasiness many Americans feel about the recent flux of immigrants." On a more alarming note, Stoter (2008) also declares that "arguably many English-only rules are linked to the building xenophobia within the nation."

As more and more non-English speaking immigrants enter the workplace, some employers are understandably concerned that a variety of languages in the workplace will impede safety, efficiency, harmony, productivity, and possibly alienate the customer base. English-only policies may be the response to such concerns. Moreover, the more culturally diverse the country and the workforce become, the more important, it is often asserted, it will be to have a common language—the English language. Employers contend these policies are necessary because speaking a language not understood by customers or fellow employees is inefficient and unproductive as well as perceived as rude and insensitive (Pedrioli, 2011). Safety concerns are also cited for English-only rules, for example, in a hospital emergency room or operating room setting, in an oil refinery or on an oil rig, or on a production line, where clear, quick, and understandable communication is critical (Pedrioli, 2011).

Employers must be careful that they do not get caught in a legal and ethical language "squeeze" between conflicting stakeholder demands, in particular the rights of people who only speak English in the workplace and the rights of other people who do not speak English or whose primary language is not English. A business manager may ponder how to avoid running afoul of language discrimination lawsuits. As characterized by scholars, "The laws, regulations, case law, and policies regarding language use in the United States form at best a patchwork and certainly have not woven themselves into a single scheme for viewing claims to language rights. International human rights treaties and interpretations by international tribunals have also failed to provide coherent analyses of claims of right in the language arena" (Gilman, 2011). The authors proceed to address this problem by cautiously venturing down the rabbit hole, knowing that this complex area of law is still evolving, both domestically and internationally.

EEOC Language Guidelines

Pursuant to power granted by the U.S. Congress, the Equal Employment Opportunity Commission established guidelines in 1980 with respect to language polices at work. The guidelines are codified in Section 1606, Volume 29, of the Code of Federal Regulations. Section 1606.1 states that national origin is defined broadly to include the language characteristics of a national origin group. The agency's English-only guidelines are found in 29 CFR 1606.7 and address situations when such workplace rules are "applied at all times," typically called "blanket" prohibitions, versus "when applied only at certain times," typically called narrow, limited, or tailored rules.

The guidelines indicate that English-only policies that apply at all times, including breaks and meals, will be subject automatically to close and strict scrutiny by the EEOC. Policies that apply only to certain times and places may be valid, yet still require the employer to demonstrate a business necessity for the policy. In essence, the EEOC guidelines result in a situation where "the mere existence of an English-only policy is sufficient to establish a prima facie case of discrimination" (Robinson, 2009). The EEOC also requires that any language policy be adopted for nondiscriminatory reasons. Consequently, any language policy would be illegal if it were promulgated with the intent to discriminate based on national origin (EEOC, Compliance Manual, 2011). For example, an employment policy that prohibits speaking some but not all foreign languages in the workplace is discriminatory and, therefore, unlawful. According to the Supreme Court, the agency's guidelines are entitled to some deference by the courts (General Electric Company v. Gilbert, 1976; Albemarle Paper Co. v. Moody, 1975).

However, employers and managers should be mindful of the basic legal premises reaffirmed in El v. Max Daetwyler Corp (2011) and Joseph v. North Shore Hospital (2011) that nothing in Title VII protects or provides that an employee has a right to speak his or her native language while on the job. In El (2011), the Court dismissed the worker's portion of the complaint alleging national origin discrimination based on the employer's requesting him to stop greeting individuals in the workplace in Arabic, because his allegations fell short of the legal standards to state a cause of language discrimination. Likewise, in Joseph (2011), the employer's summary judgment was granted against the worker's national origin discrimination claim based on the allegation that she was criticized for conversing in French, her native language. The court rejected the worker's claim that evidence of discrimination can be inferred from an English-only policy in the workplace.

Assuming that an English-only rule has been adopted by the employer for nondiscriminatory reasons, the EEOC states that the employer's language policy must pertain to specific circumstances in the workplace. The rule is permissible only if established for nondiscriminatory reasons, is narrowly tailored, and is necessary to ensure the safe or efficient operation of the employer's business (EEOC, National Origin Discrimination, 2011). The key test for the EEOC is "business necessity," though the agency admits there is no precise test for making this critical business necessity evaluation. The EEOC, however, does provide some illustrations where business necessity would justify an English-only rule, to wit: 1) to effectuate communications with customers, co-workers, and supervisors who speak only English; 2) to facilitate communications in emergency or other situations where employees must speak a common language to maintain and promote safety; 3) to effectuate cooperative work assignments where the English-only rule is necessary to promote efficiency; and 4) to enable a supervisor or manager who only speaks English to monitor the performance of an employee whose job duties require communication with coworkers or customers (EEOC, Compliance Manual, 2011). The EEOC cites a specific example of a petroleum company that operates an oil rig and that has a rule requiring all employees to speak only English during an emergency as well as when the employees perform job duties in laboratories and in processing areas where there is a danger of fire. This rule does not apply to casual conversations between employees in non-emergency situations or when the employees are not performing job duties in the laboratories or processing areas. This type of rule, says the EEOC, does not violate Title VII since it is narrowly tailored and predicated on safety requirements (EEOC, Compliance Manual, 2011, Example 20).

The EEOC also advises that the employer should notify the employees about the establishment of the English-only rule and the consequences for its violation. This notice can be accomplished by any reasonable means under the circumstances, such as meetings, e-mails, or postings. Stoter (2008) notes that the EEOC puts great emphasis on notice, "because bilingual employees may casually revert back to their native language." Furthermore, in some cases, it may be necessary for the employer to provide this notice not only in English, but also in some other languages spoken by the employees. The EEOC counsels that a "grace period" should be granted before compliance with a new English-only rule is required to ensure that all the employees have, in fact, been notified and that they have been given a chance to conform to the rule. Finally, the EEOC recommends that to minimize any adverse impact of an English-only rule on non-English speaking employees, the employer should consider implementing an "incentive" for those employees to improve their English language skills, such as English classes (EEOC, Compliance Manual, Note 50).

Language Discrimination Case Law

Nothing in Title VII protects an employee's right or desire to speak his or her native or primary language while on the job (Long v. First Union Corp., 1995). Unfortunately, even though this legal principle provides clarity and direction to business employers and managers, it is not a complete statement of the law in this area. Rather, English-only rules typically are challenged in the courts as contravening the prohibition in Title VII of the Civil Rights Act against national origin discrimination. The federal courts have ruled that English-only rules can create a discriminatory work environment based on national origin (EEOC v. Premier Operator Servs, Inc., 2000). To illustrate, in EEOC v. Synchro-Start Prods., Inc. (1999), the federal district

court stated that English-only rules may produce a discriminatory work environment based on national origin. Yet the federal courts have upheld the legality of English-only rules in the workplace if the employer can show it had a legitimate, non-discriminatory, business reason for applying the rule (Garcia v. Gloor, 1980).

A key factor for the courts in upholding an employer's English-only policy is whether it is limited to work areas or work stations and work times. To illustrate, in one federal district court case that deemed the employer's policy to be unlawful, the court underscored that the employer's Hispanic employees were "forced to be constantly on guard to avoid uttering their native language, even in their most private moments in the lunch room or on break," and also that one employee was reprimanded for speaking Spanish to her husband while at lunch in the break room (EEOC v. Premier Operator Services, Inc., 2000). Another important factor is that the employer must give adequate notice to the employees if an English-only policy is adopted, especially if the consequences of violating the policy are severe. For example, in Saucedo v. Brothers Well Service, Inc. (1979), the federal district court overturned the discharge of two Spanish-speaking employees—discharged for speaking two words of Spanish—because the employees were not given proper notice of the policy and the severe consequences for violating it. The court deemed that the discharge of the employees was the result of "racial animus" (Saucedo v. Brothers Well Service, Inc., 1979).

The Business Necessity Requirement

The courts, as well as the EEOC, have recognized that the employer has the prerogative to decide how it will conduct its business and manage its employees, including instituting language policies. The courts have enumerated several business reasons that could rise to the level of "business necessity" so as to justify an English-only rule. Safety considerations clearly can rise to the level of a business necessity (Pedrioli, 2011). For example, in one case the federal appeals court upheld an English-only policy at a hospital because communication and fluency in English were necessary for the safe and effective delivery of health care (Garcia v. Rush, 1981). In the aforementioned Saucedo v. Brothers Well Service (1979), the federal district court accepted the safety rationale and noted that well drilling is an inherently dangerous activity. The court also noted; however, that the plaintiff employees were not engaged in well drilling when they spoke Spanish. Managing interpersonal relations at the workplace is another valid reason for an English-only policy. For example, preventing or mitigating interpersonal conflicts, avoiding situations where employees who speak only English feel left out of conversations, and preventing non-foreign language-speaking employees from feeling they are being talked about in a language they do not comprehend (Roman v. Cornell University, 1999). Similarly, an English-only policy may be legitimate and necessary for an employer when its purpose is to prevent employees from intentionally using their fluency in a foreign language to isolate and intimidate employees of a different ethnic background who do not speak that language (Long v. First Union Corp., 1995). In another federal district court case, the court upheld as a legitimate justifications for an English-only rule the employer's objectives to promote safety and prevent injuries by means of effective communication on the production line and to ensure effective communication among employees and between the employees and supervisors, as well as the employer's attempt to redress a situation at work where non-Vietnamese workers believed they were being talked about by Vietnamese employees (Tran v. Standard Motors Products, Inc., 1998). In the federal district court case, affirmed by the court of appeals, of Gonzalez v. Salvation Army (1999), the legitimate business purpose accepted by the courts was the employer's objective of stopping complaints by non-Spanish-speaking employees and customers. Such was the accepted rationale in Long v. First Union Corp. (1995), where the employer, a bank, had adopted an English-only rule in response to complaints from customers as well as employees.

To compare, in Gutierrez v. Municipal Court (1988), the Ninth Circuit Court of Appeals struck down an English-only rule that forbade a Hispanic court clerk from speaking Spanish except when performing her duties as a court translator and when she was at lunch or on a break. The court held that the English-only rule had a disparate or adverse impact on the employee, but the employer did not show a sufficient reason for the policy to meet the business necessity requirement (Gutierrez v. Municipal Court, 1988). Leonard (2004) declared that "language … is plainly relevant to workplace decision-making. No one would argue seriously that the ability to speak English is unnecessary to most jobs in this country. Our business, commercial, and government culture is Anglophone. In the typical case, we expect that communication, recordkeeping, and client contact will be done in English."

English Fluency

Can an employer refuse to promote an employee or hire an applicant due to an inability to communicate in English? The EEOC maintains that generally an employer only can require that an employee be able to speak fluent English if fluency is necessary to perform the job effectively (EEOC, National Origin Discrimination, 2011; EEOC, Compliance

Manual, 2011). However, the EEOC counsels that since the degree of fluency in the English language can vary from position to position, the employer should avoid fluency requirements that apply uniformly to a broad range of dissimilar positions. Furthermore, the EEOC advises that an employee's or applicant's lack of proficiency in English may impede job performance in some circumstances and not others. The EEOC provides two examples in its Compliance Manual, to wit: In one, an applicant whose English is adequate to qualify as a cashier at a fast-food restaurant may lack the written language skills to work as a manager in the same restaurant requiring the completion of large amounts of paperwork in English. In the other example, a Central American national applies for a sales position with a small retailer of home appliances in a primarily English-speaking community. The applicant has limited oral communication skills in English. The applicant is informed by management that he is not qualified for a sales position because his ability to assist English-speaking customers effectively is limited. However, management offers to consider him for a position in the stock room. The EEOC states that excluding the applicant from obtaining the sales position does not violate Title VII (EEOC, Compliance Manual, 2011, Example 18). The "sum and substance" of the examples, according to the EEOC, is that the employer should not demand a greater degree of fluency in English than is required for the particular position.

There is case law in conformity with the EEOC guidelines regarding language capabilities. In one federal district court case, the court ruled that the employer did not violate Title VII by demoting the employee because the employee's language capabilities were too limited for the employee to create detailed and complex scientific manuscripts required for the position (Shieh v. Lyng, 1989). Yet Weeden (2007) warns that "the rejection of applicants for employment who cannot speak English may well be discriminatory if the job can be performed by a person lacking the ability to speak English."

National Origin Harassment and Discrimination

Civil rights law makes it unlawful to harass an employee because of national origin. The EEOC relates that harassment can include offensive or derogatory remarks about a person's national origin, ethnicity, language, or accent (EEOC, National Origin Discrimination, 2011). Harassment also includes ethnic slurs, workplace graffiti, or other offensive conduct. The law, however, does not prohibit simple teasing, off-hand comments, or isolated incidents that are not serious. Nonetheless, harassment becomes illegal when to a reasonable person it is so severe and frequent that it produces a hostile, offensive, or abusive work environment, or when it engenders an adverse employment decision, such as a discharge (EEOC Compliance Manual, 2011). A hostile or offensive environment can be produced by the actions of managers, supervisors, co-workers, or even non-employees, such as customers or business partners. The EEOC's Compliance Manual lists five factors that should be used to determine if national origin harassment rises to the level of creating a hostile work environment: 1) Whether the conduct was physically threatening or humiliating; 2) The frequency and repetition of the conduct; 3) Whether the conduct was hostile or patently offensive; 4) The context in which the harassment occurred; and 5) Whether management responded appropriately when it learned of the harassment. An illustration of a hostile work environment caused by language is the Tenth Circuit Court of Appeals case of Maldonado v. City of Altus (2006), where the appellate court reversed the district's court decision in favor of the city, which had adopted an English-only policy for the employees. The appeals court found sufficient evidence for a reasonable jury to find that a hostile work environment existed toward Hispanic employees, particularly because the manager told employees of the policy in private due to fears that other employees would learn of the English-only policy and use it to harass the plaintiff employees, and that the plaintiff employees had been taunted by the policy and made to feel inferior (Maldonado v. City of Altus, 2006). Accordingly, if an employer cannot justify its English-only policy by showing business necessity, or if the English-only policy is too broad, overly intrusive, or applied in a discriminatory fashion, such a policy can engender a hostile, abusive, or offensive work environment based on national origin, thereby triggering liability for harassment. If the language policy is created or applied in such a way that it engenders a work environment or atmosphere of isolation, inferiority, or intimidation on the part of the employees, then the policy could constitute national origin harassment. However, a Catch-22 situation can materialize for the employer: The employer can also be at risk legally if an English-speaking employee contends that fellow employees harassed the employee by consistently speaking a foreign language that the employee did not understand (McNeil v. Aquilos, 1993).

Implications and Recommendations

As the number of immigrant, non-English-speaking, and bilingual employees continues to increase rapidly, employers can expect even more national origin lawsuits, particularly language discrimination ones, in the coming years. Generally, employers can mitigate the risk of discriminatory employment decisions and civil rights lawsuits by establishing clear, written, objective, job-related criteria for employment positions and promotions, applying these criteria consistently to all candidates, and fairly evaluating all candidates. Similarly, such criteria should exist for discipline, demotion, and discharge of employees. The more objective and precise the criteria, and the more they are directly tied to business needs, the less chance for managers to engage in arbitrary, capricious, and discriminatory decision-making. The failure to hire someone or the discharge of an employee due to inadequate English skills, or due to a foreign accent, very well could be illegal national origin discrimination unless these employment actions are justified by legitimate business reasons.

Bilingual employees can offer special and valuable skills and knowledge that can attract new customers and clients, develop new markets, improve communication between global departments and divisions, and materially enhance a business. Such workers are plainly needed to satisfy non-English speaking customers at home and when U.S. companies expand overseas and interact globally. Bilingual employees legitimately may command premium salaries. Yet, if fluency in another language is required by the job, then the employer should specify this requirement clearly and, of course, make sure it is justifiable. In such circumstances, the employer can pay more for an employee who is bilingual. But if the additional language is not a legitimate job requirement and the employer nonetheless pays the bilingual employee more money merely because the employee can speak another language, which may come quite naturally to the employee, the employer now risks a national origin discrimination lawsuit from other non-bilingual employees as well as a deteriorating morale situation if other employees feel the bilingual employee is being unfairly and overly compensated. Consequently, the employer is best advised to take heed of the old HR adage: "Pay the position and not the person."

Regarding the highly contentious and legally problematic subject of English-only policies, the employer must recognize that no matter how well justified and how carefully crafted, English-only policies can disadvantage an employee's job opportunities and can produce an atmosphere of isolation, intimidation, and inferiority due to an employee's national origin. If an English-only rule is contemplated, an employer is well advised to weigh the business justification for such a rule against its possible discriminatory effects. A reasonable, legitimate, business justification for the rule will, of course, be required, such as improving safety, facilitating management communication, improving communication among the employees, or avoiding misperceptions and morale problems when the employees do not understand one another. Yet the employer is also advised to ascertain the likely effectiveness of the rule in fulfilling management objectives, the effect of the rule on the employees, particularly those not proficient in English, and whether there are alternatives to an English-only rule that would be as effective in achieving the employer's goals. English-only policies should be narrowly tailored to work times and work places. For example, if the employer believes it is losing sales because English-speaking customers are too intimidated to approach Spanish-speaking sales employees, or if the employer perceives that customers feel they are being treated rudely by employees speaking only in Spanish, the employer can impose an English-only policy on the employees while they are on duty because the courts and the EEOC maintain that customer preference can rise to the level of a business necessity. However, the employer should ascertain whether it is truly necessary that the policy apply to the employees while they are waiting to enter the workplace, particularly if there are no customers in this waiting area. Similarly, it would be unreasonable for the employer to require employees to speak English generally, but then to allow or insist that Spanish-speaking employees speak Spanish to customers who approach them in Spanish, so as not to lose a sale. To reprimand and punish those same employees for speaking Spanish while on their free time or during meals would be double standard and will cause problems for the employer—legally, ethically, and practically—as will a blanket language policy that requires English at all times and places in the workplace, even during employee breaks.

An employer should recognize from the forgoing legal analysis of these policies that "totally forbidding the use of another language … is likely to result in a discriminatory work environment, characterized by an atmosphere of inferiority, isolation and intimidation" (45B American Jurisprudence, 2nd ed. Sec. 861, Aug. 2011). The employer, therefore, should craft its English-only policy very carefully so that it is narrowly written to forbid the use of languages other than English only during work times. Moreover, the policy should explicitly state that employees are free to speak any language they choose during their breaks and meals or other free time, though they should be reminded to be sensitive to other employees who may not understand the language they are speaking.

The presence of a business necessity is yet another critical factor for legal analysis (Pedrioli, 2011). However, "there is no exact definition of the business necessity that employers are required to prove," as Meitus (2007) correctly observes. Nonetheless, based on an analysis of the case law, EEOC guidelines, and legal and management commentary, the authors of this article can supply a list of business justifications that can rise to the level of a "business necessity" so as to sustain an English-only policy, to wit:

1. To satisfy customers who cannot understand languages other than English.
2. To facilitate communication at work, especially when company materials are only available in English.
3. To effectuate communication for team or group work where English is absolutely necessary for efficiency.

4. To improve the English-speaking skills of bilingual employees. Also, to allow managers and supervisors who only speak English to be better able to oversee, monitor, communicate, and manage a bilingual or multilingual workforce.
5. To promote racial, ethnic, and cultural harmony at work, to improve morale, and to avoid a hostile and offensive work environment.
6. To ensure that the workplace is free of discriminatory, insulting, and abusive remarks.
7. To promote and enhance worker safety, and to prevent accidents and injuries, particularly with multilingual employees.
8. To enhance product quality and avoid product flaws and defects.

Weeden (2007) counsels that "A proper construction of the disparate impact analysis … demonstrates that an employer may not use an English-only rule without meeting the business necessity or job relatedness test independent of the EEOC guidelines." Rodriquez (2006) specifically underscores the safety rationale as one recognized by the courts and the EEOC, but adds two caveats for such English-only rules: first, in a safety situation, for example, dealing with dangerous substances and equipment, the rule must be applied only to those conversations conducted in the course of performing the dangerous job; and second, " 'safety' cannot simply be invoked … The concern for safety must be demonstrated, and the rule must be tailored to meet the purported need." Leonard (2004) emphasizes that avoiding workplace disruption is a valid reason for an English-only rule.

Leonard (2004) also underscores that "effective management requires that supervisors know what employees are saying and how they feel. Unless a supervisor is multi-lingual, conversations in (languages other than English) tend to deprive management of information that it needs to regulate the workplace.... Permitting pockets of conversation in (languages other than English) creates a risk that employers will be deprived of information that they need to manage the often complex dynamic of the workplace." Smith (2005) notes that customer preference, though not consistently accepted as a defense by the courts, is still allowed in language cases, including accent cases, as a business necessity defense when employers "feel pressured" by their customers "hostility" to employees speaking a language other than English or speaking English with an accent.

Many business justifications can rise to the level of a business necessity to validate an English-only rule (Pedrioli, 2011). The "business necessity" doctrine does recognize that the employer has an interest in controlling the workplace and managing employees; and the law also recognizes that this employer interest can supersede legally the employee's desire to speak in a preferred, typically primary, language. However, one legal commentator warns that the business-necessity standard will nonetheless require the employer "to meet a very high level of scrutiny to prevent employers from skirting enforcement of the Civil Rights Act of 1964 and masking the discriminatory purpose of their English-only workplace rules with banal justifications" (Hentzen, 2000).

In developing an English-only workplace policy, employers and managers should try to track the EEOC template articulated in the Code of Federal Regulations (at 29 CFR 1606.7). Specifically, rules that require employees to speak only English at all times in the workplace would be viewed as a "burdensome term and condition of employment" (29 CFR 1606.7(a) 2011). However, if the English-only rule is applied only at certain times "where the employer can show that the rule is justified by a business necessity" (29 CFR 1606.7(b)), and only enforced during time periods where the business interests to be protected are present, it likely will withstand the scrutiny of courts. Furthermore, it would be advisable that the employer's policy be phased in after adequate notice "of the general circumstances when speaking only English is required and of the consequences of violating the rule" (29 CFR 1606.7(c)). Therefore, it would be prudent that such a rule be included in personnel and employee handbooks and manuals, and that the workers acknowledge receipt of such a policy with a written signature.

Summary

Ethnic and cultural diversity is the "new reality" in the United States. The economy is now truly global and ever more diverse, but employers can benefit from this diversity by having a diverse labor force. Diversity enables the employer to retain talented and knowledgeable people from all segments of the U.S. population as well as the world. Diversity in employment also will allow the employer to relate well to a diverse customer base. Furthermore, greater awareness of the diversity of employees and applicants and showing greater respect for the employee's cultures, will benefit the employer and its stakeholders by achieving a more tolerant and harmonious workplace and one that is accordingly more efficient, effective, and productive.

The employer's right to set workplace policy and to manage its workforce to fulfill its business needs, including setting forth language restrictions at work, could clash with the employees' rights to maintain their ethnic identity and to express themselves culturally, including, of course, their use of language. Employers and employees can expect to see continuing tensions and conflict in the workplace as the country and its workforce become more diverse ethnically, culturally, and linguistically. The prudent as well as ethical employer, therefore, must be keenly aware of its business needs regarding

language, fully cognizant of the legal ramifications of its language policies, especially English-only rules, and be aware of the practical consequences of such rules—especially the potential negative effects on the morale, harmony, and productivity of employees to whom the rules are applied.

References

Ainsworth, J. (2010, Fall/Winter). Language, power, and identity in the workplace: Enforcement of 'English only' rules by employers. Seattle Journal for Social Justice, 9, 233–249.

Buckman, D. E (2007). Requirement that employees speak in workplace as violative of federal constitutional and statutory law, 24 A.L.R. E2d 587.

Cavico, E C., and Mujtaba, B. G. (2008). Legal Challenges for the Global Manager and Entrepreneur. Dubuque, Iowa: Kendall-Hunt Publishing Company.

Cavico, E J., and Mujtaba, B. G. (2011). Managers be warned! Third-party retaliation lawsuits and the United States Supreme Court. International Journal of Business and Social Sciences, 2(5), 8–17.

Civil Rights Act of 1964. 42 United States Code Sections 2000e-17 et seq. Thomson/West Publishing Company.

Code of Federal Regulations, Vol. 29, Sections 1606.1 and 1606.7 (2008).

Colon, M. (2002). Line drawing, code switching, and Spanish as second-hand smoke: English-only workplace rules and bilingual employees. Yale Law and Policy Review, 20, 227–267.

EEOC v. Premier Operator Services, Inc., 113 E Supp. 2d 1066 (N.D. Tex. 2000).

EEOC v Synchro-Start Products, Inc., 29 E Supp. 2nd 911 (N.D. Ill. 1999).

EEOC v. Delano Health Assoc, 593 E Supp. 2nd 741 (E.D. Cal. 2011).

EEOC Speak English Only Rules, 29 CFR 1606.07.

El v. Max Daetwyler Corp, 2011 U.S. Dist. LEXIS 49645 (W.D.N.C. 2011).

Equal Employment Opportunity Commission (2011). EEOC Compliance Manual—Section 13: National Origin Discrimination. Retrieved June 7, 2011 from: http://www.eeoc.gov/policy/docs/national-origin.html.

EEOC (March 11, 2009). EEOC Reports Job Bias Charges Hit Record High of Over 95,000 in Fiscal Year 2008.

EEOC Press Release. Retrieved March 20, 2009 from: http://www.eeoc.gov/press

EEOC (2011). National Origin Discrimination. Retrieved June 7, 2011 from: http://www.eeoc.gov/laws/types/nationalorigin.cfm

EEOC (2011). Questions and Answers for Small Employers About National Origin Discrimination. Retrieved June 7, 2011 from: http://www.eeoc.gov/policy/docs/quanda-nationalorigin.html

Equal Employment Opportunity Commission (2011). Statistics—All Statutes. Retrieved June 7, 2011 from: http://www.eeoc.gov/eeoc/statistics/enforcement/all.cfm.

EEOC (2011). Statistics—National Origin-Based Charges. Retrieved June 7, 2011 from: http://www.eeoc.gov/eeoc/statistics/enforcement/origin.cfm.

El v. Max Daetwyler Corp, 2011. ORDER re 9 Memorandum in Support of Motion, 8 MOTION to Dismiss. Signed by District Judge Richard Voorhees on 7/27/10. Retrieved on August 20, 2011 from: http://law.justia.com/cases/federal/district-courts/north-carolina/ncwdce/3:2009cv00415/57260/11

Garcia v. Gloor, 618 E2d 264 (5th Cir. 1980), cert. denied, 449 U.S. 1113 (1981).

Gareia v. Rush, 660 F. 2d 1217 (7th Cir. 1981).

Garcia v. Spun Steak Co., 998 F.2d 1480 (9th Cir. 1993), cert. denied, 512 U.S. 1228 (1994).

General Electric Company v. Gilbert, 429 U.S. 125 (1976).

Gilman, D. (2011, Summer). A "bilingual" approach to language rights: How dialogue between U.S. and international human rights law may improve the language rights framework, 24 harv. Hum. Rts. J. 1 p. 4.

Gonzalez v. Salvation Army, U.S. Dist. LEXIS 21692 (M.D. Fla. 1991), affirmed, 985 F.2d 578 (11th Cir. 1992), cert denied, 508 U.S. 910 (1993).

Gutierrez v. Municipal Court of the Southeast Judicial District, 838 E2d 1031 (9th Cir. 1988).

Hentzen, P. K. (2000, Winter). EEOC v. Synchro-Start Products: The New Face of Disparate Impact Challenges to English-Only Workplace Rules. University of Missouri-Kansas City School of Law, 69, 439–456. Retrieved on August 20, 2011 from: https://litigationessentials.lexisnexis.com/webcd/app?action=DocumentDisplay&crawlid=1&doctype=cite&docid=69+UMKC+L.+Rev.+439&srctype=smi&srcid=3B15&key=e2ae15f7a61c904dlb5030cf70aacb75

Joseph v. North Shore Hospital, 2011 U.S. Dist. LEXIS 14926 (E.D.N.Y. 2011).

Jurado v. Eleven-Fifty, 813 F.2d 1406 (9th Cir. 1987).

Leonard, J. (2004, Fall). Bilingualism and equality: Title VII claims for language discrimination in the workplace. University of Michigan Journal of Law Reform, 38, 57–127.

Leonard, J. (2007, Summer). Title VII and the protection of minority languages in the workplace: The search for a justification. Missouri Law Review, 72, 745–785.

Long v. First Union Corp., 894 E Supp. 933 (E.D. Va. 1995), affirmed, 86 F.3d 1151 (4th Cir. 1996).

Lynch, W. (2006, Fall). A nation sanctioned by immigrants sanctions employers for requiring English to be spoken at work: English-only work rules and national origin discrimination. Temple Political & Civil Rights Law Review, 16, 65–105.

Maldonado v. City of Altus, 433 F.3d 1294 (10th Cir. 2006).

McNeil v. Aquilos, 831 F. Supp. 1079 (S.D.N.Y. 1993).

Meitus, M. (2007). English-only policies in the workplace: Disparate impact compared to the EEOC Guidelines. Denver University Law Review, 84, 901–925.

Muffler, S. C., Cavico, E J., and Mujtaba, B. G. (2010, Summer). Diversity, disparate impact, and ethics in business: Implications of the New Haven firefighters' case and the Supreme Court's Ricci v. DeStefano Decision. SAM Advanced Management Journal, 75(3), 11–19.

Pedrioli, C. A. (2011, Spring). Respecting language as part of ethnicity: Title VII and language discrimination at work. Harvard Journal of Ethnic and Racial Justice, 27, 97–129.

Prado v. L. Luria & Son, Inc., 975 F. Supp. 1349 (S.D. Fla. 1997).

Robinson, A. J. (2009, May). Language, national origin, and employment discrimination: The importance of EEOC Guidelines. University of Pennsylvania Law Review, 157, 1513–1536.

Rodriquez, CM. (2006, Summer). Language diversity in the workplace. Northwestern University Law Review, 100, 1689–1758.

Roman v. Cornell University, 53 F. Supp.2d 223 (N.D.N.Y. 1999).

Saucedo v. Brothers Well Service, 464 F. Supp. 919 (S.D. Tex. 1979).

Shieh v. Lyng, 710 F. Supp. 1024 (E.D. Pa. 1989), affirmed, 897 F.2d 523 (3rd Cir. 1990).

Smith, G. B. (2005). Want to speak like a native speaker: The case for lowering the plaintiff's burden of proof in Title VII accent discrimination cases. Ohio State Law Journal, 66, 231–262.

Stoter, R. S. (2008). Discrimination and deference: Making a case for the EEOC's expertise with English-only rules. Villanova Law Review, 53, 595–635.

Sun-Sentinel (2011, July 15). Latino births in U.S. outpace immigrants, 6A.

Sun-Sentinel (2011, July 8). Youths lead the way to diversity, 2A.

Torrens, C. (2011, May 29). Some N.Y. immigrants say lack of Spanish is a barrier. Miami Herald, 9A.

Tran v. Standard Motors Products, Inc., 10 F. Supp.2d 1199 (D. Kan. 1998).

United States Census Bureau (2011). The 2011 Statistical Abstract. Retrieved June 16, 2011 from: http://www.census.gov/compendia/statab/cats/population.html

Weeden, L. D. (2007, Summer). The less than fair employment practice of an English-only rule in the workplace. Nevada Law Journal, 7, 947–981.

Critical Thinking

1. What are some benefits of language diversity in the workplace for you?
2. How many languages can you speak? What has learning another language helped you to understand?

Internet References

Canadian HR Reporter

wwwhrreporter.com

Inclusive Language Guidelines. Diversity at Work/HR Toolkit

http://hrcouncil.ca

DR. MUJTABA, the author or co-author of several books and journal articles on diversity, ethics, and business management, has worked with HR professionals around the world for the past 25 years. **DR. CAVICO'S** teaching to three levels of students encompasses government regulation of business, ethics, labor relations, and law pertaining to business, the Constitution, administration, labor, and health care. The Huizenga School has awarded him for teaching and as Faculty Member of the Year (2007). **DR. MUFFLER**, a full-time attorney, also teaches business law and ethics at the Huizenga School. He was a former legal assistant to the Florida Bar's ethics enforcement branch in Miami and a former special public defender for the 17th Judicial Circuit. In addition to publishing on legal and ethical topics, he lectures occasionally to national and local organizations.

Mujtaba, Bahaudin G.; Cavico, Frank J.; Muffler, Stephen C. From *SAM Advanced Management Journal*, vol. 77, no. 2, 2012, pp. 38–47. Copyright © 2012 by Society for Advancement of Management. Reprinted by permission.

Unit 5

UNIT

Prepared by: Maria Nathan, *Lynchburg College*

Implementing Compensation, Benefits, and Workplace Safety

One of HRs traditional functions that remain among its most important is employee compensation and benefits. Pay can be a touchy subject. In general, employees tend to assume that others make more than them. This perception creates such an equity problem that some employers have even issued policies that caution employees that they can have their employment terminated if it is found that they share pay information with another employee.

How about executives? Top leader salaries are routinely published in the United States—which brings us to an executive pay controversy. Should top leaders be paid such exorbitant amounts that read about in the newspapers? Not all countries of the world have such wide differentials between top and lower level employee pay. For example, in Japan, the differential between the various managerial levels seems to be much more modest. Still another controversy in the matter of executive pay is that some boards have not carefully thought through the incentives they provide to their executives. Executives may be tempted to pursue self-interest over that of the organization they represent. Boards learn that they don't just get what they pay for; they get what they reward.

Then, there are benefits. They are very expensive for the employer and they are probably the least understood by employees. Employees may focus upon their annual salary plus bonuses, and so on, but they usually don't recognize that their total compensation package includes some very expensive and valuable benefits. Some organizations supply employees with an easy-to-use benefits calculator so employees can more fully appreciate all that the organization does for them. This is also because the organization's full compensation package can be a source of market competitiveness for the employer when a prospective employee also factors in benefit offerings along with compensation. Of course, now more than ever—employees appreciate the flexible benefit program that allows them to use what they need most, but pass on programs that don't suit their current needs.

Another benefit that has been highlighted quite a bit in recent years has been employee retirement. Some retirement experts have suggested that there is a large percentage of workers who have not adequately saved for their later years. Now, some creative employers have made it easier for employees to save for retirement with cash-back programs, matching programs and other innovations.

HR's work on salary and benefits is necessarily very technical and detail oriented. Another HR function that requires careful attention is workplace safety. OSHA has many guidelines for safety in the workplace. OSHA emphasizes "safety first"—a tip which HR professionals and managers in general must reinforce. Safety first. There are some great guidelines around many workplaces that seek to make the employee more conscious of potentials for risk and the part the employee plays in safety. However, investigations surrounding the circumstances of any given accident or injury frequently reveal that there were things the organization could and should have done differently and/ or better. For example, awareness of fatigue effects could make the employer more careful when they assign people to certain work schedules and assignments. The employer is at least as responsible in the matter of workplace safety as is the employee.

Safety and wellness are both critical concerns for HR. Wellness is both physical and psychological. Now more employers are recognizing that there are sometimes significant threats to employee well-being to be found in the bullying and sexual harassment that may take place in the workplace. Employers and government both are working on what to do about bullying. Case law is being shaped with each passing month.

What about the boss who bullies? We are finding that toxic environments are not just about a bullying, dysfunctional boss. They are also about an organization's culture that abides poor behavior and employees who permit bullying to continue for various reasons.

As time has passed, HR has become more and more central to employee welfare, emotional well-being, and future retirement security. This advocacy function of HR is one reason why so many people who have majored in psychology as undergraduates find themselves drawn to a career in HRM. HRM is quite psychological in its regard for individual employee well-being.

Article   Prepared by: Maria Nathan, *Lynchburg College*

Making Benefits Matter

We've all heard about it. from *NCB Nightly News* to *U.S. News & World Report* to *TIME* Magazine and beyond, the message has been consistent and it has been clear.

TORRY DELL

Learning Outcomes

After reading this article, you will be able to:

- Know that employee compensation is more fully reflected in the employer's total compensation package.

- Understand why it is important to make this full compensation package known to employees.

- Know how to make benefits matter more fully to all employees.

The "baby boomer" generation, born between the end of world War II and 1964, seventy-eight million strong, is retiring.

Demographics and Workforce Shortage

A pending wave of baby boomer retirements has been on the mind of many employers, and cooperative leadership is no exception. If you consider your own family and acquaintances, you'll probably notice that people are living longer and the population over sixty is growing. The Centers for Disease Control states that life expectancy is now 77.8 years, up from 77 just ten years ago. In 2006, the U.S. Census Bureau reported that almost eight thousand people a day—or about 330 an hour—turned sixty.

The force of baby boomers has been on the forefront of discussion for some time, so this news may not be surprising. We even watched as the first of a few notable baby boomers like Bill Clinton and George Bush make headlines for turning 60. These baby boomers will be followed by 4 million of their closest friends each year celebrating their 60th birthdays through the year 2025. When we look at the decline in birth rates and the increase in population for ages over 55 we start to see the real impact of increased longevity.

Workforce Dynamics for Electric Cooperatives

For today's electric cooperatives, an aging population brings about a more urgent issue: skilled workers. The rate at which the next generation is filling bucket trucks is looking alarmingly low. About half of the 400,000 current power industry workers are eligible to retire in the next five to ten years. Just as the need for energy is soaring, the outlook for skilled labor required for construction and maintenance is becoming more and more grim. According to Russell Turner, NRECA's principal for human capital issues, "Despite some workers delaying retirements, cooperatives are facing increasing competition from Investor Owned Utilities and Muni's to retain existing workers while attracting a whole new generation of workers to deal with the technological challenges facing cooperatives."

For today's electric cooperatives, an aging population brings about a more urgent issue: skilled workers.

For electric utilities, the year 2012 will mean:

- 52% of generation technicians are expected to reach retirement eligibility
- An estimated 40% of line worker jobs will need to be filled
- 46% of engineering jobs are expected to be vacant

Even within the NRECA member community, the impact of an aging workforce is present.

Concerns about who will "fill the boots" of a retiring workforce has prompted many cooperatives to increase their focus on recruitment and training programs. As highlighted in *RE Magazine* in the April 2009 issue, solutions developed by co-ops include extensive partnerships with local vocational schools and colleges to offer training for new linemen. Norris Public Power District and Platte-Clay Electric are just a few with structured programs that work with vocational schools and colleges to offer certificate programs after classroom and field training is complete.

Randy Evans, operations manager for Norris Public Power, estimates the average age of his lineman team is 45 and he will likely see at least one member of the current team retire in each of the next five years. Randy summed up his concerns by saying: "We used to hire a lineman about every two to three years. In the last three years, we've hired five."

Danny Belcher, manager of safety & loss control of Trinity Valley Electric Co-op, echoed these same concerns: "I would say in the next six to eight years 50 percent of our lineworker knowledge will walk out the door."

Education programs and scholarships can help recruitment immensely but what are the factors that influence employees starting work today? And on the other hand, what can be done to slow the flood of skilled workforce moving toward retirement?

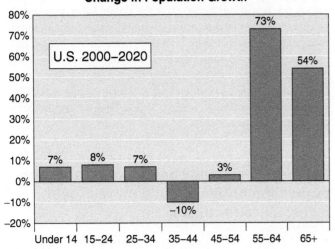

Change in Population Growth

Benefits Matter More Than You May Think

The seemingly endless sources illustrating the crushing cost of healthcare and importance of insuring your own income in retirement is having an impact on the population entering the workforce. The Employee Benefits Research Institute (EBRI) cites in their 2009 Value of Benefits Survey that over 75% of employees today rank benefits high on the list of priorities when choosing an employer.

When it comes to identifying the most important benefit, healthcare tops the list, followed closely by retirement benefits. The trend that places healthcare first may change based on the final shakeout of new healthcare legislation. Once healthcare is guaranteed or even mandated to be offered by employers, we may find that retirement benefits become what differentiates employers.

No one will disagree with the importance that employees put in their benefit packages. But what is the real impact that benefits play in differentiating one employer from another? To get to the core of how much benefits can impact retention, we can look to the 30% of employees who accepted, quit or changed jobs because of benefits. That's over one fourth of all employees basing their decision on employment because of the benefit package.

Employers are taking note. In the past, phrases like "total compensation" were mainly used in human resources departments. Now those terms and related issues have expanded to include CFOs and CEOs. In fact, we saw executives defend their benefit plans even when markets became stressed. In 2009, Charles Schwab and CFO Research services found that 60% of employers planned to commit more to their 401(k) plans in the midst of great uncertainty and depressed markets.

In addition, employees are starting to see the impact that employer-offered benefits have on their overall livelihood—now and in the future. As such, employees are beginning to place as much value on benefits as they do salary.

Our corporate office is located in a university town and of course, money is always one of the top attractions for prospective employees but today, more individuals see the long-term advantages of a good benefit package as even more of an incentive to work for a company.

One key influence likely to be a factor in employee's increased focus on benefits is what has been occurring inside the homes of most Americans. Most American families are paying more for health insurance. In 2008, the U.S. average cost of family coverage premiums was $12,298. If you

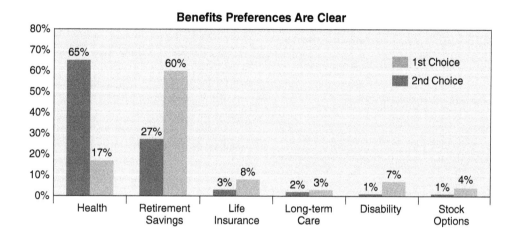

Benefits Preferences Are Clear

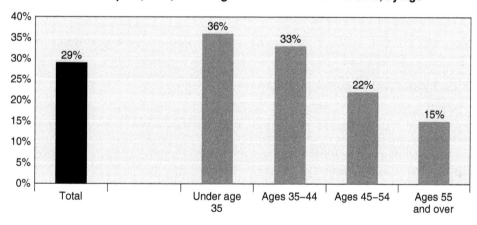

Benefits Play a Major Role in Employment Decisions Workers Who Accepted, Quit, or Change Jobs Because of Benefits, by Age

compare healthcare premiums as a percentage of median household income seven years ago to premiums two years ago, there is a dramatic increase in the percentage of household income going to cover healthcare premiums. Even more important, costs are projected to rise steadily.

Employers Are Getting Their Fair Share of Increased Cost

Increases are not just on the employee side. Most employers are paying significantly more for health insurance and are taking public steps to be sure that this is known and appreciated—in large part to help recruitment and retention.

Think about your own community. Do you know the employers who have reputations for providing strong benefit programs or have received community awards for providing noteworthy benefit programs? Probably so.

Cooperatives Are in a Position of Power

Employers can't control nationwide healthcare premium increases, financial markets or population demographics. However, there is still a great deal of power that rests within each cooperative when it comes to designing benefit programs that meet the unique needs of the workforce in each community and managing costs for the cooperative. There is also a range of flexibility that can be extended to customize these programs over time as workforce and cooperative needs change.

Retirement Realities

Customization can help, but there are benefit realities most cooperatives are facing. Years of weak investment return are hard on the bottom line for defined benefit plans. Thanks to

Year	Contributions in Billions for Single-Employer U.S. Pension Plans
2009	$ 36.3
2010	$108.6

Towers Watson simulation of large single-employer U.S. Pension Plan

legislative efforts on their behalf, electric cooperatives have smoothing techniques in the RS Plan that allow the spreading of an investment loss from a single year over several years. However, periods of extremely low investment return, such as crisis years like 2008, translate to higher funding costs that cannot be avoided. Though RS Plan funding required a significant increase in contributions beginning in 2010, conditions were even worse for most non-cooperative plans which don't have smoothing techniques. Towers Watson, a prominent actuarial and employee benefits consulting firm, stated in a recent study that contributions due nationwide for U.S. single-employer pension plans in 2010 are triple the amounts due in 2009.

Following a Strategic Approach

To get the most out of benefit programs and the increased value employees place on these programs, cooperatives will benefit by following a strategic approach. The advice to "think long-term" isn't just for employees making investment decisions. Cooperatives and other employers have a history of improving plan benefits when market performance is strong. Normal retirement dates are earlier, cost of living adjustments are more

common, benefit levels are higher and plans are overall more generous. This is good for participants but may be setting a benchmark for the long term without considering the long-term price tag. This is especially true for cooperatives where employee turnover is generally very low because some benefits, once awarded, are protected and must remain in place even if changes are made for future benefit accruals.

It helps to view employee benefit trends with an eye for what is most relevant in order to recruit and retain electric cooperative employees. Benefit features and forces affecting global employers are now reflected in employee benefit trends but may show trends that aren't applicable for electric cooperatives. For example, employees in other countries with a different cultural focus on elder care or centralized health-care systems may be less concerned about pension benefits or retiree medical. Domestic-based employers such as public, investor-owned utilities and electric cooperatives are impacted by a different set of cultural and social values and are likely to see benefits from offering a range of health plans, defined benefit options and strategic retiree medical.

It is also beneficial to consider the benefit offerings of regional competitors and other community employers. Just don't forget that this comparison should serve as a guide, not a roadmap. Following the herd and making benefit cuts to programs which cooperative employees tie to their livelihood can have devastating effects and diminish employee productivity.

The Personal Finance Employee Education Foundation reports that one-third of Americans in the workforce report that money concerns hamper work performance and/or keep them away from work. How? Employees experiencing

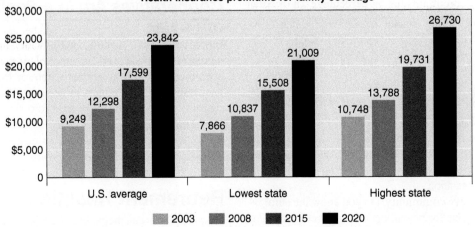

Premiums for Family Coverage 2003, 2008, 2015 and 2020

Health insurance premiums for family coverage

2003: Lowest is North Dakota: highest is District of Columbia. 2008, 2015, and 2020: Lowest is Idaho; highest is Massachusetts Data sources: Medical Expenditure Panel Survey—Insurance Component (for 2003 and 2008 premiums); Centers for Medicare and Medicaid Services, Office of the Actuary, National Health Statistics Group, national health expenditures per capita annual growth rate (for premium estimates for 2015 and 2020).

Benefit Variation Is Expanding between Global and Domestic Focused Firms—and by Workforce Focus

Employers That Are Global	Large Employers That Are Domestic–NRECA Co-ops
Low Base Pay	Base Pay Emphasis
High Incentive Pay	Low Incentive Pay
Frozen DB or Cash Balance or None	Strategic Defined Benefits Plans
401(k) Savings and Profit Sharing	401(k) Savings and Profit Sharing
High Deductible Health Plans	Range of Health Plans
No Retiree Health Benefits	Strategic Retiree Health Benefits

Targeted Hiring and Tenure Focused Employers Are Keeping DB Plans and Retiree Health

financial strain are more likely to skip preventive wellness exams that can keep them healthy and reduce medical plan costs. They take extended work breaks to get advice about what to do from co-workers. They miss work to meet with bankers to seek loan alternatives and they become distracted and make mistakes. A distracted lineman working in a storm at 50 feet above ground is not an individual most cooperatives want in their crews.

Opportunities for Employers

Legislation and public policy may dictate change or mandate minimum coverage of certain benefits. However, as Cynthia Mallet, vice president, Product & Market Strategies for MetLife stated, "With benefits, on average, representing one-third or more of the money spent to compensate each employee, there's a real opportunity for employers to better grasp the strategic role that benefits can play in workforce management."

Employee benefits are likely to rise even more to the forefront of employer conference tables and employee kitchen tables. Keeping focused on balancing benefits valued by employees with providing a total compensation package that can be supported over the long term by cooperatives is a formula that should leave most cooperatives in the best condition over time while also paying off tenfold for both current and prospective employees.

Critical Thinking

1. Why are benefits important to employees?

2. Can an outstanding benefit package be a deciding factor in a decision to accept employment?

3. Why do employees often want increased benefits rather than increased salary?

Internet References

Employee Total Compensation Calculator
www.calcxml.com/calculators/total-compensation

How to Calculate Your Compensation Package
www.ehow.com/how_5060652_calculate-compensation-package.html

The Total Compensation Blog
http://blog.compackage.com

TORRY DELL is a Senior Marketing Advisor for retirement programs at NRECA and provides financial education tools to participants and cooperatives promoting positive retirement savings and investing habits. Prior to joining NRECA in 2008, Torry managed clients for Principal Financial Group and served as a participant education consultant for an institutional retirement business.

Article Prepared by: Maria Nathan, *Lynchburg College*

Cash-Back Program Puts Money into Workers' 401(k)s

Online program doesn't require employees to change behavior or make other sacrifices to save for retirement.

ANDREA DAVIS

Learning Outcomes

After reading this article, you will be able to:

- Discuss the save or spend dilemma as it pertains to retirement planning.
- Know about the SaverNation program and how it resolves the save or spend dilemma.
- Know how an employer can help employees to save more for retirement.

Money's fun to spend, so why shouldn't it be fun to save? That's the thinking behind SaverNation, a new cash-back program for 401(k) and other workplace retirement plan participants.

SaverNation partners with over 500 online retailers in the country. Employees sign up, make their regular online purchases, and the retailers offer anywhere from 1% to 25% cash back for the online purchases. SaverNation's technology automatically converts the cash back into extra contributions for the 401(k), 403(b), 457, IRA, Roth IRA or account of choice.

"We are the only program where people can continue to buy [online] from the places they normally buy and get cash back and have someone else basically give them the money into their retirement plan so they don't have to choose between spending and saving," says Marc Robinson, founder and CEO.

The program was designed to help people overcome the save-or-spend dilemma.

"In this era of cutbacks and layoffs, this is a no-cost opportunity to offer employees a hard-dollar compensation, a new employee benefit that doesn't cost the employer anything and is easy for employees to use," says Robinson. "And it goes right to the heart of one of the most difficult problems that people have in any workplace, which is saving for retirement."

Seven years in the making, SaverNation has the support of industry heavyweights Brian Graff, CEO and executive director of the American Society of Pension Professionals and Actuaries, and Dallas Salisbury, president of the Employee Benefits Research Institute. Other key players include ERISA attorney Bruce Ashton from Drinker Biddle & Reath LLP; Dan Maddux, executive director of the American Payroll Association; and John Fiore, retired executive vice president and former chief investment officer with Bank of New York Mellon and State Street.

"One of the things we're focused on here at ASPPA is trying to increase savings, particularly for moderate-income workers and this could be a great way of doing it," says Graff. "Here's a new employee benefit you can provide without any cost."

SaverNation configures its system to whichever payroll provider an employer is currently using. "Once a month, payroll has to take instructions from us about which employees have earned at least $5 of rewards and add that to the second deduction field, which the payroll system then combines and sends to the recordkeeper as a single source," says Robinson. "There's no burden for the recordkeeper or the plan administrator, and it's very little work for payroll."

SaverNation also provides marketing materials employers and brokers can distribute to employees.

Robinson believes employers can use the program to differentiate themselves from competitors. "Employees aren't going to say, 'What's your investment lineup?' or 'Who's your plan provider?' but how easy is it to say, 'We have this cash-back program'?" he says. "It's something employers can feel innovative about and [use] to differentiate themselves."

Online Shopping as a Company Perk

Another company hoping to cash in on people's love of online shopping is workpays.me, an online platform employers can offer as a voluntary benefit. Employees shop online and pay for their purchases through payroll deductions. The site offers access to roughly 50,000 everyday and luxury items—everything from $16 bottles of perfume to $6,000 televisions. Employees can pay for the items over the course of up to 12 months with no interest.

"We're really trying to create the Amazon experience, where you can come to our site and buy anything you're looking for," says Josh Verne, president and CEO.

Another perk? Workpays.me gives anywhere from 2% to 4% of total sales back to the employer as a charitable donation or to help fund wellness and retirement programs.

The system recognizes the employee's pay cycle and breaks down payments accordingly. Every time an item is added to the cart, the site shows the employee how much it will cost per pay cycle.

Until about three years ago, Verne worked in the furniture distribution business. "When I was looking to add more benefits for employees that wouldn't cost us anything, we came up with the concept of being able to offer employees the ability to buy our furniture at no discount, but over four or six pay periods," he says. "When we sold the [furniture] business, it was my wife who said, 'Your employees used to love this benefit, why don't you look to do something like this?' And that's how we started the business."

Thirteen employers with an average group size of 6,000 employees are either already using the platform with employees or are slated to launch it soon.

So far, about 200 employers are using the program. "It's been built from an authentic place to really make a difference in people's lives by having everybody do what they normally do," says Robinson. "The participants are buying what they normally buy, HR is doing what it normally does, [and] payroll does what it normally does."

The program is available to all employees, whether they're participating in the retirement plan or not. "If they're not participating in the plan, they'll get the cash back, but not the full benefit of the program," explains Robinson. "But that gives the adviser or broker or employer the chance to say, 'You're getting this money, you might as well join the plan; it's free money.'"

Brokers, meanwhile, can use the SaverNation program to boost revenue. "As we're driving assets into the plan, they're making basis points from that revenue," says Robinson. "For clients who they feel have maxed out on their current revenue, [brokers can] put this into the clients [they] already have and watch this incremental growth."

Plan Design Feature

SaverNation is a plan design feature that "snaps on" to a workplace retirement plan.

"There's a plan amendment that doesn't have to be filed anywhere except [in] the fiduciary filings [if employers want]," says Robinson. "Then you look at the plan document. Does the plan document allow for a fixed-dollar deferral or only percentage of pay? If it's only 'percentage of pay,' you check the box that says 'either one.' Then you look and see whether there's a monthly election amount rather than quarterly or annually. And if it's not monthly, you check that box and you're done."

SaverNation was recently recognized with a 2013 Bank Innovation Award from Bank Innovation, a customer experience blog for the banking industry.

Critical Thinking

1. What devices/programs help you to save more effectively?
2. Why do you think employers should get involved in such programs?

Internet References

Employer-Sponsored Plan
www.investopedia.com/terms/e/employer_sponsored_plan.asp
For Employers Retirement Savings Education Campaign
www.savingmatters.dol.gov/employers.html
Save for Retirement
www.americasaves.org/for-savers/save-for-retirement
Types of Retirement Plans
www.irs.gov/Retirement-Plans/Plan-Sponsor/Types-of-Retirement-Plans-1

Article   Prepared by: Maria Nathan, *Lynchburg College*

Individual and Social Factors Associated with Workplace Injuries

ASHWIN KUMAR

Learning Outcomes

After reading this article, you will be able to:

- Understand why workplace injury is an important topic for employers.

- Understand major causes of employee workplace injury, especially those over which the employer can have control.

Introduction

636,000 Australians injured themselves in a work-related injury in the period 2009–2010. Of these injured Australians, 88% continued to work in their same place, 5.2% had to change their jobs, and 6.9% were no longer employed. Men continue to be the most injured individuals in workplace injuries (56%) with the highest rates of injury in the 45–49 years (72 per 1000 people) and 20–24 years (63 per 1000 people) age groups. Furthermore, 59% of these 636,000 Australians injured in workplace injuries received financial assistance from workers compensation claims, 36% did not apply for financial assistance and 5% applied but did not receive any financial assistance. The most common types of workplace injuries incurred were: sprains and strains (30%), chronic joint/muscle conditions (18%) and cuts/open wounds (16%) (Australian Bureau of Statistics, 2010). The total economic cost from workplace injuries in Australia for the 2005–06 financial year was estimated at $57.5 billion, representing 5.9% of GDP for the financial year (Australian Safety and Compensation Council, 2009). Workplace injuries also incur immeasurable personal costs to Australian workers and their families. Individual lives are altered, even lost; individual hopes and dreams of a better life are shattered. Family roles, responsibilities and relationships become strained due to changes in income earnings and the imposed challenging needs

for increased social support and increased caring needs within the home due to workplace injury. Why do Australian workers get injured in their workplaces? Is it due to their individual worker factors, or is it due to social factors associated with their work and workplace? While individual worker factors, such as: gender, age, personality, ethnicity, and substance use, do contribute to workplace injuries and fatalities, broader social and organizational workplace factors, such as: workload, work hours, work environment, safety culture, provision of quality supervision, and provision of occupational health and safety training, socially structure, and influence individual worker attitudes and behaviours in workplace injury and fatalities.

Individual Factors Associated with Workplace Injuries

Gender is associated as a contributing individual factor in workplace injuries and fatalities. In particular, more males than females are injured and prone to workplace fatalities. In the period 2009–2010, 356,229 men experienced workplace injuries in Australia. This amounts to 55.6% of the total number of reported work injuries (640,700). The most common types of workplace injuries for men were: sprain and strains (30%), chronic joint and muscle conditions (18%) and cuts and open wound injuries (16%) (Australian Bureau of Statistics, 2010). Furthermore, more males are represented in higher injury risk occupations. Of the 356,229 men who experienced work related injuries in the period 2009–2010, 30% were Technicians/Tradesman, 19% were Labourers, 15% were Machine Operators/Drivers, 18% were Manufacturing Workers, 16% were Construction Workers, and 10% were Transport/Warehousing Workers (Australian Bureau of Statistics, 2010).

The high representation of males in workplace injuries and fatalities raises some interesting questions: Why are men overrepresented in workplace injuries and fatalities? Do men cause higher rates of workplace injury and fatalities? Two sets of competing explanations are offered in current literature. The first explanation posits that men, as a gender category, engage in higher risk taking behaviours that results in higher workplace place injuries and fatalities (Berdahl, 2008; Brogmus, 2007; Islam, 2001). This view posits that men cause higher rates of injuries and fatalities due to their innate, essentialist gender based propensity to engage in higher risk taking behaviours. The second explanation posits that men, as a gender category, engage in higher employment in higher risk occupational sectors where higher workplace injuries and fatalities often occur (Gluck, 1998; Manchikanti, 2002; Smith, 2005; Sulsky, 2000). This view posits that it is not the men who cause workplace injuries, but that these men find themselves employed in high risk jobs and work environments that are more likely to cause higher rates of injuries and fatalities. The social nature and organizational factors of such high risk work environments exposes these men to higher risks and dangers related to workplace injuries and fatalities.

Age is associated as a contributing individual factor in workplace injuries and fatalities. In Australia, the highest rates of workplace injuries experienced by men were in the age groups of 45–49 years (72 per 1000 people) and 20–24 years (63 per 1000 people). The lowest age group for injured men was 65 years and over (30 per 1000 people) (Australian Bureau of Statistics, 2010). Work Safe Australia reports similar patterns in workers compensation claims for the period 2007–2008. The highest number of claims from injured workers for workers compensation were in the 45–49 years age group (13.7%), followed closely by the 40–44 years age group (12.4%) and the 35–39 years age group (11.6%). More injured males workers lodged compensation claims (88,865) than injured female workers (42,245) (Work Safe Australia, 2011).

The high representation of workplace injuries and fatalities in the age groups of 45–49 years and 20–24 years raises the interesting question: Why are workplace injuries and fatalities concentrated in these two age groups? Two sets of competing explanations are offered in current literature in relation to the age-work injury relationship. The first explanation posits that worker age-maturity factor is related to workplace injury. This view posits that young workers lack workplace maturity, thus are more injury prone and, conversely, older workers are more mature in the workplace, thus are less injury prone (Chau, 2010; Sulsky, 2000). The second explanation posits that worker age related cognitive decline is related to workplace injury (Pisarski, 2008; Pransky, 2002; Rowell, 2010; Siow, 2011; Smith, 2005). This view posits that young workers are more cognitively able, thus are less likely to be injury prone in the workplace; and, conversely, mature aged workers are less cognitively able, thus are more likely to be injury prone in the workplace.

Personality is associated as a contributing individual factor in workplace injuries and fatalities. Two sets of competing explanations are offered in current literature in relation to the personality-work injury relationship. The first explanation posits that certain types of workplace injuries appear more frequently in workers with high risk taking personality patterns (Brockner, 1988; Cellar, 2004; Chau, 1995; Nelson, Cooper and Jackson, 1995; Smith, Kaminstein, & Makadok, 1995). The implicit assumption here is that such workers are hard driving, competitive, job involved, hostile, and willing to take adverse risks to achieve goals and outcomes. The second explanation posits that workers with perceived lower personal control over their work activities are more likely to suffer from higher rates of workplace injuries and fatalities (Burkhalter, 1999; Janicak, 1996; Korzeniowska, 2004; Yoon, 2007). Furthermore, it is suggested that measures of locus of control generally focuses on generalized perceived control: workers with a so-called internal locus of control believe their own behaviours are the primary determinants of what happens to them in the workplace, whereas workers with an external locus of control believe that external influences are more important determinants of what happens in their workplace. The implicit essentialist assumption made here is that internal worker perceived personal control over their work plays an important role in external worker injuries in the workplace.

Ethnicity is associated as a contributing individual factor in workplace injuries and fatalities. Two sets of explanations are offered in current literature in relation to the ethnicity-work injury relationship. The first explanation posits that 'ethnic' workers are more likely to suffer from higher rates of workplace injury and fatalities due to a lack of adequate education, skills and training, and effective workplace communication which results in higher operational and technical errors resulting in higher workplace injuries (Loomis, 1998; Oh, 2003; Richardson, 2004; Shannon, 2009; Sulsky, 2000). The second explanation posits that 'ethnic' workers have different cultural thinking styles and approach to workplace safety and that 'ethnic' workers are more task/volume oriented rather than safety/quality oriented (Walter, 2002; Flory, 2001; Johansson, 1999). The implicit essentialist assumption made here is that cultural based thinking style, approach to workplace safety and quality of task orientation contributes to higher rates of injury in the workplace for 'ethnic' workers.

Substance use is associated as a contributing individual factor in workplace injuries and fatalities. Two sets of explanations are offered in current literature in relation to the substance use-work injury relationship. The first explanation posits that substance use, such as alcohol and prohibited drugs, impairs worker judgement, reaction time and effective decision-making (Garvey Wilson, 2003; Kunar, 2008; Petrie, 2008; Roche, 2008; Veazie, 2000). Substance use impairs cognitive abilities and effective decision-making. The second explanation posits that substance use, such as drugs and prohibited drugs, promotes higher risk taking behaviours due to loss of self-control in the workplace: substance use leads to loss of self-control; loss of self-control leads to higher risk taking behaviour resulting in higher workplace injuries (Moyers, 1999; Plurad, 2011).

While the above-mentioned individual worker factors associated with workplace injuries and fatalities are credible and empirically validated in multivariate correlational studies, they situate causality of workplace injuries and fatalities, based upon essentialist assumptions and personal characters, on the workers alone without any consideration of the social and organizational influences of the workplace. In other words, such findings often situate the 'blame' on individual workers for workplace injuries and fatalities based upon their individual attitudes, beliefs and behaviours without any examination of the mitigating social and organizational contexts of the workplace. Individual workers do not 'perform their work' in a 'social vacuum' based entirely on their individual attributes. They perform their work in 'socially structured, situated and organized' work environments. As such, a consideration of the social and organization factors associated with workplace injuries is crucial in fully understanding the complexity of workplace injuries and fatalities.

Social Factors Associated with Workplace Injuries

The lack of safety culture in the workplace is associated as a contributing social factor in workplace injuries and fatalities. Safety culture is a group phenomenon, a product of social learning and socialization about safety and the value of safety in work practices (Calmbacher, 1993; Dong, 2004; Faigenbaum, 2010; Fukuda, 1993). It is essentially the unconscious, invisible and tacit set of forces that determines both the individual and collective safety behaviour of a group of workers (Hooper, 2005). It consists of shared perceptions, thoughts, feelings and beliefs regarding safety and safe work practices. Safety culture refers to the way in which safety is managed in the workplace, and it often reflects the attitudes, beliefs, perceptions and values that employees and employers collectively share in relation to safety (Cox and Cox, 1991). How does the lack of safety culture in a workplace contribute to worker injuries and fatalities? Three sets of competing explanations are offered from current literature: 1) work environments are unsafe and remain unsafe without a safety culture (Johnson, 2002; Jones, 1981; Leiter, 2009), 2) workers are unaware and remain unaware of risks to themselves and fellow workers associated with their work practices without a safety culture (Calmbacher, 1993; Dong, 2004; Faigenbaum, 2010; Fukuda, 1993), and 3) workers are unaware and remain unaware of policies and procedures that require them to perform their jobs according to explicit statutory laws

and regulations without a safety culture (Leiter, 2009; Monforton, 2010; Patterson, 2010). Without a collective safety culture, workers are unaware of risks associated with work environments and work practices. This exposes them and fellow workers to higher rates of workplace injuries and fatalities.

The lack of supervision and/or quality supervision in the workplace is associated as a contributing social factor in workplace injuries and fatalities. Benge (2007) maintains that supervisors have a critical role in workplace injury, fatalities prevention, and maintaining and promoting an active safe culture. How does lack of supervision and/or quality supervision in the workplace contribute towards worker injuries and fatalities? Delayed response by supervisors to workers reporting work-related injury significantly influences length of injury rehabilitation (Brogmus, 2007). Negative supervisor attitudes and practices towards effectively maintaining an active safe work culture is associated with higher rates of workplace injuries (Runyan, 2007). Negative supervisor attitudes can also impede return to work and rehabilitation for injured workers (Rasmussen, 2011). The quality and time of supervisor response to reports of work-related injuries has significant effects on work injury and rehabilitation outcomes (Benge, 2007).

Excessive and unrealistic workloads in the workplace are associated as a contributing social factor in workplace injuries and fatalities. How does increasing workloads in the workplace contribute towards worker injuries and fatalities? Existing research literature suggests that increasing workloads result in higher incident reports of physical injuries, poor mental health and poor social well being for workers (Bohle, 2010; Bohle, 2004; Bohle, 2011; Costa, 2006; Donald, 1999; McNamara, 2011). Furthermore, excessive workloads result in poor work–life outcomes, more use of prescription medications, more stress, and more dissatisfaction with workers' interpersonal relationships (Niedhammer, 2008; Pisarski, 2008; Yassi, 2005). Statistics indicate that high workload is a continuing problem in many Australian industries (Australian Workers Union, 2010). Importantly, an excessive workload culture does not necessarily lead to a more productive workforce. Excessive workloads can also increase the risk of other workplace problems, such as increased absences, higher employee turnover, discrimination, employee burnout and disillusionment. Pisarski, (2008, p. 69) asserts "any organization which allows (or even promotes) a culture of excessive workload may find that it comes at a high price, which is often indirect and hidden."

Working increasing work hours is associated as a contributing social factor in workplace injuries and fatalities. The Organization for Economic Co-Operation and Development (OECD) reported that Australian full-time workers had the highest average number of total hours worked per week of all OECD countries. Australian full-time workers worked an average of 43.4 hours, followed by employees in New Zealand (43.1 hours), the United Kingdom (42.2 hours), Poland

(42.1 hours), and the United States (41.7 hours) (OECD, p. 127). How do increasing work hours contribute towards worker injuries and fatalities? Existing research literature suggests that increasing work hours results in worker fatigue (Bohle, 2010; Bohle, 2004; Bohle, 2011; Lilley, 2002; Lombardi, 2010; McNamara, 2011; Nakata, 2011; Vegso, 2007). Worker fatigue is related to: 1) the workload imposed by a job, 2) the length of shift, 3) previous hours and days worked, 4) the time of day or night and 4) unrealistic deadlines and productivity targets.

Workplace and physical environment conditions are associated as a contributing social factor in workplace injuries and fatalities. The physical aspects of a workplace environment have a direct impact on the productivity, health and safety, comfort, concentration, job satisfaction and morale of the people within it fatalities (Awan, 2010; Bates, 1996; Bohle, 2010). Furthermore, factors in the work environment that are correlated to workplace injuries include: building design and age workplace layout, workstation set-up, furniture and equipment design and quality, space, temperature, ventilation, lighting, noise, vibration, radiation and air quality (Proto, 2010; Wei, 2010; Williams, 1994; Yassi, 2005). How do workplace physical environmental conditions contribute to injuries in the workplace? Inadequately designed and poorly maintained workplaces result in poor physical working conditions that contribute to higher rates of worker injuries and fatalities.

The lack of quality occupational health and safety training in the workplace is associated as a contributing social factor in workplace injuries and fatalities). Without quality occupational health and safety training, employers and workers may be unaware of the importance of and the need for safe work practices (Calmbacher, 1993; Dong, 2004). They may be unaware of daily unsafe work practices due to "habitual, ritualised and socialised ways of doing things" (Faigenbaum, 2010, p. 67). Also, they may lack knowledge and skills associated with identifying existing and/or potential work environmental hazards, assessing risks of injuries from these hazards, implementing appropriate control measures to prevent or minimise these risks, and checking that the control strategies are effectively controlling these risks in the workplace (Wilkinson, 2002; Zierold, 2006). Furthermore, they may be unaware of legislative responsibilities associated with employer and worker roles and actions in the workplace (Zierold, 2006).

In conclusion, the above-mentioned social and organizational workplace factors associated with workplace injuries and fatalities highlight the social, situational and environmental influences on individual workers. They provide the situational background to where individual worker factors are lived and rendered operational on a daily basis. An emphasis on individual worker factors alone, based upon essentialist assumptions and personal characters, does not fully address the complexity of workplace injuries. As such, an effective and holistic understanding of workplace injury requires the crucial consideration of the social and organization factors if we are to fully understand the complexity of workplace injuries and fatalities. This understanding is crucial and urgently needed, especially if we are to make sense of why 636,000 Australians injured themselves in a work-related injury in the period 2009–2010 (Australian Bureau of Statistics, 2010).

References

Australian Bureau of Statistics, (2010, April 22). Work-Related Injuries, Australia, 2009–10. Retrieved from: http://www.abs.gov.au/ausstats/abs@.nsf/Latestproducts/6324.0Main%20Features32009-10?opendocument&tabname=Summary&prodno=6324.0&issue=2009=10&num=&view=

Awan, S., Nasrullah, M., & Cummings, K. J. (2010). Health hazards, injury problems, and workplace conditions of carpet-weaving children in three districts of Punjab, Pakistan. *Int J Occup Environ Health, 16*(2), 115–121.

Bates, G., Gazey, C., & Cena, K. (1996). Factors affecting heat illness when working in conditions of thermal stress. *J Hum Ergol (Tokyo), 25*(1), 13–20.

Benge, J. F., Caroselli, J. S., Reed, K., & Zgaljardic, D. J. (2010). Changes in supervision needs following participation in a residential post-acute brain injury rehabilitation programme. *Brain Inj, 21*(6), 844–850.

Benge, J. F., Caroselli, J. S., & Temple, R. O. (2007). Wisconsin Card Sorting Test: factor structure and relationship to productivity and supervision needs following severe traumatic brain injury. *Brain Inj, 21*(4), 395–400.

Berdahl, T. A. (2008). Racial/ethnic and gender differences in individual workplace injury risk trajectories: 1988–1998. *Am J Public Health, 98*(12), 2258–2263.

Bohle, P., Pitts, C., & Quinlan, M. (2010). Time to call it quits? The safety and health of older workers. *Int J Health Serv, 40*(1), 23–41.

Bohle, P., Quinlan, M., Kennedy, D., & Williamson, A. (2004). Working hours, work-life conflict and health in precarious and "permanent" employment. *Rev Saude Publica, 38 Suppl,* 19–25.

Bohle, P., Willaby, H., Quinlan, M., & McNamara, M. (2011). Flexible work in call centres: Working hours, work-life conflict & health. *Appl Ergon, 42*(2), 219–224.

Brogmus, G. E. (2007). Day of the week lost time occupational injury trends in the US by gender and industry and their implications for work scheduling. *Ergonomics, 50*(3), 446–474.

Calmbacher, C. W. (1993). The goal of safety training rules: reducing the threat of injury. *Occup Health Saf, 62*(3), 80–84.

Canelon, M. F. (1995). Job site analysis facilitates work reintegration. *Am J Occup Ther, 49*(5), 461–467.

Chau, N., d'Houtaud, A., Gruber, M., Monhoven, N., Gavillot, C., Petry, D., . . . Andre, J. M. (1995). Personality self-representations of patients with hand injury, and its relationship with work injury. *Eur J Epidemiol, 11*(4), 373–382.

Chau, N., Wild, P., Dehaene, D., Benamghar, L., Mur, J. M., & Touron, C. (2010). Roles of age, length of service and job in work-related injury: a prospective study of 446 120 person-years in railway workers. *Occup Environ Med, 67*(3), 147–153.

Costa, G., Sartori, S., & Akerstedt, T. (2006). Influence of flexibility and variability of working hours on health and well-being. *Chronobiol Int, 23*(6), 1125–1137.

Donald, J. (1999). What makes your day? A study of the quality of worklife of OR nurses. *Can Oper Room Nurs J, 17*(4), 17–27.

Dong, X., Entzel, P., Men, Y., Chowdhury, R., & Schneider, S. (2004). Effects of safety and health training on work-related injury among construction laborers. *J Occup Environ Med, 46*(12), 1222–1228.

Drebit, S., Shajari, S., Alamgir, H., Yu, S., & Keen, D. (2010). Occupational and environmental risk factors for falls among workers in the healthcare sector. *Ergonomics, 53*(4), 525–536.

Faigenbaum, A. D., & Myer, G. D. (2010). Resistance training among young athletes: safety, efficacy and injury prevention effects. *Br J Sports Med, 44*(1), 56–63.

Flory, M. (2001). Solving the language barrier. *Occup Health Saf, 70*(1), 37–38.

Islam, S. S., Velilla, A. M., Doyle, E. J., & Ducatman, A. M. (2001). Gender differences in work-related injury/illness: analysis of workers compensation claims. *Am J Ind Med, 39*(1), 84–9.

Janicak, C. A. (1996). Predicting accidents at work with measures of locus of control and job hazards. *Psychol Rep, 78*(1), 115–121.

Johansson, A., & Salminen, S. (1999). A minority with few occupational accidents: the case of Swedish-speaking Finns. *Am J Ind Med, Suppl 1*, 37–38.

Korzeniowska, E. (2004). [Health beliefs and health behavior in older employees of medium-size and large enterprises]. *Med Pr, 55*(2), 129–138.

Kunar, B. M., Bhattacherjee, A., & Chau, N. (2008). Relationships of job hazards, lack of knowledge, alcohol use, health status and risk taking behavior to work injury of coal miners: a case-control study in India. *J Occup Health, 50*(3), 236–244.

Lilley, R., Feyer, A. M., Kirk, P., & Gander, P. (2002). A survey of forest workers in New Zealand. Do hours of work, rest, and recovery play a role in accidents and injury? *J Safety Res, 33*(1), 53–71.

Lombardi, D. A., Folkard, S., Willetts, J. L., & Smith, G. S. (2010). Daily sleep, weekly working hours, and risk of work-related injury: US National Health Interview Survey (2004–2008). *Chronobiol Int, 27*(5), 1013–1030.

Loomis, D., & Richardson, D. (1998). Race and the risk of fatal injury at work. *Am J Public Health, 88*(1), 40–44.

Manchikanti, L., Singh, V., Fellows, B., & Pampati, V. (2002). Evaluation of influence of gender, occupational injury, and smoking on chronic low back pain of facet joint origin: a subgroup analysis. *Pain Physician, 5*(1), 30–35.

McNamara, M., Bohle, P., & Quinlan, M. (2011). Precarious employment, working hours, work-life conflict and health in hotel work. *Appl Ergon, 42*(2), 225–232.

Mikov, M., Radovanovic, M., & Mudrinic, P. (1966). [Action of alcohol on work injury]. *Med Pregl, 19*(2), 99–104.

Moyers, P. A., & Stoffel, V. C. (1999). Alcohol dependence in a client with a work-related injury. *Am J Occup Ther, 53*(6), 640–645.

Nakata, A. (2011). Effects of long work hours and poor sleep characteristics on workplace injury among full-time male employees of small- and medium-scale businesses. *J Sleep Res, 17*(2), 47–52.

Neves, I. R. (2006). [Work, exclusion, pain, suffering, and gender relations: a survey of female workers treated for repetitive strain injury at a public health clinic]. *Cad Saude Publica, 22*(6), 1257–1265.

Niedhammer, I., Chastang, J. F., & David, S. (2008). Importance of psychosocial work factors on general health outcomes in the national French SUMER survey. *Occup Med (Lond), 58*(1), 15–24.

Oh, J. H., & Shin, E. H. (2003). Inequalities in nonfatal work injury: the significance of race, human capital, and occupations. *Soc Sci Med, 57*(11), 2173–2182.

Pisarski, A., Lawrence, S. A., Bohle, P., & Brook, C. (2008). Organizational influences on the work life conflict and health of shiftworkers. *Appl Ergon, 39*(5), 580–588.

Plurad, D., Talving, P., Tang, A., Green, D., Lam, L., Inaba, K., & Demetriades, D. (2011). Alcohol Ingestion Is Independently Associated With Complications After Work Place Injuries: An National Trauma Data Bank Analysis of Injury Severity And Outcomes. *J Trauma.*

Proto, A. R., & Zimbalatti, G. (2010). Risk assessment of repetitive movements in the citrus fruit industry. *J Agric Saf Health, 16*(4), 219–228.

Pun, J. C., Burgel, B. J., Chan, J., & Lashuay, N. (2004). Education of garment workers: prevention of work related musculoskeletal disorders. *AAOHN J, 52*(8), 338–343.

Rasmussen, K., Hansen, C. D., Nielsen, K. J., & Andersen, J. H. (2011). Incidence of work injuries amongst Danish adolescents and their association with work environment factors. *Am J Ind Med, 54*(2), 143–152.

Richardson, D. B., Loomis, D., Bena, J., & Bailer, A. J. (2004). Fatal occupational injury rates in southern and non-southern States, by race and Hispanic ethnicity. *Am J Public Health, 94*(10), 1756–1761.

Runyan, C. W., Dal Santo, J., Schulman, M., Lipscomb, H. J., & Harris, T. A. (2006). Work hazards and workplace safety violations experienced by adolescent construction workers. *Arch Pediatr Adolesc Med, 160*(7), 721–727.

Runyan, C. W., Schulman, M., Dal Santo, J., Bowling, J. M., Agans, R., & Ta, M. (2007). Work-related hazards and workplace safety of US adolescents employed in the retail and service sectors. *Pediatrics, 119*(3), 526–534.

Safe Work Australia, (2011, April, 22). Online Statistics. Retrieved from: http://nosi.ascc.gov.au

Shannon, C. A., Rospenda, K. M., Richman, J. A., & Minich, L. M. (2009). Race, racial discrimination, and the risk of work-related illness, injury, or assault: findings from a national study. *J Occup Environ Med, 51*(4), 441–448.

Smith, G. S., Lincoln, A. E., Wong, T. Y., Bell, N. S., Vinger, P. F., Amoroso, P. J., & Lombardi, D. A. (2005). Does occupation explain gender and other differences in work-related eye injury hospitalization rates? *J Occup Environ Med, 47*(6), 640–648.

Smith, G. S., Wellman, H. M., Sorock, G. S., Warner, M., Courtney, T. K., Pransky, G. S., & Fingerhut, L. A. (2005). Injuries at work in the US adult population: contributions to the total injury burden. *Am J Public Health, 95*(7), 1213–1219.

Smith, L., Jeppesen, H. J., & Boggild, H. (2007). Internal locus of control and choice in health service shift workers. *Ergonomics, 50*(9), 1485–1502.

Smith, P. M., & Mustard, C. A. (2007). How many employees receive safety training during their first year of a new job? *Inj Prev, 13*(1), 37–41.

Sulsky, S. I., Mundt, K. A., Bigelow, C., & Amoroso, P. J. (2000). Case-control study of discharge from the U.S. Army for disabling occupational knee injury: the role of gender, race/ethnicity, and age. *Am J Prev Med, 18*(3 Suppl), 103–111.

Vegso, S., Cantley, L., Slade, M., Taiwo, O., Sircar, K., Rabinowitz, P., . . . Cullen, M. R. (2007). Extended work hours and risk of acute occupational injury: A case-crossover study of workers in manufacturing. *Am J Ind Med, 50*(8), 597–603.

Walter, N., Bourgois, P., Margarita Loinaz, H., & Schillinger, D. (2002). Social context of work injury among undocumented day laborers in San Francisco. *J Gen Intern Med, 17*(3), 221–229.

Wei, W., Liu, M., Fergenbaum, J., Comper, P., & Colantonio, A. (2010). Work-related mild-moderate traumatic brain injuries due to falls. *Brain Inj, 24*(11), 1358–1363.

Wilkinson, J. (2002). Creating a culture of workplace safety. *Nurs N Z, 8*(6), 14–15.

Yassi, A., Gilbert, M., & Cvitkovich, Y. (2005). Trends in injuries, illnesses, and policies in Canadian healthcare workplaces. *Can J Public Health, 96*(5), 333–339.

Yassi, A., & Hancock, T. (2005). Patient safety–worker safety: building a culture of safety to improve healthcare worker and patient well-being. *Healthc Q, 8 Spec No,* 32–38.

Yoon, H. S., & Cho, Y. C. (2007). Relationship between job stress contents, psychosocial factors and mental health status among university hospital nurses in Korea. *J Prev Med Public Health, 40*(5), 351–362.

Yoon, H. Y., & Lockhart, T. E. (2006). Nonfatal occupational injuries associated with slips and falls in the United States. *Int J Ind Ergon, 36*(1), 83–92.

Zierold, K. M., & Anderson, H. A. (2006). Severe injury and the need for improved safety training among working teens. *Am J Health Behav, 30*(5), 525–532.

Zierold, K. M., & Anderson, H. A. (2006). Racial and ethnic disparities in work-related injuries among teenagers. *J Adolesc Health, 39*(3), 422–426.

Critical Thinking

1. So what should an employer do to ensure reduced workplace injury?
2. What are the ethical implications if an employer does not take special care to ensure workplace safety for employees?
3. What do you think that you'll do differently now knowing more about workplace injury?

Internet References

DOSH – Guide to Developing Your Workplace Injury and Illness Program
www.dir.ca.gov/dosh/dosh_publications/iipp.html

Injury/Illness Incidence Rates – OSHA
www.osha.gov/oshstats/work.html

Injury and Illness Prevention Programs – OSHA
www.osha.gov/dsg/topics/safetyhealth

Rates of Serious Workplace Injuries Vary Widely by State
www.osha.gov/oshstats/work.html

Workplace Injury Prevention
www.rand.org/topics/workplace-injury-prevention.html

Unit 6

UNIT

Prepared by: Maria Nathan, *Lynchburg College*

HR and Sustainable Organizations

Sustainability is "meeting the needs and demands of today without compromising the ability of future generations to meet their requirements". Sustainability-conscious businesses seek to manage social, environmental, and economic factors in balance and from not just short term, but also the next generation perspectives.

Sustainability thinking in general is grounded in several core principles: (1) We cannot dig up from the earth at a rate faster than materials naturally return and replenish; (2) We cannot make chemicals at a rate faster than it takes nature to break down; (3) We cannot create destruction to plants at a rate faster than it takes to regrow; and (4) We cannot do things that cause others to not be able to fulfill basic needs. These precepts in turn translate to organizational practices such as zero waste, use and reuse, and conservation, and are at the essence of sustainability thinking and behavior for firms as "caretakers of the earth."

Sustainable HRM creates employee skills, motivations, values, and trust that permit their longer-term health, wellness, sustainability, and productivity. Measureable contributions to HR performance can be seen to result, including lower turnover, lower absenteeism, improved employee well-being, and overall employee engagement.

Increasingly, HR professional have come to recognize the significance of employee health, wellness, and work-life balance as critical to employee sustainability. HR has become more committed to refraining from pursuing short term, cost driven practices that could harm workers, families, and communities.

Employee health and wellness are both psychological and physical. Now, more employers are recognizing that there are sometimes significant threats to employee well-being to be found in the bullying and sexual harassment that may take place in the workplace. Employers and government both are working on what to do about bullying by bosses and others in the workplace. Case law is being shaped with each passing month. We are finding that toxic environments are not just about a bullying, dysfunctional boss. They are also about an organization's culture that abides poor behavior and employees who permit bullying to continue for various reasons.

Workplace sustainability programs can also be used to increase employee sustainability consciousness that goes beyond the organization. Employees may find that they want to try a sustainability tactic at home that was introduced at work, indicating the power of these initiatives to have lasting and far reaching effects on employees. Thus, sustainable choices at work can and do influence such choices within employees' homes as well.

Article   Prepared by: Maria Nathan, *Lynchburg College*

The Importance of Human Resource Management in Strategic Sustainability: An Art and Science Perspective

HAROLD SCHROEDER

Learning Outcomes

After reading this article, you will be able to:

- Understand how strategic sustainability has both art- and science-based perspectives.

- Know what strategic sustainability is and how it relates to HRM.

- Understand the central role that HR professionals take in sustainable HRM.

I. Introduction

According to a growing body of research evidence, many employers are struggling to incorporate sustainability in a strategic way into their business. For those that do so successfully, it is reported that the business benefits are often substantial, including an enhanced brand image resulting in increased sales, improved recruitment and retention, and greater efficiencies. When sustainability is adopted as a more peripheral or add-on way to core business, on the other hand, it often results in increased costs and can be seen as financial burden, and as a result can be readily abandoned due to economic pressures in other areas of the business (Kruschwitz and Haanaes 87).

In this article, I explain and recommend the use of an "art and science" approach to sustainability to help ensure that sustainability initiatives deliver both environmental and business benefits, and I highlight the important role of human resource (HR) specialists in this process. Although many functional areas of an organization are often involved in developing and implementing sustainability initiatives, HR specialists are uniquely placed to make a major contribution in this area due to the important people-related dimension of this type of initiative, as well as the range of art and science skills typically associated with the HR function itself. I outline some specific areas in which HR professionals can contribute to the achievement of sustainable business, and conclude by reflecting on progress and limitations in this area to date, and the ways in which this professional group should position itself for a more central role as sustainability advocates and experts.

II. The Sustainability Challenge

International sustainability surveys (Aberdeen Group; Haanaes, Balagopal, and Arthur) have found evidence of a significant gap between those organizations that have fully embraced sustainability and those who are adopting it more gradually and in a more peripheral way. While most organizations now recognize the business benefits of sustainability, the more "cautious adopters" (Kruschwitz and Haanaes 4) are struggling to measure these and are not yet gaining a competitive advantage from their sustainability initiatives in the way that the first group are. Among the organizations that have successfully adopted sustainability in a strategic way into their core business, the reported benefits include greater efficiencies, the ability to innovate, increased profits and business growth (The Aberdeen Group 22; Haanaes, Balagopal, and Arthur 78).

What often goes unrecognized is that, like other business projects, sustainability initiatives require a good mix of art and science to be successfully implemented and achieve their desired outcomes. In order to generate business as well as environmental benefits from a sustainability initiative, a transformative approach is required in which sustainability principles are incorporated into all areas of the organization, and workplace norms and behavior are modified to reflect these. Unfortunately, organizational transformations in general typically have high failure rates (Economist Intelligence Unit 5; IBM 14), and it is becoming increasingly evident from research that this can largely be attributed to a neglect of the people-related aspects of change. In the area of sustainability, projects and goals are often established without due consideration to the likely impact on employees and what will be required of them to ensure the success of the initiative. Further, sustainability initiatives are often launched without the levels of investment or the application of project management expertise and tools that would generally be allocated to other types of business project, which almost sets them up for failure from the outset.

Moreover, research indicates that sustainability is still being given a relatively low priority on the executive agenda compared with other business issues (Kruschwitz and Haanaes 87), which suggests that there are low levels of awareness of its potential business benefits among organizational leaders, leading to a "vicious circle" scenario in which inadequate attention or resources are allocated to sustainability initiatives. In one international survey of more than 4,700 executives and managers from a wide range of sectors, for example, only 28 percent reported that sustainability is a "core strategic consideration" in their organization (Kruschwitz and Haanaes 89).

III. Art and Science in Strategic Sustainability

As the above section highlights, becoming an environmentally sustainable organization represents good business sense if approached correctly, but many employers are adopting sustainability only as a peripheral or add-on project which is core to the business. When approached in this way, the sustainability program does not generally receive the level of investment or application of expertise and organizational tools necessary to ensure that it delivers the intended benefits—and project failure or termination is often the inevitable result, especially in the face of economic or workload pressures in other areas of the business.

I recommend the adoption of an "art and science" approach to sustainability as the solution to this problem and the best way of ensuring that sustainability is implemented in a way that will add measurable value to the business as well as delivering environmental benefits.

The Role of Art

In particular, there is a need to introduce a greater "art" dimension to projects in order to reduce the risks related to neglect of the people-related aspects of change. These are especially important in the context of sustainability because employees need to understand and be convinced of the need to implement the changes necessary for sustainable business, especially if these involve extra work and the benefits are intangible or only realized in the longer term.

In general, the frequent lack of attention to art in organizational change can largely be attributed to the "science"-focused nature of the formal project management discipline, which originated in industries such as construction and IT in which people-related factors are of lower importance than in other sectors and organizational contexts. In the case of sustainability, however, the successful implementation of projects relies very much on the engagement and involvement of employees throughout the organization, and securing this requires a range of skills and attributes not traditionally given high importance in project management compared with the "science" skills involved, for example, in developing a project budget, work breakdown schedule and risk management plan.

The importance in sustainability of the "soft" skills of managers and leaders was highlighted in a 2010 survey carried out by the International Society of Sustainability Professionals, with the most important being identified as including the ability to influence, inspire and motivate others, excellent communication skills and team-building abilities (Johnson 30). The importance of communications in sustainability cannot be under-estimated—a good communications strategy is needed to generate organizational learning about sustainability and about the objectives and intended benefits of the initiative to all stakeholders, and to monitor and report on progress in order to highlight the benefits and encourage all to work together to achieving its goals. It is not only necessary to convince staff about the need for sustainable working practices and address their concerns; senior executives also often need to be persuaded to give their support to the program and commit the necessary financial and non-financial resources to ensure its success. This requires sustainability champions who understand and are skilled in communicating the business benefits to senior executives and negotiating adequate investment to underpin its implementation. Other types of art skills especially important in strategic sustainability, identified from a review of the sustainability literature by Smith and Sharicz, include having a questioning, innovative and creative approach to business; the ability to build internal and external relationships and partnerships with stakeholders; strategic awareness and the ability to balance local and global perspectives, and emotional intelligence (77).

The Role of Science

All this is not to suggest that only art skills are important in the implementation of strategic sustainability, a range of "science" skills are equally important and it is achieving the right combination of art and science that is fundamental to the success of any sustainability initiative. The "science" related aspects of project management in general consist of the application of formal methods, tools and techniques in order to achieve project objectives, for example in the areas of planning, budgeting, risk management, quality control and performance measurement.

In the context of strategic sustainability, there will be a need to apply science skills from the outset in systematically reviewing current operations and practice in order to identify areas where the business can become more sustainable and what this will involve, and to develop specific sustainability goals and performance criteria. There is also a need for the application of established project management tools and techniques to scope projects and develop detailed specifications, formulate detailed implementation plans at organizational and departmental level, and determine resource requirements and the breakdown of responsibilities and required inputs. Sustainability project managers need to be able to estimate resource requirements, develop a budget, and use techniques, such as stakeholder analysis and risk analysis to maximize the likelihood of successful outcomes and minimize both inefficiencies and possibility of project failure. Additionally, they need to develop and implement performance measurement systems that can monitor and demonstrate program performance and return on investments, and convey the results in ways that will be meaningful and inspiring to stakeholders at all levels of the organization.

Combining Art and Science for Transformation

Achieving the right balance of art and science is the key to successful sustainability, as in the case of other organizational transformation projects, a point which is supported by the research evidence. International employer surveys (Haanaes, Balagopal, and Arthur; Kruschwitz and Haanaes) have revealed that the organizations generating a competitive advantage from their sustainability initiatives were most likely to be exhibiting both an analytical approach to sustainability, including the development of a formal business case as well as the use of scenario planning and strategic analysis, as well as a shift in organizational culture with an increased emphasis on intangible and qualitative business goals, such as enhanced innovation and creativity.

Indeed, strategic sustainability requires a "transformative" approach involving not just extensive changes to business processes and strategy but a significant change in mindset and corporate culture, particularly involving a shift in focus from traditional financial or quantitative indicators of business success to social and environmental indicators as well as the more intangible, qualitative factors such as improved awareness of

and attitudes toward the company brand. This involves the application of both "art" and "science" perspectives, or what might also be referred to as "right brain" and "left brain" thinking, respectively.

IV. The Central Role of HR Professionals in Sustainability

Among all functional and professional groups within an organization, HR specialists in particular can be singled out as being best placed to take on a central role in the art and science approach to sustainability. A number of key areas in which HR input is needed or in which HR specialists can potentially add value to the sustainability initiative can be identified as follows.

Raising Awareness and Promoting Dialogue

Awareness and understanding of environmental sustainability and related issues among all employees is essential for securing their engagement in and commitment to the sustainability initiative, and in developing the types of approaches and values necessary for sustainable business. The HR department with its responsibility for training will ideally be centrally involved in the development and delivery of training programs and awareness-raising materials to meet these needs, especially since the learning requirement spans all functional areas. Events and media used to raise awareness of environmental and sustainability issues may include seminars and workshops specially tailored to the requirements of the organisation, as well as newsletters or other literature, or electronic learning resources available via the organizational intranet.

One of the main objectives of interactive training events should be to promote understanding of how environmental sustainability can be achieved within specific areas of the organization, and the roles and responsibilities of individual employees in relation to this. As Colbert and Kurucz (28) and Rimanoczy and Pearson (15) highlight, HR has an important role to play in designing these to facilitate the dialogue needed to achieve this understanding, which is in turn likely to promote the sense of a community working towards shared goals, itself associated with enhanced employee engagement and other organizational benefits.

Provision of Art and Science Skills and Expertise

Overall, the HR department is responsible for ensuring that the organization possesses the right levels and combination of art and science skills necessary for successful implementation of strategic sustainability, which can be achieved either through training and development of existing employees, or recruitment. The department should take the lead in conducting an organization-wide review of skills and expertise in order to identify current strengths as well as gaps that need to be addressed, and also to ensure that the right individuals are allocated to key roles in the development and implementation of the sustainability initiative.

In doing so, the department will need to work closely with organizational leaders as well as department heads to secure the necessary levels of investment in training and recruitment, and the cooperation necessary to change or modify the jobs of individuals selected for key roles in the sustainability initiative. HR professionals will themselves need to demonstrate strengths in science as well as art skills in order to achieve these objectives including the ability to accurately estimate the budget requirements for training and recruitment and to help build a robust business case for sustainability, as well as the communications and negotiation skills necessary to convince senior executives and managers of the need for these.

HR Policies and Procedures

In order to successfully deliver the art and science skills needed for strategic sustainability, there may also be a need for the HR department to redesign its own policies and processes, especially relating to performance management, rewards and recognition, and recruitment and selection processes. There are two main objectives: first to ensure that the policies and processes are designed to provide the organization with the required mix of art and science skills for strategic sustainability, and second to ensure that sustainability-related factors are incorporated in organizational competencies and in individual, team and departmental plans and goals.

It might be argued that, traditionally, staff selection and performance appraisal procedures have been focused primarily on the assessment of "science" skills, such as formal knowledge and experience of the techniques used in a particular area of work, while the softer "art" or people-related skills have been explored less systematically. As discussed earlier, art skills are highly important in the achievement of strategic sustainability, but it is also becoming increasingly evident that both art and science are required in most jobs and should be reflected as such as job descriptions and core competencies. Widespread organizational benefits can then be expected to ensue from a redesign of selection and assessment systems to ensure that both art and science skills are being properly evaluated. Doing so may involve, for example, an increased reliance on more qualitative or holistic methods in recruitment and performance evaluation, such as in-depth interviews or the use of 360 degree appraisals to complement more structured knowledge tests.

Incorporating specific sustainability-related goals into job descriptions and core competencies will also help to ensure that employees are motivated to work toward sustainability goals and that these receive similar levels of attention as any other criteria against which individuals and teams are formally assessed. They should be linked to the organisation's rewards and recognition systems, including for example performance-related pay systems, promotion eligibility criteria, or "employee of the month" schemes (Daily and Huang 1548). These types of reward systems might also be used to reinforce a direct emphasis on sustainability, for example by introducing some form of "sustainability award" for outstanding achievements in this area.

More generally, as Colbert and Kurucz observe, HR strategy and processes are instrumental in supporting the implementation of new business directions, such as sustainability, not only by ensuring that the right skill and expertise are available, but by promoting the development of "organizational capital" such as good teamwork, employee empowerment and a positive culture (28). These are likely to evolve as the art and science skill balance of the organization improves, but can also be stimulated by the use of specific types of training, such as brainstorming sessions, teambuilding events, and consensus-building workshops.

Socially Responsible Employment

It can be argued that sustainability begins "at home" and that being a socially responsible employer goes hand in hand with being an environmentally sustainable organization, since a company is likely to be judged on its corporate social responsibility performance overall.

HR specialists can ensure that the organization and its suppliers comply with or exceed employment standards and provide favorable terms and conditions of employment to their staff and contractors (Glade; Rimanoczy and Pearson 14). They can act as source of information, guidance and support both to the parent organization and its supply chain participants on how to be social responsible employers, and arrange training in this area if necessary.

In general, high-quality HR policies and practices integrated with business and sustainability goals are likely to promote positive employee-related outcomes, such as improved morale, increased engagement, higher productivity, and improved retention (Meisinger 8; Schramm 88; Wilkinson, Hill, and Gollan 1497) and improve the company's brand image which in turn is likely to increase sales and increase the organization's attractiveness to potential recruits. On this point, HR professionals should also ensure that the organization's sustainability policy and achievements to date are included in marketing and recruitment strategies and materials (Colbert and Kurucz 28).

Sustainability Champions and Change Management Specialists

The types of art and science skills already held by many HR specialists and needed in their day to day work make them ideally suited to take on key roles—either on a full- or part-time basis—in the development and implementation of sustainability initiatives. There is evidence from previous research that companies with dedicated sustainability leaders tend to exhibit stronger sustainability performance and gain greater business benefits from their initiatives (Aberdeen Group 3). Such leaders may a central role in driving progress towards sustainability goals through collaboration and communication with internal and external stakeholders and in ensuring that sustainability stays firmly on the core business agenda.

HR professionals are usually skilled communicators and effective negotiators, with high levels of people acumen but also an astute understanding of business needs and how best to develop a company's human resources to meet these. The nature of HR work also requires expertise in planning, budgeting, risk management and a range of other science-related skills. Few other professional groups exhibit such a strong combination of the art and science skills that are also essential for driving progress toward sustainability objectives.

Performance Measurement

Finally, it will be crucial to monitor and measure progress toward the organizational sustainability goals, in order to highlight and capitalise in business terms on their achievements, reveal areas where improvements are needed, and demonstrate the return on investment of various measures and activities such as training courses or recruitment for sustainability-related posts. Overall, this will require an art and science approach to capture the tangible and non-tangible dimensions of performance in sustainability, including for example energy efficiencies and a reduction in waste, as well as the changing attitudes and behavior of employees.

HR professionals will need to play a central role in relation to the performance measurement of employee-related aspects of sustainability, by developing appropriate metrics and designing and implementing data collection methods and tools. These might include, for example, the analysis of recruitment data as well as the design and implementation of staff surveys and interviews to measure or explore changing attitudes toward environmental issues and their impact on workplace behavior.

V. Conclusion

To date, HR professionals have not been centrally involved in sustainability initiatives to the extent that their skills and expertise can contribute real value in the ways outlined above (Harmon, Fairfield, and Wirtenberg 17). A likely reason for this is that many organisations are not yet approaching sustainability in a strategic way, or acknowledging the need for the sort of art- and science-based approach which HR professionals are ideally placed to support. The available evidence suggests that there is little consensus about which functional area of an organization should lead its sustainability initiative, and this is likely to be

one of the weaknesses that may undermine an organization's approach to sustainability and perhaps even result in its demise.

However, researchers in this area have argued that this HR professionals as a group also need to become more proactive in understanding business trends, opportunities and risks in the area of sustainability, as well as the perspectives and concerns of relevant internal and external stakeholders and how to ensure that these are effectively engaged in the strategy (Harmon, Fairfield, and Wirtenberg 17). This understanding can then be converted into HR policies and processes designed to support strategic sustainability and generate business benefits which will help convert even the most skeptical stakeholders to the cause. In other words, HR specialists need to become advocates of as well as experts in sustainability, and business partners to senior executives in its overall implementation.

References

Aberdeen Group. The Sustainable Supply Chain. Author, 2010. Retrieved from http://www.aberdeen.com/Aberdeen-Library/6676/RA-supply-chainsustainability.aspx

Colbert, Barry A. and Elizabeth C. Kurucz. "Three Conceptions of Triple Bottom Line Business Sustainability and the Role for HRM." People and Strategy 30, 1 (2007): 21–29.

Daily, Bonnie F. and Su-chun Huang. "Achieving Sustainability through Attention to Human Resource Factors in Environmental Management." International Journal of Operations & Production Management 21, 12 (2001): 1539–1552.

Economist Intelligence Unit. The Burning Platform: How Companies are Managing Change in a Recession. Author, 2009. Retrieved from http://www.celerantconsulting.com/Downloads/ResearchReviews/Celerant%20-%20EIU_Burning%20platform.pdf

Glade, Brian. "Human resources: CSR and Business Sustainability—HR's Leadership Role." New Zealand Management [online]. Retrieved from http://www.management.co.nz/Editorial.asp?eID=32475&Wcat=69

Haanaes, K., Balagopal, B. and D. Arthur. "First Look: The Second Annual Sustainability & Innovation Survey." MITSloan Management Review, 52, 2 (2011).

Harmon, Joel, Fairfield, Kent D and Jeana Wirtenberg. "Missing an Opportunity: HR Leadership and Sustainability." People and Strategy, suppl. Special Issue: Transitioning to the Green Economy 33, 1 (2010): 16–21.

IBM Corporation. The Enterprise of the Future: IBM Global CEO Study 2008. Author, 2008. Retrieved from www.ibm.com/enterpriseofthefuture.

Johnson, D. "Sustainability: Spin or Substance? " ISHN.com 45, 5, 1 (May 2011): 28–30.

Kruschwitz, N. and K. Haanaes. "First Look: Highlights from the Third Annual Sustainability Global Executive Survey." MIT Sloan Management Review 53, 1 (2011, Fall).

Meisinger, Susan. "HR's Role in Social Responsibility and Sustainability." HRMagazine 52, 12 (2007): 8.

Rimanoczy, Isabel and Tony Pearson. "Role of HR in the New World of Sustainability." Industrial and Commercial Training 42, 1 (2010): 11–17.

Schramm, Jennifer. "Promoting Sustainability." HRMagazine 56, 3 (2011): 88.

Smith, Peter, A.C. and Carol Sharicz. "The shift needed for sustainability." The Learning Organization 18, 1 (2011): 73–86.

Wilkinson, Adrian, Hill, Malcolm and Paul Gollan. "The sustainability debate." International Journal of Operations & Production Management 21, 12 (2001): 1492–1502.

Critical Thinking

1. What is sustainability and why is it important to business?

2. What are the business benefits of organizational sustainability practice?

3. What is the role of HRM in strategic sustainability?

Internet References

A Guide to Building Sustainable Organizations from the Inside Out
http://www.abcdinstitute.org/docs/CFWText.pdf

Center for Sustainable Organizations, Innovating for Sustainability
http://sustainableorganizations.org/

Centre for Sustainable HRM and Well Being, Australian Catholic University
http://www.acu.edu.au/about_acu/faculties,_institutes_and_centres/law_and_business/law_and_business_research/centre_for_sustainable_human_resource_management_and_wellbeing

Article   Prepared by: Maria Nathan, *Lynchburg College*

Building Sustainable Organizations: The Human Factor

Although most of the research and public pressure concerning sustainability has been focused on the effects of business and organizational activity on the physical environment, companies and their management practices profoundly affect the human and social environment as well. This article briefly reviews the literature on the direct and indirect effects of organizations and their decisions about people on human health and mortality. It then considers some possible explanations for why social sustainability has received relatively short shrift in management writing, and outlines a research agenda for investigating the links between social sustainability and organizational effectiveness as well as the role of ideology in understanding the relative neglect of the human factor in sustainability research.

JEFFREY PFEFFER

Learning Outcomes

After reading this article, you will be able to:

- Know what is meant by the terms *sustainability* and *human sustainability*.

- Understand the relationship between human sustainability and organizational effectiveness.

- Explain why human sustainability has been given much less attention than environmental sustainability.

There is growing public and business interest in building sustainable organizations and increasing research and educational interest in the topic of organizational sustainability. The Academy of Management has a division called Organizations and the Natural Environment, and there are numerous journals and research papers concerned with ecological sustainability. There are growing numbers of higher education programs focused on sustainability and an Association for the Advancement of Sustainability in Higher Education (Fountain, 2010). Marcus and Fremeth (2009) noted that this enthusiasm for what they called "green management" came from people's expectations for how managers and the organizations they lead should conduct their business to protect the

environment. As Ambec and Lanoie (2008, p. 46) noted, "firms are facing growing pressure to become greener."

As it is operationalized in the literature, sustainability is defined in part by an effort to conserve natural resources and avoid waste in operations. Conservation and the more efficient use of resources naturally lessen the burden of economic activity on the environment and helps to ensure that the activity can be sustained over time because the resources required will not be exhausted. Sustainability also appears to encompass activities that renew and recycle what it is used, once again with the goal of ensuring that the ecosystem that supports life and lifestyle can and will be preserved. Other aspects of sustainability include preserving what is—as in preserving threatened plant and animal species and, in cultural sustainability, preserving the values, arts, culture, and food of "communities threatened by globalization and modernization" (Navarro, 2010, p. 20). In the physical sciences, much of the research on sustainability has focused on the amount of stress an ecosystem can tolerate as well as principles for restoring ecological balance. In management, research attention has focused on the possible links between profitability and sustainability as well as the factors that cause organizations to pursue different sustainability strategies (e.g., Ambec and Lanoie, 2008).

Although sustainability clearly could encompass a focus on human as well as physical resources—in fact, the Academy of

Management division on the natural environment has as one of its foci "managing human resources for sustainability"—there is a much greater emphasis on the physical rather than the social environment[1] both in the research literature and in the actions and pronouncements of companies. To illustrate this point, a search of Google Scholar finds 20,800 entries for the term "ecological sustainability," 53,000 for "environmental sustainability," but just 12,900 for "social sustainability," and a paltry 569 for "human sustainability." And even a cursory review of the management literature shows that virtually all of the articles focused on sustainability are primarily concerned with the effects of organizations on the physical as contrasted with the social environment (e.g., Ambec & Lanoie, 2008; Bansal, 2002; Marcus & Fremeth, 2009). Even when there is concern with the social effects of organizational activities, these concerns are mostly directed to the consequences of economic development and resource exploitation for the viability of indigenous cultures (Bansal, 2002) rather than the consequences of management practices for every individual's health and well-being and the richness of social life as assessed by participation in civic activities (e.g., Putnam, 2000).

Environmental sustainability is important, and nothing in this paper should be taken to imply that this is not the case. Nonetheless, this emphasis on the natural environment raises an interesting research question: Why are polar bears, for instance, or even milk jugs more important than people, not only in terms of research attention, but also as a focus of company initiatives?

In 2008, Doug McMillon (Colvin, 2008), the CEO of Sam's Club, a division of Wal-Mart, expounded on the innovation in milk jugs and the fact that his company had introduced a new jug that was able to increase the shelf life of milk, reduce the cost between 10 and 20 cents, and eliminate more than 10,000 delivery trips, thereby conserving energy. In 2005, Lee Scott, Wal-Mart's CEO, made the first speech in the company's history broadcast to all of its associates. In that speech, also made available to Wal-Mart's 60,000 suppliers, Scott committed the company to the goals of being 100% supplied by renewable energy, creating zero waste, and selling products that sustain resources and the environment (Plambeck & Denend, 2007). Meanwhile, Wal-Mart paid its employees almost 15% less than other large retailers, and because of the lower pay, its employees made greater use of public health and welfare programs (Dube et al., 2007). In 2005, 46% of Wal-Mart employees' children were either uninsured or on Medicaid, a state program to provide medical care to low-income people (Rosenbloom & Barbaro, 2009). Compared to Costco, Wal-Mart offered fewer medical and other benefits, although these lower costs did not result in higher profits per employee (Cascio, 2006).

Wal-Mart's relative emphasis on the physical environment over its employees is far from unusual. British Petroleum, a company that touts its environmental credentials in its advertising and other presentations, was one of the first major oil companies to devote significant investment to alternative energy, and at one point wanted BP to also stand for "beyond petroleum." Apparently less concerned about its people, the company paid a record fine of $87 million for an explosion in its Texas City, Texas, refinery that killed 15 workers (Greenhouse, 2009). The fine penalized the company not for the explosion but also for numerous safety violations found during a subsequent investigation and a failure to correct those deficiencies even after the fatal explosion.

Even as businesses have appointed "eco-managers" (Hsu, 2010) to oversee company efforts to become more energy efficient and environmentally conscious, and even as companies track and publicly report carbon emissions from their activities (e.g., Kaufman, 2009), one would be hard-pressed to find similar efforts focused on employees. Just as there is concern for protecting natural resources, there could be a similar level of concern for protecting human resources. For example, there has been no groundswell of reporting on employee physical and mental health and wellness, even though that might be an interesting and informative indicator of what companies are doing about the sustainability of their people. This lack of concern is puzzling given that health-care costs, which as noted below are related in part to what companies do in the workplace, are an enormous problem in the United States and throughout the industrialized world.

In this paper, I want to first make the case for broadening our dependent variables in management research from a focus on profitability and other indicators of firm performance, such as shareholder return and productivity on the one hand and environmental sustainability practices and social responsibility on the other, to also include organizational effects on employee health and mortality. Being a socially responsible business ought to encompass the effect of management practices on employee physical and psychological well-being. Indeed, there is a large epidemiological and public health literature that suggests there may be important organizational effects on human health and life span. The available evidence suggests that there is a good likelihood of finding some interesting research results if we continue to expand our understanding of the connections between organizational practices and human well-being.

Then I want to open up the question as to why employee health has received relatively short shrift in discussions of organizational effects on the environment and the implications of such effects for sustainability. In so doing, I argue that an ideology of the primacy of markets (Davis, 2008) and shareholder interests and the associated idea that market outcomes are fair and just (Jost, et al., 2003), with sentient individuals making informed choices, may help explain the constrained focus of our research attention. The paper concludes with some implications for building a research focus on human sustainability.

Broadening Our Dependent Variables: Organizational Effects on Employee Mortality and Morbidity

In assessing and evaluating countries and other political units, measures of population health (e.g., infant mortality and life span) are frequently used as indicators of societal effectiveness and the level of country development. Cornia and Paniccia (2000) examined explanations for the dramatic increase in age-adjusted mortality, particularly for men, in Eastern and Central Europe during the 1980s and 1990s, taking these decreases in life span to be evidence of dysfunctional social conditions. Marmot and Bobak (2000) explored the "missing men of Russia"—the enormous increase in mortality and consequent reduction in average life span for men following the collapse of the Soviet Union, once again implying that the health of a society's people reflects at least to some degree the functioning of that society. Indeed, Marmot (2004, p. 247) explicitly argued that "health functions as a kind of social accountant. If health suffers, it tells us that human needs are not being met." Similarly, Gakidou, Murray, and Frenk (2000, p. 42) wrote that "health is an intrinsic component of well-being," and the economist Deaton (2003, p. 115) also noted that "health is a component of well-being."

What is true for countries or other political units is also true for organizations. The health status of the workforce is a particularly relevant indicator of human sustainability and well-being because there is evidence that many organizational decisions about how they reward and manage their employee have profound effects on human health and mortality. A few of the many ways company decisions affect the health and welfare of their people follow.

The Provision of Health Insurance

In the United States, in contrast to every other advanced industrialized country, access to health insurance—and, as a consequence, access to health care for working-age people who are not so poor as to be covered by increasingly limited social welfare programs—depends on whether or not one's employer voluntarily chooses to offer medical insurance as a benefit. Approximately half of the U.S. population today receives health insurance through an employer, and the evidence shows that the proportion of employers offering health insurance has declined while the amount employees pay for their coverage has increased. The Kaiser Family Foundation reported that between 1999 and 2009, worker contributions to health insurance premiums increased by 128%, while the proportion of companies offering health benefits fell from 66% to 60%.

These employer decisions about offering health insurance and the cost to employees, something that can also affect access, are consequential because there is a great deal of evidence showing that having health insurance affects health status. Levy and Meltzer (2001), reviewing the large literature on the connection between health insurance and health status, noted that hundreds of studies showed that the uninsured had worse health outcomes than people with access to insurance. Wilper et al. (2009) recently replicated the results of an earlier panel study (Franks, Clancy, & Gold, 1993) showing significantly higher mortality for people without health insurance. This result held when age, gender, income, education, race, smoking, alcohol use, exercise, body mass index, and initial physician-rated health were all statistically controlled. Based on their empirical results and population parameter estimates, Wilper and his colleagues estimated that there were more than 44,000 excess deaths per year in the United States because of lack of health insurance. Another study looking at the effects of health insurance on health used the fact that a random event, one's birthday, affects access to health insurance. At age 65, U.S. residents become eligible for Medicare, federally provided health insurance. Using this fact and data on health status, Card, Dobkin, and Maestas (2009) found that access to Medicare resulted in a 20% reduction in deaths for a severely ill patient group compared to similarly ill people who did not have access to Medicare because they had not yet turned 65.

Other studies show that people without health insurance are, not surprisingly, less likely to obtain various preventive screening tests for blood pressure and elevated cholesterol, Pap smears, and so forth (e.g., Potosky et al., 1998; Sudano & Baker, 2003). Such screening reduces mortality and morbidity through the early detection of harmful physical conditions (Sudano & Baker, 2003). Moreover, the data show that even short periods of not having health insurance substantially reduces the utilization of preventive services (Schoen & DesRoches, 2000; Sudano & Baker, 2003).

Having health insurance also affects people's economic well-being, because medical bills are a large contributor to personal bankruptcy. Himmelstein et al. (2005) studied a sample of personal bankruptcy filers in five federal courts. About half of the people filing for bankruptcy cited medical causes. "Medical debtors were 42 percent more likely than other debtors to experience lapses in coverage" (2005, p. W5-63). When employers decide to drop or curtail medical coverage, there are health and economic well-being consequences for their people.

In addition to providing, or not providing, health insurance, some employers have recently begun implementing health and wellness programs for their employees, which can also have important effects on health. Because most large employers are self-insured, any savings from better employee health and reduced medical expenditures flow directly to company profits. An evaluation of one such program at GlaxoSmithKline (Stave, Muchmore, & Gardner, 2003), covering more than 6,000 employees continuously employed from 1996 to 2000, reported an increased use of stress reduction techniques, more eating of fruits and vegetables, and an average cost savings of $613 per participant, largely because of reduced disability expenses.

The Effects of Layoffs

Employers decide on whether or not to have layoffs, how many people they will lay off, and who will get laid off. Budros (1997) has shown that layoffs are not just a consequence of economic conditions facing companies, a point made also by Cappelli (1999) in his discussion of the changing nature of the employment relationship. Budros found that layoffs are "contagious," in the sense that they spread through similarly situated and socially connected firms, which appear to model others' layoff behavior.

Research has shown that layoffs are very harmful to the physical and mental health of those laid off. There is consistence evidence that job loss is a significant predictor of reported symptoms of psychological disorders (Catalano, 1991). Being laid off increases the likelihood that an individual will engage in violent behavior by some 600% (Catalano, Novaco, & McConnell, 2002). One study reported that job displacement increased the death rate of those laid off by about 17% during the following 20 years, so that someone laid off at age 40 would be expected to live 1.5 fewer years than someone not laid off (Sullivan & von Wachter, 2007). A study of plant closings conducted in Sweden, a country with a relatively generous social safety net, nonetheless found that mortality risk increased 44% in the four years following job loss (Eliason & Storrie, 2009). A New Zealand study reported that unemployed 25-to-64-year-olds had more than twice the odds of committing suicide (Blakely, Collings, & Atkinson, 2003), which helps explain the cause of the increased mortality following layoffs. Another New Zealand study, based on an eight-year follow-up of workers from a meat processing plant that closed compared to a neighboring plant that remained open, found an increased risk of self-inflicted harm that resulted in hospitalization or death and also an increased risk of being hospitalized with a mental health diagnosis (Keefe et al., 2002). And downsizing is associated with negative changes in work behavior, increased smoking, less spousal support, and twice the rate of absence from work because of sickness (Kivimaki, Vahtera, Pentti, & Ferrie, 2000).

Work Hours and Work-Family Conflict

Employers determine the hours people work and when they work, subject to federal and state regulations and any union-bargained contracts. There has been an intensification of work, particularly in the United States (e.g., Rousseau, 2006). Americans work longer hours than workers in most European countries and now exceed the working hours of even Japanese (Yang et al., 2006). A report by the National Institute for Occupational Safety and Health (2004) summarized the extensive evidence on the harmful effects of long working hours and shift work on people's health-related behaviors as well as on-the-job injuries and employees' health status.

There is a reasonably extensive body of evidence connecting work hours to poor health outcomes. Some of this research focuses on hypertension. For instance, Yang et al. (2006), after summarizing studies showing the connection between hours worked and hypertension in Japan, reported their findings from analyzing the California Health Interview survey. They found that compared to people who worked less than 40 hours a week, those who worked more than 51 hours were 29% more likely to report having hypertension, even after statistically controlling for variables such as socioeconomic status, gender, age, diabetes, tobacco use, sedentary lifestyle, and body mass index.

Long work hours increase the likelihood that people will face a conflict between work and family responsibilities. Work-family conflict is a form of stress and has been found to influence health and health-related behaviors. Frone, Russell, and Barnes (1996), using two random samples of employed parents, found that work-family conflict was related to alcohol use, depression, and poor physical health. Moreover, work-family conflict is related to anxiety, substance abuse, and substance dependence (Frone, 2000). Depending on the type and degree of work-family conflict and the particular disorder being investigated, employees were between 2 and 30 times more likely to experience a significant mental health problem if they experienced work-family conflict compared to people who did not.

Work Stress and the Consequences of Job Design

Organizations design jobs, and job design has important psychological consequences—for instance, for motivation—as the large literature on job design attests (e.g., Hackman & Oldham, 1980). Job design also has important effects on people's physical well-being. One important dimension of job design is the amount of control people have over their work. High job demands that people cannot control, because they have little or no discretion over the pace and content of their work, coupled with work that is socially isolating, produce job stress. Marmot and colleagues have done extensive studies on the effects of job stress, emanating from an absence of control over one's work, on health outcomes ranging from metabolic syndrome (Chandola, Brunner, & Marmot, 2006) to cardiovascular disease and mortality (e.g., Marmot, 2004). Using both retrospective and prospective panel studies, Marmot reported large effects of job stress on mortality and morbidity.

Much of this research was stimulated by studies of the British civil service. These studies, called the Whitehall studies, showed that, controlling for numerous individual characteristics such as family background, serum cholesterol levels, blood pressure, and so forth, it was nevertheless the case that the higher someone's rank in the bureaucracy, the lower that person's risk of cardiovascular disease and death from heart attack (e.g., Marmot et al., 1997).

Inequality

The Whitehall studies are just part of a larger literature showing the connection between inequalities in health outcomes and inequality in individual attributes ranging from income to education. Wildman (2003, p. 295) reviewed papers reporting substantial "income-related inequalities in health in a number of developed countries," noting that the United Kingdom and the United States were high-inequality countries. Marmot (2004) reported that virtually all diseases followed a status gradient and that gradients in both income and education were important in understanding differences in health. It is not just the case that people with more income, higher education, and better jobs are more likely to enjoy better health and live longer lives— although that is clearly the case (see Marmot, 2004, for a review of this research). Some argue that there is an effect of inequality, particularly income inequality, on the average health status of a population. Lynch et al. (2001) argued that income inequality in the United States in the 1990s caused as much loss of life as the combined mortality resulting from lung cancer, diabetes, motor vehicle crashes, homicide, and AIDS combined. Although the effect of inequality on average health outcomes remains a contested issue (e.g., Deaton, 2003), there is growing concern about inequality in health outcomes within societies and increasing research attention to the causes and consequences of a number of forms of health-relevant inequality.

The research and policy link to organization studies is clear: Many, although certainly not all, of the inequalities in social systems that result in inequalities in health are produced in and by organizations. Because most people work for organizations rather than being self-employed, income inequality is produced in part by decisions made by employers about how much wage dispersion to have, both within and across organizational levels, and who and what types of people will obtain higher and lower level positions and incomes (e.g., Baron & Bielby, 1980;

Pfeffer and Langton, 1988). The organizations literature has a number of studies exploring the effects of wage dispersion on various outcomes ranging from satisfaction to indicators of organizational performance (e.g., Bloom, 1999; Cowherd & Levine, 1992; Pfeffer & Langton, 1993; Siegel & Hambrick, 2005). The importance of inequality for health suggests two important extensions to this line of research: first, including health outcomes as a dependent variable in studies of the consequences of wage dispersion, and second, renewing efforts to understand the factors that create greater or lesser inequalities in income, power, job responsibilities, time pressure, and other such dimensions inside organizations. If inequality is consequential for health, we need to better understand how that relationship operates inside organizations and what factors produce inequality in the first place.

The foregoing is only a partial review of a large epidemiological literature that potentially ties organizational decisions to health outcomes. There seems to be overwhelming evidence that organizational decisions about whether to offer health insurance and choices about layoffs, work hours, job design, and the degree of inequality created by wage structures have profound effects on employee physical and mental health and even people's life-spans. There are other aspects of the work environment that are also likely to be important and might productively be studied, including whether or not people have paid sick days, the amount of vacation they receive and take, and the emotional climate of the workplace, including whether or not there is bullying and verbal abuse. If we want to understand employee psychological and physical well-being and if we want to assess the effects of management decisions on people, health outcomes would seem to be one productive focus of research attention. That's because organizational effects on psychological well-being frequently manifest themselves in people's health status, as, for instance, in the effect of socioeconomic status on physical health as operating through its effect on negative emotions (Gallo & Matthews, 2003). Moreover, health-care costs are important both to companies and to society.

Why Does Human Well-Being Receive Relatively Short Shrift?

Given the profound effects of organizations and work arrangements on the psychological and physical well-being of the people who work in them and the growing interest in sustainability, it is interesting that the human dimension of sustainability remains largely in the background. In both social psychology and economics, there is increasing research attention to happiness as an important dependent variable in and of itself (e.g., Diener, Suh, Lucas, & Smith, 1999; Frey & Stutzer, 2002;

Oswald, 1997; Ryff, 1989). And as already noted, health is considered an important indicator of well-being for both individuals and societies.

However, in the management literature, the focus on a somewhat related topic, job satisfaction has evolved over time to largely although not exclusively consider the connection between job satisfaction and turnover—which is costly to the firm—and also the relationship between job satisfaction or its conceptual cousin, employee engagement, and customer service and other dimensions of organizational performance. Although there is obviously a large and important literature on work-family conflict and its consequences, once again a focus of at least some significant fraction of this literature is on the consequences of such conflict for organizational well-being, as reflected in absenteeism, sickness, turnover, and job performance.

This is not to say there is no interest in social responsibility and people for their own sake, but in the management literature, such concerns are often, although not invariably, coupled with their connection to profits, costs, or productivity. This is scarcely the first time this point has been made. Walsh, Weber, and Margolis (2003, p. 859) have noted that while the Academy of Management was founded to deal with society's objectives and the public interest along with organizational economic performance, over time the field "has pursued society's economic objectives much more than it has its social ones." March and Sutton (1997, p. 698), in their critique of performance as a dependent variable, commented that organizational researchers lived in two worlds, one of which "demands and rewards speculations about how to improve performance."

Why some topics get attention and others don't, and how research questions are framed are themselves important topics for research and theoretical exploration. As Ferraro, Pfeffer, and Sutton (2005, 2009) have argued, theories matter, not just because theories influence the institutional arrangements, norms, and language of organizational management, but also because theories focus both research and public policy attention. Molotch and Boden (1985) described three faces of power. The first face is the ability to prevail in explicit conflicts over decisions. The second face of power concerns the capacity to set agendas—whether or not there will be any decisions over which to fight and what such decisions will entail. They defined the third face of power as "the struggle over the linguistic premises upon which the legitimacy of accounts will be judged" (Molotch & Boden, 1985, p. 273), and argued this aspect of power was the least visible and accountable and possibly therefore the most potent. In the present context, how we talk—or don't—about sustainability and what is considered legitimately included and excluded from such discussions affects what we study, how we study it, and by extension, what becomes included in public policy debates as well.

There are undoubtedly many reasons that the sustainability of the physical environment has received more emphasis than have people. One possibility is that the consequences of organizational actions on the physical environment are frequently much more visible and, therefore, salient. You can see the icebergs melting, polar bears stranded, forests cut down, and mountaintops reshaped by mining, and experience firsthand the dirty air and water that can come from company economic activities that impose externalities. Reduced life expectancy and poorer physical and mental health status are more hidden from view. Even the occasional and well-publicized act of employee or ex-employee violence has multiple causes and is often seen as aberrant behavior outside of the control and responsibility of the employer.

Another explanation for the relative attention to physical versus human sustainability is the differential actions taken to make sustainability salient. Organizations and groups focused on improving the physical environment have taken steps to increase the visibility of what companies do—reporting on carbon emissions and measures of environmental compliance, for instance, and trying to ensure that these reports generate news coverage. Partly as a result of this public attention, laws have been passed in numerous countries mandating environmental compliance to various standards and requiring assessments of environmental impact before certain forms of economic development can take place. These laws, at a minimum, ensure the availability of more data to assess physical environmental effects. And while between 1980 and 2006 there was a 62.3% increase in the number of U.S. federal staff dealing with the environment, during that same period there was a *decrease* of 34.5% in staff in agencies overseeing the workplace (Dudley & Warren, 2005). These changes in federal staffing oversight also provide some indication of shifting social priorities and alterations in the focus of public policy attention.

One lesson for those interested in human sustainability is that developing a consistent set of measures or indicators of the construct, gathering data on them, and publicizing such data might provide more impetus for focusing on the human sustainability implications of what organizations do. Another implication is that federal and state regulation and oversight matter—both for the substantive effect and as a signal of what society values.

Both environmental and social sustainability confront one issue: the belief that the sole goal of companies should be to maximize profits and the idea that "markets work well to reach optimal use of scarce resources" (Ambec & Lanoie, 2008, p. 45) so that markets should generally be left unimpeded. Davis (2008, 2009) has provided an account of the rise of shareholder (as contrasted with stakeholder) capitalism and the associated primacy of economic criteria in business and public decision making and has noted the growing importance of the market-like aspects of many domains of life, ranging from housing to employment. Because all forms of sustainability contravene both the idea of economic performance above all else and the inviolability of markets, much more research is needed to understand the waxing and waning of managerial ideas and ideology. A model for such an investigation is Barley and Kunda's (1992) exploration of the cycling of managerial discourse related to employee control between normative (cultural) and rational (economic) bases. The point is that ideas and ideology are themselves important topics of study and such an analysis is inextricably linked to variation in the interest in sustainability in any of its forms or manifestations.

In many respects, sustainability represents a set of values and beliefs. As such, it is an ideology. Unfortunately, as nicely documented by Jost (2006, p. 651), "the end of ideology was declared more than a generation ago by sociologists and political scientists." Jost, Nosek, and Gosling (2008) also detailed the resurgence of ideology as an explanatory construct in many branches of psychology and illustrated its explanatory usefulness. Ideology and belief may be even less frequent topics of study in management, with its emphasis on performance, efficiency, and rationality. However, as Tetlock (2000) demonstrated, political ideology can be empirically uncovered, dimensionalised, and, most important, used to explain how managers decide what course of action to take in realistic scenarios concerning topics ranging from correcting safety defects to corporate accountability. If we are to understand why human sustainability receives relatively short shrift, ideology, how and why it develops, and how it affects decisions will need to be a part of the research agenda.

Another factor that may explain the difference between environmental and human sustainability derives from the different actors in the two systems and the presumption of choice. Few would argue that trees "choose" to be cut down, that the air or water decides to be dirty, or that polar bears make decisions that result in the disappearance of food and habitat. Therefore, there is an implicit assumption that people must act on behalf of the environment, threatened species of plants and animals, and possibly even indigenous populations because these entities can't act on their own behalf. Employees, however, have choices, and exercise their choices in a labor market in which they compete for jobs and employers compete for talent. Presumably if they don't like the conditions of their jobs, including the degree of inequality, the amount of stress, or the absence of health insurance, employees can decide to work elsewhere. At the limit, if the conditions of work are really life-threatening, as the evidence shows, employees can choose unemployment over ill health and/or premature death.

Ideas about market outcomes being fair—even if they sometimes aren't (Blount, 2000)—the primacy of markets (Davis, 2008), and the fact that people are capable of making choices—even if such choices are constrained and socially influenced—lead naturally to a very different approach to human sustainability. Threatened plants and animals and the natural world need protection, but sentient humans making free choices in competitive markets can, and should, fend for themselves. This line of argument, coupled with the finding that profitable companies are believed to be more ethical than unprofitable ones (Jost et al., 2003)—as one way of justifying their profitability and as an example of the tendency to attribute good qualities to an entity that is successful—lead to greater reluctance to find human sustainability problematic and requiring intervention.

Although I have highlighted two factors—visibility of consequences and ideology—as helping to account for the relative emphasis on environmental as opposed to human sustainability, there are undoubtedly many other factors at work. The fundamental message is that we need to understand what subjects receive attention and why, as well as the beliefs and values that form the foundation for our theorizing—not just for the topic of sustainability but for many others, as well. The evidence suggests that these are important and underexplored issues.

What If We Took Human Sustainability Seriously? A Research Agenda

Throughout this article I have highlighted questions that could productively receive research attention. In this concluding section, I offer some additional suggestions that logically follow from the literature reviewed in this article.

As Ambec and Lanoie (2008) noted, one of the major issues addressed by research on environmental sustainability has been whether or not adopting sustainability practices imposes net costs on companies, thereby eroding their competitiveness, or whether the benefits of being "green" more than outweigh any costs incurred. Completely parallel questions and issues confront a focus on human sustainability. First, just as in the case of environmental pollution, companies that do not provide health insurance, lay people off, pay inadequate wages, and have work arrangements that stress and overwork their employees also impose externalities that others pay for even as they save on their own costs. That's because some portion of the extra costs of increased physical and psychological illness fall on the broader health system through, for instance, increased use of public health and emergency room facilities. Second, just as green companies enjoy reputational benefits that help in brand building and product differentiation, so, too, we might expect that companies with better records of human sustainability could enjoy benefits in attracting and retaining employees and also in building a reputation that could attract additional consumer demand. Therefore, whether or not it pays to be a company that offers a system high in human sustainability, and how the various costs and benefits balance and under what conditions, would be an important focus for research.

There are some data that suggest that human sustainability may pay off for companies. Each year the Great Place to Work Institute, in conjunction with *Fortune,* publishes a list of the best places to work. Most of those places are noted for their provision of good working conditions and benefits, including vacations, sick days, health insurance, training, and jobs that provide people autonomy and challenge. The Institute's Web site shows data indicating that companies on the list consistently outperform benchmark indices over varying periods of time, indicating that, at least as measured by stock market performance, it is good to be a great place to work. How and why these returns accrue remains to be explored in more detail. But it is quite likely that, just as in the case of environmental sustainability, human sustainability pays. Indeed, the literature on the positive effects of employee-centered management practices is extensive (e.g., Becker & Huselid, 1998). If so, that raises a third question: if it does pay to be green, whether "green" is assessed in environmental or human terms, or both, then why is it so difficult to get companies to adopt practices consistent with sustainability?

Another implication of the research cited may help to explain one of the paradoxes of the U.S. health-care system—why it costs so much even as it does not deliver measurable health benefits, as assessed by indicators ranging from infant mortality to life expectancy to survival rates for various serious illnesses, that are no better than in many other industrialized countries. Once again, there are undoubtedly many answers to this important question. But one possibility is this: If health status is affected by what happens to people on the job, the relatively poor health-care outcomes in the U.S. might result from a laissez faire labor market that leaves even the provision of paid sick days and paid vacation at the discretion of employers. In other words, differences in the distribution of working conditions across different countries (or, for that matter, other political units such as states or even industries) could possibly help account for differences in the differences in health outcomes. Because of differences in unionization rates (by industry and sector) and differences across states in both formal regulation of working conditions and the vigor with which such regulations are enforced, there is a great deal of natural variation in working conditions that research has shown to be relevant to health and mortality. Exploring whether those variations also account for variations in health-care outcomes and costs would be fruitful.

Wilper et al. (2009) estimated that there are more than 44,000 excess deaths in the United States annually because people lack health insurance. Some, although not all, of the absence of health insurance results from employer decisions. If one added to the portion of these deaths resulting from employer actions the mortality coming from layoffs, company-generated inequalities in income and control over work, and all the other factors briefly reviewed in this article, the resulting number would be both interesting and important. It might spark some serious effort to prevent deaths from employer decisions. There is already a great deal of employer and public policy focus on individual choices such as diet and exercise. Attention to the role of the employer in individual health status would round out the picture.

There is no reason why building sustainable companies should focus just on the physical and not the social environment. It is not just the natural world that is at risk from harmful business practices. We should care as much about people as we do about polar bears—or the environmental savings from using better milk jugs—and also understand the causes and consequences of how we focus our research and policy attention.

Note

1. In this paper I use the term social environment to include organizational effects on people and small groups. Just as physical sustainability considers the consequences of organizational activity for material, physical resources, social sustainability might consider how organizational activities affect people's physical and mental health and well-being— the stress of work practices on the human system—as well as effects of management practices such as work hours and behaviors that produce workplace stress on groups and group cohesion and also the richness of social life, as exemplified by participation in civic, voluntary, and community organizations.

References

Ambec, S., & Lanoie, P. (2008). Does it pay to be green? A systematic overview. *Academy of Management Perspectives, 22,* 45–62.

Bansal, P. (2002). The corporate challenges of sustainable development. *Academy of Management Executive, 16,* 122–131.

Barley, S. R., & Kunda, G. (1992). Design and devotion: Surges of rational and normative ideologies of control in managerial discourse. *Administrative Science Quarterly, 37,* 363–399.

Baron, J. N., & Bielby W. T. (1980). Bringing the firms back in: Stratification, segmentation, and the organization of work. *American Sociological Review, 45,* 737–765.

Becker, B. E., & Huselid, M. A. (1998). High performance systems and firm performance: A synthesis of research and managerial implications. *Research in Personnel and Human Resources Management, 16,* 53–101.

Blakely, T. A., Collings, S. C. D., & Atkinson, J. (2003). Unemployment and suicide: Evidence for a causal association? *Journal of Epidemiology and Community Health, 57,* 594–600.

Bloom, M. (1999). The performance effects of pay dispersion on individuals and organizations. *Academy of Management Journal, 42,* 25–40.

Blount, S. (2000). Whoever said that markets were fair? *Negotiation Journal, 16,* 237–252.

Budros, A. (1997). The new capitalism and organizational rationality: The adoption of downsizing programs, 1979–1994. *Social Forces, 76,* 229–250.

Cappelli, P. (1999). *The New Deal at Work.* Boston: Harvard Business School Press.

Card, D., Dobkin, C., & Maestas, N. (2009). Does Medicare save lives? *Quarterly Journal of Economics, 124,* 597–636.

Cascio, W. F. (2006). The economic impact of employee behaviors on organizational performance. *California Management Review, 48,* 41–59.

Catalano, R. (1991). The health effects of economic insecurity. *American Journal of Public Health, 81,* 1148–1152.

Catalano, R., Novaco, R. W., & McConnell, W. (2002). Layoffs and violence revisited. *Aggressive Behavior, 28,* 233–247.

Chandola, T., Brunner, E., & Marmot. M. (2006). Chronic stress at work and the metabolic syndrome: Prospective study. *British Medical Journal, 332,* 521–525.

Colvin, G. (2008, October 16). How Sam's Club sees the future. *Fortune.* Retrieved February 15, 2010, from http://money.cnn .com/2008/10/15/news/companies/Wal-Marts_rising_star_ colvin.fortune/index.htm.

Cornia, G. A., & Paniccia, R. (Eds.). (2000). *The mortality crisis in transitional economies.* Oxford, UK: Oxford University Press.

Cowherd, D. M., & Levine, D. I. (1992). Product quality and pay equity between lower-level employees and top management: An investigation of distributive justice theory. *Administrative Science Quarterly, 37,* 302–320.

Davis, G. F. (2008). The rise and fall of finance and the end of the society of organizations. *Academy of Management Perspectives, 23,* 27–44.

Davis, G. F. (2009). *Managed by the Markets: How Finance re-shaped America.* Oxford, UK: Oxford University Press.

Deaton, A. (2003). Health, inequality, and economic development. *Journal of Economic Literature, 41,* 113–158.

Diener, E., Suh, E. M., Lucas, R. E., & Smith, H. L. (1999). Subjective well-being: Three decades of progress. *Psychological Bulletin, 125,* 276–302.

Dube, A., Graham-Squire, D., Jacobs, K., & Luce, S. (2007). *Living Wage Policies and Wal-Mart: How a Higher Wage Standard Would Impact Wal-Mart Workers and Shoppers.* Berkeley, CA: U.C. Berkeley Center for Labor Research and Education.

Dudley, S., & Warren, M. (2005). *Upward trend in regulation continues: An analysis of the U.S. budget for fiscal years 2005 and 2006.* George Mason University, Mercatus Center, 2006 Annual Report, Regulators' Budget Report 27.

Eliason, M., & Storrie, D. (2009). Does job loss shorten life? *Journal of Human Resources, 44,* 277–302.

Ferraro, F., Pfeffer, J., & Sutton, R. I. (2005). Economic language and assumptions: How theories can become self-fulfilling. *Academy of Management Review, 30,* 8–24.

Ferraro, F., Pfeffer, J., & Sutton, R. I. (2009). How and why theories matter: A comment on Felin and Foss (2009). *Organization Science, 20,* 669–675.

Fountain, H. (2010, January 3). Urban environment: Sustainability comes of age. *New York Times,* Education Life, p. 20.

Franks, P., Clancy, C. M. & Gold, M. R. (1993). Health insurance and mortality: Evidence from a national cohort. *Journal of the American Medical Association, 270,* 737–741.

Frey, B. S., & Stutzer, A. (2002). What can economists learn from happiness research? *Journal of Economic Literature, 40,* 402–435.

Frone, M. R. (2000). Work-family conflict and employee psychiatric disorders: The national comorbidity survey. *Journal of Applied Psychology, 85*(6), 888–895.

Frone, M. R., Russell, M., & Barnes, G. M. (1996). Work-family conflict, gender, and health-related outcomes: A study of employed parents in two community samples. *Journal of Occupational Health Psychology, 1*(1), 57–69.

Gakidou, E. E., Murray, C. J. L., & Frenk, J. (2000). Defining and measuring health inequality: An approach based on the distribution of health expectancy. *Bulletin of the World Health Organization, 78,* 42–54.

Gallo, L. C., & Matthews, K. A. (2003). Understanding the association between socioeconomic status and physical health: Do negative emotions play a role? *Psychological Bulletin, 129,* 10–51.

Greenhouse, S. (2009 October 30). BP faces record fine for '05 refinery explosion. *New York Times,* p. B1.

Hackman, J. R., & Oldham, G. R. (1980). *Work redesign.* Reading, MA: Addison-Wesley.

Himmelstein, D. U., Warren, E., Thorne, D., & Woolhandler, S. (2005). MarketWatch: Illness and injury as contributor to bankruptcy. *Health Affairs-Web Exclusive,* W5-63–W5-73.

Hsu, T. (2010, January 2). Corporate eco-managers turning companies green. *San Francisco Chronicle,* p. D2.

Jost, J. T. (2006). The end of the end of ideology. *American Psychologist, 61,* 651–670.

Jost, J. T., Blount, S., Pfeffer, J., & Hunyady, G. (2003). Fair market ideology: Its cognitive-motivational underpinnings. *Research in Organizational Behavior, 25,* 53–91.

Jost, J. T., Nosek, B. A., & Gosling, S. D. (2008). Ideology: Its resurgence in social, personality, and political psychology. *Perspectives on Psychological Science, 3,* 126–136.

Kaufman, L. (2009, December 20). Coming clean about carbon: Industries disclose emissions to claim the high ground. *New York Times,* p. B1.

Keefe, V., Reid, P., Ormsby, C., Robson, B., Purdie, G., Baxter, J., & Ngati Kahungunu Iwi Imcorporated (2002). Serious health events following involuntary job loss in New Zealand meat processing workers. *International Journal of Epidemiology, 31,* 1155–1161.

Kivimaki, M., Vahtera, J., Pentti, J., & Ferris, J. E. (2000). Factors underlying the effect of organizational downsizing on health of employees: Longitudinal cohort study. *British Medical Journal, 320,* 971–975.

Levy, H., & Meltzer, D. (2001). *What do we really know about whether health insurance affects health?* (Working Paper No. 6). Ann Arbor, MI: University of Michigan, Economic Research Inititiative on the Uninsured.

Lynch, J., Davey-Smith, G., Hillemeier, M., Shaw, M., Raghunathan, T., & Kaplan, G. (2001). Income inequality, psychosocial environment and health: Comparisons across wealthy nations. *Lancet, 358,* 194–200.

March, J. G., & Sutton, R. I. (1997). Organizational performance as a dependent variable. *Organization Science, 8,* 698–706.

Marcus, A. A., & Fremeth, A. R. (2009). Green management matters regardless. *Academy of Management Perspectives, 23,* 17–26.

Marmot, M. (2004). *The Status Syndrome: How social standing affects our health and longevity.* London: Times Books.

Marmot, M., & Bobak, M. (2000). International comparators and poverty and health in Europe, *British Medical Journal, 321,* 1124–1128.

Marmot, M. G., Bosma, H., Hemingway, H., Brunner, E., & Stansfeld, S. (1997). Contribution of job control and other risk factors to social variations in coronary heart disease incidence. *Lancet, 350,* 235–239.

Molotch, H. I., & Boden, D. (1985). Talking social structure: Discourse, domination, and the Watergate hearings. *American Sociological Review, 50,* 273–288.

National Institute for Occupational Safety and Health (2004). *Overtime and extended work shifts: Recent findings on illnesses, injuries, and health behaviors* (Publication No. 2204-143, May). Washington, DC: Author.

Navarro, M. (2010, January 3). Sustainable cultures: A step beyond anthropology. *New York Times, Education Life,* p. 20.

Oswald, A. J. (1997). Happiness and economic performance. *The Economic Journal, 107,* 1815–1831.

Pfeffer, J., & Langton, N. (1988). Wage inequality and the organization of work: The case of academic departments. *Administrative Science Quarterly, 33,* 588–606.

Pfeffer, J., & Langton, N. (1993). The effect of wage dispersion on satisfaction, productivity, and working collaboratively: Evidence from college and university faculty. *Administrative Science Quarterly, 38,* 382–407.

Plambeck, E. L., & Denend, L. (2007). Wal-Mart's sustainability strategy. (Case No. OIT7–71). Stanford, CA: Stanford University, Graduate School of Business.

Potosky, A. L., Breen, N., Graubard, B. I., & Parsons, P. E. (1998). The association between health care coverage and the use of cancer screening tests: Results from the 1992 National Health Interview Survey. *Medical Care, 36,* 257–270.

Putunam, R. D. (2000). *Bowling alone: The collapse and revival of American Community.* New York: Simon and Schuster.

Rosenbloom, S., & Barbaro, M. (2009, January 25). Green-light specials, now at Wal-Mart. *New York Times,* p. BU1.

Rousseau, D. M. (2006). The shift in risk from employers to workers in the new employment relationship. In E. E. Lawler, III & J. O'Toole (eds.), *America at Work: Choices and Challenges* (pp. 153–172). New York: Palgrave Macmillan.

Ryff, C. D. (1989). Happiness is everything, or is it? Explorations on the meaning of psychological well-being. *Journal of Personality and Social Psychology, 57,* 1069–1081.

Schoen, C., & DesRoches, C. (2000). Uninsured and unstably insured: The importance of continuous insurance coverage. *Health Services Research, 35,* 187–206.

Siegel, P. A., & Hambrick, D. C. (2005). Pay disparities within top management groups: Evidence of harmful effects on performance of high-technology firms. *Organization Science, 16,* 259–274.

Stave, G. M., Muchmore, L. & Gardner, H. (2003). Quantifiable impact of the contract for health and wellness: Health behaviors, health care costs, disability, and workers' compensation. *Journal of Occupational and Environmental Medicine, 45,* 109–117.

Sudano, J. J., & Baker, D. W. (2003). Intermittent lack of health insurance coverage and use of preventive services. *American Journal of Public Health, 93,* 130–137.

Sullivan, D., & von Wachter, T. (2007). *Mortality, mass layoffs, and career outcomes: An analysis using administrative data* (Working Paper No. 13626). Cambridge, MA: National Bureau of Economic Research.

Tetlock, P. E. (2000). Cognitive biases and organizational correctives: Do both disease and cure depend on the politics of the beholder? *Administrative Science Quarterly, 46,* 293–326.

Walsh, J. P., Weber, K. & Margolis, J. D. (2003). Social issues and management: Our lost cause found. *Journal of Management, 29,* 859–881.

Wildman, J. (2003). Income related inequalities in mental health in Great Britain: Analysing the causes of health inequality over time. *Journal of Health Economics, 22,* 295–312.

Wilper, A., Woolhandler, S., Lasser, K. E., McCormick, D., Bor, D. H., & Himmelstein, D. U. (2009). Health insurance and mortality in US adults. *American Journal of Public Health, 99,* 2289–2295.

Yang, H., Schnall, P. L., Jauregui, M., Su, T., & Baker, D. (2006). Work hours and self-reported hypertension among working people in California. *Hypertension, 48,* 744–750.

Critical Thinking

1. What can organizations do to help "sustain" their employees?
2. Why have employees generally been ignored in the discussion of sustainability?
3. What can be done to remedy this situation?

Internet References

A World Institute for Sustainable Humanity
　　www.awish.net
Sustainability, Resilience, and Human Systems
　　www.garrisoninstitute.org/sustainability-resilience-and-human-systems
The Human Sustainability Institute
　　www.humansustainabilityinstitute.com

JEFFREY PFEFFER is the Thomas D. Dee II Professor of Organizational Behavior at the Graduate School of Business, Stanford University.

Acknowledgment—I gratefully acknowledge the advice, encouragement, and inspiration of Nuria Chinchilla from IESE, who encouraged me to think about the issue of human sustainability in both societies and companies. The helpful comments of the editor and the reviewers substantially clarified the arguments.

Article   Prepared by: Maria Nathan, *Lynchburg College*

Discrimination and the Aging American Workforce: Recommendations and Strategies for Management

FRANK J. CAVICO AND BAHAUDIN G. MUJTABA

Learning Outcomes

After reading this article, you will be able to:

- Understand how U.S. employment law treats alleged age discrimination.

- Know employer defenses that exist for the age discrimination lawsuit.

- Consider management strategies that might be used to ensure the employer is effectiveness minded yet legally compliant.

An Overview of Age Discrimination in Employment

The global workforce is becoming older. In the United States, the Bureau of Labor Statistics reported that 76.9 million people in the workforce are age 40 or older (Grossman, 2008). More people are living longer and working longer, by either choice or, particularly in today's uncertain economic times, necessity. The increasing age of the workforce, the presence of age bias in society generally, together with the fact that the consequences of unemployment fall more harshly on older people, make the topic of age discrimination in employment a significant one—legally, ethically, and practically. Moreover, as "older" employees get even older, their pension and health care costs increase for their employers, thereby making older employees more attractive targets for workforce downsizing. Furthermore, not only are older employees disadvantaged in their efforts to retain employment, but also to regain employment when they are discharged from their jobs. Weak economies also affect older workers more harshly, particularly since, when business is not good, employers may feel compelled to reduce the number of their most expensive employees, who are typically their oldest workers. Moreover, in a tight economy, older workers are most likely to have a more difficult time securing another job, let alone a comparable job. Today, therefore, many older workers are remaining in the workforce, and the percentage of older workers in the U.S. workforce is projected to expand. Sherman (2008) reported on a study by the American Association of Retired Persons that the percentage of people 65 and older who continue to work has grown from 10.8% in 1985 to 16% in 2007. Moreover, for people aged 55 to 64, the numbers have increased from 54.2% in 1985 to 63.8% in 2007. Dealing with older workers in the workforce, particularly as the workforce ages, emerges as a very important legal matter indeed.

In contrast to intentional age discrimination, covert discrimination can exist against older employees. This form of discrimination is subtler, and human resource managers should be wary of it. Research has revealed that unintentional code words often are used during the interview process, such as "we're looking for go-getters" and people who are "with-it," to describe desirable employees. Generally, these buzzwords seem not to apply to people who are experienced, just "old." However, as will be seen, the phase "over-qualified" and other such words and phrases may be code words indicating age discrimination intent. According to Clark (2003), about two-thirds of all U.S. companies use performance as at least one factor when deciding who to lay-off during tough economic times. Many firms use the forced ranking system, viewed by executives as the "fairest and easiest way to downsize." Unfortunately, older workers seem to get the worst of it, as larger portions of them lose their jobs, possibly due to biases and because they earn more income and benefits than their younger counterparts (Mujtaba, Cavico, Edward, and Oskal, 2006).

The Civil Rights Act of 1964, the most important civil rights law in the United States, prohibits discrimination by employers, labor organizations, and employment agencies on the basis of race, color, sex, religion, and national origin. Regarding employment, the scope of the statute is very broad, encompassing hiring, apprenticeships, promotion, training, transfer, compensation, and discharge, as well as any other "terms or conditions" and "privileges" of employment (Mujtaba and Rhodes, 2006). The Act applies to both the private and public sectors, including state and local governments and their subdivisions, agencies, and departments. An employer subject to this Act is one who has 15 or more employees for each working day in each of 20 or more calendar weeks in the current or preceding calendar year. One of the principal purposes of the Act is to eliminate job discrimination in employment (Cavico and Mujtaba, 2008). The focal point of this is Title VII of the Civil Rights Act, which deals with employment discrimination.

Discrimination, in employment or otherwise, can be direct and overt or indirect and inferential. Typically, there are two types or categories of employment discrimination claims against employers involving hiring or promotion. The first theory of recovery, "disparate treatment," involves an employer who intentionally treats applicants or employees less favorably than others based on one of the protected classes of color, race, sex, religion, national origin, age, or disability (Mujtaba, 2010). The other legal avenue claimants may travel to prove discrimination is called "disparate impact" or "adverse impact," and does not require proof of an employer's intent to discriminate. Both categories are discussed further in this article.

ADEA and EEOC

The Age Discrimination in Employment Act (ADEA), passed in 2005 promotes the employment of older persons based on their ability and not their age, prohibits arbitrary age discrimination in employment, and assists employers and employees in finding ways to meet the problems arising from the impact of age on employment (Mujtaba and Cavico, 2010). The law recognizes the grave problems resulting from age discrimination against older workers, particularly long-term unemployment, as well as the burden that age discrimination places on commerce and the free flow of goods and services. One important objective of the ADEA was to eliminate age discrimination against older job applicants. It was believed that the eliminating age discrimination would reduce long-term unemployment

of older workers, thereby diminishing poverty among the elderly.

The ADEA prohibits an employer from failing or refusing to hire a protected individual, or discharging an employee within the protected age category, or otherwise discriminating against such individuals because of their age regarding compensation and the other terms and conditions of employment. The ADEA specifically makes it illegal for an employer to refuse or fail to hire a person, or to discharge an employee, or to otherwise discriminate against any person with respect to compensation, terms, conditions, or privileges of employment, including hiring, firing, promotion, layoff, compensation, benefits, job assignments, and training, due to this person's age (Mujtaba, 2010). Moreover, it is illegal for an employer to limit, segregate, or classify its employees in any way that would deprive a person of employment opportunities or otherwise adversely affect a person's status as an employee because of age. The Equal Employment Opportunity Commission (EEOC) is a federal government regulatory agency empowered by the U.S. Congress to make anti-discrimination laws in the form of administrative rules and regulations pursuant to civil rights laws enacted by Congress as well as to administer and enforce civil rights laws, including the ADEA.

The EEOC is permitted to bring a lawsuit on behalf of an aggrieved employee, or the aggrieved employee may bring a suit for legal or equitable relief. In either case, the ADEA provides the right to a jury trial. Over the past decade, as the number of older workers has increased the number of age discrimination claims filed with the EEOC has also increased. The ADEA is a federal law, but almost all states also have some type of anti-discrimination age law, some of which may provide more protection to an aggrieved employee than the federal law does.

According to EEOC, for the fiscal year 2008, which ended September 30, the agency received the unprecedented number of 95,402 workplace discrimination claims, representing a 15% increase from the previous year. Charges based on age discrimination and retaliation saw the largest annual increases (EEOC Press Release, 2009). To compare, for the 2004 fiscal year, the Commission received 17,837 charges of age discrimination, resolved 15,792 age discrimination charges, and recovered $60 million for charging parties and other aggrieved individuals (not including monetary benefits obtained through litigation). The EEOC reports that age discrimination claims are still a major factor, although the percentage of such claims declined in the mid-1990s compared with previous data. This decline is attributed in part to sharp growth in the over 40 population.

The most recent data from the Equal Employment Opportunity Commission (EEOC) report the number of age discrimination lawsuits and the monetary benefits obtained by the agency. (Note that the EEOC's data do not include monetary benefits obtained by litigation.) Pursuant to all civil rights laws that the EEOC enforces, the agency received 80,680 complaints of discrimination in 1997 and 99,992 in 2010. Again pursuant to all statutes, the agency obtained $176.7 million for employees in 1997 and $319.4 million in 2010.

Regarding the Age Discrimination in Employment Act (ADEA), in 1997 the agency received 15,785 complaints of age discrimination; by 2010 that number was 23,264. Also regarding the ADEA, in 1997 the agency obtained $44.3 million for employees, but by 2010 that total had more than doubled to $93.6 million. To compare, for race-based claims pursuant to Title VII, the agency in 1997 received 29,199 complaints, which had increased to 35,890 in 2010. In 1997, the EEOC obtained $41.8 million for the victims of race discrimination, which more than doubled to $84.4 million in 2010—but was lower than the total of monetary benefits obtained for the victims of age discrimination. Regarding the Americans with Disabilities Act (ADA), the EEOC received 18,108 claims of disability discrimination in 1997, a total that increased to 25,165 in 2010. Under the ADA, the EEOC obtained $41.3 million for victims of disability discrimination in 1997, which rose to $76.1 million by 2010. This was less than the amount obtained for age discrimination, though the number of disability claims filed with the agency exceeded the number of age discrimination claims.

Finally, regarding sex-based discrimination charges pursuant to Title VII, the most recent EEOC data show a substantial increase over all categories. In 1997, 24,728 such claims were filed with the EEOC, which increased to 29,029 in 2010. In 1997 the EEOC obtained $72.5 million for the victims of sex discrimination, but by 2010 that amount had increased sharply to $129.3 million, surpassing all other categories, including age. Age claimants, however, still received more than race-based Title VII and ADA claimants, even though in the case of race there were materially more claims filed with the EEOC.

The Age Discrimination Lawsuit: Procedural and Substantive Elements

A. Employee's Initial or Prima Facie Case

When the EEOC finds "reasonable cause," it sends the aggrieved party a "right-to-sue" letter which allows the employee to proceed to the federal courts. The agency itself may go to court on behalf of the complaining employee, or the employee may also choose to be represented by private legal counsel. Regardless, in either situation, the prima facie case is the required initial case that a plaintiff asserting discrimination must establish. Prima facie means the presentment of evidence

that, if left unexplained or not contradicted, would establish the facts alleged. Generally, in the context of age discrimination, the plaintiff employee must show that: 1) he or she is in an age class protected by the ADEA; 2) he or she applied for and was qualified for a position or promotion for which the employer was seeking applicants; 3) he or she suffered an adverse employment action, for example, the plaintiff was rejected or demoted despite being qualified, or despite performing at a level that met the employer's legitimate expectations; and 4) after the plaintiff's rejection or discharge or demotion, the position remained open and the employer continued to seek applicants from people with the plaintiff's qualifications. These elements give rise to an inference of discrimination. The burden of proof and persuasion is on the plaintiff to establish the prima facie case of discrimination by a preponderance of the evidence. However, based on the Supreme Court case of O'Connor v. Consolidated Coin Caterers Corp. (1966), it is not necessary for the plaintiff's prima facie case to show that he or she was replaced by a person under 40 years of age, the ADEA minimum age. That is, the fact that one person protected by the ADEA lost out on a job opportunity to another person also protected by the ADEA is irrelevant, so long as the aggrieved party lost out because of age. Of course, as a practical matter, the fact that a person's replacement is substantially younger than the person replaced should emerge as a far more reliable indicator of age discrimination.

B. The Disparate Treatment Theory

Disparate treatment, as noted, means intentional discrimination. The employer simply treats some employees less favorably than others because of their age (or other protected characteristic). Proof of a discriminatory intent on the part of the employer is critical to a disparate treatment case. The plaintiff can demonstrate this intent by means of direct or circumstantial evidence, but the employer's liability hinges on the presence of evidence that age actually motivated the employer's decision. A disparate treatment case will not succeed unless the employee's age actually formed a part to the decision-making process and had a determining effect on the outcome. Of course, if the motivating factor in the employer's decision was some criterion other than the employee's age, there is no disparate treatment liability.

C. Direct Evidence

This is evidence that clearly and directly indicates the employer's intent to discriminate; that is, the proverbial "smoking gun." In building a case, one commentator noted that "… offering direct proof of motive in the form of ageist slurs or other incriminating behavior is a more common approach, and one that is likely to be more effective. Such evidence must, however, be evaluated on a case-by-case basis (Labriola, 2009). An example of direct evidence would be a memo to terminate all older men since they are technologically less knowledgeable and capable and resist technological changes. Illustrations would be statements that the employee is too old for certain work, or too old to make tough decisions, that the employee should be spending more time with his or her family, or playing golf or fishing, as well as constant questioning of the employee as to his or her retirement date or plans. Concrete examples of actual "ageist" language of a demeaning and derogatory nature that can provide evidence of discriminatory intent include "that old goat," "too long on the job," "old and tired," and "he had bags under the eyes" (Quirk, 2008). Also evidencing an intent to discriminate are such remarks as "We need young blood around here," "Let's bring in the young guns" (Quirk, 2008), and the employee "needs special treatment because she is getting old" (Pounds, 2009). In another case, the Second Circuit Court of Appeals found that allegations that two waitresses were repeatedly assigned less desirable work stations and work shifts than younger wait-staff were sufficient to make a claim for age discrimination. In the case, the employer made comments to the waitresses to "drop dead," "retire early," "take off all that makeup," and "take off your wig," thereby giving rise to a claim of age discrimination as well as a hostile work environment (Laluk and Stiller, 2008). In another Second Circuit case, the appeals court further noted that the probative value of age comments did not depend on how offensive they were. For example, a supervisor's assertion that the plaintiff "was well suited to work with seniors" was not offensive, yet it indicated discriminatory intent. The court found that considering the supervisor's remarks in the context of all the evidence, the remarks were sufficient to sustain a reasonable inference that the supervisor was motivated by age discrimination in discharging the plaintiff (Laluk and Stiller, 2008).

Nevertheless, not every type of age insult will be found actionable by the courts (Labriola, 2009). Consequently, the further the discriminatory memo, remark, or comment is made from the time of discharge, the greater the risk that a court will brand it as a "stray remark," and find it too remote to qualify as direct evidence of discrimination (Labriola, 2009). Similarly, the more ambiguous and general the comment, or the more the statement can be subject to varying interpretations, the less likely a court will declare it direct evidence of age discrimination (Labriola, 2009). Another important factor in determining the viability of a statement as direct evidence of age discrimination is whether the statement was made by a decision-maker or a person with supervisory, managerial, or executive authority.

D. Circumstantial Evidence

Age discrimination is an intentional legal wrong. Since proof of this wrongful intent—discriminatory or otherwise—is notoriously difficult for a plaintiff to obtain, the courts at times permit discriminatory motive to be inferred from the facts of the case. Age bias can thus take the form of broad assumptions about older workers that cannot be shown to be supported by the facts. Examples would be oral or written statements that infer age bias, such as comments that older workers are "over-qualified" or "computer illiterate" or reflect other negative assumptions. Another example would be when an employer discharges a successful and experienced older worker and replaces him or her with a person with no or less experience or with different and lesser academic credentials. Other problematical situations would arise from suspicious timing or even from differences in treatment, such as better treatment of similarly situated employees not in the protected class. Regarding differences in treatment, if it is systematic and rises to the level of a pattern, or as one court said, a "convincing mosaic," the inference of age bias and deliberate discrimination is naturally much stronger. Burden-shifting typically arises in a discrimination case when the plaintiff uses the disparate treatment legal theory. That is, the plaintiff (the aggrieved employee) is arguing that his or her employer intentionally discriminated against him or her because of a protected characteristic, such as age pursuant to the Age Discrimination in Employment Act or race pursuant to Title VII of the Civil Rights Act. To sustain his or her initial burden of proof, the plaintiff must introduce evidence that the employer intended to discriminate against the employee, who thereby suffered an adverse employment action due to age, race, or other protected characteristic. The evidence the employee can offer can be direct evidence of discrimination, such as an express comment indicating a bias against older workers, or circumstantial, such as a comment that an employee is "over-qualified," which can be the basis of an inference of a discriminatory animus. Once the plaintiff establishes this initial or prima facie case, the burden then shifts to the employer to present a legitimate, bona fide, nondiscriminatory reason for the adverse employment action. Next, if the employer can meet this burden, the burden shifts back to the plaintiff employee to demonstrate that the purportedly legitimate reason offered by the employer is, in fact, fake and a mere pretext for an underlying discriminatory motive.

Yet the courts have made it somewhat easier for plaintiff employees to present circumstantial evidence of age discrimination by ruling that the federal district court judges have the authority to allow what is called "me, too" evidence of age discrimination. Such evidence basically consists of supporting evidence from other employees at a company that they also had been discriminated against because of their age. In deciding whether to admit such evidence, a judge must determine whether the evidence of discrimination by the same or other supervisors or managers is closely related to the plaintiff's circumstances.

E. Pretext

In a circumstantial case, when the defendant contends that its rationale was an appropriate, legitimate, and nondiscriminatory business one, the plaintiff is allowed to show that the proffered reason was really a pretext for discrimination. Pretext means that the employer's stated reason was fake, phony, a sham, a lie, not that the employer made an error in judgment or a bad decision. A pretexual reason is one designed to hide the employer's true motive, i.e., an unlawful act of age discrimination. The courts have allowed the employer's explanation to be foolish, trivial, or even baseless, as long as the employer honestly believed it. The genuineness of the reason, not its reasonableness, is the key. The plaintiff bears the burden of showing that the employer's proffered reason was a pretext. The plaintiff, however, need not show the pretext beyond all doubt. He or she need not totally discredit the employer's reasons for acting, but rather must provide sufficient evidence to call into question and to cast doubt on the legitimacy of the employer's purported reasons for acting. Providing such evidence of pretext allows the plaintiff to contend that the reason given by the employer for the discharge or demotion or negative action was something other than the reason given by the employer. The following types of evidence have been used by the courts to enable the plaintiff to demonstrate pretext: 1) disparate treatment or prior poor treatment; 2) disturbing procedural irregularities or the failure to follow company policy; 3) use of subjective criteria in making employment decisions; 4) the fact that an individual who was hired or promoted over the plaintiff was obviously not qualified; and 5) substantial changes over time in the employer's proffered reason for the employment decision (Tymkovich, 2008).

However, there are limits as to what a court will accept as evidence of pretext. To illustrate, for many years attorneys have encouraged employers to publish and widely disseminate written policy statements of their commitment to nondiscrimination. Attorneys have argued that the published policies were an important defense tool in any subsequent lawsuit (Corbin and Duvail, 2008). In the case of Hoard v. CHU2A, Inc. Architecture Engineering Planning (2007), the Court of Appeals for the Eleventh Circuit addressed the legal relevance of an employer's failure to have a published anti-discrimination policy, and concluded that the failure did not demonstrate that the employer's stated reason for its adverse employment action was pretextual. In Hoard, the plaintiff, a fifty-eight year old man, brought a lawsuit against CHU2A alleging age discrimination as prohibited by the Age Discrimination in Employment Act. After an adverse district court decision, the employee, Hoard, argued on appeal that the absence of a published policy by the employer constituted adequate evidence of pretext. The district court entered summary judgment in favor of CHU2A, deciding that Hoard failed to establish any evidence of pretext to rebut the employer's stated, legitimate, nondiscriminatory reason for the adverse employment action taken against him. The appeals court summarily rejected the employee's contention, affirming the district court's decision (Corbin and Duvail, 2008). Nonetheless, it is still prudent—legally, morally, and practically—for an employer to have a written and communicated anti-discrimination policy.

Once sufficient evidence of pretext is shown, a judge may allow a jury, as finder of fact, to infer that the true reason for the action was improper age discrimination. The failure of the employer to give any reason, foolish or not, for the discharge of an older worker at the time of termination has been construed as evidence that the employer's asserted business reason, for example, allegedly poor performance, when given much later, was merely a pretext for discrimination. The prudent employer is well advised, therefore, despite a certain management prevailing opinion to the contrary, to provide in a direct and unambiguous manner at the time of discharge, an appropriate business-related reason for the discharge even of an employee at-will, and to have a written record of the transaction.

F. The Disparate Impact Theory

Disparate impact discrimination, as noted, means unintentional discrimination on the part of the employer. In a disparate impact case, the employer's policies and practices are neutral on their face in their treatment of employees, yet they fall more harshly or disproportionately on a protected group of employees, and they cannot be justified by legitimate, reasonable, and non-discriminatory business reasons. The disparate impact theory has long been a widely used and accepted means of establishing illegal discrimination under Title VII of the Civil Rights Act.

The Supreme Court in 2005 handed down a major decision regarding the disparate impact doctrine and age discrimination in employment in the case of Smith v. City of Jackson, Mississippi (2005). The decision expanded the protection afforded older workers pursuant to the ADEA. The decision allowed protected workers over the age of 40 to institute age discrimination lawsuits even when evidence was lacking that their employers purposefully intended to discriminate on the basis of age. As a result, the decision substantially lessened the legal burden for employees covered by the statute by allowing aggrieved employees to contend in court that a presumably neutral employment practice nonetheless had an adverse or disparate or disproportionately harmful impact on them. However, the Court also allowed the employer to defend such an age discrimination case by interposing that the employer had a legitimate, reasonable, and job-related explanation for the "neutral" employment policy. The Supreme Court case initially was brought by older police officers in Jackson, Mississippi, who argued that a pay-for-performance plan instituted by the city granted substantially larger raises to employees with five or fewer years of tenure, which policy, the officers contended, favored their younger colleagues. The lower courts had dismissed the lawsuit, ruling that these types of claims were barred by the statute. The U.S. Supreme Court, however, in a 5-3 decision, ruled that the officers were entitled to pursue the age discrimination lawsuit against the city. Justice John Paul Stevens, writing for the majority, stated that the Age Discrimination in Employment Act of 1967 was meant to allow the same type of "disparate impact" legal challenges for older workers that minorities and women can assert pursuant to the Civil Rights Act. Yet Justice Stevens also noted in the decision that the same law does allow employers the legal right to at times treat older workers differently. It is important to note that pursuant to the Civil Rights Act, employers can successfully defend a disparate impact case only by showing the "business necessity" for a neutral but harmful employment policy, which is, it seems, a much more difficult test to meet than the "reasonable" explanation standard of the ADEA. In the Supreme Court Smith case, the defendant, City of Jackson, successfully articulated a reasonable factor other than age underlying its pay plan, namely reliance on seniority and rank. The city's decision to award larger raises to lower-level employees to bring salaries in line with that of neighboring police forces was found to be a decision based on "reasonable factors other than age" and motivated by the city's legitimate objective of attracting and retaining police officers. Moreover, under the reasonable-factors-other-than-age standard, it was not necessary, the Court ruled, for the city to consider whether the method it adopted was the most reasonable method of achieving its goals.

It is important to remember that a disparate impact case is materially different from a disparate treatment case. In a disparate impact case, the plaintiff need not prove an intentional act of discrimination by the employer in order to recover. In essence, the plaintiff will first have to show that there is a statistical disparity, and that younger and older employees are affected differently by the policy or practice. Then he or she will have to demonstrate that the challenged practice was based on age. In a disparate impact case, moreover, the plaintiff cannot establish his or her initial case by pointing to a general policy of the employer that produced the disparate impact. Rather, the plaintiff must isolate and identify the employer's specific age-motivated policies or practices that are allegedly responsible for any perceived disparities, and then link them to the disparity. That is, a close nexus, or connection, must be established between the specific practice and any observed statistical significance to prove illegal discrimination.

In 2009 the U.S. Supreme Court made it even more difficult for a claimant to prove age discrimination. The Court in Gross v. FBL Financial Services (2009) ruled that age must be the key factor in the employment determination, as opposed to being a reason for the improper decision. The Court used the common law "but for" test as the legal standard in a modern day age discrimination context; that is, the employee must show by a preponderance of the evidence that "but for" the illegal age discrimination the negative employment determination would not have occurred (Legislation, 2009). One commentator (Fleischer, 2009) noted that "this is a higher standard than that imposed on other victims of discrimination who must show that discrimination was a 'motivating or substantial factor' in the decision." Therefore, even if the motivating factor is correlated with age, for example, in making pension plan or health care plan changes or engaging in a reduction-in-force to eliminate high salaries or reduce health care costs, the employer can still avoid liability under the ADEA if the discriminatory age motivation was not the key factor in the decision. The result, according to Fleischer, is that "since many older workers are paid more, they are let go because of their salaries. Proving age was the 'but for' reason for termination will be impossible because the employer will be able to point to the salary savings as the real motive." This Court ruling thus provides further support for the employer because the federal courts have ruled that age and years of service or rank can be deemed to be "analytically distinct," and, consequently, the employer can take cognizance of one while ignoring or downplaying the other. In such a case, the employee must identify the specific aspects of the plan that caused the disparate impact. Similarly, even though an employee's deteriorating level of competence may be related to his or her advancing age, the poor performance factor can be deemed reasonable and legitimate. Of course, the employer in such situations should be able to distinguish these motivating factors and to demonstrate that the motivating factor, such as rank or years of service, or a legitimate concern with perceived too-high salaries, or poor performance, was in fact the non-age-connected motivating factor and thus a "reasonable" one.

G. Employer Defenses—Generally

The ADEA affords the employer certain statutory defenses to age discrimination lawsuits. An employer is allowed to take an action otherwise prohibited to comply with the terms of a legitimate employee benefit plan or a bona fide seniority system (though generally a seniority system cannot require the involuntary retirement of employees). An employer is also permitted to justify a disciplinary decision or a discharge on grounds of "good cause." Furthermore, similar to Title VII of the Civil Rights Act, an employer is allowed to discriminate on the basis of age where age is a bona fide occupational qualification reasonably necessary to the normal operation of the particular business. Finally, and most significantly, the ADEA provides a defense to an age discrimination lawsuit when the employer can demonstrate that the differentiation is based on "reasonable factors other than age." Of course, defining a bona fide occupational qualification as well as a reasonable factor other than age can be difficult, and, therefore, are often determined by the federal courts on a case-by-case basis. The EEOC itself cautions that no precise and unequivocal determinations can be made as to the scope of these defensive provisions. Finally, it should be noted that there is some debate in the legal community as to whether the "reasonable factors other than age" provision in the ADEA is a safe-harbor totally precluding employer liability if applicable, or merely an affirmative defense provided to employers and, significantly, one that must be affirmatively asserted or lost. To be safe, the employer is well advised to treat the "reasonable factor" defense as an affirmative one. The ADEA also contains defenses for bona fide seniority plans and employee benefit plans.

H. The Bona Fide Occupational Qualification Exception (BFOQ)

The employer can also defend an ADEA lawsuit by interposing the bona fide occupational qualification doctrine (BFOQ). Pursuant to this doctrine, the employer will be obligated to show that the challenged age criteria is reasonably related to the normal operation of the employer's business, and that there is a factual basis for believing that only employees of a certain age would be able to do the particular job safely or effectively. That is, the employer must demonstrate that all or substantially all persons excluded from the job in question are in fact not qualified due to age. Age certainly can be a relevant factor in certain jobs and rise to the level of a bona fide exception, such as in professional sports (Savage, 2008). A job notice or advertisement which specifies or limits age is illegal pursuant to the ADEA; however, the employer may do so when age is demonstrated to be a valid qualification reasonably necessary to the normal operations of the business. Examples of this would include airline pilots, police, firefighters, and bus drivers, as well as others for whom certain physical requirements are a necessity for efficient job performance. It must be underscored that with the BFOQ defense, the employer admits that age was a factor in the decision to fire or to not hire, and the employer has a legally justifiable excuse for the need to rely on age. This defense is limited however. To prevail, the employer must demonstrate that it had reasonable factual cause to believe that all or substantially all of the older persons would be unable to perform the duties of the job in a safe and efficient manner. If the employer's rationale in invoking the BFOQ is public safety, the EEOC will require that the employer demonstrate that the challenged age restriction does in fact effectuate that public policy goal and that no reasonable alternative exists that would better or equally advance the goal with a less discriminatory effect.

Courts, moreover, have construed the BFOQ defense narrowly in all civil rights cases, though the mandatory retirement of airline pilots has been upheld. The EEOC itself counsels that the exception will have only limited scope and application.

I. The Reasonable Factor Other Than Age (RFOA) Defense

This ADEA provision allows the employer to defend an age discrimination claim by demonstrating that "reasonable factors other than age" prompted the employment policy or practice in question. That is, the employer can argue that age did not motivate the decision to fire or to not fire, but that another nondiscriminatory reason, such as poor job performance, was the true reason behind its action. When this defense is raised against an individual claiming discriminatory treatment, the burden is on the employer to demonstrate that the "reasonable factors other than age" actually exist. This test emerges as a much more efficacious defense than the "business necessity" test under the Civil Rights Act. In the latter, the employer must ascertain whether there are alternative ways to achieve its objectives without resulting in an adverse impact on a protected class; whereas in the former, the "reasonableness" inquiry does not encompass such a search for alternatives. So long as the "factor" is not improperly age-connected, is reasonable, and advances the employer's goals, such as financial considerations, it will be sufficient as a defense. The employer under the ADEA does not have to search for a less discriminatory alternative or even the "most reasonable" approach; rather "merely" a "reasonable" one will suffice for a defense. Furthermore, "reasonableness" does not require the employer's decision to be absolutely necessary, or wise, or even well-considered merely reasonable and nondiscriminatory. The employer is even allowed to have "mixed motives"; that is, once the employer presents evidence of the "reasonable factors other than age," the policy or practice will be validated legally even if age played a part in the promulgation of the policy or the implementation of the practice. However, in discharge situations, especially in a reduction-in-force, employers must be careful of the criteria used to retain and terminate workers. Reasons and ratings based on specific skills and knowledge will be easier to sustain as objective and fair, but subjective criteria such as "flexibility" and "creativity" could be problematical. "Loose" standards could be construed by a jury as a pretext for age discrimination (Savage, 2008).

Management Strategies and Recommendations

Due to the aging of the workforce, civil rights laws, particularly the ADEA, must be increasingly concerned with encouraging the greater employment of older workers. AARP (American

Association of Retired Persons) concludes that "policymakers may want to think about how the ADEA might be modified to provide more protection against age discrimination in hiring" (Neumark, 2008). An "older worker," according to the laws in the U.S., is a worker 40 years of age or older. Unfortunately, many firms have shown patterns of discrimination against "older workers" in the U.S., especially when it comes to hiring.

The U.S. Age Discrimination in Employment Act presents leaders and managers with many challenges. Although the U.S. Supreme Court has ruled that the disparate impact theory now extends to age discrimination lawsuits, employers must realize that the theory is much narrower under the ADEA than pursuant to Title VII of the Civil Rights Act. The narrowness of the disparate impact theory in the age context means that the statute's coverage—and the employer's potential liability therein—is much more limited in age discrimination employment cases. In particular, the "reasonable factor other than age" provision in the law means that certain employment criteria and practices that are legitimate and routinely used by employers could well be legal despite their adverse impact on older employees as a group. This test, moreover, further narrows the application of the ADEA. For other civil rights lawsuits, the employer must explore alternative ways to achieve its objectives without resulting in an adverse impact on a protected class. Yet due to the reasonable-factor doctrine, the employer is not obligated to search for alternatives.

To sustain a defense when confronted with an ADEA disparate impact age discrimination lawsuit, an employer must produce credible and relevant evidence that the challenged policy or practice was based on reasonable factors other than age. Moreover, this factor, or factors, if reasonable and not age-related and consistent with the employer's goals, need not be absolutely necessary. The ADENs reasonable-factor test is not the "business necessity" test of Title VII of the Civil Rights Act. Furthermore, the employer does not have to search for the "most reasonable" approach. All that is required is a "reasonable" rationale for the action and evidence that the employer relied on this non-age-related reasonable factor. Accordingly, only "unreasonableness" will engender employer liability. Relying in some circumstances on rank, seniority, or years of service when making decisions may be reasonable regardless of their relationship to age. Actually, there are many factors—age-related but arguably sufficiently distinct—that an employer could cite as reasonable ones, such as the following: recruiting concerns, such as attracting or keeping technically knowledgeable and capable employees; reputation concerns, such as honoring commitments to hire recent graduates or to recruit and hire at particular schools; budgeting concerns, such as reducing payroll costs by eliminating higher-salary positions or off-shoring and outsourcing; performance concerns, such as making

decisions based on performance or review ratings, evaluations, or needed skills; and dealing with the ramifications of mergers and other fundamental change and restructuring, such as workforce reductions, lay-offs, reductions-in-force, and downsizing. What the employer cannot do is to use these rationales as a subterfuge to pull off the wholesale elimination of older workers. Such a ploy would make the factor age-related and unreasonable and consequently illegal. Yet once the separation from age is achieved and reasonableness is determined, the employer prevails. The Supreme Court in Smith v. City of Jackson recognized that necessary and legitimate job requirements and classifications may exist that have a greater adverse impact on older employees than younger ones. Such a "reasonableness" standard emerges as an employer friendly one.

Statistical analysis can be employed as a tool to avoid age discrimination lawsuits, especially disparate impact claims based on age. Birk (2008) provided detailed guidance and recommendations on the use of statistical analysis to avoid disparate impact lawsuits based on age in the context of a reduction-in-force. When contemplating laying off workers due to business reasons, an employer must be aware of the potential for disparate impact claims based on age by employees who are over 40. It is possible that companies may be targeting older employees in certain lay-offs since older workers are generally the highest paid and have the most expensive benefits (Levitz and Shishkin, 2009). Birk, accordingly, urges employers to use statistical analysis, not after litigation has begun, but before the lay-offs, to ascertain the risk of age discrimination claims. Says Birk: "If the employer's statistical self-analysis uncovers disparities between the proposed impact of the RIF (reduction-in-force) on protected older workers versus that of younger workers, the company is able to proactively make changes in its RIF decision to avoid such an impact" (Birk, 2008). As discussed extensively in the disparate impact section, to establish an initial disparate impact case, the plaintiff employee must demonstrate an employment policy or practice that has a disparate, that is, negative or adverse, impact on employees protected by the ADEA compared with younger workers.

A statistical analysis will test the statistical significance of any disparity in the lay-off or termination of younger versus older workers. Then, "If the observed number of terminations is statistically significant from what would have been expected randomly, statistical evidence of disparate impact discrimination may be established" (Birk, 2008). A critical question to be answered is what is a "statistically significant finding?" According to Birk, in such a disparate impact age case,

Experts will generally require either a statistical significance measure of 1% to 5% to show a correlation with age. These numbers, while not hard-and-fast, have generally been accepted by courts in disparate impact cases. When dealing with large samples, many courts have found that if the difference between the expected value and the observed number is greater than two or three standard deviations, most experts would find the results not likely to have been random. Theoretically, the higher the number of standard deviations associated with a particular result, the less likely that a random and nonbiased selection process would have generated the result in the absence of discrimination (Birk, 2008).

It is recommended that the statistical analysis be conducted by experts, because even though the comparison of younger and older workers appears simple, "the calculations and factors to be considered are complex" and also "the failure to do a proper analysis will negate the value of the analysis as a legal challenge" (Birk, 2008). She also recommends using regression analysis. Regression analysis is "a method of statistical analysis in which the relationship between two or more variables is examined to determine if there is an association between the variables" (Birk, 2008). The objective of such an analysis is to ascertain "… the possibility of disparate impact based on age in a RIF situation [by] determining if there was a correlation between the employees being laid off and their age" (Birk, 2008). Such an analysis, notes, Birk, "does not determine if employees were actually laid off because of their age, but rather whether it is likely that such a result would have happened by chance" (Birk, 2008). The underlying data will be the key to analyzing the reduction-in-force and its consequences. As such, data for each employee to be laid-off or potentially laid-off must be carefully collected, collated, and analyzed. Concomitantly, the criteria for choosing the employees to be laid-off must be clearly ascertained. To develop these criteria, the employer must have a clear understanding of the business and economic rationales for the lay-offs, for example, restructuring or reorganizing, centralizing or outsourcing functions or services, upgrading services thereby requiring a more educated and skilled workforce, or closing certain plants or locations completely. The proper grouping of employees emerges as another important element to the analysis, for example, comparing blue-collar employees to be laid-off to the blue-collar labor pool, and similarly comparing white-collar workers. Geographic boundaries as well as time periods for the lay-off must also be considered. After grouping the employees in an appropriate manner, they must be evaluated on objective, age-neutral, criteria to determine which will be subject to the reduction-in-force. Assuming that age-neutral criteria were used but the lay-offs still produced a disparate impact based on age then, as discussed extensively in the legal analysis, the employer must be prepared to show to a court that "reasonable factors other than age" were carefully, objectively, and fairly used to effectuate the reductions. Such use of statistical analysis, counsels Birk, is "a proactive and valuable preventative step to limit an employer's risk of age-related litigation as a result of that RIF" and thus a "wise decision economically" and "an important human resource management tool" (Birk, 2008).

Summary

This article examined the laws of age discrimination in the United States and provided a detailed explication of the U.S. Age Discrimination in Employment Act (ADEA) and other age-related laws. The article also discussed the nature and role of the Equal Employment Opportunity Commission in implementing and enforcing age discrimination law. The purposes of the ADEA were to promote the employment of older persons predicated on their capabilities and not their age, to prohibit arbitrary age discrimination in employment, as well as to assist employers and employees to solve problems stemming from the impact of age on employment. This article focused on the plaintiff's challenging legal burden in the U.S. for establishing a successful case of age discrimination against his or her employer. Moreover, if the employee is suing under a disparate impact theory, he or she must realize that the employer defendant need only produce evidence of "reasonable factors other than age" to justify, and thereby to sustain legally, its employment policy or practice. U.S. multinational business firms, as well as foreign firms operating in the U.S., must be aware of U.S. civil rights law. Beyond that, these firms also must be aware of the far-reaching extraterritorial rule that a U.S. company employing U.S. citizens anywhere in the world generally will be subject to a civil rights lawsuit if these employees are discriminated against based on the protected categories.

One theme to this work is that prudent and wise employers and managers are well-advised to be cognizant of the ADEA as well as other important civil rights anti-discrimination statutes. This article sought to provide to leaders and managers with practical strategies, tactics, and recommendations to comply with age discrimination laws, to maintain fair employment practices, and to handle an actual age-based discrimination lawsuit. The authors hope that the information and insights will be helpful to managers and employers who seek to attain a legal and ethical, fair and equitable, efficient and effective, and value-maximizing workplace.

References

Age Discrimination in Employment Act (2005). Sections 621–634. Thompson/West Publishing Company.

Age Discrimination in Employment Act of 1967, Public Law 90–202, 29 United States Code, Sections 621–634, http://www.eeoc.gov/policy/adea.html.

Age Discrimination in Employment Act, Help Wanted Notices or Advertisements (2008). 29 Code of Federal Regulations, Section 1625.4. Thomson/West Publishing Company.

Age Discrimination in Employment Act, Employment Applications (2008). 29 Code of Federal Regulations, Section 1625.5. Thomson/West Publishing Company.

Birk, M. (2008, April). RIFs: Use statistical analysis to avoid disparate impact based on age. Legal Report, Society for Human Resource Management, pp. 5–8.

Cavico, E J. and Mujtaba, B. G. (2006). Age Discrimination in Employment: Cross Cultural Comparison and Management Strategies. BookSurge Publishing (An Amazon.com Company, USA).

Cavico, E J. and Mujtaba, B. G. (2008). Legal Challenges for the Global Manager and Entrepreneur. Dubuque, Iowa: Kendall Hunt Publishing Company.

Civil Rights Act of 1991 (2005). 105 U.S. Statutes, Sections 1071, 2000. Thomson/West Publishing Company.

Clark, K. (2003). Judgment day. Money and Business. U.S.News. com. Retrieved on January 13, 2003 from http://www.usnews .com/usnews/biztech/articles/030113/13performancehtm.

Corbin, P. R. and Duvail, J. E. (2008). Eleventh Circuit Survey: January 1, 2007—December 31, 2007: Article: Employment discrimination. Mercer Law Review, Volume 59, pp. 1137f.

Corbin, P. R. and Duvail, J. E. (2007). Employment discrimination. Mercer Law Review, Volume 58, pp. 1187f.

EEOC v. Arabian American Oil Company, 499 U.S. 244 (1991).

EEOC Compliance Manual (1993, October 20). EEOC Enforcement Guidance on Application of Title VII to Conduct Overseas and to Foreign Employers Discriminating in the U.S., Notice 915.002, p. 2169.

EEOC (2011). Equal Employment Opportunity Commission— Statistics. Retrieved October 27, 2011 from: http://www1.eeoc .gov//eeoc/statistics/enforcement.

Equal Employment Opportunity Commission (2008). Age Discrimination. Retrieved May 28, 2008 from http://www.eeoc .gov/types/age.html.

Equal Employment Opportunity Commission (2008). Employee Rights When Working for Multinational Employers. Retrieved May 28, 2008 from http://www.eeoc.gove/facts/multi-employers.html.

Equal Employment Opportunity Commission (2008). Employers and Other Entities Covered by EEO Laws. Retrieved May 28, 2008 from http://www.eeoc.gov/abouteeo/overview_coverage.html.

Equal Employment Opportunity Commission (2009, March 11). EEOC Reports Job Bias Charges Hit Record High of Over 95,000 in Fiscal Year 2008. EEOC Press Release. Retrieved March 20, 2009 from http://www.eeoc.gov/press.

Equal Employment Opportunity Commission (2008). The Equal Employment Opportunity Responsibilities of Multinational Employers. Retrieved May 28, 2008 from http://www.eeoc.gov/ facts/multi-employers.html.

Fleischer, R. A. (2009, July 13). Another bad right turn by the Supreme Court. The Miami Herald, p. 7G.

Griggs v. Duke Power (1971). 401 U.S. 424.

HR Guide to the Internet: Disparate Treatment. Retrieved on July 5, 2009 from: http://www.hr-guide.com/data/G701.htm.

Isbell v. Allstate Insurance Company, 418 F.3d 788 (7th Circuit 1995), certiorari denied, 126 S.Ct. 1590 (2006).

Labriola, D. J. (2009). But I'm Denny Crane!: Age discrimination in the legal profession after Sidley. Albany Law Review, Volume 72, pp. 367–386.

Laluk, S. S. and Stiller, S. P. (2008). 2006–2007 Survey of New York Law: Employment Law. Syracuse Law Review, Volume 58, pp. 955f.

Legislation (2009, June 19). High court makes age discrimination harder to prove. The Miami Herald, p. 3C.

Levitz, J. and Shishkin, P. (2009, March 11). More workers cite age bias after layoffs. The Wall Street Journal, pp. D1, D2.

Mahajan, R. (2007, May). The naked truth: Appearance discrimination, employment, and the law. Asian American Law Journal, 14(10), 165–213.

Mahoney v. RFE/RL, Inc., 47 E3rd 447 (D.C. Cir. 1995).

McDonnel Douglas Corp. v. Green (1973). 411 U.S. 792.

Meacham v. Knolls Atomic Power Laboratory (2008). 128 Supreme Court 2395.

Morelli v. Cedel, 141 F.3d 39, 42–43 (2nd Cir. 1998).

Mujtaba, B. G. (2010). Workforce Diversity Management: Challenges, Competencies and Strategies (2nd edition). ILEAD Academy; Davie, Florida.

Mujtaba, B. G., and Cavico, F. J. (2010). The Aging Workforce: Challenges and Opportunities for Human Resource Professionals. ILEAD Academy: Davie, Florida.

Mujtaba, B. G., Cavico, F., Edwards, R. M., and Oskal, C. (2006, January). Age discrimination in the workplace: Cultural paradigms associated with age in Afghanistan, Jamaica, Turkey, and the United States. Journal of Applied Management and Entrepreneurship, 11(1), 17–36.

Mujtaba, B. G. and Rhodes, J. (2006). The aging workface: Best practices in recruiting and retaining older workers at publix. The 2006 Pfeiffer Annual: Human Resource Management (Edited by Robert C. Preziosi), pp. 87–95. ISBN: 0-7879-7824-8.

Neumark, D. (2008). Reassessing the age discrimination in employment act. Research Report #2008-09. AARP Public Policy Institute, Washington, D.C.

O'Connor v. Consolidated Coin Caterers Corp, 116 U.S. 1307 (1996).

Older Workers Benefit Protection Act (2008). Public Law 101–433. Retrieved May 28, 2008 from http://www.eeoc.gov/policy/adea .html.

Pounds, M. H. (2009, April 30). Job discrimination claims have risen dramatically in South Florida. The Sun-Sentinel, pp. 1D, 2D.

Pounds, M. H. (2009, March 12). Keep right attitude, be 'ageless' to thrive in today's workplace. The Sun-Sentinel, pp. 1D, 2D.

Quirk, B. (2008, May 7). Don't let 'em call you an old fart. Madison Capital Times, p. 42.

Quirk, J. (1993). A Brief Overview of the Age Discrimination in Employment Act A (ADEA). Reviewed June 1999. Available online at http://my.shrm.org/whitepapers/ documents agediscrimination.

Savage, D. G. (2008, June 20). Court backs strong age bias protection. The Houston Chronicle, p. 6.

Sherman, M. (2008, February 18). Court to Rule on Age Bias. The Miami Herald. p. 3A.

Sherman, M. (2008, February 18). Justices to Hear Plenty on Age Bias. Madison Capital Times, p. A 4.

Sherman, M. (2008, February 18). Supreme Court mulls five age discrimination cases. Tulsa World, p. A 24.

Smith v. City of Jackson, Mississippi, 125 S. Ct. 1536, 544 U.S. 228 (2005).

The ADA: Your Responsibilities as an Employer (2003). Equal Employment Opportunity Commission. Retrieved on June 23, 2005 from http://www.eeoc.gov/facts/adal7/html

Yeatts, D.E., Folts, W., and Knapp, J. (2000). Older Workers' Adaptation to a Changing Workplace: Employment Issues for the 21st Century. Retrieved October 1, 2003 from Biomedical Reference Collection: Comprehensive.

Yost, P. (2008, February 27). Peers' Testimony to Age Bias Eyed. The Miami Herald, p. 3A.

Critical Thinking

1. Why might more problems with age discrimination lawsuits be expected in the United States?

2. What do you think managers can do to assure they are aware of biases against older workers?

3. How would you feel if you were an older worker in the face of ageism in your workplace?

Internet References

A Focus on Age Discrimination in the Workplace

www.nytimes.com/2013/07/25/opinion/a-focus-on-age-discrimination-in-the-workplace.html?_r=0

Age Discrimination in the Workplace

www.aarp.org/work/employee-rights/info-06-2012/age-discrimination-ma1788.html

Nine Signs of Age Discrimination

http://jobs.aol.com/articles/2011/05/17/top-signs-of-age-discrimination

DR. CAVICO, Professor of Business Law and Ethics, has received two citations for excellence in teaching. Recent law review publications address trade secret law, the law of intentional interference with contract, and a comparative legal and ethical analysis of whistleblowing in the private sector, among other subjects. **DR. MUJTABA**, Professor of Human Resources Management, also twice-named Faculty Member of the year, has researched human resource issues and worked with professionals in many countries around the world, providing insights in ethics, culture, and management.

Cavico, Frank J.; Mujtaba, Bahaudin G. From *SAM Advanced Management Journal*, vol. 26, no. 4, Autumn 2011, pp. 15–26. Copyright © 2011 by Society for Advancement of Management. Reprinted by permission.

Article   Prepared by: Maria Nathan, *Lynchburg College*

Generational Differences in the Workplace: Personal Values, Behaviors, and Popular Beliefs

JANE WHITNEY GIBSON, REGINA A. GREENWOOD, AND EDWARD F. MURPHY, JR.

Learning Outcomes

After reading this article, you will be able to:

- Differentiate different generations in the workplace. Understand why generational differences are important for HRM professionals to consider.

- Offer ideas for possible HR programs that are able to address generational difference in the workplace.

Introduction

Much attention has been given in recent years to the intergenerational conflict in the workplace caused by diversity in values related to age. While different beginning and ending dates are attributed to the Baby Boomer, Generation X, and Generation Y cohorts, the popular and academic literature agree on a core group of values found among these workers. These values in turn lead to speculation about what these workers want occupationally and how to motivate them to be both committed and productive organizational members.

Baby Boomers, for example, are thought to be competitive and loyal workaholics who value individual freedom and dedication to task. Generation X, on the other hand, crave more of a balance between work and family, are more cynical, informal, fun-loving and independent. Generation Y is characterized as socially sensitive, optimistic, ambitious, curious, technologically adept, and easily bored. This paper will build a profile of generational values based on both popular and academic articles.

The current study then looks at these popularly accepted beliefs about generational values and compares them to results

of a study using the Rokeach Value Survey. Do the personal values of the three generations as reported by members of those cohorts reflect the popular concepts? Specifically, the top ten instrumental and terminal values as reported by the survey respondents are analyzed in terms of their "fit" with the previously mentioned model. If there is a degree of congruence, what would it mean for managers who lead these three generations on a daily basis? The paper will conclude with a discussion of implications for managers. We begin by suggesting a central research question and then by proposing the generational profiles based on the literature.

The Research Question

This study examines the commonly accepted profile of characteristics of Generation X, Y, and Baby Boomers and uses the Rokeach Value Survey for an empirical study of values among representatives of each generation in the U.S. The research question is: Will an empirical study of values support descriptions of the generations found in the literature?

Generational Profiles

Generational research dates back to Mannheim (1953) who defined generations as a group of people born and raised in the same general chronological, social and historical context. A discussion of generational differences often looks at values held by each age cohort. Morris Massey (2005) raised awareness of how these differences play out in the workplace through a series of popular films beginning with "What You Are is Where You Were When" which implied that one's values depended on where you were during the value formation years

(0–20 years) and what you experienced during that time. While there is considerable disagreement as to beginning and closing years for each generation, the following dates are reflected in the current study. The Baby Boomer generation is defined as 1946–1964 as suggested by Strauss and Howe (1997) and Egri and Ralston (2004). The same sources used 1965–1979 as the years for Generation X, and so do we. Finally, this study uses the dates 1980 to present for Generation Y as per Eisner (2005) and Murphy et al. (2006).

The Baby Boomers

The Baby Boomer generation, approximately 85 million strong, is the largest cohort currently in the workplace (Trunk, 2007) and the one with the most power by virtue of their high numbers in leadership positions. Baby Boomers are reputed to be loyal and competitive workaholics (Crampton & Hodge, 2007) whose serious and dedicated attitude toward work has been influenced by the Vietnam War and the economic prosperity following World War II (Patota, Schwartz & Schwartz, 2007). This same prosperity may account for their reputed self-absorption (Weil, 2008) and a feeling of entitlement (Lyons, 2005). This indulgence was expressed by many young Baby Boomers who grew up in the 1960s by the mantra of sex, drugs, and rock and roll (Brandt, 2008). Boomers experienced much social change in their early years and therefore embrace change and growth (Crampton & Hodge, 2007). In addition, Massey (1979) says the Boomers value success, teamwork, inclusion and rule-challenging. Likewise, they have proven their determination to fight for a cause. (National Oceanographic . . .)

Generation X

Many Generation X adults grew up in dual worker families which gave rise to the new term, "latch-key kids." Thus, they are self-reliant, fun-loving, and independent (Lyons, 2005). They are also less loyal than the Boomers having witnessed high numbers of divorces and corporate downsizing. (Crampton & Hodge, 2007). Unable as a generation to enjoy the career success of their predecessors, the Generation X'ers are more concerned with career options, balance of work and non-work lives, and express cynicism toward Corporate America (Crampton & Hodge, 2007). At work, they are computer literate and want a fun environment (Patota, Schwartz & Schwartz, 2007) but they are far more mobile than the Baby Boomers, moving from job to job to improve their careers (Johnson & Lopes, 2008).

Generation X'ers experienced economic uncertainties, the beginning of the AIDS epidemic and the end of the Cold War, as well as corporate and government scandals, all feeding into their distrust of authority. (Johnson & Lopes, 2008). Instead, they rely on personal entrepreneurial effort, independence and creativity (National Oceanographic...). At work, they demand fulfilling work (Merrill, 2008) but may be seen by their Baby Boomer bosses as "slackers" who lack loyalty (Rottier, 2001).

Generation Y

Generation Y saw the insecurities of the Cold War replaced by Columbine, 9/11, and celebrity scandals. They were raised with MTV, cell phones, IPods, and computer games and are totally at home with instant communication and social networking. This digital generation is optimistic, realistic, globally aware, and inclusive by nature (McNamara, 2005). Less indulged than the X generation, the Millennials accept diversity and different types of families (Alch, 2008); they are civic-minded and prone to volunteerism (Leyden, Teixeira & Greenberg, 2007). Like the generation before them, they value work/family balance and independence (Yeaton, 2008) but they are also curious, questioning (Kehril & Sapp, 2006) and results-oriented (Streeter, 2007).

In the workplace, Millennials can try the patience of their Baby Boomer bosses and their Gen X colleagues. Their entrepreneurial, answer-seeking behaviors coupled with their sense of personal responsibility and need for feedback (Martin, 2005) can be diminished by their dissatisfaction with entry-level jobs and their tendency to change jobs frequently (Wallace, 2001). Millennials want a say in how they do their work; they are collaborative (Alch, 2008) and work well within the modern empowered workplace as long as there are enough challenges and opportunities to keep them interested (Martin, 2005).

Table 1 shows a list of descriptors that may be drawn of each generation from the academic and popular articles consulted above.

Method

The Rokeach Value Survey (RVS) has been used since 1968 to study instrumental and terminal values of individuals in a variety of national, international, multinational, and professional settings. Terminal values according to Rokeach measure "the ultimate end goals of existence, such as wisdom, equality peace, or family security," while instrumental values measure "the behavioral means for achieving such end-goals, for instance, the importance of being honest, ambitious, forgiving, or logical" (Rokeach & Ball-Rokeach, 1989, p. 776).

The RVS requires respondents to rank order both instrumental and terminal values in terms of their relative importance to the respondents. Between 2003 and 2008 working adults were surveyed using the RVS. From that initiative, 5,057 surveys were found to be usable for this study and analyzed. Of these,

Table 1. Generational Descriptors

Baby Boomers	Generation X	Generation Y
Sandwich generation	Latch-key kids	Netters
Company loyalty	Lack of loyalty	"Contract" mentality
Idealistic	Reactive	Civic-minded
Self-absorbed	Self-reliant	Self-centered
Workaholic	Work/life balance	Multi-taskers
Tech conservatives	Computer savvy	Tech experts
Entitled	Cynical/skeptical	Easily bored
Traditional family	Divorced family	Many family forms
Wary of authority	Independent	Crave feedback
Competitive	Entrepreneurial	Serial Entrepreneurs
Materialistic	Fun-loving	Volunteers
Training	Life-long learning	Distance learning
Comfortable with change	Creative	Crave challenge
Optimistic	Want fulfilling work	High maintenance
Security oriented	Career options	Collaborative

1,464 were classified as Baby Boomers, 1,440 belonged to Generation Y and 2,153 were Millennials.

Findings

Table 2 shows the ranking of terminal values by generation and Table 3 shows the instrumental values by generation as developed by this study. Note that the top 10 are in bold for easy reference. Our examination will focus on these top 10 values, since they were designated the most important values by our respondents

An examination of Table 2 shows a good deal of congruence between the generational value profiles described above and in Table 1 and the value profiles of Table 2. "Health" and "family security" ranked # 1 and 2 for all three generations. It is logical that "health" edged out "family security" for the older generation who may face more health issues and fewer family responsibilities than the younger generations. It is notable that "freedom" (independence and free choice) ranked as relatively more important to the Generation X and Generation Y respondents just as their popular profiles would suggest. Likewise, the high ranking of "true friendship" (close companionship) by Gen Y supports the networking, socially conscious profile of the Millennials. Also, Gen Y, with its high need for "accomplishment" (making a lasting contribution) supports their craving for challenge and civic-mindedness. Additionally, just as we would expect, Gen X's value for "pleasure" (an enjoyable,

leisurely life) was higher than the other generations. One of the most notable value differences is Generation X's relatively high value on "inner harmony" (freedom from inner conflict) as compared especially to the Gen Y respondents who ranked "inner harmony" near the bottom of the list. Managers could conclude from this that while Gen X will struggle to avoid such conflict, Gen Y will be little affected by it.

Table 3 shows similar congruence between the value profile described above and the results of our survey. Interestingly, "honest" and "responsible" were the # 1 and #2 means-to-an-end described by each of the three cohorts. There are, however, some interesting points of comparison. Gen Y ranked "independence" higher than the Baby Boomers and much higher than Gen X who is known for their self-reliance. This may be a result of the fact that Gen X, by virtue of their upbringing, has been independent from an early age while Gen Y aspires to this degree of self-sufficiency. Likewise, Gen Y respondents put a higher priority on "ambition" than the other two groups. It may be argued that the Baby Boomers translate "ambition" as hard-working while Gen Y defines this same instrumental value as aspiring which would support each of their profiles. Interestingly, the Baby Boomer respondents ranked "broad-minded" (open mindedness) very low while the same value was in the top eight for the other generations. This could give evidence to the reputed self-absorption of the Baby Boomers. On the other hand, only the Baby Boomers ranked "forgiving" as a top 10 value. This may well tie in with their company

Table 2. Ranking of Terminal Values by Generation

Terminal Value Ranking	Baby Boomer	Generation X	Generation Y
# 1 (most important)	Health	Family security	Family security
# 2	Family security	Health	Health
#3	Self-respect	Freedom	Freedom
#4	A comfortable life	A comfortable life	True friendship
#5	Freedom	Inner harmony	Self-respect
#6	Wisdom	Self-respect	A comfortable life
#7	True friendship	True friendship	A sense of accomplishment
#8	Salvation	Wisdom	Wisdom
#9	Inner harmony	Mature love	Mature love
#10	A sense of accomplishment	Pleasure	Salvation
#11	Mature love	A sense of accomplishment	An exciting life
#12	An exciting life	Salvation	Equality
#13	Pleasure	An exciting life	Pleasure
#14	A word at peace	Equality	National security
#15	National security	A world at peace	A world at peace
#16	Equality	National security	Inner harmony
#17	A word of beauty	Social recognition	Social recognition
#18	Social recognition	A world of beauty	A world of beauty

Table 3. Ranking of Instrumental Values by Generation

Terminal Value Ranking	Baby Boomer 1946–1964	Generation X 1965–1979	Generation Y 1980–present
# 1 (most important)	Honest	Honest	Honest
# 2	Responsible	Responsible	Responsible
#3	Loyal	Capable	Loving
#4	Capable	Loyal	Independent
#5	Independent	Loving	Ambitious
#6	Loving	Courageous	Loyal
#7	Ambitious	Logical	Broadminded
#8	Logical	Broadminded	Capable
#9	Forgiving	Independent	Self-controlled
#10	Self-controlled	Helpful	Intellectual
#11	Intellectual	Ambitious	Helpful
#12	Courageous	Intellectual	Logical
#13	Helpful	Self-controlled	Courageous
#14	Polite	Forgiving	Clean
#15	Broadminded	Polite	Forgiving
#16	Clean	Clean	Polite
#17	Imaginative	Imaginative	Obedient
#18	Obedient	Obedient	Imaginative

loyalty in the face of downsizing and corporate scandal. Likewise the fact that Gen X did not rank "self-controlled" (restrained and self-disciplined) among their top 10 values seems to reinforce their priority for having fun. More telling is the relatively low ranking of "loyalty" for Gen Y who is known for job-hopping and quick boredom if career opportunities are not immediately apparent. The one big surprise in Table 3 is the fact that the Baby Boomers and Gen X ranked "capable" (competent, effective) as a considerably higher value than Gen Y who are reputed to be results-oriented. The fact that Gen X ranked "capable" higher than the other two cohorts may be a result of their self-reliance and independence rather than any goal-orientation.

Implications for Managers

Among the many challenges facing managers today is effectively dealing with a diverse workforce. Such diversity is not limited to gender, religious, ethnic, and racial backgrounds but also relates to the various generational values found in the workplace today. This study has confirmed that there are gross differences among the Baby Boomers, Generation X and Generation Y, but the reader should be cautioned against overgeneralizing or stereotyping any given individual by virtue of his/her membership in a particular generational cohort. It should be helpful, however, to be more sensitive to these gross generational differences in order to bridge what is commonly called the generation gap. Just as cultural sensitivity to other diverse factors is important to effective management, so too is an appreciation for the differences that exist among your workers because of their age-related value systems.

The Baby Boomer generation is found in senior and high-level positions throughout the private and public sectors. This huge cohort of individuals is characterized by hard work, resistance to authority, and a feeling of having earned the right to be in charge. Managers can likely motivate them with money and overtime, recognize them with praise and position, and expect them to be loyal. Unlike the generation before them, they embrace change and will champion a good cause. As these Baby Boomers retire from the workforce, they will be replaced by Gen X.

Generation X, however, reflects the independence and self-reliance they earned as children and tend to be suspicious and cynical. They value family-work balance more than the other two generations and are not particularly loyal to their employer because they don't expect their employer to be loyal to them. Managers should try to make work meaningful and fun for this cohort and understand their skepticism for what it is: a reflection of their honest observations about the relationship between employer and employee.

Generation Y are the children of the Boomers and, as such, elicit the same incongruity of values that one expects between parents and children. The Millennials personify all the tech savvy, social networking, and constant connectedness that drives Boomers crazy and they bring to the workplace their need for instant gratification. Managers should try to make work exciting and relevant for this group, being careful to show them verifiable career opportunities if they exist. Where Boomers will do their job and like to be left alone, Gen Y wants attention and feedback.

Conclusion

The authors began with a research question asking if an empirical study of values would support descriptions of the Baby Boomer, Gen X, and Gen Y characteristics found in the literature. Responses from over 5,000 working adults using the Rokeach Value Survey confirmed that the generational profiles shown in both public and academic literature are accurate and therefore useful to managers in understanding and bridging the generation gap caused by these differences. An anecdote from one author's recent past might serve as an example.

When the author was presenting a paper on fun as an effective workplace strategy at a conference several years ago (Jeff coat & Gibson, 2006), two men presumably in their mid to late 1950s argued vociferously that work "should not be fun." These Baby Boomers were just as serious in their outlook as the Gen X attendees who jumped to the author's defense and a heated argument ensued. The lesson for management is to expect these arguments and realize that not everyone will agree on the look and feel of the workplace. The challenge is to provide enough motivational stimulation and communicate in various modalities in order to reach all your employees and not just the ones who agree in principle with your values and beliefs.

References

Alch, M. L. (June 2008). Get ready for a new type of worker in the workplace: the net generation. *Supervision* 69(6), 18–21.

Brandt, J. R. (June 2008). Talkin' bout my generation. Retrieved July 22, 2009 from http://www.industryweek.com.

Crampton, S. M. and Hodge, J. W. (2007). Generations in the workplace: Understanding age diversity. *The Business Review, Cambridge*, 9(1), pp 16–23.

Egri, C. and Ralston, D. (2004). Generation cohorts and personal values: A comparison of China and the US, *Organization Science*, 15, pp. 210–220.

Eisner, S. P. (Autumn, 2005). Managing generation Y. *SAM Advanced Management Journal*, 70(4), 4 (4 pages)

Jeff coat, K. and Gibson, J. W. (February, 2006). Fun as Serious Business: Creating a Fun Work Environment as an Effective Business Strategy, Journal *of Business and Economic Research*, 4, (2).

Johnson, J. A. and Lopes, J. (2008). The intergenerational workforce revisited, *Organizational Development Journal*, 26, (1), pp. 31 – 37.

Kehrli, S. and Sopp, T. (2006). Managing generation Y. *HRMagazine*, 51(5), pp. 113 (4 pages)

Leyden, P., Teixeira, R. and Greenberg, E. (2007). The progressive politics of the millennial generation. *New Politics Institute*. Retrieved May 8, 2008 from http://www.newpolitics.net/node/360?full_report=1

Lyons, S. (November 2005). Are gender differences in basic human values a generational phenomenon? *Sex Roles: A Journal of Research*. Retrieved May 13, 2008 from http://wwwfindarticles.com/p/articles/mi_m2294/is_9-10_53/ai_n16084047/print

Mannheim, K. (1953). Essays on sociology and social psychology. New York: Oxford University Press: NY

Martin, C. A. (2005). From high maintenance to high productivity: What managers need to know about Generation Y. *Industrial and Commercial Training*, 37(1), 39–44.

Massey, M. (1979). *The People Puzzle*. Brady, NY.

Massey, M. (2005). *What you are is where you were when—again!* Enterprise Media, Cambridge, MA.

McNamara, S. A. (June, 2005). Incorporating generational diversity. *AORN Journal*. Retrieved May 20, 2008 from http://findarticles.com/p/articles/mi_mOFSL/is_6_81/ai_n15394405

Merrill, D. (May 2008). Boomers pass the workplace torch. *The Lane Report, 23(5)* p. 34+.

Murphy, E. F. Jr., Greenwood, R., Ruiz-Gutierrez, J., Manyak, T. G., Mujtaba, B. and Uy, A. (August, 2006). Generational value changes: Their history and a cross-cultural empirical test, Paper presented at the Academy of Management Meeting, Atlanta, Georgia.

National Oceanographic and Atmospheric Association of Diversity. Tips to improve interaction among the generations: Traditionalists, Boomers, X'ers and Nexters. Retrieved May 20, 3008 from http://www.honolulu.hawaii.edu/intranet/committees/FacDevCom/guidebk/teachtip/interencom

Patota, N., Schwartz, D. and Schwartz, T. (2007). Leveraging generational differences for productivity gains. *Journal of American Academy of Business, Cambridge*, 11(2), pp. 1–11.

Rokeach, M. and Ball-Rokeach, S. J. (May, 1989) Stability and change in American value priorities. *American Psychologist*, 44(5), pp. 775–784.

Rottier, A. (October 2001). Generation 2001: Loyalty and values – Generation X and work. *Workforce*. Retrieved July 29, 2008 from http://findarticles.com/p/articles/mi_mOFXS/is_10_80/ai_7935245?tag=rbxcra.2.a.3

Strauss, W. and Howe, N. (1997). *The Fourth Turning: What the Cycles of History Tell Us Abut America's Next Rendezvous with Destiny*. New York: Broadway Books.

Streeter, B. (December 2007). Welcome to the new workplace. *ABA Banking Journal*, 99(2), 7, 6 pages.

Trunk, P. (2007). What Generation Y really wants. *Time*. Retrieved May 20, 2008 from http://www.time.com/time/magazine/article/0,9171,1640395,00.html

Wallace, J. (April, 2001). After X comes Y—echo boom generation enters workforce. *HRMagazine*. Retrieved July 29, 2008 from http://findarticles.com/p/articles/mi_m3495/is_46_ai_73848314

Weil, N. (2008). Welcome to the generation wars: As Boomer bosses relinquish the reins of leadership to Generation X both are worrying about Generation Y. For the good of the enterprise, everyone needs to do a better job of getting along. *CIO*, 21(8).

Yeaton, K. (April 2008). Recruiting and managing the 'why?' generation: Gen Y. *The CPA Journal*, 78(4) 68, 5 pages.

Critical Thinking

1. What are distinct characteristics of baby boomers, generation X, and generation Y employees?

2. How should managers use this understanding in their leadership, motivation of, and communication with employees?

3. How does a manager reach out to employees when there are critical differences in values and beliefs between manager and employee?

Internet References

AACSB Vision: Aging Workforce Demographics, AACSB International
   http://www.aacsb.edu/vision/themes/future-roles-of-management-in-society/aging-workforce-demographics

Demographic Change and the Future Workforce, Department of Labor
   https://www.dol.gov/dol/aboutdol/history/herman/reports/futurework/conference/trends/trendsI.htm

The Aging U.S. Workforce, Stanford Center on Longevity
   http://longevity3.stanford.edu/wp-content/uploads/2014/01/The_Aging_U.S.-Workforce.pdf

The State of Diversity in Today's Workforce, Center for American Progress
   https://www.americanprogress.org/issues/labor/report/2012/07/12/11938/the-state-of-diversity-in-todays-workforce/

JANE WHITNEY GIBSON, Professor of Management for Nova Southeastern University teaches management, leadership, human resource management, and organizational behavior at the graduate and undergraduate levels in both traditional and online formats. Gibson is the Editor of *The Journal of Applied Management and Entrepreneurship* and an editorial board member of several management journals. She is active in the Academy of Management, the SAM Advanced Management Society and the Southern Management Association and has written books and articles in her areas of academic interest.

EDWARD F. MURPHY, JR., Adjunct Professor of Business and Management for Embry Riddle Aeronautical University teaches Bachelor's Degree and Master of Business Administration courses throughout California. He is a retired United States Air Force officer and serves as an education and strategic planning consultant. Dr. Murphy's research interests are in strategic planning, organizational and societal culture, socialization, cross-cultural similarities and differences, sex roles, gender roles, values, aviation human factors, and situational leadership.

REGINA A. GREENWOOD, Professor of Business and Management at Nova Southeastern University teaches management, business strategy, and management history courses at the graduate and undergraduate levels. Dr. Greenwood is also the co-Historian and co-Archivist for the Academy of Management. She has published numerous research papers in her areas of interest: management history, strategy, cross-cultural factors, and lean management.

Whitney Gibson, Jane; Greenwood, Regina A.; Murphy, Jr., Edward F. "Generational Differences In The Workplace: Personal Values, Behaviors, And Popular Beliefs," *Journal of Diversity Management (JDM)*, [S.l.], v. 4, n. 3, p. 1–8, 2009. Copyright © 2009 by Clute Institute. Used with permision via CC (BY) 3.0.

Article   Prepared by: Maria Nathan, *Lynchburg College*

Eye of the Beholder: Does Culture Shape Perceptions of Workplace Bullying?

STUART D. SIDLE

Learning Outcomes

After reading this article, you will be able to:

- Know what workplace bullying is.
- Consider what the experience of the bulllied employee might be.
- Know that bullying perceptions may vary by national culture.

Would someone considered to be a belligerent bully by workers in one division of a global company be viewed the same way by employees in other geographic locations of the same company? Perhaps part of the answer to this question in today's global economy is that it depends on the national culture of the employees in particular locations. And since executives are increasingly managing diverse, global teams it is more important than ever to understand the cross-cultural differences that may impact workplace dynamics.

Although recent cross-cultural studies have produced findings that help leaders manage in this complex environment, much remains to be done. For instance, while the negative consequences of workplace bullying on employees have been clearly documented, most of this research has been conducted in Western cultures. Virtually no studies have examined workplace bullying across Eastern cultures—raising the question of whether research based in Western cultures will generalize to other parts of the globe.

New research by Jennifer Loh (University of New England, Australia), Simon Lloyd D. Restubog (University of South Wales), and Thomas J. Zagenczyk (Clemson University) sheds light on whether exposure to bullying has the same impact on workers across cultures. Specifically, Loh and her colleagues compared Australian and Singaporean employees to see if there were differences between these cultures in how workplace bullies impacted victims' attitudes toward their jobs and relationships with their co-workers.

Incidentally, this research is timely in light of the introduction of the Singapore-Australia Free Trade Agreement (SAFTA) in 2003. Not only has this agreement created increased trade opportunities between these nations, but it has also sparked a greater need for cross-cultural understanding between business leaders in both countries.

Loh and her colleagues also thought that these two cultures would be useful to compare given their clear differences around the acceptance of formal, hierarchical power differences (what cross-cultural research pioneer Geert Hofstede calls "power distance"). High power distance cultures such as Germany, China, and Singapore tend to accept status differences between bosses and subordinates as the norm. For example, employees in these cultures tend to be reluctant to question the demands of an authority figure. Conversely, low power distance cultures such as the United States, the Netherlands, and Australia tend to expect more egalitarian relationships between supervisors and subordinates. For example, workers in these cultures are more likely to be on a first-name basis with supervisors and are more likely to question the supervisory authority, especially when they believe they are being treated unfairly.

Consequently, Loh and her colleagues expected that employees in Singapore, a high power distance culture, would be more tolerant of bullying supervisors than employees in Australia, a low power distance culture. Their data came from a mail survey of over 300 Australian and Singaporean employees (a survey with an impressive 58% response rate). All respondents were post-graduate business students in their respective countries. The survey questionnaire assessed employees' experiences with workplace bullying, their level of job satisfaction, and feelings toward their co-workers (e.g., whether they feel like a member of the group or an outsider).

Overall, Loh and her colleagues found that regardless of culture, workplace bullying lowered employees' feelings of job satisfaction. In essence, bullying may signal to employees that they are not appreciated, respected, or valued. And in turn, workers do not want to be committed to a team or to a manager who bullies them. To make matters worse, individuals who are bullied tend to be perceived by their fellow workers as either outsiders or lower status individuals— reactions that further isolate bullying victims. Consequently, bullied employees feel that they lack meaningful relationships in the workplace and their morale suffers. In fact, Loh and her colleagues found that, regardless of culture, employees who experienced the wrath of a workplace bully felt alienated from their co-workers.

While both Australian and Singaporean employees were similar in terms of experiencing a negative reaction to workplace bullying, Loh and her colleagues also found compelling differences across the two cultures. Essentially, Australian employees rated their job satisfaction much lower than their Singaporean counterparts when bullying was involved. Moreover, Australian employees reported more intense feelings of alienation from their co-workers following bullying incidents than did Singaporean employees.

In a nutshell, this study suggests that while bullying may be a universally unpleasant experience for employees, the degree of distress it causes seems to be influenced by national culture. Loh and her colleagues explain that the differences in the intensity of the consequences probably relates to the differences in each culture's level of power distance. Essentially those in higher power distance cultures have a higher tolerance for this type of behavior because they may see some expressions of power especially from supervisors as standard behavior (e.g., delivering corrective feedback in public in a stern manner). In contrast, employees in low power distance cultures may tend to perceive these same behaviors as extraordinarily harsh. Loh and her colleagues suggested that another reason for the difference in the impact of bullies across cultures stems

from the fact that job satisfaction and work-group identification are outcomes that tend to be more strongly embraced by employees with a Western or individualistic orientation. Conversely, Singaporeans and employees in other Eastern cultures are more likely to have a collectivistic attitude toward work and are more focused on organizational and team outcomes rather than on their individual experiences and personal treatment by supervisors.

Indeed, this study serves as a reminder to leaders in global organizations of the importance of viewing their workforce through a cross-cultural lens to create an environment where all employees around the world feel satisfied and committed to the firm. That said, Loh and her colleagues believe more research on bullying is needed, both across cultures and in multicultural work settings. After all, managers and employees alike are increasingly spending time collaborating in diverse, global work environments—where key differences in values, perceptions, and belief systems nonetheless exist.

Critical Thinking

1. Why might perceptions of bullying vary depending upon global geographic location?

2. What do you think are the effects of workplace bullying?

3. What would you do if you were bullied? What would you do if you felt an inclination to bully another?

Internet References

Harassment
www.eeoc.gov/laws/types/harassment.cfm

What's Behind a Rise in Workplace Bullying?
www.usatoday.com/story/news/health/2013/10/08/hostile-workplace-less-productive/2945833

Workplace Bullying
www.huffingtonpost.com/tag/workplace-bullying

Workplace-Bullying Laws on the Horizon?
www.shrm.org/hrdisciplines/safetysecurity/articles/Pages/Workplace-Bullying-Laws.aspx

Article   Prepared by: Maria Nathan, *Lynchburg College*

Investigating Sexual Harassment Complaints: An Update for Managers and Employers

RICHARD TROTTER AND SUSAN RAWSON ZACUR

Learning Outcomes

After reading this article, you will be able to:

- Know what sexual harassment is according to the Civil Rights Act of 1964.

- Grasp what the employer's responsibility is in the event of a complaint of sexual harassment.

- Understand what procedural issues might cause a court or jury to find an employer liable for failing to conduct a proper investigation.

Employers ignore sexual harassment complaints at their peril. They must navigate amid a number of federal statutes that define and affect their responsibility to maintain a harassment-free workplace. Employers must have an effective and well-publicized anti-harassment policy, they must investigate any claims, and they should administer appropriate discipline, as warranted. This article focuses on the crucial investigation stage. It provides detailed guidance on procedures, conduct, and the final written report to help protect employees from such behavior and from false charges, as well as protect employers from suits alleging liability regarding such claims.

Investigating sexual harassment complaints is a critical aspect of any employer's efforts to create a workplace that is free from discrimination under Title VII of the Civil Rights Act of 1964. The Equal Employment Opportunity Commission (EEOC) defines sexual harassment as unwelcome sexual advances, requests for sexual favors, and other verbal or physical conduct of a sexual nature when submission to such conduct

is a term or condition of employment, is used as the basis for an employment decisions, unreasonably interferes with an individual's work performance, or, even without submission, the conduct creates an intimidating, hostile, or offensive working environment (EEOC, 2009).

An employer's responsibility in the area of sexual harassment includes an understanding of relevant law, a well-developed and publicized sexual harassment policy, training for employees and managers to help them understand and carry out the policy, and a procedurally and substantively proper investigation procedure. Appropriate discipline or remedy must follow a finding of harassment. Employers must be aware that having a sexual harassment policy is not enough to protect them against liability if they fail to properly investigate employee complaints.

This paper focuses on procedural issues that can cause a court or jury to find an employer liable for failing to conduct a proper investigation. It provides updated legal background based on Title VII, the Electronic Communications Privacy Act of 1986, and the Fair and Accurate Credit Transactions Act of 2003. It also provides insights from legal, academic, and practitioner literatures, relevant source materials, information on the role of electronic media, and best practices for initial intake managers and investigators.

Sexual harassment complaints are a critical aspect of work life for all employers. They consume valuable resources, create morale and productivity issues and may result in negative publicity. More than 11,700 sexual harassment complaints were filed with the EEOC in fiscal year 2010. In that same year, the resolution of 12,700 cases resulted in more than $48 million in recovered benefits for charging parties and other aggrieved individuals, exclusive of any monetary benefits obtained through litigation (EEOC, 2010). A review of EEOC press releases for the past two years reveals details of sexual harassment settlements with such well-known businesses as Lowe's Home Improvement Warehouse, Cheesecake Factory, McDonald's, Dunkin' Donuts, IHOP, Lenscrafters, and Dollar General, among others (EEOC, 2011). The consent decrees in these cases often call for enhanced sexual harassment policies and training for employees, managers, and investigators.

Guidance for employers in developing policies and training programs is available from the EEOC and human resource literature. Policy guidance is provided on the EEOC Web site (EEOC, 1999). Policy formation and training are addressed by others as well (Trotter and Zacur, 2004; Levy and Paludi, 2001; Orlov and Roumell, 1999). Training guidance is updated in an extensive review of practitioner and research literature by Perry, Kulik, and Field (2009). Assuming an employer has a clear sexual harassment policy and that appropriate training has taken place, this paper focuses on the next phase: the investigation of sexual harassment complaints.

We begin by updating the legal background, then review best practices for investigations including procedural design issues, conducting the investigation, and possible outcomes. Title VII lawsuits have been distinguished by the courts as having either disparate impact on, or disparate treatment of, protected classes or groups. Disparate impact cases are "generally statistically-based group cases alleging that … facially neutral employer policies have a disparate or adverse impact on a protected Title VII group" (Bennett-Alexander and Hartman, 2009). Disparate treatment cases involve intentional discrimination on the part of the employer against member(s) of a protected Title VII group (based on race, religion, gender, color, or national origin) (Ibid.). Case law pertaining to sexual harassment investigations applies to disparate treatment cases as opposed to disparate impact cases. These cases are highlighted in the sections that follow dealing first with United States Supreme Court cases and then with lower court rulings.

Supreme Court Rulings on Sexual Harassment

In recent years the courts, practitioners, and scholars have recognized the growing importance of workplace investigations in protecting employee rights and as a means of insulating employers from litigation if the investigations are properly conducted (Morgan, Owens, and Gomes, 2002). The most recent U.S. Supreme Court decision related to sexual harassment investigations was Crawford v. Nashville (2009), where a witness in a sexual harassment investigation was later fired. Crawford, a long-term employee of the Metropolitan

Government of Nashville, was fired, along with all other witnesses, after reporting the sexually-based behavior of a newly hired employee relations director. Crawford had been reluctant to report the behavior earlier for fear of reprisal and had done so only after the assistant director of human resources had interviewed her as part of the investigation. Crawford sued her employer under Title VII of the Civil Rights Act of 1964 which protects employees who oppose unlawful employment actions. The Supreme Court decision stated that section 704 (a) of Title VII makes it unlawful for an employer to discriminate against an employee who has made a charge, testified, assisted, or participated in any manner in an investigation, proceeding, or hearing related to this aspect of the law. Therefore, the Court held that Title II's anti-retaliation provision's protection extends to an employee who speaks out on discrimination in answering questions during an employer's internal investigation.

Other U.S. Supreme Court decisions have confirmed the need for employers to conduct a "reasonable" investigation if a complaint arises. In the following two cases, harassed employees sued their employers. In Burlington Industries v. Ellerth (1998), the threats of a manager who had been rebuffed were found to be sufficient to hold the employer responsible under Title VII (Orlov and Roumell, 1999). In Faragher v. City of Boca Raton (1998), the employer was found to be responsible for unreported sexually-harassing conduct of its supervisory staff (Orlov and Roumell, 1999). Both were determined to be hostile-environment sexual harassment cases since no adverse employment action (e.g., firing, failure to promote, significant change in responsibilities or benefits) resulted for the complaining employee in either situation. Still, in both it was reaffirmed that employers may be held liable for not establishing, disseminating, and consistently enforcing a policy that prohibits sexual harassment. It was also made clear that employers must exercise reasonable care to prevent and promptly correct any sexually harassing behavior by its supervisors or managers.

The Supreme Court's holdings in the Ellerth and Faragher cases have also provided employers with an affirmative defense when a supervisor's harassing behavior does not cause any tangible employment action, such as termination, but does create a hostile environment. These rulings allow an employer to avoid liability by showing that reasonable care was taken to prevent the harassment, prompt action was taken to correct the harassment after it occurred, and the victim failed to take advantage of corrective opportunities provided by the employer. This defense is not permitted where there is tangible unfavorable job action by a supervisor (Bennett-Alexander and Hartman, 2009). If tangible damages resulted from supervisor harassment, the employer may be held strictly liable (regardless of lack of knowledge or absence of negligence). Employer liability has been found by the courts in four instances: (1) supervisor harassment of an employee (with tangible employment action), (2) supervisor harassment of an employee (with no tangible employment action), (3) harassment by co-worker(s), and (4) harassment by a third-party (client, customer, or service person associated with the employer's business).

The following cases clarify and strengthen the legal basis of sexual harassment and are briefly cited here to provide a more complete background for the reader. The first Supreme Court case to deal with sexual harassment was Meritor Savings Bank, FSB v. Vinson (1986) in which the harassed employee sued her employer. In this case, a female employee claimed that due to fear of job loss, she accepted the sexual advances of her supervisor. The court found that harassing a subordinate because of the subordinate's sex is a form of discrimination on the basis of sex and is a violation of Title VII (Orlov and Roumell, 1999). The opinion of the Court further stated that claims of sexual harassment do not have to be based on quid pro quo "tangible" or "economic" losses in the workplace, such as discharge or demotion, and that subjecting an employee to a "hostile or abusive work environment" because of that person's sex would be sufficient to alter the person's terms or conditions of employment and be considered sexual harassment under Title VII (Bland, 2000). The Court found that the employer had no notice of the supervisor's activity but this did not prevent liability and that the employer's grievance policy was generic rather than a specific sexual harassment policy that would encourage employees to seek help.

The second case to deal with sexual harassment was Harris v. Forklift Systems, Inc. (1993) in which the harassed employee sued her employer. In that case, the company president made a female employee the target of sexual jokes, insults, and other sexually based overtures. The Supreme Court found that the workplace environment was such that a "reasonable person" would find it to be sexually hostile or abusive and that it was not necessary for the employee to suffer psychological or other injury. This case was significant for its further clarification of what was meant by hostile environment. Sexually harassing behavior by co-workers toward an employee of the same sex was also found to be covered by Title VII in Oncale v. Sundowner Offshore Services, Inc. (1998).

In 1999, the Equal Employment Opportunity Commission issued revised enforcement guidelines (EEOC, 1999) emphasizing the importance of prompt, thorough, and impartial investigations conducted by well-trained investigators. Given the Supreme Court's rulings and the EEOC's revised guidelines, clearly employers must conduct rigorous, proper, and effective investigations when allegations of impropriety first arise regardless of whether there was alleged harassment by a supervisor (resulting in either tangible or no tangible employment action), a co-worker, or a third-party (customer, client, or service person). Indeed the failure to investigate may be regarded as strong evidence that the employer condones, albeit implicitly, of the offending behavior.

Lower Court Rulings Pertaining to Sexual Harassment Investigations

One of the landmark cases on the elements of reasonable investigation is Silva v. Lucky Stores, Inc. (1998), in which the alleged harasser unsuccessfully challenged his dismissal. In that case the California appellate court found that an employee fired for having engaged in sexual harassment could not prevail if there had been an appropriate investigation leading to a substantiated finding that harassment had occurred. The following facts were cited in the court opinion to substantiate an appropriate investigation: Lucky had a written policy specifying how sexual harassment allegations were to be investigated, the policy was to treat complaints seriously, investigate immediately, treat the matter confidentially, conduct interviews in a private area, listen to allegations, make complete notes, attempt to identify all persons involved, interview the accused employee and all witnesses, record notes on a witness interview form and/or obtain a written statement from each witness, and have a neutral third party do the investigation (in this case, a trained human resources representative). The accused was notified of the charges promptly, given an opportunity to present his version of the events, and allowed to clarify, correct, or challenge information provided by witnesses. The investigator asked relevant, open-ended questions and attempted to elicit facts rather than opinions or suppositions. He encouraged those he spoke with to let him know if they wanted to talk again. He gave critical witnesses an opportunity to clarify, correct, or challenge information provided by other witnesses that was contrary to their statements. After the investigator interviewed all the other witnesses, the accused was given another opportunity to comment on the information that had been gathered.

Holly D. v. California Institute of Technology (2003) provides an example of case law where an employer was shielded from damages due to a reasonable investigation. In this case, the plaintiff (complaining employee) brought a hostile-environment claim against the employer alleging that she had been harassed. After investigation, the employer found insufficient evidence of sexual harassment. Later, the plaintiff sued the employer, providing evidence that she did not present during the employer's investigation. The employer prevailed against a claim for damages by the plaintiff because the employer's investigation into the harassment was found to be reasonable.

Baldwin v. Blue Cross Blue Shield of Alabama (2007) is another example in which an employee appealed an unfavorable decision in a hostile-environment case. The Eleventh Court of Appeals found in favor of the employer because it considered the employer's investigation of the complainant's allegation of harassment reasonable under the circumstances. That court noted that under both Faragher and Ellerth there is no requirement for courts to micromanage the internal investigations of employers. It should be noted, however, that courts may have varying interpretations of the degree of rigor required of employers in the investigation of sexual harassment charges.

Two cases in which the investigations were flawed and the employers were, therefore, subject to liability are Beldo v. University of Massachusetts (1998) and Fuller v. City of Oakland (1995). In Beldo, an investigation that involved one interview between the investigating supervisor and the alleged perpetrator who was a friend and no other interviews, not even with the complainant, was held to be inadequate. In Fuller, the investigator failed to interview the accused promptly, did not corroborate the allegations (when it would have been easy to do so), failed to interview an important witness for the complainant, and failed to give sufficient weight to evidence in the complainant's favor.

In addition, there are two wrongful discharge cases that dealt with situations where the accused harasser successfully prevailed against the employer because of defects in the investigation process. In Kestenbaum v. Pennzoil (1988), the New Mexico Supreme Court affirmed a judgment in excess of $1 million in a wrongful discharge case brought by the alleged harasser because the investigator relied on rumors and failed to assess credibility. In Sassaman v. Gamache (2009), the person accused of being the harasser successfully sued his employer claiming gender discrimination because the employer stated during the investigation that the alleged harasser probably did what he was accused of doing because he was a male. The appellate court found that the statement was evidence of (male) gender discrimination against the plaintiff, who was the alleged harasser in the case. This underscores the importance of proper employer conduct and awareness of the fact that suit against the employer can be brought by the alleged harasser as well as the person alleging harassment. In contrast, in Scherer v. Rockwell International (1992) an effective investigation resulted in a favorable ruling for the employer who was being sued by the alleged harasser.

Managers must recognize that courts review the employer's investigative process in cases where the investigations lead the employer to conclude that the harassment was sufficiently severe to result in the discharge of the accused employee. The rights of the accuser must be balanced with those of the accused. From these cases, some guidance for effective investigation procedures can be determined. The employer's sexual harassment policy must contain clear references to the investigation procedure, including steps to be followed, who should do the investigation, assurance of every effort to ensure confidentiality, fair treatment of all parties, documentation of findings, and an opportunity for the accused to review the findings and comment. It has been found that observers' perceptions of the fairness of the employer's investigation influence whether the employee chooses to seek assistance outside the organization (Elkins, Phillips, and Ward, 2008).

Guidance for Conducting Sexual Harassment Investigations

Due Process

In evaluating the degree to which an investigative procedure can insulate an employer from a subsequent lawsuit for "negligent investigation," some fundamental due process principles must be observed. Bernice R. Sandier, an expert witness in sexual harassment cases, provides a comprehensive online resource for sexual harassment investigations (Sandier, 2011). She begins with a review of the basic due process rights that include the following: Informing the alleged harasser of the concerns raised and allowing an opportunity to respond before any disciplinary action is taken; fair and equal treatment, so that if one party is allowed to bring an attorney, the other is allowed to do the same; prompt investigation beginning within a few days with quick completion; confidentiality assured to the extent possible; and assigning an investigator who is free of any conflict of interest in the matter. Each of these aspects should be covered in an effective investigation process.

Complaint Procedure

Guidance for a legally sound complaint procedure is provided by the EEOC in its Enforcement Guidance document (EEOC, 1999b). According to that document, the employer should have a sexual harassment policy and complaint procedure that can be easily understood by the workforce. It is distributed to each employee, contained in the employee handbook, posted in central locations, and supported by training of all employees, if feasible. The following elements should be in the procedure: A clear explanation of the prohibited conduct; assurance of no retaliation for bringing a complaint; a clear complaint process that tells how to bring a complaint with a choice of at least two different employer representatives, including a male and female if possible (Bland and Stalcup, 2001); assurance of confidentiality to the extent possible; assurance of a prompt, thorough, and impartial investigation; timelines for filing charges; and assurance that the employer will take appropriate action when it determines that harassment has occurred. Kass, Kleinman,

Pesta, and Samson (2004) suggest that the policy also include specific examples of behavior that would be interpreted as sexual harassment and list the consequences of being accused of violating the policy. They recommend that the employer require employees to sign a statement acknowledging that they have read and understood the policy.

The Intake Manager

In many organizations, regardless of size, the first intake person (the one who initiates any next steps) may not be an official part of the investigation team but may simply be the first one to learn of the sexual harassment complaint. These individuals should be trained to refer to the policy and to help the employee contact the correct person. Suppose, however, that an employee is clearly upset and that the contact person is not immediately available. In this case, managers and supervisors should be trained to act as the initial intake person, understanding that their behavior may well set the tone for how the employee perceives all of the company's actions to follow (Orlov and Roumell, 1999). Orlov and Roumell (1999) provide detailed guidance on how to proceed. The manager should display a great deal of sensitivity for the employee while bearing the responsibility to represent the employer's legal interest. The initial intake manager should meet with the complainant in a private office or meeting room, be fully attentive without allowing interruptions from outside sources, try to get the facts, remain impartial, not render any opinion or make expressions of sympathy, make clear that the company's sexual harassment prevention policy will be followed (at this point, review the actual policy with the employee), and give assurance that the complaint will remain confidential to the fullest extent possible, that no retaliation will be permitted, and that the employee will be kept informed of the progress of the investigation. The initial intake manager should record everything that happens in this meeting, including the date and time, and review these notes with the employee to be sure that they are accurate. It would also be advisable to have the employee sign the notes indicating their accuracy. These notes should be provided to the investigator who will pursue the complaint.

The Investigator

The designated investigator should be neutral and experienced. The employer should avoid assigning anyone with less authority than the accused to do the investigation. If a high-ranking employee is implicated, it is best to consult an attorney or bring in an outside investigator, or both. However, the employer's attorney should not necessarily conduct the investigation since this person would most likely be defending the employer should a discrimination case later go to court. If there is litigation either by the person claiming harassment or by the accused

(should that person be discharged), it is likely the employer will use this investigation as part of its defense.

The employer will have to decide whether to use an in-house investigator or someone from the outside. Each has benefits. It is generally less expensive and speedier to use someone from the inside. However, there may be no inside person with the requisite skill and neutrality to do an effective investigation. While outside investigators are more expensive, they usually appear to be more neutral and have greater experience. If the employee making the complaint is known to be litigious, if the allegations are against someone with significant authority, or if for other reasons the employer believes litigation is likely, it is a good idea to go with an outside investigator (Dorfman, Cobb, and Cox, 2000).

An issue that caused some consternation for employers with regard to outside investigators was addressed by the Fair and Accurate Credit Transactions Act of 2003 (FACT). FACT reversed a previous statutory provision that required employers to obtain the consent of the accused in order to retain a neutral, experienced, outside, third-party to investigate a sexual harassment complaint. That law amended the Fair Credit Reporting Act of 1970 as amended by The Consumer Reporting Reform Act of 1996. This is critical because an opinion under the 1996 amendment, known as the Vail letter, had stated that the FCRA applied to workplace harassment investigations conducted by third parties (Fliegel and Arena, 2004). Gardner and Lewis (2000) thoroughly reviewed the implications of this 1996 opinion for sexual harassment investigations, which stated that employers would have to "obtain consent of the accused in order to have a neutral, experienced third party investigate a sexual harassment complaint" and would have to provide a copy of the investigative report to the accused (Ibid.). This would cause delays in investigations, reduce confidentiality, and could have a chilling effect on those who might have key information about the case (Ibid.). Fliegel and Arena (2004) discuss FACT and its application to current investigations, providing helpful guidance to employers so that they will maintain "safe harbor" protection under the 2003 law. Their recommendations include the following: employers conducting in-house investigations into employee misconduct will not be subject to FCRA; if third-party investigators are used, employers should restrict disclosure of the investigation report and its contents in accordance with FCRA and consider adopting a policy of providing only a summary of the report to the victim to comply with EEOC guidance.

Whether designated from within or outside the employing organization, the investigator should have the following characteristics: knowledge and training in issues dealing with sexual harassment including an understanding of relevant legal issues and familiarity with the institution's sexual harassment policies; credibility with the institutional community and the ability to be neutral, maintain confidentiality, and represent the institution in a fair manner; ability to make tough decisions regarding the truthfulness and credibility of the parties and witnesses; ability to be fair and refrain from drawing conclusions until the investigation is finished. The investigator should be sympathetic in a neutral way as well as nonjudgmental and not defensive. Complete written records of all information, interviews, and determinations should be kept. The investigator may need to take immediate action when necessary, such as removing offensive materials from the workplace or graffiti from a wall or obtaining protection for someone who is being stalked, and, therefore, should be in a position to do so (Sandier).

Is an Investigation Necessary?

Once the complaint has been made to the appropriate investigator, it is important to begin work as soon as possible—but after a brief time for reflection. Sandier suggests that an employer should take a short time to make some determinations before beginning an investigation. She suggests that the employer assess whether the complaint is amenable to informal resolution and whether the complainant wants to attempt this. The employer should also assess whether the complaint is so serious (for example sexual abuse or assault, attempted assault, possibility of physical danger) that the organization must intervene even if a formal complaint is lacking. The employer should assess whether the complaint fits the timelines in the company's policy and whether the complaint, in fact, presents a sexual harassment issue. Finally, if the compliant is anonymous, the employer will need to determine what action to take (Sandier).

Interviewing Guidelines

A legally valid investigation should include an interview of the complainant, the alleged harasser, and corroborating witnesses plus any individuals who saw the complainant upset or spoke to him or her about the incident. These contemporaneous or indirect witnesses can affect a complainant's credibility, especially if the witness is not a close friend or family member but rather a co-worker (Oppenheimer, 2004). In each interview, the investigator should be and appear as nonjudgmental and neutral as possible; ask open-ended questions, and not suggest answers to questions. For specific questions, refer to the list provided by the EEOC (1999b). Further guidance for the investigator includes: asking follow-up questions to get as much detail as possible; suppressing emotional response to any answer; assuring all interviewees that confidentiality will be protected as much as possible; documenting the person's answers and making sure he or she reads your notes and signs them as accurate; and keeping your own separate notes about appearance, demeanor, accuracy of memory, and overall credibility (Orlov

and Roumell). Keep all notes in an "investigation file" separate from employee files (Bland and Stalcup, 2001).

Interviewing the Complainant

Before interviewing the complainant, Sculnick (1983) advises the investigator to verify whether the employee is represented by a union whose collective bargaining agreement contains an EEO nondiscrimination clause. If so, the investigator should inform the complainant that union assistance is available. If the complainant does not desire this assistance, then the employer "may resolve the complaint so long as the result is consistent with the collective bargaining agreement" (Ibid.). It may also be helpful to review the personnel files of the complainant and the accused for background facts and documentation of any similar problems in the past.

The investigator should begin the interview with a review of the employer's sexual harassment policy, emphasizing confidentiality insofar as possible and that retaliation will not be permitted. The investigator should then get specific facts: who was involved and exactly what happened; find out whether there was a pattern of previous episodes of similar behavior toward the employee; get the specific context in which the conduct occurred (where? what time?); and ask for evidence in the form of any documents such as journals, calendar entries, notes, or electronic communications to support her or his claim. For readers seeking more detailed guidance, Abell and Jackson (1996) provide an extensive list of questions for such interviews.

Evidence today may often involve electronic media: E-mail, text messages, tweets, and the computer screens of co-workers may all be evidence of either direct harassment or a hostile environment. Major employers have terminated employees for forwarding sexually explicit e-mails to co-workers; for accessing x-rated sites and downloading pornographic videos and pictures; for distributing pornographic images via e-mail; and for sending jokes, photos, and sexually explicit videos to co-workers (Towns and Johnson, 2003). When a supervisor is misusing e-mail or the Internet for sexual images, the courts have come down more harshly on employers (Ibid.). Soewita and Kleiner (2000) report that a major corporation agreed to a $2.2 million settlement in a suit brought by four of its employees after attorneys found evidence of sexual harassment on the firm's own e-mail server. The complainant may provide copies of messages received or tell of images seen on the computer screens at work, in which case the employer may need to investigate further. Deleted images and transmissions can be readily retrieved by technology specialists. In technology investigations, the employer should be aware of the Electronic Communications Privacy Act of 1986 (ECPA), which prohibits interception and disclosure of wire, oral, or electronic communications and the unauthorized accessing of stored electronic images. The ECPA does not prohibit employers from reviewing communications after they have been received by intended recipients, however (Ibid.).

The investigator should next ask for names of those who were told about the incident or concern by the complainant and those who may have observed the victim's reaction or changes in behavior by either party (Sandier). It is important to explore whether the complainant may have any motive to dissemble or exaggerate. The investigator should give the complainant an opportunity to describe the consequences and harm resulting from the alleged harassment and to suggest a desired result of the investigation (Ibid.).

Interviewing the Alleged harasser

When dealing with the alleged harasser, every effort must be made to ensure a fair proceeding. The allegations may later prove to be unfounded and the employer could risk legal action by this individual if the investigation is improperly handled (Pappas, 2009). Those accused of inappropriate behavior have been known to sue their employers for emotional distress, defamation, and wrongful discharge (Morgan et. al., 2002). In this regard, Bland and Stalcup (2001) advise that the internal investigation and discipline documents should not label offenders as "harassers" but rather as persons who have engaged in inappropriate workplace behavior. No immediate action should be taken against the accused before the facts are known. If deemed necessary, the accused can be sent home with pay while the investigation begins.

In the interview, the investigator should (1) inform the alleged harasser of the complaint of sexual harassment and that a full and complete investigation will be conducted in compliance with the employer's policy, including appropriate statements about confidentiality and no retaliation; (2) provide the specific allegations including dates, places, and names of complainants; and (3) assure that there will be an opportunity to respond to the allegations. The investigator should seek specific and detailed responses to questions, ask if others have knowledge of the events in question or could corroborate all or some of the alleged harasser's statements, and explore fully any statements or suggestions by the alleged harasser that the complainant participated in the alleged conduct. The interviewer should note any admissions to having engaged in any inappropriate behavior or misconduct. The alleged harasser should be informed that further interviews may be necessary to gather more facts or respond to statements by the complainants. The investigator should advise the alleged harasser that she or he is encouraged to return any time with additional information, new facts, or a response in writing (Sandier).

The Investigation Report

The written report should include the following:

1. Interviewing data. Complainant's name, respondent's name, type of complaint, date filled, name of office that received the complaint, and names of investigators.
2. Background information. The history of the relationship between the parties and other details surrounding the complaint, such as what unit or office each worked in, how long they have worked there, job titles, documented incidents that may be relevant.
3. Summary of the complainant's specific allegation.
4. Findings from the investigation pertaining to each allegation.
5. Conclusions, specifically whether or not sexual harassment occurred. If it did not occur, the allegation was either unsubstantiated or information was insufficient to make a determination.
6. If sexual harassment did occur, recommendations for corrective action. In rendering a decision, the proper "burden of proof" is the "preponderance evidence" used in civil proceedings, not the "beyond a reasonable doubt" standard used in criminal proceedings.
7. Right of appeal including the name of the person to whom the appeal is addressed, the limit for appeal, and conditions for appeal (Sandier).

Rendering a Decision and Applying Appropriate Remedy

Options for an appropriate resolution of the sexual harassment complaint may include the following: a formal apology to the complainant, a transfer or reassignment of the complainant ensuring that there can be no perception of punishment, disciplinary action for the person who engaged in inappropriate workplace behavior (oral and written warning, reprimand, suspension, probation, transfer, shift reassignment, demotion, denial of a prospective promotion or pay raise, instructions to not be alone with the complainant, or discharge). Any forms of discipline short of discharge should be accompanied by a warning that similar misconduct in the future may result in immediate discharge. If discipline is imposed, document the reasons why. Provide remedial counseling and training on sexual harassment. Also, take the opportunity to re-communicate your policy. Carefully and fully document the investigation, the discipline, and any remedial steps. Conduct follow-up interviews with the parties to inform them of the company's actions (Orlov and Roumell, 1999).

After a determination is made, the employer should send the report or a summary, as dictated by employer policy, to the complainant, the alleged harasser, and other need-to-know parties, administer appropriate disciplinary action, and schedule regular meetings with the complainant and the disciplined employee to ensure that the remedy is effective and there is no retaliation.

Concluding Comments

To minimize liability for sexual harassment claims, the courts have held that employers should demonstrate three things: an effective anti-harassment policy, investigation of harassment complaints, and appropriate discipline for the harassing employees. The focus of our discussion has been on the investigative process. Managers should be aware that timeliness and fairness are important elements of a sexual harassment investigation in order to withstand the scrutiny of the courts. The case law strongly supports the need for investigations to commence within a reasonably short time. The employer should take action to stop the harassing activity, with appropriate corrective action—often disciplinary in nature—after the investigation. If these actions are not taken, the employer could be subject to liability. Employers have successfully protected themselves when they have conducted a careful, well-detailed investigation followed by appropriate discipline.

It is critically important for managers to be aware that suits imposing liability on the employer can succeed if employers have ineffectively addressed the issue of sexual harassment in any of the following ways: an inadequate or nonexistent sexual harassment policy; inadequate investigation of complaints; failure to balance the rights of the accused harasser with the rights of the person alleging harassment; failure to discipline, inadequate discipline, or provide an inappropriate remedy (i.e., transferring the victim to a less-desirable position or location to separate him or her from the harasser).

This paper has sought to make managers and employers aware of the responsibilities involved in dealing with sexual harassment complaints in today's workplace. We have presented the legal background for these investigations, highlighted best practices for investigation procedures, discussed the role of information derived from electronic media as part of the investigatory evidence, and identified appropriate remedies. Armed with this information, leaders can make better decisions on preventing sexual harassment, addressing allegations, and conducting investigations with respect and regard for the interest and well-being of employees and the employer.

The authors recommend that employers consult experienced employment legal counsel and consider any state and local laws that may pertain to their particular situation. It should be noted that courts at the federal and state levels may vary in their interpretations of the degree of rigor required in a sexual harassment investigation. We hope that this article and good counsel will lead to properly conducted, timely investigations that can "serve essentially to provide a cloak of invincibility to an employer" (Reisman, 2007) facing actual or potential legal action pertaining to harassment or wrongful discharge.

References

Abell, N.L. and Jackson, M.N. (1996). Sexual harassment investigations-Cues, clues and how-to's. The Labor Lawyer, 12, 17–52.

Baldwin v. Blue Cross Blue Shield of Alabama, 480 F. 3d 1287 U.S. App (2007).

Beldo v. University of Massachusetts, 20 MDLR 105, 113 (1998).

Bennett-Alexander, D., and Hartman, L.P. (2009). Employment law for business. Boston: McGraw-Hill Irwin.

Bland, T. (2000, January). Get a handle on harassment. Security Management, 62–67.

Bland, T.S. and Stalcup. S.S. (2001). Managing harassment. Human Resource Management, 40(1), 51–61.

Burlington Industries v. Ellerth, 118 S. Ct. 2257 (1998).

Crawford v. Metropolitan Government of Nashville, 129 S. Ct. 846 (2009).

Dorfman W., Cobb, A.T., and Cox, R. (2000). Investigations of sexual harassment allegations: Legal means fair—or does it? Human Resource Management, 39(1) 33–49.

Elkins, T.J., Phillips, J.S., and Ward, S.G. (2008). Organizational sexual harassment investigations: Observers' perceptions of fairness. Journal of Managerial Issues, 20(1), 88–108.

Equal Employment Opportunity Commission (2010): http://www.eeoc.gov/eeoc/statistics/enforcement/sexual_harassment.cfm

Equal Employment Opportunity Commission Regulations: 29 C.ER. Part 1604.11 (2009).

Equal Employment Opportunity Commission (2011): http://www.eeoc.gov/eeoc/newsroom/release

Equal Employment Opportunity Commission (1999): Policy guidance on current issues of sexual harassment: http://www.eeoc.gov/policy/docs/currentissues.html

Equal Employment Opportunity Commission (1999b): Enforcement guidance on vicarious employer liability for unlawful harassment by supervisors. http://www.eeoc.gov/policy/docs/harassment.html

Faragher v. City of Boca Raton, 118 S. Ct. 2275 (1998).

Fliegel, R.M. and Arena, R.D. (2004). The impact of the FACT Act on employee misconduct investigations and implications for FCRA and Title VII compliance. The Labor Lawyer, 20, 97–106.

Fuller v. City of Oakland, 47 E3d. 1522-U.S. Court of Appeals, 9th Circuit (1995).

Gardner, S. and Lewis, K. (2000). Sexual harassment investigations: A portrait of contradictions. SAM Advanced Management Journal, 65(4), 29–36.

Harris v. Forklift Systems, Inc., 510 U.S. 17 Supreme Court (1993).

Holly D. v. California Institute of Technology, 339 E3d. 1158 U.S. Court of Appeals, 9th Circuit (2003).

Kass, D.S., Kleinman, L.S., Pesta, B.J., and Samson, Y (2004). Current developments in sexual harassment case law: Questions and answers. ALSB Journal of Employment and Labor Law, 10, 67–75.

Kestenbaum v. Pennzoil 766 P. 2d 280,288 (N.M. 1988) cert. denied 490 U.S. 1109 (1989).

Levy, A.C. and Paludi, M.A. (2001). Workplace sexual harassment, 2nd ed., Upper Saddle River, NJ: Prentice Hall.

Meritor Savings Bank, FSB v. Vinson, 477 U.S. 57 Supreme Court (1986).

Morgan, J.F., Owen, J.M., and Gomes, G.M. (2002). Union rules in non-union settings: The NLRB and workplace investigations. SAM Advanced Management Journal, 67(1), 22–27.

Oncale v. Sundowner Offshore Services, Inc., 118 S. Ct. 998 (1998).

Oppenheimer, A. (2004). Investigating workplace harassment and discrimination. Employee Relations Law Journal, 29(4) 61–62.

Orlov, D. and Roumell, M.T. (1999). What every manager needs to know about sexual harassment. New York: Amacom.

Pappas, M.P. (2009, June). Damned if you do, damned if you don't: Terminating accused harasser can lead to liability for "sex stereotyping." ASAP Newsletter, de 1–2.

Perry, E.L., Kulik, C.T., and Field, M.P. (2009). Sexual harassment training: Recommendations to address gaps between the practitioner and research literatures. Human Resource Management, 48(5), 817–837.

Reisman, J.E. (2007). How to investigate workplace misconduct and avoid the HP syndrome. Supervision, 68 (4), 12–15.

Sandler, B.R., Investigating sexual harassment complaints— Procedures for investigations at http://bemicesandler.com/id40_m.htm, retrieved 7/12/2011 from electronic address.

Sassaman v. Gamache,—F.3d—(2nd Cir. May 22, 2009).

Scherer v. Rockwell International, 975 F. 2d 356, 360–361 (7th Cir. 1992).

Sculnick, M.W. (1983). A policy and procedure for handling harassment complaints. Employee Relations Today, 10(2) 161–175.

Silva v. Lucky Stores, Inc., 65 Cal. App. 4th 256. 76 Cal. Rptr. 2d 382 (1998).

Soewita, S. and Kleiner, B.H. (2000). How to monitor electronic mail to discover sexual harassment. Equal Opportunities International, 19(617) 45–47.

Towns, D.M. and Johnson, M.S. (2003). Sexual harassment in the 21st century—E-harassment in the workplace. Employee Relations Law Journal, 29(1), 7–24.

Trotter, R. and Zacur, S.R. (2004). Corporate sexual harassment policies—Effective strategic human resource management. Journal of Business and Economic Research, 2(3), 63–70.

Critical Thinking

1. What do you anticipate will be the most difficult aspects surrounding the investigation of a sexual harassment allegation by an employee?
2. Why do you think people sexually harass others?
3. Do you think that a person alleging sexual harassment would do this for reasons other than that a sexual harassment actually occurred?

Internet References

Facts about Sexual Harassment
www.eeoc.gov/facts/fs-sex.html

Sexual Harassment Training Online
www.workplaceanswers.com

Workplace Harassment Prevention Training Workplace
www.shrm.org/multimedia/webcasts/Documents/1012harassment_2.pdf

In addition to teaching management-related courses, **DR. TROTTER** is an arbitrator. He has published his decisions, as well as a book and academic journal articles, and has made presentations at professional meetings. **DR. ZACUR**, a professor of Management and formerly Dean of the Merrick School of Business at the University of Baltimore, has published three books, journal articles, and serves as a management consultant and leadership coach. Before her academic career, she worked in human resources.

Article   Prepared by: Maria Nathan, *Lynchburg College*

Recognizing and Overcoming Toxic Leadership

GEORGE A. ZANGARO, KELLY YAGER, AND JOSEPH PROULX

Learning Outcomes

After reading this article, you will be able to:

- Know the symptoms of toxic leadership.

- Know how to address toxic leadership.

- Understand the workplace context that abides toxic leadership.

It was difficult for the novice nurse, a cheerful and competent practitioner, to get out of bed. That queasy, nauseous feeling had already begun, and she knew that the headache would not be far behind. What was this, some sort of infectious process or a virus perhaps? Could this dread of getting up and going out to work, possibly be related to something on the job? Indeed it was, and the "infection" had to do specifically with a toxic leader.

Toxic leaders can be devastating to personnel at all levels in an organization and can ultimately lead to the dismantling of the organization. Most people have worked for leaders who display some level of toxicity. The following provides some examples of toxic behaviors. The purpose of this article is to assist nursing leadership in recognizing a toxic nurse manager and in taking the appropriate steps to reduce the spread of the toxicity in the organization.

The Nurse Manager Who

- has a staff meeting and spends thirty minutes talking about how wonderful he or she is, and during the process takes credit for others' accomplishments.

- blames the staff nurses when discharge times have increased on the unit over the past 3 months.

- shares information with the inner circle of loyal followers but not with others.

- refuses to consider a staff nurse's idea for a new way to give report to oncoming nurses during shift change, stating that the current way works fine and no change is needed.

- is easily annoyed by simple requests from the staff, is not engaged in conversation with the staff or does not listen to their concerns.

Impact on Nursing

The U.S. health system continues to struggle with a critical shortage of nurses. It is anticipated that there could a shortage of approximately 500,000 nurses in the U.S. by 2025 (Buerhaus, Staiger, & Auerbach, 2008). Due to the challenges with the U.S. economy, hospital administrators are requiring significant contributions from leadership at all levels, specifically from the nurse managers on inpatient units. Nurse managers are expected to ensure a positive work environment that fosters satisfaction and retention of nurses. With the shrinking pool of registered nurses, it is becoming increasingly difficult to recruit new nurses.

Effective hospital leadership at the executive level as well as at the unit level is crucial in today's unstable economic environment. Studies have identified a significant relationship between effective leadership and job satisfaction (Laschinger & Finnegan, 2005; Upenieks, 2003; Wilson, 2005), commitment (McGuire & Kennerly, 2006) and intent to stay (Force, 2005; Johnson & Rea, 2009). Each of these outcomes contributes to a healthy and productive work environment. In today's market there is a high demand for leaders who serve as coaches, empower staff, and inspire staff to excel. To be successful in these difficult times a nurse manager must value the staff and make staff members his or her top priority. Unfortunately, there are nurse managers in organizations today who demoralize staff, promote their personal agendas, and go out of their way to protect their reputation regardless of the negative impact to the organization. They are known as toxic leaders.

Toxicity is defined as "the degree to which a substance can harm humans or animals" (Webster's, 2009). Repeated exposure to a toxic organism can have long lasting effects on an individual. Staff members who are repeatedly exposed to a toxic nurse manager will either accept the leadership style and adapt to toxic behaviors, or will reject it and leave the environment. In a hospital setting, the effects of toxic management can spread rapidly through a nursing unit if the culture of the unit supports it. The effects of toxicity can have a significant impact on the individual employees on the unit and the organization.

One of the greatest challenges in addressing toxic leadership in an organization is simply that it is widely tolerated by employers (Flynn, 1999; Kimura, 2003; Padilla, Hogan, & Kaiser, 2007; Reed, 2004). Flynn (1999) reports that apathy leads to the organizational culture that makes toxic leadership acceptable, while other researchers state that workers eventually accept the situation of poor leadership as normal. Poor interpersonal skills also play a role in this problem. Too often, belittling, embarrassing, yelling, and blaming become the main forms of communication (Kimura, 2003; Reed, 2004). This leads to controlling information and the isolation of workers, which can escalate the problem (Wilson-Starks, 2009).

Symptoms of a Toxic Nurse Manager

Toxic nurse managers are not always easy to identify. A toxic manager is defined as "the manager who bullies, threatens, yells. The manager whose mood swings determine the climate of the office on any given workday. Who forces employees to whisper in sympathy in cubicles and hallways. Call it what you want—poor interpersonal skills, unfortunate office practices— but some people, by sheer, shameful force of their personalities, make working for them rotten" (Flynn, 1999, p.40). Behaviors displayed by toxic managers include:

Self-Centeredness

Self-centered toxic nurse managers are focused on advancing their careers and exhibit little concern for staff morale or professional growth and tend to ignore the organization's vision. They are rigid in their thinking and hide their weaknesses and failures from their own supervisors (Kimura, 2003). When interacting with a self-centered manager he or she will use "I" when speaking about accomplishments on the unit and not give credit to the staff who were responsible for the accomplishment. Self-centered nurse managers typically place blame on and complain about the staff on the unit. The self-centered toxic manager will search for followers who will do exactly what they request and these individuals will become the manager's "inner circle." These staff members will likely adopt the toxic behaviors displayed by their leader.

Exploiting Others

Toxic nurse managers will take credit for successful initiatives on a unit, but give no credit to the nurse(s) who initiated, planned and executed them. More importantly, when a problem occurs with a particular initiative on the unit, the toxic nurse manager will blame the staff nurses and accept no responsibility for the problem.

Controlling Behavior

The toxic nurse manager must be in control of every aspect of the unit at all times. In order to maintain control, toxic nurse managers withhold information from the staff, are secretive, and give very little, if any, autonomy to the staff. This behavior results in stagnation or a lack of progress on the unit. The controlling nurse manager will eventually create a culture on the unit that is resistant to change.

Disrespecting Others

The toxic nurse manager who yells, bullies, threatens and speaks to staff in a condescending tone is demonstrating a broad lack of respect. This may occur in a person-to-person contact or in coercive emails. As an example, a new staff nurse fresh from orientation has made a medication error and must complete an incident report. The toxic nurse manager decides to discuss the error with the new staff member, instead of this being a private counseling session the nurse manager ridicules the staff member in front of her peers. What should have been a positive learning experience for the new staff nurse turned into a humiliating experience for the staff nurse.

Suppresses Employees' Innovation and Creativity

Nurse managers who suppress employees' innovative thinking and creativity are not permitting the employees to "think outside of the box." He or she controls all information and forces employees to follow the manager's vision for the unit. The toxic leader has staff convinced that he or she can guide them to accomplish unrealistic goals as long as they follow his or her vision. This behavior leads to employees feeling unappreciated.

Inadequate Emotional Intelligence

Emotional intelligence is defined as "the ability to manage ourselves and our relationships effectively." It consists of four fundamental capabilities: self-awareness, self management, social awareness, and social skill (Goleman, 1998). Nurse managers who lack emotional intelligence can be described as those who yell at staff, make irrational decisions, lack self-awareness of one's emotions, or are unable to control disruptive impulses. The nurse manager who displays some or all of these characteristics on a busy chaotic nursing unit is the one to avoid.

Recognizing Toxic Nurse Managers

The use of a 360-degree evaluation is one of the best ways to recognize a toxic nurse manager. A 360-degree evaluation permits the manager's supervisor to receive input from all individuals in the nurse manager's sphere of influence (Davidson, 2007). This performance appraisal instrument provides a supervisor with feedback on the nurse manager's work performance. The evaluation can be given to the nursing staff, unit clerks, patients and any other departments that interact with the particular unit manager that is being evaluated. This approach will permit the nurse manager to see how his or her behavior and leadership style is viewed by others in the organization.

Another suggestion is to conduct focus groups with the nursing staff on the unit and other employees who interact with the toxic nurse manager on a regular basis. Focus groups permit the nursing supervisor to obtain in-depth meaning and understanding through the use of probing questions and nonthreatening discussion. A drawback to focus groups is that employees may not be willing to publicly express their concerns in front of co-workers. Individual interviews can be very time consuming, but if a nursing supervisor feels that the staff is not willing to speak publicly, they are an option. Of particular importance in this process is for the nursing supervisor to assess the climate on all shifts, not just the day shift.

A nursing supervisor may also track the turnover rate on the toxic nurse manager's unit. Units with high turnover rates should raise a red flag for the supervisor. When a staff nurse feels that there is no resolution that will occur in a toxic work environment he or she will leave the organization. Turnover is very costly to the organization and disruptive to unit cohesiveness. Additionally, research indicates that increased workplace incivility results in decreased productivity in the health care system (Hutton, & Gates, 2008). Decreased productivity in a hospital represents another significant financial burden for the institution.

Addressing Toxicity

Addressing toxicity requires involvement from organizational executives as well as staff nurses. The approaches to be taken by these roles are explored in this section.

Nurse Executive Role

First, the job description should state that the incumbent is required to treat all employees in a respectful and professional manner. It has actually been suggested that the particular behaviors that will not be tolerated by the organization are stated in writing (Flynn, 1999). Second, when selecting the team to conduct the interview the nurse executive should ensure that there are a variety of staff on the team so that diverging viewpoints are represented. This will also increase the odds of identifying a toxic individual in the interview process. Finally, the nurse executive must ensure that he or she clearly communicates the objectives for the interview, rules of engagement and has everyone sign to document agreement to the hiring process.

During a hiring interview, the nurse executive can attempt to identify a toxic leader through using a behavioral-based interview approach. Behavioral-based interviewing is used to determine how an individual has reacted to, and managed prior problem situations (Hoevemeyer, 2006). This interview technique does not focus on what the interviewee might do in a future situation, but rather what he or she has done in a previous situation. For example, the interviewer might ask, "Could you provide me with an example of how you handled a difficult situation with a co-worker?" or "Could you describe a situation where you used appropriate delegation to complete a task?" Behavioral questions will permit the interviewer to determine if the interviewee is the right fit for the job by assessing the skills that are needed to be successful in the new job. Also the leadership should tell the prospective employee they will be evaluated on whether or not they have met these human resource objectives that relate to managing employees in a positive way. The executive must ensure that the prospective employee understands that toxic behavior could end his or her tenure in the organization, but on the other hand nontoxic behavior will be rewarded and recognized by superiors.

Despite the best hiring practices toxic nurse managers will still emerge in the organization. Once a toxic nurse manager has been identified, it is important for the nurse executive to address this toxicity as quickly as possible. The nurse executive should take an identify-verify-rectify approach to address a toxic situation. Begin by investigating the situation, interviewing people close to the situation. Verifying facts will help to determine if this truly is a toxic situation, isolated incident, or the result of a disgruntled employee. If it is determined to be a toxic situation then the nurse executive should confront the nurse manager and rectify this situation as quickly as possible.

Nurse executives have the power and authority in the organization to address toxicity issues with a nurse manager. One of the most important issues for the nurse executive is to ensure that he or she is honest with the nurse manager and states things as they are so that the nurse manager gets a clear picture of his or her behavior. When conducting this counseling session be firm, but reasonable in your approach. Always document these types of sessions in the event of future occurrences or if disciplinary action needs to be taken at a later date. The nurse executive may set some reasonable goals for the nurse manager to achieve.

Nurse managers are often selected from within the unit and promoted quickly to a new role that he or she is not ready for. For many of these nurses who are unprepared for a managerial role toxic behavior tends to be displayed as a defensive or survival mechanism. In these situations, the new nurse managers are taking an autocratic type approach to leadership to ensure compliance from the staff (Kerfoot, 2007). In this case it would be appropriate for the nurse executive to take a mentoring or coaching type role and assist the new nurse manager in being a successful leader. The nurse executive may provide the nurse manager with an effective leadership style to emulate and also offer educational classes to ensure success.

Nurse executives are encouraged to obtain mentors for leaders who have been identified as toxic. The mentor can guide the nurse manager into creating a common vision on the unit that encourages participation by all staff. This vision should be developed by the manager and staff on the unit. This strategy has been identified as one that generates cohesiveness and increases communication and employee pride (Burritt, 2005; Failla & Stichler, 2008; Huston, 2008). In doing this the nurses will become re-energized and empowered (Burritt, 2005; Failla & Stichler, 2008). Empowering the nursing staff, creating a strong sense of community and instituting changes that will inspire confidence, excite the nursing staff, instill creativity and autonomy, and stimulate personal growth results in a healthy work environment (Failla & Stichler, 2008; Gratton & Erickson, 2007).

How to Survive a Toxic Manager

It is important for nurse executives to foster a culture in which the staff nurse feels safe and is comfortable approaching a nurse executive for advice or assistance when dealing with a toxic nurse manager. The following depicts behaviors that are recommended for a staff nurse to practice when confronted with a toxic nurse manager. These behaviors are suggested to assist the staff nurse to understand how to best approach a toxic situation. Even though the nurse manager possesses positional power and authority on the unit, as a staff nurse you can quietly lead from the middle and be just as effective. Leading from the middle can be accomplished by working with the other staff

nurses to make subtle changes that are satisfying to the staff, but not contributing to the toxicity on the unit.

The Staff Nurse Should:

- never approach a toxic nurse manager alone, always seek safety in numbers and confront the manager as a group (Lipman-Blumen, 2005).
- align themselves with other nurse managers or executives for appropriate support.
- never lose control of your emotional intelligence when interacting with a toxic nurse manager.
- not get frustrated and feel like it is a hopeless situation.
- attempt to develop ways to exert a positive influence on the nurse manager by remaining professional and calm in difficult situations.
- avoid condemning or criticizing the nurse manager and spend your time more wisely by developing a strategic plan to overcome the adversity the toxic nurse manager is spreading on the unit.

Implications

The literature demonstrates that the implications of toxic leadership on the nursing profession are very costly in terms of staff turnover. There are many contributing factors to this problem. Among the most commonly mentioned problems are the lack of leadership training and professional development activities offered for nurses in leadership roles (Kerfoot, 2007). Very often, a person has had only "field-specific" training, as opposed to managerial or leadership training (Flynn, 1999). Furthermore, findings have shown that a major barrier in obtaining leadership training is the current work schedule and job demands of nurses which lead to them being unable to get away to attend training and workshops (O'Neil, Moorjikian, & Cherner, 2008).

The impact of toxic leadership on the nursing profession is substantial. Combining toxic leadership with the stressful nature of the job itself leads to lackluster work, poor morale, decreased productivity, increased absenteeism, and high turnover (Dyck, 2001; Kimura, 2003; Pearson & Porath, 2005; Shirey, 2006; Wilson-Starks, 2009). Employees begin to feel cynical and frustrated, leading to decreased energy, enthusiasm, and self-esteem (Lencioni, 2007). Both physical and psychological problems such as hypertension, ulcers, headaches, anxiety, depression, and anger also occur due to the stress of poor leadership (Dyck, 2001; Sutton, 2007). In addition to these physical symptoms, toxic leadership causes de-motivational behavior, which affects a nursing unit's morale and general culture (Reed, 2004). This organizational stress places the purpose of the organization in jeopardy (Padilla, Hogan, Kaiser, 2007; Reed, 2004). Unhealthy work environments created by organizational stress may produce bad outcomes for both the staff and patients.

A final implication of toxic leadership is that in toxic environments employees have to decide to conform to the current work environment, transfer to another unit or to leave the organization entirely. Unfortunately some employees are not maneuverable due to a lack of education, or they just simply cannot afford to change jobs because they are economically dependent on their current job. As a result, many employees accept toxic leadership, willingly conform to this leadership style and become the next generation of toxic leaders (Sutton, 2007; Wilson-Starks, 2009). In the current economy nursing executives cannot afford to allow this toxic cycle to continue and spread into the next generation of future nursing leaders. Toxic leadership will spread and produce systematic damage in an organization.

Summary

Toxic managers do not save the organization money rather they cost it money in recruitment fees. They have infectious, devastating cumulative effects on the person, unit and organization. Nurse executives are in the position to stop this toxicity in the workplace and create healthy work environments for nurses. There is not a shortage of great leaders in nursing, but we need them to mentor and coach new nurse managers to help eliminate toxic behaviors. Let's remove toxic managers, empower nursing staff, and create good leaders for the next generation of nurses to emulate.

References

Buerhaus, P.I., Staiger, D.O., & Auerbach, D.I. (2008). The Future of the Nursing Workforce in the U.S.: Data, Trends, and Implications. Boston, MA: Jones and Bartlett.

Burritt, J.E. (2005). Organizational turnaround: The role of the nurse executive. The Journal of Nursing Administration, 35 (11), 482–489.

Davidson, M.L. (2007). The 360 degree evaluation. Clinics in Podiatric Medicine and Surgery, 24(1), 65–94.

Dyck, D. (2001). The toxic workplace. Benefits Canada, 25 (3), 52–58.

Failla, K.R. & Stichler, J.F. (2008). Manager and staff perceptions of the manager's leadership style. The Journal of Nursing Administration, 38 (11), 480–487.

Flynn, G. (1999). Stop toxic managers before they stop you! Workforce, 78 (8), 40–44.

Force, M. (2005). The relationship between effective nurse managers and nursing retention. Journal of Nursing Administration, 35(7/8), 336–341.

Goleman D. (1998). Working with emotional intelligence. New York: Bantam Books.

Gratton, L. & Erickson, T.J. (2007). 8 ways to build collaborative teams. Harvard Business Review, 85(11), 101–109.

Hoevemeyer, V.A. (2006). High-impact interview questions: 701 behavior based questions to find the right person for every job. New York: American Management Association.

Huston, C. (2008). Preparing nurse leaders for 2020. Journal of Nursing Management, 16, 905–911.

Hutton, S. & Gates, D. (2008). Workplace incivility and productivity losses among direct care staff. AAOHN Journal, 56(4), 168–175.

Johnson, S.L., & Rea, R.E. (2009). Workplace bullying. Journal of Nursing Administration, 39(2), 84–90.

Kerfoot, K. (2007). Bossing or serving? How leaders execute effectively. Nursing Economics, 25 (3), 178–188.

Kimura, H. (2003). Overcome toxic management. Nursing Management, 34(1), 26–29.

Laschinger, HKS, Finnegan, J. (2005). Using empowerment to build trust and respect in the workplace: A strategy for addressing the nursing shortage. Nursing Economics, 23(1), 6–13.

Lencioni, P. (2007). The three signs of a miserable job: A fable for managers (and their employees). San Francisco: Jossey-Bass.

Lipman-Blumen, J. (2005). The allure of toxic leaders: Why followers rarely escape their clutches. Ivey Business Journal, Jan/Feb,1–8.

McGuire, E., & Kennerly, S.M. (2006). Nurse managers as transformational and transactional leaders. Nursing Economics, 24(4), 179–185.

O'Neil, E., Moorjikian, R.L., & Cherner, D. (2008). Developing nursing leaders: An overview of trends and programs. The Journal of Nursing Administration, 38 (4), 178–183.

Padilla, A., Hogan, R., & Kaiser, R.B. (2007). The toxic triangle: Destructive leaders, susceptible followers, and conducive environments. The Leadership Quarterly, 18, 176–194.

Pearson, C.M., & Porath, C.L. (2005). On the nature, consequences and remedies of workplace incivility: No time for "nice"? Think again. Academy of Management Executive, 19(1), 7–18.

Reed, G. (2004). Toxic leadership. Military Review, 84(4), 67–71.

Shirey, M.R. (2006). Authentic leaders creating healthy work environments for nursing practice. American Journal of Critical Care, 15 (3), 256–267.

Sutton, R.I. (2007). The no asshole rule: Building a civilized workplace and surviving one that isn't. New York: Hachette Book Group.

Upenicks, V. (2003). What constitutes effective leadership? Perceptions of magnet and nonmagnet nurse leaders. Journal of Nursing Administration, 33(9), 456–467.

Webster's online dictionary. No date. Available at: www.websters-online-dictionary.org/definition/toxicity. Accessed April 21, 2009.

Wilson, A. Impact of management development on nurse retention. Nursing Admin Quarterly, 29(2), 137–145.

Wilson-Starks, K.Y. Toxic leadership. From the President and CEO. www.transleadership.com. Accessed March 15, 2009.

Critical Thinking

1. Is it possible for you to be toxic in some contexts but not in others?
2. What would you do if you were in a leadership role and witnessed toxicity in the workplace?
3. Why do you think toxicity is tolerated in the workplace?

Internet References

Bad Bosses
www.ebosswatch.com/Bad-boss

How to Fix a Toxic Workplace
www.inc.com/top-workplaces/2010/how-to-fix-a-toxic-workplace.html

Identifying a Toxic Workplace-Kickbully-Where the Fight Begins
www.kickbully.com/toxic.html

The "Dark Side" of Leadership: The Impact of a Bad Boss
www.forbes.com/sites/alicegwalton/2013/02/07/the-dark-side-of-leadership-the-impact-of-a-bad-boss-can-go-viral-though-the-office

When Your Workplace Is Toxic
http://psychcentral.com/blog/archives/2011/06/25/when-your-workplace-is-toxic

Article   Prepared by: Maria Nathan, *Lynchburg College*

Finding and Fixing Corporate Misconduct

What 300,000 employees said about unethical cultures.

DAN CURRELL AND TRACY DAVIS BRADLEY

Learning Outcomes

After reading this article, you will be able to:

- Comprehend the relationship between ethics and culture.

- Know how an organization can evolve to one of higher integrity.

- Understand what management must do to curb corporate misconduct.

In 2009, senior management teams restructured departments and business units, and in many cases dramatically reduced the size of their companies. Upset by these changes, employees became cynical about their companies' ethical cultures and the integrity of the people who work with them. That cynicism translated directly into a rise in serious instances of fraud and misconduct.

In 2008, as the economy worsened, misconduct rose by 20% during the second half of the year. In 2009, by contrast, overall misconduct levels reportedly declined from the first half of the year to the second half.

But a survey conducted by the Corporate Executive Board's Compliance & Ethics Leadership Council (CELC), provides compelling evidence for why this finding does not tell the whole story.

According to the results from more than 300,000 employees in over 75 countries, this "decline" in misconduct during 2009 is actually misleading, as it pertains to less severe and risky behaviors such as the misuse of company resources or other "inappropriate behavior."

In fact, the real story in 2009 was that more serious types of misconduct (e.g., conflicts of interest, insider trading and improper payments) rose during the year. Observations of bribery and corruption were up more than 100%, and observations of insider trading were up 300%. At a time when regulators are on the warpath for precisely these kinds of violations, such behaviors tremendously increased risk for companies.

Consistent with this trend, and with the ongoing recession, CELC research found that the number of highly disengaged employees increased in 2009. At the beginning of the year, the proportion of such employees was one in ten. But by the end of 2009, it rose to one in five. (The data is based on the attitudes and work habits of thousands of employees.) Based on CEB's productivity models, this widespread disengagement not only created fertile ground for misconduct, but also decreased employee output by about 5%.

The fact is that while many have reported that overall misconduct was on the decline, the most troubling types of misconduct are actually on the rise. And they have increased to a staggering degree. Companies must not just be on guard, but learn how to prevent employees from wanting to skirt the rules—or even the law—in the first place. Prevention starts from within.

The Culprit: Employee Perceptions of Culture

Misconduct levels were shown to reveal themselves in employee perceptions of culture. Business units with the weakest ethical cultures had the highest levels of misconduct—in 2009, these units experienced five times more misconduct than those with the strongest ethical cultures. When employees perceive a weak ethical culture, misconduct does not just increase—it multiplies.

In contrast to popular opinion, CELC research also found that misconduct does not vary by region. Europe and North America, for example, have nearly identical overall levels. That said, different business units in different locations within a company often do show varying levels of misconduct. But this disparity is not a national culture issue—it is a business culture issue. Weak business units within an otherwise average company can have sky-high misconduct levels.

Perhaps more disconcerting is that misconduct is rarely reported. This means that companies need to be diligent, creative and persistent in their efforts to detect and mitigate serious compliance risks and uncover information about employee misconduct.

A companywide assessment is a good place to start. By comparing business units' performance on such ethical culture measures as clarity of expectations, tone at the top, comfort speaking up, and levels of observed misconduct, companies can pinpoint business units that present a cultural risk to the company.

When it comes to perceptions of ethical culture, employees can generally be divided into four ethical risk groups: "Integrity Champions," who are most positive about the culture, and present the least risk; "Casual Supporters," who are somewhat positive about the culture and present minimal cultural risk; "Agnostics," who are on the fence about their company's ethical culture and present a cultural risk to the company; and "Disaffected," who have the most negative perceptions of the culture at their company and thus present the greatest cultural risk.

Agnostics and Casual Supporters, in particular, report greater levels of uncertainty about observing instances of misconduct than other employees, and also report the misconduct that they do observe at much lower rates than do Integrity Champions. Their lack of certainty about what they are observing, and their possible negativity about their firm's ethical culture, suggests that awareness and education are the keys to reaching these Agnostic and Casual employees. Targeted communication and training can greatly impact the reporting rates for this segment of a company's population.

Organizational Justice for a Culture of Integrity

So how can executives restore a strong culture of integrity? Looking at the best-performing business units, it is clear that the key to a strong culture of integrity is an element called organizational justice. Organizational justice has two parts: (1) the belief among employees that the company does not tolerate unethical behavior, and (2) the belief that

---

Evolutionary Stages in Your Corporate Culture of Integrity

The best way to prevent employee misconduct is not a draconian enforcement strategy. It is promoting a culture of integrity and openness.

Enron famously had a "no harm, no foul" culture where potential whistleblowers were either too apathetic or too concerned about their own advancement and profit to care what others were up to. Whether it was simply looking the other way or actual ignorance, most workers were unaffected by the executive pillaging going on across all levels of the business. And once that becomes endemic, it is tough to reverse course.

Creating and nurturing a culture where malfeasance cannot occur is not easy. But your best resources are right in front of you: your employees. By recognizing where your workers are in this evolution, you can start to determine how high the hill is that you have to climb.

These are the four general employee types that you can either identify as a part of the solution—or a part of the problem.

Integrity Champions

Those who are very positive about the culture. These are the key influencers in the company who can help turn others into positive employees.

Casual Supporters

Employees who are somewhat positive about the culture but not particularly engaged one way or the other.

Agnostics

"Fence-sitters," these people may present some cultural risk to the company and can be influenced if the culture takes a change for the better—or for the worse.

Disaffected

These employees with the most negative perceptions of the culture at their company present the greatest risk.

management responds quickly and consistently to unethical behavior when it occurs.

In other words, organizational justice is strong when employees believe that their company will take action on its policies and values. And it encapsulates the maxim that actions speak louder than words.

Organizational justice is singularly powerful in driving a culture of integrity throughout the company. When employees believe that the company has strong organizational justice, the company's integrity index (an overall measure of integrity) rises, and misconduct drops significantly. And while every aspect of culture affects employees' perceptions of corporate integrity, organizational justice is by far the most powerful single factor—accounting for more index movement than all other cultural factors combined.

How can management teams enhance organizational justice? The key is for the organization to visibly enforce the company's ethical commitments. This is no small task. Many management teams are either unwilling to do this or just do not know what to do.

For those firms willing to do what is necessary, there are three key steps: (1) equip managers to decisively deal with unethical behavior, (2) show the whole employee population—using real instances from within the company—that the company deals decisively with misconduct, and (3) close the loop with employees who report misconduct so that they know that appropriate actions were taken.

Companies need to be accountable, consistent and transparent when taking action on misconduct. These efforts should focus on the top and middle leadership of the organization. Employees who believe that their senior leaders have high integrity feel more connected to the values of the company. Viewing it at another level, an employee who believes that his or her manager behaves ethically and demonstrates corporate values

will consistently show better performance in the workplace—including working harder and longer hours.

Corporate values in action lead to a more ethical work environment, and possibly even better corporate performance. With some hard data in hand, we now know with precision how corporate integrity, corporate misconduct and corporate performance relates to one another. These connections are clear, and they are too strong to be ignored.

Critical Thinking

1. What role does corporate culture play in corporate misconduct?
2. Do you think that senior management plays a role in establishing the corporate culture?
3. How can a corrupt corporate culture be changed?

Internet References

Controlling Corporate Misconduct
www.nationalaffairs.com/public_interest/detail/controlling-corporate-misconduct

If I Witness Corporate Misconduct, What Should I Do?
http://whistleblowers.com/if-i-witness-corporate-misconduct-what-should-i-do

Preventing Corporate Misconduct
http://raportroczny.lotos.pl/en/risk-management/preventing-corporate-misconduct

The Spreading Scourge of Corporate Corruption
www.nytimes.com/2012/07/11/business/economy/the-spreading-scourge-of-corporate-corruption.html

DAN CURRELL is managing director of the Compliance and Ethics Council at the Corporate Executive Board. **TRACY DAVIS BRADLEY,** PhD, is senior director of the council at CEB.

Article   Prepared by: Maria Nathan, *Lynchburg College*

Inclusive Thinking, Grievances, Amending Policies

SHARI LAU

Learning Outcomes

After reading this article, you will be able to:

- Understand what is meant by "inclusive thinking."
- Know how to create a more inclusive work environment.

How can we get our managers to think more inclusively? "Do we have to buy Joe a larger office chair to accommodate his obesity?" frustrated managers may ask. "Must we let Sarah leave early every Friday so she can be home before sundown?"

Less often, they ask what they can do to help find Joe a chair that makes him more comfortable or suggest that Sarah telecommute on Fridays.

True inclusion in the workplace encompasses the way people behave and the way they think. It's one thing to get Joe that chair; it's another to really want Joe to have it.

While all people have personal biases, prejudices and cultural expectations, HR professionals can help managers transform their thinking to create a more inclusive environment.

An inclusion initiative can lay the framework for the change to and the maintenance of an inclusive workplace. In implementing the initiative, HR professionals should seize opportunities to demonstrate more-inclusive thoughts to managers. For example, when training managers on the Americans with Disabilities Act and their role in providing reasonable accommodations, HR professionals should stress that business leaders are enthusiastic about making such accommodations—as opposed to being forced to provide them. Point out that, in the long run, making accommodations is less expensive than not making them. Show how support for Joe is related to the inclusion initiative and the company's values. Explain how support from managers may make employees more loyal to the company, more engaged in their work and more productive.

Don't just tell managers what they have to do—show them how changing their attitude toward providing accommodations helps the company achieve its goals and values and helps them meet expectations of them as leaders.

Ideally, inclusive thinking permeates all work activities, not just accommodations. For instance, in creating job descriptions, work with managers to develop a list of abilities that support inclusion. If employees complain that managers don't listen to their ideas, show managers how a variety of opinions and proposed solutions can increase their own knowledge and perceptions and may be the catalyst for an innovative process or product. An employee who uses a wheelchair, for instance, may bring a special perspective to the design of a product; an employee who tends to think quietly first, then formulate ideas, might notice gaps or flaws that people who generate ideas quickly might miss. By infusing these types of thoughts into daily actions, HR professionals help set the example and lead managers toward inclusion.

Critical Thinking

1. What are the effects of a non-inclusive environment? Why would a manager do this?
2. Can you think of how and why you would create a more inclusive environment within your class, among your social network?

Internet References

Society for Human Resource Management
www.shrm.org.

What Is Inclusive Thinking?
www.ehow.com/about_6128665_inclusive-thinking_.html

Article   Prepared by: Maria Nathan, *Lynchburg College*

Values-Driven HR

Juniper Networks is turning words on the wall into behaviors in action.

BILL ROBERTS

Learning Outcomes

After reading this article, you will be able to:

- Know what a values-driven organization is.
- Know how to create a values-driven organization culture.

Folks at Juniper Networks Inc. have lofty goals. Last year, one goal embraced by company leaders was to help end worldwide slavery. As Juniper employees see it, this goal aligns with the company's values, talent, technology and another lofty goal to change the world—in part, by designing and developing hardware and software for high-performance networks.

Led by its chief executive officer and HR executive, the 15-year-old Sunnyvale, Calif., enterprise is in the process of re-energizing company values among its more than 9,100 employees in 46 countries. As corporate leaders seek more effective ways to put values into action, they want to align corporate giving with those values.

Hence, the Juniper Foundation supports Not for Sale, a nonprofit in Half Moon Bay, Calif., whose mission is to abolish slavery, indentured servitude and other human trafficking and to use social and other technologies in that effort. Some high-tech companies have begun to target these issues because perpetrators can be found within their sprawling supply chains. Juniper contributes money, technology and expertise. "We want to do more than write checks," explains Steven Rice, executive vice president of HR.

Rice says supporting Not for Sale is just one example of how Juniper's leaders strive to create a culture where the company that customers see on the outside matches the one on the inside. The notion of narrowing the gap between values as words on the wall and values as behaviors is starting to permeate HR processes from recruiting to talent management. In pursuit of this quest, Juniper's HR professionals draw on recent research and emerging practices regarding corporate values, cultural transformation and the neuroscience of leadership.

A Page from Juniper's Values Blueprint

Value

We are about trust.

Definition

We inspire confidence in colleagues, customers and partners by always acting with integrity, fairness, respect and reliability.

Behaviors

- Acts with the highest level of honesty and integrity.
- Shares agendas and objectives, encouraging feedback and discussing things in an open, collaborative and respectful manner.
- Takes responsibility and delivers on commitment.
- Acts confidently but never arrogantly.
- Respects decisions and supports them with enthusiasm and follow-through.
- Assumes positive intentions, viewing conflict as an opportunity to find constructive solutions that help all succeed.

Finding the Way

Juniper's approach represents the future of corporate leadership, says Chris Ernst, co-author of *Boundary Spanning Leadership* (McGraw-Hill, 2010) and a senior faculty member at the Center for Creative Leadership in Greensboro, N.C. He calls Juniper a bellwether for "creating more connected, collaborative, cross-boundary ways of working. The pieces are in place, but there is hard work ahead for Juniper."

Rice similarly believes that the journey has just begun. The values, known as The Juniper Way, are as follows: We are authentic, we are about trust, we deliver excellence, we pursue bold aspirations, we make a meaningful difference.

"One definition of our values is to be confident but not arrogant," says Rice, an effervescent proponent of the cause. Rice spent 25 years in HR at Hewlett-Packard Co. in Palo Alto, Calif., before joining Juniper in 2006, where he leads a global HR team of 108. The team includes an HR leader assigned to each business unit, centers of excellence in various disciplines, and a shared services group that relies heavily on employee and manager self-service for HR transactions.

Tone at the Top

After its launch in 1996, Juniper became one of the most watched Internet startups. Its mission was simple and bold: "Connect everything. Empower everyone." Facing formidable rivals, Juniper emerged as one of the leading providers of switches, routers, software and other networking equipment for global networks such as the New York Stock Exchange. In 2011, annual revenue topped more than $4 billion, up 9 percent from 2010 and a record for the company. The company was less affected by the recession than many other businesses, growing its workforce every year since 2009.

Juniper has always attracted some of the best and brightest talent—veterans and new grads with master's and doctoral degrees in science, math, engineering and computer science—to work on hardware systems, computer chip designs, network architecture and software. More than 4,200 employees conduct research and development. The company has a reputation as an innovative, collaborative, high-performance meritocracy. So why focus on values and culture?

Enter Kevin Johnson, a longtime Microsoft executive who became chief executive officer in September 2008, replacing Scott Kriens, who remains chairman of the board.

"Juniper was founded with a thought leadership agenda: to be a disruptive innovator in new ways to power the networks that power the world today," Johnson says. At the core: "When people around the world are connected, it is transformative for business, society, education, social causes, for the good and advancement of people."

Johnson spent his first year clarifying strategy with his leadership team, including Rice. Thus was born The New Network, a theme that encapsulates Juniper's dedication to fast, flexible hardware and software for networks capable of handling ubiquitous voice, data, video and other traffic, wired or wireless, at ever-increasing volume and speed.

With that strategy in place, Johnson turned to culture. "There was an opportunity to shape the cultural values and environment that will allow great people to do their best work," he says. "We had to embrace the concept of the importance of talent and culture in achieving goals. It is not HR's responsibility, but the business leaders' responsibility. And that is where the CEO has a role to play." Rice agrees: "I am the caretaker of the culture; the executive team owns the culture."

As caretakers, Rice and his HR team face the challenge of making sure the company hires, develops, retains, and properly compensates and recognizes workers that have the requisite science, engineering and business skills, plus the personal traits of collaboration and high energy. While offering competitive salaries and benefits, Juniper needs people who are willing to collaborate across business units, driven to innovate, and passionate about their work and how it will change the world, according to Rice.

Ernst, who studied Juniper in his research, says as many as three-fourths of organizational change efforts fail because the focus is misplaced on management systems, structure and process, rather than on leadership. "Real change requires a change in leadership," he says. "And leadership is about culture, beliefs and values." Ernst is conducting workshops with Juniper's executive team "so they can role-model collaborative behavior for the entire organization. This is one way Juniper is trying to beat the odds," he says.

Juniper Networks Inc.

Products and services: Designs, develops and sells products and services for network infrastructure.
Ownership: Publicly held (NYSE: JNPR).
Key executives: Kevin Johnson, chief executive officer; Steven Rice, executive vice president of HR.
2011 revenue: $4.5 billion.
Employees: More than 9,100.
Locations: Headquarters in Sunnyvale, Calif., with operations in 46 countries. The largest concentrations of employees are in the Silicon Valley, the Boston area and India.
Connections: www.juniper.net, www.juniper.net/us/en/company/careers.

Values-Centric Cultures

Rice and Greg Pryor, HR vice president for leadership and organization effectiveness, retained Ann Rhoades, head of People Ink Corp. in Albuquerque, N.M., to help build what she calls a values-centric culture. She uses Juniper as an example in her book *Built on Values* (Jossey-Bass, 2011).

Rhoades says some Juniper executives were initially confused by the new approach. They said, "We have great values, why change them?" But Rhoades says those values "were not defined. They did not have behaviors behind them." To infuse values into the culture, they must be spelled out as behaviors that are sought, developed and prized. In her patent-pending process, a group of employees examines existing values and explores new ones, defines them, and identifies behaviors associated with them. The result is a values blueprint.

Juniper chose more than 200 employees from around the world—including new hires, senior engineers, managers and the CEO—to participate in creating the blueprint. "I had a chance to listen and understand the perspectives of others," Johnson says. To identify behaviors associated with desired values, the group used the Organizational Cultural Inventory from Human Synergistics Inc. and produced a draft blueprint in two days.

The 35-member executive team reviewed the blueprint and then held discussions among 120 top leaders. "The executive staff decided on its own, without any coaching, to share this in small sessions with employee groups of no more than 100," Pryor says.

Thus was born the Trio Tour: Groups of three senior executives, often including Johnson, conducted 75 meetings with groups of employees, mostly in person but some virtual, to promote the strategy, the values and the company's promise to customers: a workforce dedicated to innovation, collaboration, authenticity, trust, high performance and leadership in its field. "We framed this incredibly powerful culture work as a renewal of our culture and values, like a long-married couple would renew their wedding vows," Pryor says.

Rhoades applauds the executives' rare commitment to the values rollout.

Hiring to Build the Brand

Rice's HR team began to look for ways to infuse the values throughout talent management processes. The goal was to hire, retain and develop people who have the right skills and knowledge and who share the company's values, too. "If the customer sees you as team-oriented and such and the customer service guy is different, you have a problem," Rice says. "You have to hire against the brand."

Performance Management Redux

When asked which Juniper value was least apparent in practice, employees said trust. They cited the annual performance review as an example of lack of trust.

Employees expressed concern about the lack of positive feedback, the forced labeling from a ranking system, and even the use of words like "review" and "appraisal."

"We fundamentally rethought our performance management process," says Greg Pryor, HR vice president for leadership and organization development. "It was inspired by the managers who brought this to our attention."

The old performance review was a typical backward-looking process to identify where the employee needed to improve and involved rating each employee. A distribution curve was imposed on the ratings of the entire population.

The process was replaced with a semiannual "conversation day." On these days, employees and managers discuss areas for improvement and areas for new growth, set stretch goals, and align the goals with employees' career aspirations. There is no rating given or a specific measure of improvement expected.

Internal surveys indicated that 93 percent of employees participated in the first conversation day and 66 percent of participants found it "helpful" to "extremely helpful," Pryor says. Conversation days would not be possible without other practices introduced by HR. For example:

- Goal alignment became a separate activity. Employees and managers set goals aligned with the business unit's and the company's overall strategy. More employees are included in this activity than were included in the past.
- Compensation planning now involves a statement of guidance that gives local managers more leeway in distributing merit pay, rather than rigid guidelines for doing so.
- Instead of imposing a distribution curve on employees' ratings, there is now relative laddering within each occupational and geographical group. There are 300 such ladders.
- Detailed talent scenarios for each group now give managers and employees guidance for steps to take based on the scenario in which each employee best fits.

—Bill Roberts

In Rice's view, a strong culture has these three components:

- Employees who agree with the mission.
- The ability to identify, keep and develop those types of employees.
- Willingness on the part of corporate leaders to let values drive decisions—from talent management processes to corporate giving.

Juniper's HR team began to identify key attributes, based on the values, that should be sought in any employee and to create about 300 job descriptions (called "architectures") that include the skills, knowledge, behaviors and values associated with each role in the company. The central values of collaboration, authenticity and trust define employees the company calls its J Players. "Our aspiration is 100 percent J players," Rice says.

In conversations and through other communications, business-unit leaders and others asked employees where The Juniper Way fell short in practice. Trust came up, with the annual performance review seen as a culprit. "We got feedback that our existing performance management process was not consistent with the values," Pryor says, so HR professionals revamped the process.

About this time, Pryor discovered David Rock, founder and CEO of Results Coaching Systems LLC, with headquarters in New York City and Sydney, Australia. Rock coined the term "neuroleadership" and founded the NeuroLeadership Institute to promote leadership training.

He uses a model for influencing behavior called SCARF—which stands for status, certainty, autonomy, relatedness and fairness. The model gave Pryor and Rice hard evidence to show engineers and scientists, who were initially skeptical of some of the changes included in the new performance management process.

Culture Shift

Juniper executives point out that the changes are rooted in the need to achieve authenticity with customers. "We are dealing with the most richly informed buyers in history," says Lauren Flaherty, executive vice president and chief marketing officer, who adds that when companies don't act genuinely, they "do so at their own peril."

Flaherty and Rice work together on overseeing the brand and values rollout internally and externally. "You always hope that what you present to the marketplace externally has an authentic origin from within. But you often hope more than it is reality," Flaherty says.

Juniper is different from most companies, she admits. "It has a very open, collaborative culture. It is not burdened by turf. Synergies are seen as a good thing. That's why you can get a marketing team and HR team to work together to change the external face and internal face of the company."

Juniper's efforts are unusual, even for Silicon Valley standards, but other HR executives are taking note. "There is a cultural shift happening more generally, and a lot of HR organizations are waking up to it," says Paul Whitney, vice president of HR and site services for Infinera Corp., an optical networking company based in Sunnyvale, Calif. Whitney is familiar with Juniper's leaders' efforts.

Ernst acknowledges that Juniper might appear to be so different that it does not offer any direct analogy to traditional industries. But he cautions that more corporate leaders are experiencing or soon will experience similar demands for creativity, flexibility and collaboration.

"Even in government, education and family-owned business, all organizations are dealing with challenges they have not seen before and need to learn to work in new ways," Ernst says.

Critical Thinking

1. What do you think about Juniper Foundation's lofty goals?
2. What are your values? How readily can you list your top five values? How readily can you prioritize these?
3. How do you think employees respond to a values-driven work environment?

Internet References

Creating a High Performance, Values-Aligned Culture
www.kenblanchard.com/getattachment/Leading-Research/Research/A-Values-Aligned-Culture/Blanchard_Creating_a_High_Performance_Values-Aligned_Culture.pdf

The New Leadership Paradigm: Servant Leaders in Values
www.examiner.com/article/the-new-leadership-paradigm-servant-leaders-values-driven-organizations

Values-Driven Leadership
http://cvdl.org/values-driven_leadership/definitions.asp

BILL ROBERTS is technology contributing editor for HR Magazine and is based in Silicon Valley.

Unit 7

UNIT

Prepared by: Maria Nathan, *Lynchburg College*

International Human Resource Management

Many organizations are global in some facet or another. For example, they may off-shore or they may have a subsidiary in a foreign country. Globalization tends to create much change within the organization. Foreign exchange, bank intermediaries across countries, different time zones and different languages. . . . A whole another layer of complexity has been added to the business equation.

So too with HRM. Globalization creates especial concerns for the HR function. Some teams of researchers have been studying the employee who goes to work in a foreign country on behalf of their company. These expatriates may be gone for short stints or long ones. How do they manage life abroad? Researchers are finding that they must train employees who will go overseas if they are to go full term in their assignment. Furthermore, the family of the employee must be socialized, so they know what to expect. Many expatriate stints that have ended early were because of employee family problems that developed while their family was living overseas. Expatriates also frequently find that they have been forgotten at home. While they were away and learning amazing things and doing exciting work, people at home got on with their lives. An employee returns home expecting to be a hero and finds he is not considered a hero by those at home.

Yet more than a few top executives aver that any employee seeking promotion to top levels of the organization should be required to live in a foreign country for a time. These employees become more valuable because of what they've become as a result of their overseas work. Maybe soon employers will learn how to integrate their expatriates back into the workplace in a gratifying and meaningful way for all involved.

So the HRM person is prone to many sorts of headaches that are distinctly about the global scope of the organization. Benefits programs, pay, culture, leadership, employee relations, and followership—are frequently very different from country to country. One size fits all does not fit comfortably for those involved. As time passes, more organizations are finding new and interesting innovations that suit their business needs. For example, some organizations have off-shored their corporate headquarters for various important business reasons. Some organizations have relied upon offshoring so much that they are advised to be careful that their organizations haven't become "hollow corporations."

There is much to be learned about what works and doesn't work among global employers. We know a lot about what doesn't work so far! We are finding that there is a regionalization thrust in global business in which organizations in countries that are closer geographically are tending to work together more and more. This reduces many of the distance, language, culture, time zone, and other obstacles. We shall see what regionalization does for global business and international HRM in the future.

In the military, there is an acronym that still gets used—K.I.S.S.—keep it simple, stupid. Yes, let's keep what is already a highly complex matter as simple as possible.

Article   Prepared by: Maria Nathan, *Lynchburg College*

HR Best Practices Can Lead to a Better Expat Experience

Mentoring employees before and during an expat assignment is among the effective preparation strategies for adjusting to a new country

KATHY GURCHIEK

Learning Outcomes

After reading this article, you will be able to:

- Know what is meant by "expat."

- Appreciate what the expat experience might be like.

- Consider that HR has an integral role in the preparation of a company's expatriates for assignment.

Employees who have accepted international assignments adjust and perform better in the host country when effective HR management practices are implemented, according to a report included in a compilation of research that the SHRM Foundation recently released.

The findings in Crossing Cultures: Unpacking the Expatriate Learning and Adjustment Process over Time are based on responses from 171 expatriates surveyed 30 days before leaving for their assignments and then nine more times over the first nine months of their international assignment. The respondents—nearly ¾ of whom were men, and most of whom had a spouse and children moving with them—were from three multinational organizations. Their assignments spanned 38 countries in Africa, the Americas, Asia, Australia and Europe.

The study found that the expat's psychological well-being, language fluency and training before relocation had a positive overall effect on adjusting in the first nine months of the international experience. The findings, the researchers wrote, underscore the importance of HR practitioners understanding the expat's adjustment process. HR professionals must make sure their organization:

- Addresses the employee's need to develop language fluency in the international assignment.

- Offers psychological screening to assess readiness for an international assignment, including an individual's openness to having an international experience.

- Provides strong support before and during the assignment, including setting clear expectations about the employee's role and performance and giving feedback and assistance.

- Provides the employee with a self-assessment tool prior to the international assignment to help set realistic expectations for adjusting to the host country.

- Provides a mentor in the host country. A former, current or more experienced expatriate to offer an insider's perspective can be especially helpful; a host-country national who is a distinguished organizational leader also would be a good choice.

- Maintains a connection between the expatriate and the home-based organization.

Mentors, Support Team

Cynthia Biro, global co-head of Skills Village at PeopleTicker, an information provider based in the New York City area, found that mentors in the host country helped her when she opened offices in various international locations. In preparation, her employer arranged for expatriates in those countries to contact her about a month before she left the U.S. Once she was in the host country, each expat spent several hours, on different days, introducing Biro to the area, including showing her where to shop for food and taking her on tours of the city to expose her to various areas and to learn the city's history, she noted in a Society for Human Resource Management (SHRM) discussion on LinkedIn.

"I cannot tell you how much it helped me in my management and expansion efforts whilst [I was] onsite. Everyone was much more approachable in the office, because we had 'off time' and 'warm introductions' beforehand. I highly suggest this strategy for others. I also had language classes, and they helped, but the introducing of expats prepared me best."

At defense technology company Raytheon, a support team is assigned to an employee who accepts an international assignment, said Randa G. Newsome, vice president of HR and based in Waltham, Mass. The team includes a sponsor, an in-country supervisor and an HR point of contact and it remains active throughout the employee's preparation, deployment and repatriation.

"The support team is responsible for understanding the employee's assignment and career aspirations, and for engaging in regular communication and activities to help the employee fulfill development goals throughout their assignment," she said in an e-mail to SHRM Online. "Most important, the support team works to place the employee in a meaningful company role upon their return—one that aligns with their career aspirations and benefits from their international experience and acumen."

Preselection Criteria, Screening

Spell out pre-selection criteria for expat assignments, said Suzanne Garber, CEO of Gauze, a Philadelphia-based global database of hospitals, in an email to SHRM Online. She has been an expat and has managed and helped other expats prepare for their assignments.

"The onus is on the hiring manager to ensure that cultural compatibility is one of the determining factors to awarding an expat assignment. Without fully understanding this component of the expat assignment, it may be doomed to fail," she noted. "Many rising executives know that obtaining an expat position is one way to propel one's career into super-stardom. . . . However, all who are chosen are not best suited. Why not? Because while the job specs were carefully crafted, the cultural aspects were not. Culture, in an expat position, trumps credentials."

Not everyone will adapt well to a new country or culture, wrote Vancouver, Canada-based HR consultant Debra Walker in an e-mail to SHRM Online.

"Tests that show adaptability, resourcefulness, problem-solving, thinking on one's feet, ability to work in grey [areas]—and even introversion vs. extroversion review—are good to

incorporate, so that individuals that will not adapt well will have a clearer picture before they even leave home soil."

Most multinational firms do not have a standard screening process to identify traits—such as resourcefulness and a high tolerance for ambiguity—that make for a successful expat, said James P. Johnson, PhD, professor of international business at Rollins College Crummer Graduate School of Business in Orlando, Florida.

"These qualities cannot be taught in a brief pre-departure cross-cultural training program. Instead, efforts should be made to identify candidates that have these traits, and to train them in the technical aspects of the international assignment, rather than select the person who has the technical skills and assume that he or she can acquire the necessary soft skills that are essential to international success," he said in an e-mail to SHRM Online.

Language, Cross-cultural Training

Learning the host country's language is important, said Johnson, who has worked in Finland, Great Britain, Mexico, Spain, and the former Yugoslavia.

"It can go a long way in developing relations with employees, colleagues, customers and neighbors," he said, but advised being realistic in one's expectations. "Traditional language training is time-intensive and crash courses can be expensive. In addition, many firms that offer language training require the employee to do it in his or her free time or take vacation days to attend a crash course."

He also thinks cross-cultural training should be a mandatory component of an international assignment.

"Less than 50 percent of firms require it, although many are getting better in realizing that training is not only essential for the employee, but for spouses [or significant others] and family members" accompanying the employee, he noted in an e-mail. Family members should have access to training as well for help securing a driver's license, for example, and locating babysitters, schools and English-speaking medical providers.

And Gauze's Garber stressed that additional cultural training is a must, even if the assignee has visited, worked in or previously lived in the host country.

"It is imperative to get a briefing on what's going on in the country now. This includes an update from a political, gastronomical, religious, and security perspective."

Richard Phillips, managing director at Britam, a risk management and training consultancy in London, has employed more than 1,000 staff members in expatriate roles over the last 11 years—most commonly in "quite challenging environments," he said in an e-mail to SHRM Online.

"The single most important part of their preparation is making absolutely sure they understand the living and working environment they are about to enter—warts and all! To avoid wasting time and money, do this first and check as part of your quality process. It is human nature to look at the positives of a role and skip the bits you don't know much about."

"Make sure your candidates are fully appraised of the challenges, issues and differences to their previous experience to avoid them wanting to return five minutes after arrival."

Critical Thinking

1. What expatriate experiences can lead to a better experience abroad?

2. Would you be interested in working as an expatriate for a firm someday? In what country would you like to be based?

3. Do you know someone who served in an expatriate assignment? Did you ever talk to them about it?

Internet References

Best Resources for Expatriates
http://www.transitionsabroad.com/listings/living/resources/

Expat Exchange: Resources for Expats
http://www.expatexchange.com/expatresources

Living Abroad and Expatriate Resources
http://www.contrariantraveler.com/resources/expatriates.html

KATHY GURCHIEK is the associate editor at *HR News*.

Article   Prepared by: Maria Nathan, *Lynchburg College*

Offshored Headquarters

Global human resources becomes a top priority—fast—when foreign companies buy U.S. operations.

ALLEN SMITH

Learning Outcomes

After reading this article, you will be able to:

- Understand unique challenges of offshoring a corporate headquarters.

- Reflect upon HR's role in managing the offshored headquarters.

I t's not every day that companies such as General Motors (GM)—once the largest private employer in the world—go bankrupt. Sichuan Tengzhong Heavy Industrial Machinery Co.'s purchase of the Hummer brand as part of GM's bankruptcy plan, announced June 2, may not be just the end of an era for GM. It may signal the purchase of other U.S. businesses by companies based abroad, a trend that shouldn't be too surprising in light of the global economy.

Of the four most populous countries—China, India, the United States and Indonesia—only the United States was predicted to have a shrinking gross domestic product (GDP) in 2009. Last June, the Organisation for Economic Co-operation and Development, based in Paris, projected that the GDP in China would grow by 7.7 percent in 2009, India's would rise 5.9 percent and Indonesia's 3.5 percent.

Would you be ready if your corporate headquarters suddenly went offshore? Any merger can be challenging for HR professionals, but that's especially true when the C-suite suddenly flies across the globe.

Fortunately, HR leaders can learn lessons from those who have been through this. When Doosan, based in Seoul, South Korea, bought the Bobcat unit from Ingersoll Rand Co. in 2007, the acquired company launched a familiarization program for employees on both sides of the Pacific, even sending U.S. employees to Seoul to immerse themselves in Korean culture, says Bonnie Guttormson, SPHR, director of compensation and benefits at Doosan in West Fargo, N.D.

Bridging cultural differences is not the only challenge, according to Jay Warren, an attorney with Bryan Cave LLP in New York. During foreign takeovers, HR leaders must run on "a compliance track and business-culture track." One challenge on the compliance track: the need to "manage upward," which means not simply telling executives what they may want to hear but instead informing them if standard business operating procedures in their countries would lead to legal challenges in the United States.

After hearing bits and pieces about the at-will rule, owners of foreign companies may overestimate how much leeway U.S. employers have in dismissing employees, cautions Laurence Stuart, an attorney with Stuart & Associates PC in Houston and a member of the Society for Human Resource Management (SHRM) Labor Relations Special Expertise Panel. Stuart has come across a "cowboy mentality" among some new foreign owners of U.S. businesses—purchasers who assume that when an employee must be terminated, "anything goes."

Beginners' Mistakes

"There will be a huge difference" among foreign buyers that have US. operations and foreign buyers purchasing their first U.S. ventures, according to Donald Dowling Jr., an attorney with White & Case LLP in New York.

For HR professionals who already have been through mergers, much about foreign takeovers may seem the same as with new U.S. owners. Dowling says many urgent issues remain largely the same: post-merger integration, layoffs, internal restructuring, new reporting relationships, alignment of HR offerings and policies, and so forth.

That said, HR employees will face additional layers of complexity when purchasers are based abroad, Dowling says, noting that his wife works at a French-owned company. "When the foreign-based buyer has other existing U.S. operations, it will likely aim toward integrating this new operation with its other U.S. business lines," he says. "When the foreign-based buyer is taking its first steps into the U.S. via this acquisition, that is where the cultural and HR problems are likely to be most acute."

Stuart "has seen activity among foreign buyers looking for U.S. companies." He suspects this trend will intensify "if other economies get strong before us." In Texas, he sees the most activity among owners of international private equity firms based in Europe who are eyeing energy-related businesses.

Different Lens

Many foreign professionals have the "misconception that the U.S. employment market is not heavily regulated. That obviously is not correct," Stuart notes.

While the United States does not have the kinds of national and local severance and termination protection common in the European Union (EU), he says many U.S. laws protect classes of individuals from discrimination. That "makes the U.S. market more heavily regulated than Europe, but the risks aren't as obvious."

Foreign executives may be used to more-unionized settings but unfamiliar with laws such as the Americans with Disabilities Act and the Family and Medical Leave Act. Consequently, he cautions, sometimes "they don't understand the role documentation procedures and policies have in reducing risks."

Foreign executives may be used to more-unionized settings but unfamiliar with laws such as the Americans with Disabilities Act and the Family and Medical Leave Act.

Stuart recommends employment law training to familiarize new owners with US. laws and their applications.

Dowling notes that "EU executives come from a culture that has complex and intrusive employment regulations—far more so than under U.S.-style employment at will." But, he says misunderstandings arise because the at-will rule has given rise to a highly evolved—to a European, a disproportionate—series of equal employment opportunity, discrimination and harassment regulations.

As a result, European executives purchasing U.S. businesses "need to reorient their thinking" about employment law

compliance, according to Dowling. From the European perspective, "the good news is that the U.S. state and federal systems impose far fewer employment laws and rules than they are used to. The bad news is that Americans look at employment relationships through the lens of discrimination." And, he says, "To a European executive, Americans appear over-concerned with what the European might see as political correctness."

However, Dowling doesn't think foreign executives necessarily are surprised by the compliance risks in the United States: "European executives hear horror stories about U.S. court judgments—multimillion-dollar verdicts, runaway juries, class actions and unpredictable results," he notes. But they still "will need to be shown where the land mines lie."

Dowling adds that U.S. unionization laws constitute a separate issue, and he advises incoming businesses to develop a U.S. union strategy.

Stuart recalls several foreign-based clients that have unions in Europe and have been "pushed into signing global codes of conduct" that simply weren't practical for U.S. operations. For example, in global codes of conduct, foreign businesses may have provisions prohibiting mandatory overtime, even though mandatory overtime may be an industry norm in the United States and a feature many workers want. Or, global codes of conduct may specify the intervals for employees to have days off, even though seven-day workweeks while employees are offshore are common in the energy sector, he adds.

Stuart recommends that U.S. HR professionals and attorneys conduct due diligence and look into overseas policies that would be unlawful if applied in the United States. For example, mandatory retirement is common overseas.

HR professionals shouldn't be surprised if colleagues at acquiring companies do not understand the exempt/nonexempt distinctions under federal and state wage and hour laws, as well as other state-specific requirements, according to Baker & McKenzie attorneys Susan Eandi, Ute Krudewagen, John Raudabaugh and Carole Spink.

In addition, foreign employers often do not understand that employee benefits are provided at the employer's discretion in most circumstances, or that the amount and quality of benefits a company provides affects its ability to attract and retain employees, the Baker & McKenzie attorneys add.

Face to Face

There's much for U.S. employees to learn about the prevailing culture of an overseas purchasing company's C-suite.

At Bobcat, employees were used to having the C-suite overseas even before Doosan purchased it, since Bobcat was owned by Ingersoll Rand, a global construction equipment business based in Ireland. But, to help get employees on the right cultural track,

Online Resources

For more about HR professionals' role when a foreign business buys domestic operations, see the online version of this article at www.shrm.org/hrmagazine. For other resources on employment law, visit www.shrm.org/law.

some Bobcat employees were paid to travel to Seoul following Doosan's acquisition. Guttormson says the company started flying over top-level executives and is working its way down the organization. She is slated to be in the next group to visit.

Guttormson recommends familiarization training for employees in the United States as well as for those in the purchasing company, even if the purchaser seems to be a good match, as was the case with Doosan. Familiarization training might include an introduction to cultural differences. For example, Guttormson notes that Korean culture is "very hierarchical, so where here in the United States we're very free to talk with higher officials about differences, there the process is to go through the hierarchy."

To smooth the way for foreign travelers in the United States, Dowling recommends that employers start getting visas early.

Employees' Fears

Cultural differences intimidate some, according to Thomas Belker, SPHR, GPHR, managing director of HR for OBI—one of the world's largest home improvement companies, located in 15 countries—based near Cologne, Germany. "We say it is a global world, but nonetheless many line managers have never been exposed to dealing with cultural differences," he notes. "Nor do they necessarily understand anything about foreign laws and their impact on HR processes. There is quite normally a huge gap caused by resentment or a lack of understanding of foreign HR issues."

Belker, a member of the SHRM Global Special Expertise Panel, recommends starting with minor changes and paying close attention to employees' initial reactions.

Michelle Haste, an attorney with Crowell & Moring in London, recommends that HR leaders stay in "close contact with U.S. employees who may be fearful of acquisition by a foreign entity." She says HR executives from the purchaser and the seller should cultivate relationships that enable "full and frank communication on the differences."

Reset Expectations

One point of discussion should be the cultural work expectations, such as whether employees can speak freely or are expected to be subordinate to managers, advises Brenda Cossette, SPHR, HR director for the City of Fergus Falls, Minn., and a member of the SHRM Labor Relations Special Expertise Panel.

The foreign company can have very different values, and it may put a premium on running extremely efficient operations compared to some of our U.S. companies, Cossette says. "Employee loyalty to the new brand name or new company is a real difficult issue since many smaller companies are often bought up by foreign companies," she explains. "These small companies are proud of being a local company, and now a foreign company only sees them in terms of sales or diversification of their product lines."

According to Cossette, many Asian companies don't have big bonuses and stock plans for leaders, raising concerns among U.S. executives who depend on those plans—assuming these executives aren't laid off following the purchase.

Role Clarification

Stuart notes that in some jurisdictions, the HR function may even "be purely administrative as opposed to being strategic business partners."

HR leaders should be sure they understand what the decision-making process will be following the acquisition. Will all decisions flow through headquarters abroad, or will the new C-suite choose not to get involved in day-to-day activities?

HR leaders should be sure they understand what the decision-making process will be following the acquisition.

The answer affects liability in lawsuits, says Warren, explaining that if a foreign company acquires a publicly traded U.S. company through stock acquisition but does not get involved in decision-making, the parent company would have no legal liability.

However, if the foreign purchaser doesn't trust U.S. officers to make decisions and starts calling the shots, it would be treated as liable, he cautions. So, the acquiring company "may want to keep itself separate."

Managing Upward

Managing upward always is a challenge, but particularly with officers based abroad—and when there are cultural and linguistic divides.

"Most of us try to listen to get to what the boss wants," Warren notes. But HR leaders should be quick to recognize when bosses overseas are inadvertently asking them to implement changes that would fly in the face of domestic law. Warren says that takes "active and patient listening."

The challenge, he notes, is to respond "in a way that does not lead to friction, not to say, 'That's not the way we do things here.'" He recommends that HR professionals make sure they understand what bosses are asking—and then, make sure it's legal stateside.

Critical Thinking

1. How are mergers with offshored companies more complicated than simply domestic companies?

2. Why are cultural considerations important?

3. What are some of the implications for HR?

Internet References

Offshoring—Society for Human Resource Management
www.shrm.org/Research/FutureWorkplaceTrends/Documents/0402WorkpcVisions.pdf

Offshoring's Impact on Human Resources
http://smallbusiness.chron.com/offshorings-impact-human-resources-25748.html

Article   Prepared by: Maria Nathan, *Lynchburg College*

"People Analytics" Are Helping Employers Make Savvier Hires

Jeffrey J. Selingo

Learning Outcomes

After reading this article, you will be able to:

- Understand what "people analytics" are.

- Appreciate how "people analytics" can help an employer to hire people more effectively.

It's that time of year when a crop of new college graduates floods the job market looking for work. But how those with freshly minted bachelor's degrees eventually match up with employers is often a haphazard process for an economy as advanced as that of the United States.

Employers don't plan far in advance for their hiring needs. They evaluate candidates during interviews based largely on gut instinct, and rely heavily on the halo effect of credentials from elite universities.

Anyone who has ever done the hiring for a job has a story about a mistaken hire. According to one survey by the Corporate Executive Board, hiring managers regretted making offers to one in five people on their staffs.

Increasingly, companies are embracing new technology and data analytics in making their talent decisions. It's called "people analytics," and it follows in the footsteps of professional sports teams that use data to evaluate talent—a process made famous by the book and movie "Moneyball," about how the Oakland Athletics fielded an inexpensive, yet competitive, baseball team.

Human resources offices at major companies now harness thousands of pieces of data to figure out why and how their workers are hired, fired and promoted. This shift could transform how students find employment when they leave college and forever change the value of the degree as the sole signaling device that someone is job ready.

Today, 4,500 companies have at least one employee focused on people analytics; half the companies created those positions after 2010.

Credit Suisse is one. The global banking firm has had various new hires that didn't pan out. Meanwhile, others who had summer internships there turned down offers for full-time jobs in favor of positions at other banks, tech companies or private-equity firms. Bank officials were worried about getting a reputation as a place where new hires failed or didn't stay long.

"With all of the challenges we face in the market for top university recruits, hiring mistakes can end up harming our brand," said William Wolf, who until recently was head of talent acquisition and development at Credit Suisse.

One of Credit Suisse's early goals was to study hiring successes to see how possible it was to identify recruits who would "survive and thrive." As Wolf defined it, those are employees who stay for more than two years and perform well.

The people analytics team at Credit Suisse tried to determine whether certain experiences in a student's background could better predict success at the company. Wolf's team looked at dozens of variables on résumés and in the screening process and asked a series of questions: Do athletes outperform non-athletes? (They don't.) Does evidence of accomplishment in music matter? (It doesn't among undergraduates, but sustained accomplishment among graduate students does.) Foreign language competency? (Doesn't help.)

Some of the answers led to changes in Credit Suisse's screening and interviewing process. For example, historically the bank had emphasized quantitative reasoning in hiring given the number of calculations young bankers do every day. So it tended to favor applicants with high GMAT scores, SAT math scores and college grade-point averages.

But the data team discovered that attributes such as leadership counted for much more than expected, and the bank developed new scoring guidelines that emphasized leadership across the board, and not just leadership itself. For example, students who had earned the top spot through skill or dedication, such as a captain of a varsity athletic team, were more likely to succeed than those popularly elected to, say, student government.

Whether the data will significantly change the list of top colleges and universities Credit Suisse typically recruits from remains unclear. Wolf acknowledged that campus hiring is still done by an army of volunteer screeners and interviewers who apply their judgment to candidates. So a student with a 3.8 GPA from Big State U may be asked tougher questions than a student with a similar GPA from an Ivy League school because the interviewer uses a higher standard, thinking that hiring the Big State U candidate is a risk.

As a result, it's difficult to say whether hires from one school perform better than those from another, given the different human filters. "Our team tries to improve the judgment of recruiters by arming them with analytical information when it appears their biases have led to poor decisions," Wolf said.

Wolf hopes that by emphasizing data and results over traditional biases recruiters will become more confident about hiring students from nontraditional colleges. Over time, he believes, the school name on the diploma will matter less to hiring managers. Already, by using virtual recruiting, the bank is hiring from a broader range of schools, and that helps Credit Suisse reach more students who want to make banking a long-term career, not a ticket to be punched on the way to a hedge-fund job.

The future of what people analytics might mean for new college graduates goes well beyond what is listed on résumés and academic transcripts.

It is being built by the likes of a Silicon Valley start-up called Knack, which makes video games for smartphones.

Knack's games are not purely for entertainment, however. They measure the users' resourcefulness, numerical reasoning and risk-taking. In one game, Wasabi Waiter, for example, the task is to deliver sushi orders based on the facial expressions of a growing number of customers who suddenly appear on the screen. Users give out menus, deliver a lineup of food from meals piling up in the kitchen and clear dishes. Meanwhile, behind the scenes, the game tracks every move, noting how well a user prioritizes, solves problems and learns from mistakes—all skills employers want. In just 10 to 20 minutes, the game collects enough information to make an assessment of abilities.

Royal Dutch Shell's innovation team uses Knack to find the best ideas of the hundreds proposed at the company. Knack also is working with colleges to open the games to students so they can demonstrate their skills to potential employers well before they hit the job market. Students earn badges as they play the games, such as Leadership, Grit and Logistical Reasoning, which they can display online for potential employers to discover. Eventually, Guy Halfteck, Knack's founder, hopes the games will help short-circuit the long and ineffective recruitment process for new college graduates.

"The interview process will change its form and function," Halfteck said. "Instead of using the interview process to filter out the best candidates, you'll start the interview process with only the best candidates."

Selingo is a contributor to The Washington Post's Grade Point blog. This article is adapted from his new book, "There Is Life After College: What Parents and Students Should Know About Navigating School to Prepare for the Jobs of Tomorrow" (William Morrow, an imprint of HarperCollins).

Critical Thinking

1. How are "people analytics" being used by HR managers in hiring decisions?
2. What do you think of Knack's video game for smart phones being used by employers for prospective hires?
3. Would you like a selection tool such as is used by Royal Dutch Shell in your interview protocol? Explain.

Internet References

Google Analytics 360
www.google.com/analytics/marketing.
People Analytics and Planning for Workforce Performance
http://www.acendre.com/solutions/people-analytics
People Analytics Resource Center,' www.workday.com
https://www.workday.com/en-us/pages/bersin-resource-center.html

JEFFREY J. SELINGO is the author of There Is Life After College, a book about how today's graduates launch into their careers, and the best-selling College (Un)Bound. He is the former editor of the Chronicle of Higher Education, a professor of practice at Arizona State University, and a visiting scholar at Georgia Tech's Center for 21st Century Universities.

Unit 8

UNIT

Prepared by: Maria Nathan, *Lynchburg College*

Human Resource Information Systems, Metrics, and Analytics

The sheer amount of data available to firms is formidable. It is therefore more difficult to spot and gather actionable data given the sheer volume of data that is available.

More and more, firms are using dashboards and cloud-based searchable depositories. They are using data more effectively and digging deeper into the data in search of useful segments. They gather this information on a quarterly or even more frequent basis. The information may be segmented by division, department, or job-level . . .

HR functions are using dashboards more frequently with time. They might choose 8–12 metrics. They cover every functional facet of HR: Recruitment metrics include employee referral rates; retention metrics include high/low performer performance differentials; compensation/benefits metrics includes appraisal rating to salary ratio; diversity/culture metrics include employee happiness. Development metrics include employee satisfaction with development.

It is not just that metrics are used, but also how the metrics are used. It is not just about providing data that shares status updates but dynamic data that supports decision making. The HR function has much to gain from metrics that elucidate costs, recruiter efficiency, time to fill, quality of hire, source of hire, and employee referrals. There are many more metrics that might be calculated depending upon the HR purpose. However, using fewer meaningful measures is probably better than using too many metrics that may not even do a good job of capturing a concept or relationship with clarity.

This moves us on to predictive analytics that permit the firm to make informed decisions about the future. Wayne Gretzky's advice, "Skate to where the puck is going to be, not where it has been" is what is here referred to. For example, a firm can anticipate which high value employees are most likely to leave the firm. Competitive analytics may also prime a firm to know when a key figure in a competitor firm has left or if the competitor has planned a change of strategy.

There is so much more work ahead for firms seeking to use analytics and metrics for insight and action. There is also quite a volume of data and many metrics that remain underused that may be mined in the years ahead.

Article   Prepared by: Maria Nathan, *Lynchburg College*

HR Dashboard and Useful Metrics: Bringing More Insight and Life to Your Dashboard

Darcy Jacobsen

Learning Outcomes

After reading this article, you will be able to:

- Understand what a dashboard is.

- Consider why a dashboard could be indispensable to a manager.

- Imagine what an HR dashboard might look like for an HR generalist.

Last Friday, we talked about some of the principles behind building a great HR dashboard, and today I wanted to share a few metrics I think are worth considering. Ultimately, in choosing your 8–12 metrics, you will have to rely on your own instincts and on feedback from those around you. To get you started, I've listed below some of your options—as well as some key metrics I think you should consider—that could bring more insight and life to your dashboard.

Recruitment Metrics

If your HR group is currently gathering metrics, they're likely based on recruitment. This would include metrics, such as vacancies, average days open, cost per vacancy, cost per hire, temporary staffing, agency costs, and search fees. Some companies also track hiring manager satisfaction and candidate satisfaction.

Consider Tracking

1. Hiring manager interviews to offers ratio (by manager): Tracking how many interviews it takes to get to an average

offer will give you a sense of how efficient recruitment is across your departments, and which managers might need assistance or guidance with their hiring processes.

2. Yield ratio (percentage of hires by recruitment source): Are you tracking the relative efficiency of your recruitment sources to determine which are most effective and valuable for future investment? Shouldn't you be?

3. Employee referral rates by department or business units: One of the key questions NetPromoter uses to determine customer satisfaction scores is: "How likely is it that you would recommend [your company] to a friend or colleague?" Tracking actual referrals gives you a real time answer to this question when it comes to employee satisfaction, and a deep comparative insight about each area of your business.

4. Quality of hire: The quality of hire metric is not an easy one to get at, but Steve Lowisz at ERE.com believes it is one of the most important hiring metrics you can track. He suggests using a formula that derives QoH by averaging job performance rating of new hires, the percentage of new hires reaching acceptable productivity with acceptable time frame, and the percentage of new hires retained after one year. I would argue you can also include the amount of recognition that new hires receive, to get a more complete picture of how the hire is regarded throughout the organization.

Retention Metrics

Retention is another area many HR departments are already tracking. These stats might range from simple average tenure to metrics like 90-day retention rate, monthly or annual turnover rates and average turnover costs. This is also where many companies collect data from exit interviews.

Consider Tracking

1. Retention rate of critical employees: It isn't enough to have a high retention rate, if you're still losing key talent. Use HCM tools and recognition data to identify and flag your key contributors, cultural energizers and future leaders, and then look specifically at your retention rates among those groups.

2. High/low performer retention differential: Likewise, it makes sense to do a comparison of departures by performance review ratings, to determine if there are patterns there that should be addressed.

3. Resignation rates by department: Parsing resignation data by manager and department can highlight potential issues in a given group or with a given manager.

Compensation/Benefits Metrics

Because it is directly related to money and the bottom line, Compensation and Benefits is a focal point for many senior executives. They want to be sure they are getting a maximum ROEI (Return on Employee Investment). Metrics here might include average compensation (or average compensation by employee level), benefit cost per employee, benefit as a percentage of salary, benefits as a percentage of revenue (or operating expenses), overtime, healthcare costs, or recognition spend.

Consider Tracking

1. Appraisal rating-to-salary ratio: Get ahead of your voluntary turnover rate and ensure that your best employees won't be tempted away by higher salaries by tracking the percentage of employees who are rated in the top performance appraisal level and who are paid above the average salary for their position (and vice versa).

2. Recognition reach in key populations: Do your top employees feel appreciated at your company? Are they building critical relationships with peers and managers that will keep them happy and productive? How big is your winners circle where it matters? One simple way to see this is to track recognition reach for key groups like high potentials or flight risks.

Culture and Diversity Metrics

More and more HR pros are taking closer note of culture and diversity metrics, in order to better measure and improve the experience of working in their organizations. Engagement and satisfaction have long been annual survey staples, but some companies are also employing short pulse surveys to keep tabs on those metrics more regularly. Companies are also tracking diversity—whether by race, military service or gender—by looking at (for example) how many women are in their workforce; new hire groups, or being promoted into management

and executive levels. Union percentage is also another important indicator of worker population mix.

Consider Tracking

1. Strength of company values: Use performance review data and real-time recognition data to measure the comparative strength of your company core values. Track by department, business unit or company-wide. If your R&D department is being recognized for "teamwork" but not "innovation," you might have a problem on your hands.

2. Employee happiness: Even a few years ago, employee happiness was considered fluffy and irrelevant. Now, companies are beginning to understand the enormous impact of employee happiness and its effect on morale and productivity. Consider pulse surveys, or at the very least adding a few questions to your satisfaction or engagement surveys to measure this critical stat. (Also, consider attending next Thursday's webinar on happiness, co-hosted by Jessica Miller-Merrell and our own Derek Irvine.)

3. Average workforce age/projected retirements: Tracking average workforce age can give you some important psychographic detail on your employees and help you to estimate and prepare for future talent and leadership crunches due to retirement.

Staffing/Performance/Productivity Metrics

Staffing metrics are bread and butter numbers that connect your workforce and the results that they drive. It begins with simple headcount and encompasses metrics such as absenteeism, workforce productivity (dollars spent on people/revenue or profit generated), performance goals (number of performance goals met or exceeded / total number of performance goals), revenue per employee, and labor costs as a percentage of revenues. It also might triangulate against stats like operating margin, profit, and number of defects.

Consider Tracking

1. HR to staff ratio (employees/HR team members): One thing HR practitioners sometimes forget to do is look out for their own needs. Be sure you're adequately tracking the ratio of HR to staff to ensure that your team grows along with your business.

Development Metrics

Employee development is poised to become one of the most critical issues of the decade, as increasingly development is being positioned as a differentiator of employee brand. Metrics from this group include stats such as: number of promotions from within, average length of time before promotion, average salary raise per promotion, percentage of employees receiving training, number of certifications, number of training development hours, training cost per employee, and stats on tuition reimbursement.

Consider Tracking

1. Employee satisfaction with development: Use survey data to track the percentage of your employees who are satisfied with the learning and growth opportunities provided by your organization.

2. Social graphs and percentage of employees reached by recognition: Ensure that you are facilitating communication and maximizing positive feedback loops in your organization by encouraging bonds of recognition among employees. Recognition analytics will let you visualize real-time relationships and communication among workgroups. The data can also be mapped against performance ratings to highlight potential problem areas.

Health, Safety, and Sustainability Metrics

Health, safety, and sustainability are other rising concerns for many organizations, and therefore deserve a spot on some HR dashboards. Statistics might include: worker's comp incident rates and cost per employee, number of documented safety violations, number of accidents, wellness campaign participation and results, safety incident rates, safety training expenses per employee, and recycling initiatives.

Consider Tracking

1. Number of safety/wellness/sustainability award nominations: Awards and recognition are a great way of seeing real-time engagement in your initiatives, because they are a measure not only of the achievement of those receiving the awards, but the commitment of those who are nominating their peers.

These are just some of the forward-looking metrics you might consider including in your dashboards. In addition, there will also be industry-specific metrics you may want to consider tracking for your organization (such as per diem time for healthcare systems, or intellectual property filings for R&D organizations).

Can you think of any creative or insightful metrics you'd add to this list?

Critical Thinking

1. What does an HR dashboard look like? Why is it used by HR professionals?

2. What are some especially useful metrics that could be included on an HR dashboard?

3. Design an HR dashboard for a company for which you've worked. Why did you choose the metrics you chose?

Internet References

70 HR Metrics with Examples
http://business.simplicable.com/business/new/70-HR-metrics-with-examples

Change Your Company with Better HR Analytics
https://hbr.org/2013/12/change-your-company-with-better-hr-analytics

Top 10 HR Metrics—Knowing the Numbers and How to Use Them
http://www.unicornhro.com/articles/top-ten-hr-metrics--knowing-the-numbers-and-how-to-use-them

---

DARCY JACOBSEN is a content marketing manager for Globoforce. Darcy Jacobsen spends most of her days submerged in reports, tweets, research articles, and other delicious information about the current state of employee recognition and engagement. Her goal is to find the good stuff and pass as much of it as possible on to you! Darcy has a BS and an MA in history from Boston University.

Article

Prepared by: Maria Nathan, *Lynchburg College*

Human Resource Information System as a Strategic Tool in Human Resource Management

EBENEZER ANKRAH AND EVANS SOKRO

Learning Outcomes

After reading this article, you will be able to:

- Know how the use of HRIS supports effectiveness of the strategic human resource manaement function.

- Understand the relationship between HRIS and cost and time savings.

- Understand why it is important for employees—not just HR staff—to be thoroughly educated about HRIS.

Introduction

The use of Human Resource Information Systems (HRIS) has been advocated as an opportunity for human resource (HR) professionals to become strategic partners with top management (Lengnick-Hall and Moritz, 2003). The idea has been that HRIS would allow for the HR function to become more efficient and to provide better information for decision-making. The question remains whether HRIS has fulfilled its promise. In its most basic form HRIS is a system used to acquire, store, manipulate, analyze, retrieve and distribute pertinent information about an organization's human resources. It is often regarded as a service provided to an organization in the form of information (Tannenbaum, 1990). However, the promise is that, as the use of these systems become more widespread, higher level forms of HRIS will evolve.

Lengnick-Hall and Moritz (2003) have postulated that HRIS will be implemented at three different levels: the publishing of information; the automation of transactions; and, finally, a change in the way human resource management is conducted

in the organization by transforming HR into a strategic partner with the line business. In their view, the evolution of HR as promoted by HRIS evolves from information to automation and from automation to transformation. They note that while HRIS has been widely deployed, a transformation of human resource management has occurred in relatively few organizations. The evolution that Lengnick-Hall and Moritz propose, along with others (e.g., Walker, 2001), revolves around the perspective that HRIS will create informational efficiencies and cost savings such that HR departments can turn their attention to providing better analysis of current data and creative uses of the HRIS to provide better and more accurate data upon which to base strategic decisions. Overman (1992), concluded that the potential advantages of HRIS are faster information processing, greater information accuracy, improved planning and program development, and enhanced employee communications.

Problem of Research

Organizations become more complex and as the amount of information they need increases the need for automated information systems increase dramatically. The organization determines what kind of information it will need by deciding what kind of decision it will be making based on the HRIS information and which will be the decision maker. Because these needs are likely to change over time, it is also necessary to build a certain amount of flexibility. However, Human Resources Information Systems (HRIS) is more than a simple aggregation mechanism for inventory control and accounting; it is the foundation for a set of management tools enabling managers to establish objectives for the use of their organization's human resources and to measure the extent to which those objectives have been achieved. As managers come to recognize both the essentiality and feasibility of sophisticated management information systems for monitoring human resources, more and more computerized personnel management information systems such as HRIS will be installed (Orlando and Johnson, 2004).

A significant problem with deciding whether HRIS benefits the organization is that of measuring the effect of HR and more particularly HRIS on the bottom line. There are few clear cut ways to measure the value of HRIS. While there are measurements for administrative HRIS such as cost reductions in HR departments, it is difficult to measure precisely the return on investment and specific improvements in productivity within the HR, there is a link between Human Resource Information Systems (HRIS) and strategic human resources. To gain vital information to be able to compete in a competitive environment, the study seeks to have an in depth analysis of the issue at hand. These and other related issues provided the foundation for this research to be carried out in order to investigate the strategic role of HRIS in human resource management. The main objective of the study is to identify specifically, how the use of Human Resource Information Systems (HRIS) contributes to the effectiveness of strategic human resources management and to examine the strategic importance of using HRIS at the workplace.

Research Focus
Development and Role of HRIS

Recent developments in technology have made it possible to create a real-time information-based, self-service, and interactive work environment. Personnel Information Systems have evolved from the automated employee recordkeeping from the 1960s into more complex reporting and decision systems of late. Today, managers and employees are assuming activities once considered the domain of human resource professionals and administrative personnel. HRIS meet the needs of a number of organizational stakeholders. Typically, the people in the firm who interact with the HRIS are segmented into three groups: HR professionals, managers in functional areas (production, marketing, engineering etc.), and employees. HR professionals rely on the HRIS in fulfilling job functions (regulatory reporting and compliance, compensation analysis, payroll, pension, and profit sharing administration, skill inventory, benefits administration etc.). Thus, for the HR professional there is an increasing reliance on the HRIS to fulfill even the most elementary job tasks. As human capital plays a larger role in competitive advantage, functional managers expect the HRIS to provide functionality to meet the unit's goals and objectives. Moreover, managers rely on the HRIS's capabilities to provide

superior data collection and analysis, especially for performance appraisal and performance management.

Additionally, it also includes skill testing, assessment and development, résumé processing, recruitment and retention, team and project management, and management development. Finally, the individual employees become end users of many HRIS applications. The increased complexity of employee benefit options and the corresponding need to monitor and modify category selections more frequently has increased the awareness of HRIS functionality among employees. Web-based access and self-service options have simplified the modification process and enhanced the usability of many benefit options and administration alternative for most employees.

Apparently, data entry in the past had been one way, but today, scanning technology permits scanning and storage of actual image off an original document, including signatures and handwritten notes. The maintenance function updates and adds new data to the database after data have been entered into the information system. Moreover, the most visible function of an HRIS is the output generated. According to Kovach et al., (1999), to generate valuable output for computer users, the HRIS have to process that output, make the necessary calculations, and then format the presentation in a way that could be understood. However, the note of caution is that, while it is easy to think of HR information systems in terms of the hardware and software packages used to implement them and to measure them by the number of workstations, applications or users who log onto the system, the most important elements of HRIS are not the computers, rather, the information. The bottom line of any comprehensive HRIS have to be the information validity, reliability and utility first and the automation of the process second.

Impact of HRIS on Human Resource Management

The human resource strategy has a significant role in supporting the implementation of the strategy of an organization. Strategic human resource management seeks an answer to the question: How does an organization plan, organize, control and develop human resources to carry out its strategy and to renew its competitive position?

HRIS have tremendous effects on the system of Human Resource Management (HRM). In this direction, a lot of the literature covering the link between human resource management and firm performance is based on the universalistic or "best practices" perspective that "implies a direct relationship between particular approaches to human resources and performance". Many researchers have empirically supported universalistic predictions especially in context where HRIS is concerned. First there are those who focus on a single or several HRM practices and examine their effect on various performance measures. There are also similar studies examining the effect of bundles, or systems, of HRM practices on performance. This stream of research implies that firms should create a high degree of internal consistency among their HR activities. A detailed diagram of an integrated HRIS oriented to strategic needs of organizations is provided by Smith in 1980. Categories in the input transformation and output sections could be used as criteria for an HRIS. Various criteria mainly related to technical and database management systems, but informative to HRIS development, are scattered throughout the article:

a) Data files should be integrated for easy cross-referencing among various departments and redundancy of data minimized.
b) Crucial data should be available on request (i.e. online). Critical information includes: the location of key employees, essential skills data, and promotion and performance information.
c) Appropriate variables for measurement are: employee turnover; absenteeism; type of grievances; frequency of accidents; requests for transfers; trends in personnel costs.
d) Quantifiable measures can include: attitudinal data correlated with demographics, performance and costs.
e) Standard and unplanned reports should be available on a timely basis, including immediate feedback on employee turnover, financial ratios and recruiting results. More sophisticated reporting for career profiles, job applicants' review, etc., is desirable.
f) Advanced features, such as matching current personnel to future needs of an organization, succession planning, organizational change models and identification of prospective future managers and facilitation of their growth and development, which would enhance their performance.

Costs and Benefits of HRIS

An HRIS system represents a large investment decision for companies of all sizes. Therefore, a convincing case to persuade decision makers about the HRIS benefits is necessary. The common benefits of HRIS frequently cited in studies included, improved accuracy, the provision of timely and quick access to information, and the saving of costs (Lederer, 1984; Wille and Hammond, 1981). Lederer (1984) discussed why the accuracy and timeliness of HRIS is very important in terms of operating, controlling, and planning activities in HR. In addition, Kovach et al. (2002) listed several administrative and strategic advantages to using HRIS. Similarly, Beckers and Bsat

(2002) pointed out at least five reasons why companies should use HRIS. These are:

a) Increase competitiveness by improving HR practices.
b) Produce a greater number and variety of HR operations.
c) Shift the focus of HR from the processing of transactions to strategic HRM.
d) Make employees part of HRIS, and
e) Reengineer the entire HR function.

Ball (2001) reviewed the issues surrounding the use of HRIS by personnel and human resources departments in smaller organizations. The study enquired as to the nature of information stored electronically in three core areas: personnel, training and recruitment. Additionally, the paper evaluated system usage in terms of previous research, its sophistication, and other debates, which apply to larger firms. The study employed empirical data, which profiled system usage by 115 UK companies in the service sector in terms of information stored on personnel, training and recruitment and information processing features used. Ball (2001) revealed that the more people employed in an organization, the more likely the HR function was to hold information electronically both on the individual and the organization. Similarly, the more people organization employed, the more likely it was that information analysis with HRIS would occur. However, only half of the firms who employed less than 500 employees, and those who used only core HR modules, rather than additional training and recruitment modules used HRIS. Moreover, the more people employed by the organization the less likely it was to purchase additional non-core HR modules. Consequently, organizations that had purchased HRIS were more likely to buy additional modules. In general, HRIS had wider usage administratively, although those who used HRIS in training and recruitment were beginning to move away from this. Finally, time and attendance were the most frequent integrated additional modules (Ibid).

The findings from Ball (2001) reveal that organizational size is a clear determinant of, first, whether an organization has an HRIS at all and, second, whether it adopts certain modules over others, and third, how information is used and analyzed. Similarly, the type of software chosen by new HRIS users was typically a low-cost option. In-house database development was an equally popular option for smaller organizations adopting HRIS for the first time. This was in line with Thaler-Carter's (1998) observations that smaller organization would go for low cost and low risk HRIS purchases, typically cheaper, supplementary software that were flexible or in-house HRIS development.

In a more recent study, Hussain et al. (2006) investigated the use and impact of human resource information systems on human resource management professionals. The aim was to assess and compare the specific areas of use and to introduce a taxonomy that provides a framework for academicians. They also sought to determine whether HRIS usage was strategic, a perceived value-added for the organization, and its impact on professional standing for HR professionals. The results showed that, on average, few differences existed between SME and large company HRIS usage. Further, the authors observed that the professional standing has been enhanced by the specific HRIS usage for strategic collaborating, but cautioned that it was not as pronounced as that experienced by those other professions. Invariably, the researchers noted that for senior HR professionals, strategic use of HRIS was increasingly the norm, irrespective of company size. In addition, they observed that strategic use of HRIS enhanced the perceived standing of HR professionals within organizations; senior non-HR executives however did not share this view.

Theoretical Framework

HRIS literature (e.g. Beadles *et al.*, 2005; Kovach *et al.*, 2002; Ball, 2000; Overman, 1992) is replete with the strategic role HRIS plays to enhance management decisions. It has been established that the potential advantages of HRIS are faster information processing, greater information accuracy, improved planning and program development, and enhanced employee communications. This study, following from previous studies, will focus on four key areas in which HRIS is noted to influence HRM and organizational performance. They are:

- Savings in cost and time.
- Contributions to strategic decision making.
- Quality of information effects.
- Commitment to employee development.

Therefore, the study worked with the research model below:

Methodology of Research
General Background of Research

In this study, a conclusive research design was used. This is because by reviewing literature, needed information and constructs have been clearly specified. Additionally, this study intends to test four HRIS hypotheses (Cost and Time Savings, Decision Making Contributions, Quality Information Effects, Employee Development Commitments) and understand the specific relationships HRIS has with HRM. For this study, the target population was HR professionals, HR directors, HR managers in Ghana. Particularly, these respondents were drawn from three industries: Telecommunications, Banking, and Foods and Beverages.

Sample of Research

A Proportionate Sample size of eighty (80) was used for this study representing eighty percentage of the total population. However, due to time and financial constraints, only 63 responses were obtained. Some responded questionnaires were found to be incomplete and others wrongly filled; thus only 57 were used for further analysis.

Research Instrument, Procedures and Data Analysis

The survey was developed using questionnaires as the main instrument for data collection. Likert-type items on a five point scale and open-ended questions were employed on the survey to measure the perceptions of the HR directors in regard to the impact of the HRIS on HR processes, the time spent on various HR activities, the expense of HR activities, levels and use of information within the organization, the role of the HR department, and strategic decision making. Both qualitative and quantity data analysis techniques were used in analysing the data.

For purposes of this study, reliability of data is tested on the scales used to measure the four independent and one dependent variable using the Cronbach's alpha coefficients. Ideally a value above 0.7 confirms the internal consistency of the scales. The results, as shown in Table 1 *Reliability Statistics* above, indicate that three of the scales used to measure Decision Making

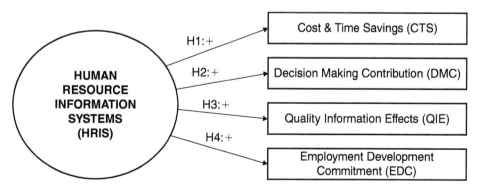

Figure 1 Research Model: Conceptualising the Strategic Role of HRIS.

Table 1 Reliability Statistics

Scale	Cronbach's Alpha	Number of Items
Cost & Times Savings (CTS)	0.598	3
Decision Making Contribution (DMC)	0.826	3
Quality Information Effects (QIE)	0.734	3
Employment Development Commitment (EDC)	0.855	3
HRIS Use	0.678	3

Contribution (DMC), Quality Information Effects (QIE) and Employment Development Commitment (EDC) have internal consistency with Cronbach values of 0.826, 0.734, and 0.855 respectively. Whiles HRIS was near to record undisputed internal consistency in its scales by the 0.678 value, scales for Cost & Time Savings lacked consistency.

Results of Research
Evaluating the Model

The importance of the impact of HRIS on the four dependent variables can be evaluated using the effect size statistic (*see Table 2*): **Partial Eta Squared** (Pallant, 2003). Partial Eta Squared represents the proportion of the variance in the dependent variables (CTS, DCM, QIE, and EDC) that can be explained by the independent variable (HRIS). Eta squared represents the proportion of variance of the dependent variable that is explained by the independent variable. Values for eta squared can range from 0 to 1.

To interpret the strength of eta squared values the following guidelines can be used (from Cohen, 1988):

- 0.01 = small effect;
- 0.06 = moderate effect; and
- 0.14 = large effect.

Based on these criteria, the following findings can be drawn about the impact of HRIS use on our various independent variables.

> *Hypothesis 1 (H$_1$): The greater the use of HRIS, the higher the operational savings in terms of cost and time*

This hypothesis is supported by the statistic Partial Eta Squared = 0.673. Since this value is greater than Cohen's 0.14, it suggests that HRIS is positively correlated (i.e. has a massive impact) to cost and time savings. This, according to Pallant (2003) means, converted to percentages, HRIS uses accounts for 67 percent of the variance in cost and time savings in an organization. The results reflect findings from previous

studies (e.g. Kovach and Cathcart, 1999) which suggest that a key advantage of HRIS is that processing costs is reduced. Even more strongly, Ngai and Watt (2006) found that the perceived benefit of a "quick response and access to information" had the highest mean score in their survey. Similarly, Teo *et al.* (2001) reported in their study that the advantage of a more timely management reporting as a result of HRIS adoption was the leading benefit.

> *Hypothesis 2 (H$_2$): The greater the use of HRIS, the better the contributions to strategic decision making*

This hypothesis is also supported by the statistic Partial Eta Squared = 0.673. Using Cohen's standard, it can be concluded that HRIS has a massive impact on decision making in an organization. Statistically, HRIS contributes not less than 67 percent of strategic input to decision making. Our findings here corroborate the assertions of Lengnick-Hall and Moritz (2003) who reported that the functions provided by HRIS allow a strategic type and amount of information to be provided to top management and the HR department which helps to make better decisions. Particularly, Beadles *et al.* (2005) found that one area where respondents believed that the system did aid in making decisions concerns promotions, with 60% responding that it provides useful information.

> *Hypothesis 3 (H$_3$): The greater the use of HRIS, the better the quality of information effects*

Considering the Partial Eta Squared = 0.410, this hypothesis has been statistically proven. Although the strength is a little lower than CTS and DMC, it passes Cohen's criteria, and thus it can be concluded that HRIS contributes 40 percent of quality information to firms. Beadles *et al.* (2005) also found a positive yet moderate relationship between HRIS and quality of information. The deduction here is that quality information can be seen as means to an end (i.e. better DMC) and not necessarily a distinct achievement in itself; thus separating

Table 2 Tests of Between-Subjects Effects

Source	Dependent Variable	Type III Sum of Squares	df	F	Sig.	Partial Eta Squared
Corrected Model	CTStot	72.398[a]	7	7.654	0.000	0.673
	DMCtot	126.775[b]	7	7.643	0.000	0.673
	QIEtot	58.168[c]	7	2.581	0.037	0.410
	EDCtot	165.050[d]	7	4.763	0.001	0.562
Intercept	CTStot	786.742	1	582.259	0.000	0.957
	DMCtot	921.463	1	388.884	0.000	0.937
	QIEtot	770.100	1	239.178	0.000	0.902
	EDCtot	993.184	1	200.621	0.000	0.885
HRIStot	CTStot	72.398	7	7.654	0.000	0.673
	DMCtot	126.775	7	7.643	0.000	0.673
	QIEtot	58.168	7	2.581	0.037	0.410
	EDCtot	165.050	7	4.763	0.001	0.562
Error	CTStot	35.131	26			
	DMCtot	61.607	26			
	QIEtot	83.714	26			
	EDCtot	128.714	26			
Total	CTStot	998.000	34			
	DMCtot	1239.000	34			
	QIEtot	1012.000	34			
	EDCtot	1378.000	34			
Corrected Total	CTStot	107.529	33			
	DMCtot	188.382	33			
	QIEtot	141.882	33			
	EDCtot	293.765	33			

a. R Squared = 0.673 (Adjusted R Squared = 0.585)

b. R Squared = 0.673 (Adjusted R Squared = 0.585)

c. R Squared = 0.410 (Adjusted R Squared = 0.251)

d. R Squared = 0.562 (Adjusted R Squared = 0.444)

them as distinct scales is likely to yield such a moderate effect.

Hypothesis 4(H₄): The greater the use of HRIS, the higher the commitment to employee development

Similarly this hypothesis is supported by the statistic Partial Eta Squared=0.562. Since this value is greater than Cohen's 0.14, it suggests that HRIS is positively correlated to employee development commitments. Percentage-wise according to Pallant's (2003) elucidation, HRIS use accounts for more than half of the variance in employee development commitments. This may not be as strong as the impacts on CTS and DMC, but

according to Ball (2001), who reported a relatively low impact of HRIS on employee development (e.g. skills matching and training), the reason is because using HRIS to perform such tasks can be more complex and analytical in nature and thus lower patronage.

Summary of Major Findings

According to the data analysis, it was found that a greater percentage of our respondents were males (58.8%) while lesser percentage were female (41.2%) and that the age range was from 21 to 40. Even further, all our hypotheses were strongly supported with the statistical findings.

Our assumption about cost and time savings in Hypothesis 1 (The greater the use of HRIS, the higher the operational savings in terms of cost and time) is statistically supported, and that there is a relatively strong and positive relationship between HRIS use and cost and savings, which also means that organizations that divert concerted efforts towards HRIS adoption and use have a high likelihood of cutting down cost and saving time. Decision making contributions (Hypothesis 2) − The greater the use of HRIS, the better the contributions to strategic decision making) also have high tendencies of improving effectiveness of HR decision if HRIS use is widely implemented. It was found that HRIS use will improve quality decisions by not less than 67 percent. Similarly, our assumption that HRIS will go a long way to add value to organizational competitive advantage and enhance the development of employees is statistically supported. A few concerns from our open-ended questions also provided considerable responses. Many respondents appear to be concerned about the cost of implementing a thorough HRIS system in organizations. Even beyond implementing, there are genuine qualms as to whether the systems can be maintained efficiently and cost-effectively.

Conclusion

In all, 57 HR stakeholders were sampled from three different organizations. In spite of the major revelation that HRIS use contributes a great deal to enhance variables such as cost and time savings (CTS), decision making contributions (DMC), quality information effects (QIE) employee development commitment (EDC), it is also worth noting that there is much that needs to be considered by the organizations in terms of HRIS planning, implementation and sustenance.

References

Ball, K. (2001). The Use of Human Resource Information Systems: a Survey. *Personnel Review, 30* (6): 667–693.

Bamberger, P., Meshoulam, H. (2000). *Human Resource Strategy: Formulation, Implementation, and Impact.* Beverly Hills, CA: Sage,

Beadles, N., Lowery, C. M., & Johns, K. (2005). The Impact of Human Resource Information Systems: An Exploratory Study in the Public Sector. *Communications of the IIMA 39,* 5 (4).

Broderick, R., Boudreau, J. W. (1992). Human Resource Management, Information Technology and The Competitive Edge. *Academy of Management Executive, 6* (2). 7–17.

Brown, D. (2002). eHR − Victim of Unrealistic Expectations. *Canadian HR Reporter, 15* (16), 1–6.

Davenport, T. H. (1993). *Process Innovation.* Boston, MA: Harvard Business School Press.

Florkowski, G. W. (2006). The diffusion of human-resource information-technology innovations in U.S. and non-U.S. firms. *Personnel Review, 35* (6), 684–710.

Haines, Victor Y., Petit, A. (1997). Conditions for Successful Human Resource Information Systems. *Human Resource Management, 36* (2), 261–275.

Gardner Sharyn, D., Lepak David, P., Bartol Kathryn, M. (2003). Virtual HR: The Impact of Information Technology on Human Resource Professional. *Journal of Vocational Behavior, 63* (2), 159–179.

DeSanctis, G. (1986). Human Resource Information Systems − A Current Assessment. *MIS Quarterly, 10* (1), 15–27.

Gupta, A. (2000). Enterprise Resource Planning: the emerging organizational value Systems. *Industrial Management and Data Systems, 100* (3), 114–118.

Hendrickson, R. (2003). Human Resources Information Systems: Backbone Technology of Contemporary Human Resources. *Journal of Labor Research,* XXIV (3).

Kotler, J. (1996). *Leading Change.* Boston, MA: Harvard Business.

Kossek, E. E., Young, W., Gash, C. D., Nichol, V. (1994). Waiting For Innovation in The HR Department: Godot Implements a HRIS. *Human Resource Management, 33* (1), 135–159.

Kovach, K. A., Cathcart, C. E. Jr. (1999). Human resource information systems (HRIS): providing business with rapid data access, information exchange and strategic advantage. *Public Personnel Management,* 275–281.

Kovach, K. A., Hughes, A. A., Fagan, P., Maggitti, P. G. (2002). Administrative and strategic advantages of HRIS. *Employment Relations Today, 29* (2), 43–48.

Lawler, E. E., Mohrman, S. A. (2003). HR as a strategic partner: what does it take to make it happen. *Human Resource Planning, 26* (3), 15–29.

Lederer, A. L. (1984). Planning and developing a human resource information system. *The Personnel Administrator, 29* (8), 27–39.

Lengnick-Hall, Mark L., & Moritz, S. (2003). The Impact of e-HR on the Human Resource Management Function. *Journal of Labor Research, 24* (3), 365–379.

Martinsons, M. G. (1994). Benchmarking human resource information systems in Canada and Hong Kong, *Information & Management, 26,* 305–316.

Ngai, E.W.T., Wat, F. K. T. (2006). Human resource information systems: a review and empirical analysis. *Personnel Review, 35* (3), 297–314.

Mayfield, J., Mayfield, M., & Lunce, S. (2003). Human Resource Information Systems: A Review and Model Development. *Advances in Competitiveness Research, 11* (1), 139–151.

Overman, S. (1992). Reaching for the 21st Century. *HR Magazine, 37,* 61–63.

Sadri, J., Chatterjee, V. (2003). Building organizational character through HRIS. *International Journal of Human Resources Development and Management, 3* (1), 84–98.

Tannenbaum, S. I. (1990). Human Resource Information Systems: User Group Implications. *Journal of Systems Management, 41* (1), 27–32.

Tansley, C., Newell, S., William, H., (2001). Effecting HRM-style practices through an integrated human resource information system An e-Greenfield site? *Personnel Review, 30* (3), 351–370.

Targowski, A. S., & Deshpanade, S. P. (2001). The Utility and Selection of an HRIS. *Advances in Competitive Research, 9* (1) 42–56.

Teo, T., Soon, G. L., Fedric, A. N. (2001). Adoption and Impact Of Human Resource Information Systems (HRIS). *Research in Practice in Human Resource Management, 9* (1), 101–117.

Ulrich, D. (2001). Human Resource Champions: From e-business to e-HR. *HRIM Journal, 5,* 90–97.

Walker, A. J. (2001). How the Web and Other Trends are Changing Human Resources. In Alfred J. Walker, Ed., *Web-Based Human Resources.* New York: McGraw-Hill, 2001.

Watson, W. (2002). e-HR: Getting Results Along the Journey—*2002 Survey Report.* Watson Wyatt Worldwide.

Wright, P. M., McMahan, G. C. (1992). Theoretical perspectives for strategic human resource management. *Journal of Management, 18,* 295–321.

Wright, P., & Snell, S. (1991). Toward an integrative view of strategic human resource management. *Human Resource Management Review, 1* (4), 203–225.

Critical Thinking

1. How is HRIS a strategic tool for the HR function?

2. What additional insights does a cost/benefit analysis of HRIS permit?

3. What does the conceptual model in Figure 1 help you to understand?

Internet References

HRIS Software, HRIS and HR

www.geniushr.com

Types of HRIS Systems

www.ehow.com/list_6890587_types-hris-systems.html

Article   Prepared by: Maria Nathan, *Lynchburg College*

Playing IT Big Brother
When Is Employee Monitoring Warranted?

BRUCE GAIN

Learning Outcomes

After reading this article, you will be able to:

- Determine when employee monitoring is illegal.
- Understand when employee monitoring is ethical.

Instant messaging, YouTube videos, personal email accounts, and social networking sites represent an ever-burgeoning number of attention-grabbers that can prevent users from getting their work done. On a business level, time-wasting Internet use represents lost productivity and, ultimately, money lost.

Of more concern is the possibility that a user will use enterprise property to download viruses, transmit sensitive company information, or use enterprise property to break the law. A recent worst-case scenario involved Societe Generale, one of the largest banks in Europe, and its now-famous French rogue trader who, left virtually unchecked, allegedly lost the bank $7.1 billion.

What is an admin to do? The immediate reaction for many admins might be to invest in increasingly smarter employee monitoring technologies that facilitate tight surveillance and control to make sure employees are not using the enterprise's machines and network to do things they shouldn't. But how far should monitoring of small to midsized enterprises go? When does it cross the line between employee and company rights?

There are no black-and-white answers to these questions. The solution you adopt should take into account your enterprise's particular needs, user education, and ultimately a common-sense approach when it comes to employee monitoring.

Enterprises Jump on the Bandwagon

Whether it is in response to employees using online outlets such as instant messaging and consumer websites or just a more paranoid business climate, the use of employee monitoring is rapidly increasing. The technologies are also increasingly cheaper to implement.

"Surveillance is now routine business practice among American employers both large and small as the cost and ease of introducing [surveillance products] have dropped," says Jeremy Gruber, legal director for The National Workrights Institute.

Adam Schran, chief executive and founder of Ascentive (www.ascentive.com), which offers Internet monitoring software, says employee monitoring as well as blocking and filtering product sales have become a $300 million-a-year market. "There are more distractions out there," he says. "A few years ago, [potential customers] said it was like Big Brother. Now they are saying, 'Here is my credit card number.'"

100% Legal

Enterprises in the United States today also have much leeway when it comes to monitoring what their employees do at the workplace. There are few mandates or court decisions that prohibit enterprises from tracking employees' activities.

"Employees have few if any rights when it comes to electronic surveillance in the workplace," Gruber says. "Only two states, Connecticut and Delaware, even require that employers give notice of monitoring, let alone actually regulate the monitoring itself."

But just because tight surveillance is not illegal does not necessarily make it ethical—or something that IT will necessarily want to put into place, Gruber says. "While there are some legitimate threats that form the basis for surveillance, they are often exaggerated, and rarely is the surveillance tailored to meet the specific objective or balanced with employee privacy concerns," he notes. "Employees are working longer hours than they ever have before. It should be acceptable to allow for reasonable personal and private use of computers and other forms of electronic communication, but only a minority of employers allows for reasonable-use policies, and even then the surveillance continues uninterrupted."

On a practical level, the advantages of catching people who are not doing their work or are doing what they shouldn't might not outweigh the disadvantages of employees who resent being watched.

"You can lock down their systems and monitor them to the point that they cannot do anything except use company software," says Ira Herman, co-CEO of Logic IT Consulting (www.logicitc.com). "But a lot of times, employees will ask 'Why are you being mean and locking us down?'"

In situations where professionals are paid for results, some employees think that it is none of management's business if they take a break and use their work Internet connection for personal reasons, provided they get their work done. For users of this mindset, heavy-handed surveillance is especially prone to backfire for employees who work in creative fields, Schran says. "If you work for a company that is too strict and you are a creative type, why would you want to stick around?" he asks.

One solution is to allow for employees to have a certain amount of privacy time when their Internet and computer use remain private.

"Some software can turn on private time features and turn off the monitoring so the employee can go on YouTube and email their kids and spouses," Schran says. "You can use it for an hour or 90 minutes a day. But it is the folks that are spending four to six hours a day on YouTube who are going to get caught anyway."

Middle Ground

The degree to which employees' computer and Internet use needs to be monitored varies from enterprise to enterprise. Strict surveillance of financial services industry personnel is often legally required, for example. But an administrator of a 700-user network for an airline components firm will not have the same concerns.

Indeed, network activity and PC usage need to be monitored to a certain extent for any enterprise. If employees are spending an inordinate amount of time watching streaming video content, for example, the network's bandwidth can surfer. In this case, using monitoring technology to determine whose personal use of the network is causing problems is warranted.

Monitoring Tips

It is relatively easy to monitor and track practically everything users do on their machines and the network, but creating a working policy that addresses both employees' privacy concerns and the security needs of the enterprise requires some finesse. Following certain guidelines can help achieve the right balance between locking down users' PCs and giving them free rein to do whatever they want. Here are some things to keep in mind:

- It is crucial to educate users about what activity is prohibited and that any electronic communication they make with the enterprise's equipment is subject to monitoring.
- The degree to which your enterprise's employees need to be actively monitored varies depending on each user's position and business activity.
- Your legal department will likely tell you that most electronic surveillance is allowed, but that does not necessarily mean any and all means of monitoring is ethical (or good for employee morale).

"The cost implications are things that come into my mind as what you have to watch for," notes Andras Cser, an analyst for Forrester Research. "You look at where your bandwidth goes to. If you start seeing activities that really are out of the normal and ordinary, then you start interfering."

One approach for SMEs might be to adopt a policy prohibiting downloads or installation of any kind of third-party software and access to certain kinds of websites. The guidelines might also allow for reasonable personal use of the network and computer equipment, such as for communicating with spouses or even taking a break from work to read an online newspaper. But employees should also be aware that usage might be watched to prevent problems from arising, such as when the monitoring system alerts you that someone is slowing down the network by regularly downloading large video files.

"There are two extremes when it comes to employee monitoring, and the answer is somewhere in between," Cser says.

Ultimately, your monitoring policy will have to take into account the specific needs of your enterprise and should evolve as the network's infrastructure, users, and applications change over time. The right approach is less about gaining control than it is about striking a balance between your users' privacy concerns and how to prevent employees from disrupting the network. Cser says, "As far as I am concerned, this is more about common sense and saving costs."

Critical Thinking

1. Do employers have the right to monitor the IT activity of their employees?

2. Should employers monitor the IT activity of their employees?

3. What actions should an employer take when they find an employee abusing his or her IT account?

4. Do employees have the right to expect IT privacy at work?

Internet References

Email, Phone, and Social Media Monitoring in the Workplace – Know Your Rights as an Employer

www.sba.gov/community/blogs/email-phone-and-social-media-monitoring-workplace-%E2%80%93-know-your-rights-employer

Is it Legal for Employers to Monitor Employees at Work?

http://smallbusiness.chron.com/legal-employers-monitor-employees-work-16563.html

Workplace Monitoring Laws, Society for Human Resource Management

www.shrm.org/legalissues/stateandlocalresources/stateandlocalstatutesandregulations/documents/state%20surveillance%20and%20monitoring%20laws.pdf

Article
Prepared by: Maria Nathan, *Lynchburg College*

Bring Your Own Device

More employers are allowing employees to use their own technology in the workplace.

DAVE ZIELINSKI

Learning Outcomes

After reading this article, you will be able to:

- Know what is meant by "consumerization" of workplace technology.

- Understand how "consumerization" of workplace technology affects the HR function.

- Know what HR should do to accommodate "consumerization" of workplace technology.

It began with a simple question posed by frustrated employees: "Why is the laptop or smart phone I use at home so much better than what I have in the workplace?" When executives at companies such as software maker Citrix Systems began taking the question to heart, the bring-your-own-device movement was born. Today, fueled by the growing popularity of Apple's iPad and iPhone, more organizations are allowing workers—beyond just the executive and information technology staffs—to use personal mobile devices at work.

It's not just a preference by younger workers that's spurring companies to adopt bring-your-own-device policies. Business leaders find that offering greater choice in work technologies can:

- Boost productivity and satisfaction levels of most employee generations.
- Reduce capital equipment costs.
- Lift some computer support burdens from the IT staff.
- Others say bring-your-own-device programs aid in recruiting.

According to a July 2011 study from the Aberdeen Group, a Boston-based human capital research firm, 75 percent of 415 surveyed organizations around the globe are now allowing employees to use their own mobile devices for business purposes. In addition, a fall 2011 survey of 1,663 IT workers in the U.S. by Forrester Research found that 48 percent of the respondents now buy the smart phone they want and use it for work. Given the mushrooming popularity of tablets—which are less expensive than most laptops—most experts expect the trend to grow.

This "consumerization" of workplace technology has implications for human resource functions. While positives include enhanced productivity and morale, the use of personally owned devices for work also presents threats to data confidentiality, security and employee privacy.

What happens, for example, if an employee leaves the company but still has sensitive company data on a dual-use iPhone or iPad? What if hackers prey on the less-mature security features of an HR manager's preferred smart phone or carrier network, embedding malicious software or gaining access to personally identifiable information copied there for temporary use? And if an employee breaks copyright law in downloading material from the Internet to a personal device while on the job, is the organization subject to legal action?

Human resource, legal and line executives must understand these issues before launching any bring-your-own-device programs.

Power of Choice

Citrix Systems is a pioneer. It launched a bring-your-own-device program in 2008 after a survey found that many employees were happier with their home computing devices than those in the workplace. Participating employees each receive $2,100 to purchase their choice of laptop along with a three-year service warranty, says Brandy Fulton-Moorer, vice president of human resources. With an average three-year cost of $2,600 to procure, manage and support an enterprise-supplied laptop, executives say the program represents a cost savings to the company.

About 20 percent of 6,800 worldwide employees use the program, including members of Fulton-Moorer's HR department. "We have people who've purchased their own laptops or iPads, and some like to have separate devices for different work purposes or situations, with one being company-provided and the other employee-owned," Fulton-Moorer says.

Citrix takes data security and employee privacy issues seriously, Fulton-Moorer says, employing homegrown "virtualization" technologies to ensure that sensitive HR data remains centrally managed and locked down on servers so it can't be transferred to employee-owned devices.

As a multinational company, Citrix's HR professionals have to keep up with data privacy regulations around the world. In countries with stringent privacy laws, for example, employers aren't allowed to monitor the activities of employee-owned devices on a corporate network, even if that smart phone or tablet resides on business premises. That means multinationals often have different policies for different global regions; as a result, employees in some regions remain ineligible for bring-your-own-device programs.

"Data privacy rules tend to be different or more restrictive outside of the United States, and we strive to adhere to the highest common denominator," Fulton-Moorer says.

Despite technology safeguards, she says, training HR staff regarding access to and use of sensitive corporate data remains paramount. The more private the data are, Fulton-Moorer says, the tighter they should be locked down.

Social Security numbers or health care data "shouldn't even be visible to most HR staff," Fulton-Moorer says. On the other end of the spectrum sits sensitive data that should be highly secured but that employees need to access regularly, such as performance evaluations.

The proliferation of dual-use devices in the workplace presents legal, data security and compliance issues for all companies.

"HR team members have to access evaluations to coach and provide services to individuals they support, but there is never a need to copy or load them onto personal devices, and our technology doesn't allow them to do so," Fulton-Moorer says.

Freedom with Accountability

At consumer products company Kimberly-Clark in Irving, Texas, executives' fondness for Apple's iPhone led to a new policy allowing employees to connect their own mobile devices to the corporate network for business purposes.

Some 3,000 Kimberly-Clark employees now use their personal smart phones or tablets to access corporate e-mail, calendars and contacts. Should their device be lost or stolen, or if they attempt to enter an invalid password a maximum number of times, all the information on the device is "wiped" remotely through the company's mobile-device management system. Employees sign an agreement consenting to this arrangement, since such destruction runs the risk of wiping out personal information like family photos or contacts.

Martin Evans, vice president of human resource business enablement, says the program helps employees be more productive, positions the company as progressive to potential recruits and sends workers a positive message. Specifically, it says that the company will treat them like adults, it demonstrates that the company cares that they have the right tools to do their jobs well, and it acknowledges that there are different work style preferences, Evans says. Anecdotal evidence shows that the bring-your-own-device program gets "a strong positive reception."

At Carfax, a Centreville, Va., provider of vehicle history information, executives say a bring-your-own-device initiative boosts productivity and helps attract candidates. Employees can apply for an interest-free loan from the company for up to $2,000 to buy their devices, and they have two years to pay the loans back.

"It's a good feeling from a recruiting perspective when we talk to a candidate who says, 'I don't want to give up my personal smart phone, I love it and have had it forever' and we tell them they won't have to carry a second, corporate-owned phone," says Toni Amey, vice president of human resources at Carfax.

About 800 employees participate in a two-year-old bring-your-own-device program at Kraft Foods, the Northfield, Ill., food and beverage conglomerate, says Mike Cunningham, chief technology officer. Kraft provides a stipend for workers to purchase Apple or Windows devices of their choice. Not everyone is eligible, however. Managers who frequently handle personally identifiable information, for example, including some members of the legal and HR departments, aren't allowed to participate.

Cunningham says the program creates a lower-cost model from an IT perspective, and it has clear employee satisfaction and recruiting benefits.

The program "strengthens work/life balance for our employees," Cunningham says. "No two people work exactly the same, and by giving employees the freedom to choose the computer that best suits their work style, we think we're accommodating their work needs in a more proactive way."

Rather than giving employees a stipend, Sybase, a Dublin, Calif.-based software provider, picks up the monthly service fees for personal devices used for work, says Jim Swartz, chief information officer. With their managers' approval, employees order services such as text messaging, international service and certain data plans.

In return, participating employees agree to let Sybase install security software on their devices to perform remote data wipes should the equipment be lost or stolen. Data encryption technologies provide additional security.

"The program is designed to help our employees be more productive from anywhere, anytime from almost any mobile device," Swartz says. "From an HR standpoint, employees can do things like conduct personnel requisition approvals and make or approve vacation requests from their mobile devices."

Ensuring Data Security

The proliferation of dual-use devices in the workplace presents legal, data security and compliance issues for all companies—and such issues are heightened in heavily regulated industries such as government, health care or financial services. In addition, although data security features for the iPhone and the iPad have improved, experts say they still can't match protections provided by Research In Motion's venerable BlackBerry. Although not invulnerable, the BlackBerry is known for its ability to combat hacker incursions and malicious software. Yet it has become a less popular choice in bring-your-own-device programs.

According to the 2011 iPass Global Mobile Workforce Report, iPhone now holds 45 percent of the worldwide smart phone market share among mobile workers, which is up from 31 percent a year earlier. In 2010, BlackBerry held the top spot.

Under bring-your-own-device policies, more responsibility for security protections such as keeping anti-virus software up-to-date falls to workers instead of technicians in IT departments. IT is typically only responsible for troubleshooting problems on employee-owned devices associated with corporate software, not the operating systems.

Making employees responsible for the security of their own technology devices represents the best safeguard against sensitive information reaching an employee-owned device. Many employers protect such data with "virtualization" technologies that keep the data or intellectual property locked on servers in central data centers, even when accessed remotely by mobile devices.

Many corporate leaders embrace the idea that, once they're educated on the risks, employees will take better care of devices they own.

According to Citrix Systems' policy, "Never have unencrypted data that is subject to regulation on your mobile device, which includes personally identifiable information," says Kurt Roemer, chief security strategist. A protected network folder holds HR applications at the company, Roemer says, and employees must use virtualization technologies to access it.

"The system prevents anyone from cutting, copying, pasting or saving any data to their local mobile device that the company doesn't want them to," Roemer says. "Our technology makes sure just keystrokes, mouse clicks and screen refreshes are moving across the corporate network, not actual files or data."

So, for example, an HR specialist can no longer copy an Excel file with salary information to his laptop to work on at home.

Many corporate leaders embrace the idea that, once they're educated on the risks, employees will take better care of devices they own—even from a data security perspective—than they will company-supplied laptops or smart phones.

With employee ownership, "They're more diligent about keeping devices updated, want them set up a certain way and welcome use of virtualization technologies, since they keep sensitive data from being stored on their devices," Roemer says.

Critical Thinking

1. Why do you think that use of personal devices in the workplace enhances employee performance?
2. How is the work-home balance improved with dual-use devices?
3. How has IT improved security features of employee dual-use devices?

Internet References

Bring Your Own Device

www.shrm.org/publications/hrmagazine/editorialcontent/2012/0212/pages/0212tech.aspx

The "Bring Your Own Device" to Work Movement

www.mondaq.com/unitedstates/x/177472/Employee+Rights